A HISTORY OF EDUCATION
DURING THE MIDDLE AGES
AND THE TRANSITION TO MODERN TIMES

A HISTORY OF EDUCATION

DURING THE MIDDLE AGES AND THE TRANSITION TO MODERN TIMES

BY

FRANK PIERREPONT GRAVES
(PH.D., COLUMBIA)
DEAN OF THE SCHOOL OF EDUCATION AND PROFESSOR
OF THE HISTORY OF EDUCATION IN THE
UNIVERSITY OF PENNSYLVANIA

GREENWOOD PRESS, PUBLISHERS
WESTPORT, CONNECTICUT

Originally published in 1920
by The Macmillan Company, New York

Reprinted from an original copy in the collections
of the Brooklyn Public Library

First Greenwood Reprinting 1970

Library of Congress Catalogue Card Number 79-104274

SBN 8371-3933-3

Printed in the United States of America

TO MY WIFE

HELEN WADSWORTH GRAVES

PREFACE

THIS book is a continuation of my *History of Education before the Middle Ages*, and holds in general to the same point of view and method of approach. It may, however, be used quite independently of that volume as a textbook or a work of reference upon educational history between the sixth and the eighteenth centuries. In either case, it is hoped that a sufficiently clear and detailed account is given to afford an accurate picture of the period covered, and to interest students in some of the more important origins of modern educational procedure. The extensive quotation of the sources and the selected lists of supplementary reading should contribute materially to these ends.

No apology is necessary, I trust, for continuing to view the educational process from the standpoint of the development of individualism. The period of the Middle Ages and the subsequent four centuries of reaction lend themselves to this method of interpretation with engaging facility. Nevertheless, I have striven never in the interest of this method to slur the facts nor force their construction, and have deferred all serious attempts at generalization until after the data have been presented. As in the former volume, I have also undertaken to furnish a background and a perspective for the history of education by interweaving a liberal measure of political material. Although this part of the narrative is, because of the growing complexity of the times under consideration, necessarily less connected than in my work upon ancient education, such an historical setting may tend to acquit me of the charge of pedagogical aeroplaning. At any rate, a life-line of general history is sadly needed by the average student of education.

In making this work accurate, I have received aid from several quarters. I am much indebted to my colleagues, Professors E. H. McNeal and Clarence Perkins, for the pains they have expended in checking up the descriptions of an historical layman, and to my former colleague, Professor J. H. Coursault, of the University of Missouri, for his frank but kindly criticism of the educational facts in the book and of my method of presenting them. I owe an even larger debt to my colleague, Professor A. E. Davies, who has throughout the preparation of this treatise been ever at my service as a critic and guide, and has found time in a very busy life to make many suggestions and improvements.

F. P. G.

JULY 1, 1910.

CONTENTS

PART I

THE MIDDLE AGES

CHAPTER I

THE PROBLEM OF THE MEDIÆVAL PERIOD 1
The Middle Ages as a Period of Assimilation. The Middle Ages as a Period of Repression.

CHAPTER II

MONASTICISM AND THE MONASTIC SCHOOLS . . . 4
Rise and History of Monasticism. The Rule of Benedict. The Libraries, Multiplication of Manuscripts, and Original Writings of the Monasteries. Organization of the Monastic Education. The Three Ideals of the Monastic Education. The Monastic Course of Study and the Seven Liberal Arts. The Methods of Teaching and the Texts Used in the Monastic Schools. How Monasticism Affected the Middle Ages and Civilization in General.

CHAPTER III

CHARLEMAGNE'S REVIVAL OF EDUCATION 25
Rise of the Franks and the Empire of Charlemagne. Charlemagne's Improvements in Administration. Charlemagne's Efforts to Improve Learning. Alcuin and the Palace School. Educational Improvement in the Monastic and Other Schools. The Course of Study and the Organization in the Schools. The School of Alcuin at the Monastery of Tours. Rabanus Maurus and Other Pupils of Alcuin.

CONTENTS

CHAPTER IV

THE REVIVAL OF EDUCATION UNDER ALFRED . . . 36
    Alfred's Desire to Extend and Improve Education. The Establishment of Schools and the Importation of Educators. Alfred's Personal Assistance to Learning and Education. Significance of Alfred's Educational Work.

CHAPTER V

THE MOHAMMEDAN LEARNING AND EDUCATION . . . 40
    The Rise of Moslemism and Its Absorption of Greek Culture. The Brothers of Sincerity and Their Scheme of Higher Education. The Moorish Colleges. Elementary Education. Stimulating Effect upon Europe of the Moslem Education.

CHAPTER VI

THE EDUCATIONAL TENDENCIES OF MYSTICISM AND SCHOLASTICISM 47
    The Nature and Rise of Christian Mysticism. The Education in Mediæval Mysticism. The Development of Mysticism. The Character of Scholasticism. The History of Scholastic Development. The Tendency of Scholasticism. Its Educational Organization and Content. The Method of Presentation. Scholasticism and Its Influence. The Relations of Mysticism and Scholasticism to Education.

CHAPTER VII

THE EDUCATION OF FEUDALISM AND CHIVALRY . . 63
    The Origin of Feudalism. Chivalry and Its Development. The Ideals of Chivalric Education. The Three Stages of Education Preparatory to Knighthood. Knighthood. Training of Women. The Effects of Chivalric Education.

CHAPTER VIII

THE EDUCATIONAL WORK OF THE FRIARS 72
 The Purpose of the Friars. Their Organization and Methods. Their Influence upon Education and Progress.

CHAPTER IX

THE MEDIÆVAL UNIVERSITIES 76
 General Causes of the Rise of Universities. The History and Purpose of the Universities. Privileges Granted to Universities. Organization of the Universities. The Courses of Study. The Methods of Study. Degrees. The Value of the University Education and Its Effect upon Civilization.

CHAPTER X

THE DEVELOPMENT OF CITIES AND NEW SCHOOLS . . 96
 The Rise of Commerce and Cities. The Gild, Burgher, and Chantry Schools.

CHAPTER XI

THE PASSING OF THE MIDDLE AGES 100
 The Growth of National Spirit. The Development of Vernacular Literature. Mediæval Art. Summary of the Middle Ages.

PART II

THE TRANSITION TO MODERN TIMES

CHAPTER XII

THE RENAISSANCE AND HUMANISTIC EDUCATION . . 106
 The General Tendencies of the Renaissance. The Renaissance and the Revival of Learning. Humanism and the Humanists.

CHAPTER XIII

THE HUMANISTIC EDUCATION IN ITALY 110

Causes of the Awakening in Italy. Petrarch and His Influence. The Development of Greek Scholarship. Chrysoloras and His Pupils. The City Tyrants as Humanists. The Court School at Mantua and Vittorino da Feltre. The Relation of the Court Schools to the Universities. Attitude of the Humanists toward the Church. Ideals of the Humanistic Education. The Content, Method, and Organization. Decadence of the Italian Humanism and the Rise of Ciceronianism.

CHAPTER XIV

THE HUMANISTIC EDUCATION OF THE NORTH . . . 140

The Spread and Character of Humanism in the Northern Countries. The Development in France. Budæus. Corderius. Collège de Guyenne. Classical Studies in the German Universities. Groot and the Hieronymian Schools. Wessel, Agricola, Reuchlin, and Hegius. Jakob Wimpfeling. Erasmus, the Leader in Humanistic Education. The *Fürstenschulen* and the *Gymnasien*. Melanchthon and His Organization of Schools. Sturm's *Gymnasium*. The Early Humanistic Movement in England. Greek at Oxford. Greek at Cambridge. Humanistic Influences at the Court. Elyot's *Governour*. Vives. Ascham's *Scholemaster*. John Colet and His School at St. Paul's. Humanism in the English Grammar Schools. Formalism in the Grammar Schools. English Grammar and Public Schools To-day. The Grammar Schools of America. The Aim of Humanistic Education in the North. The Connection of Northern Educational Organization with the Reformation. The Course of Study. The Formalization of Humanistic Education.

CHAPTER XV

EDUCATIONAL INFLUENCES OF THE PROTESTANTS . . 179

General Causes of the Reformation. Luther's Revolt. Educational Features of Luther's Religious Works. Luther's Chief Educational Works. The Civic Aim of Education. The Organization of Education by the State. Industrial and Academic Training. Religious, Humanistic, and Other Content of Education. Rationality in Method. Melanchthon, Sturm, Bugenhagen, Trotzendorf, and Neander. Zwingli's Revolt. Zwingli's Educational Foundations and Treatise. Calvin's Revolt. Calvin's Encouragement of Education, and the Work of Corderius. Spread of Calvinist Education. Knox and the Elementary Schools of Scotland. Henry VIII's Revolt. Effect upon Education. The Civil and Universal Aim of Protestant Education. The Foundation of Elementary Schools. Effect upon Secondary Schools and Universities. The Curricula. The Lapse into Formalism.

CHAPTER XVI

THE EDUCATION OF THE CATHOLICS 208

The Council of Trent. Loyola and the Foundation of the Society of Jesus. The *Constitutiones* and the *Ratio Studiorum*. The Lower and Upper Colleges. The Humanistic Curriculum of the Lower Colleges. The Philosophical and Theological Courses in the Upper Colleges. The *Prælectio*. Memorizing. Reviews. Emulation. Corporal Punishment. Estimate of the Jesuit Schools. The Oratorian Schools. The Little Schools of the Port Royalists. The Curriculum and Texts. Methods. The Closing of the Little Schools. La Salle and the Christian Brethren. The Aim, Organization, Curriculum, Method, and Results. Catholic Education of Girls. Fénelon. Religious and Repressive Aim of Catholic Education. The Organization of Catholic Schools and Universities.

The Humanistic and Religious Curricula. The Teachers and Methods. Results of Education during the Reformation.

CHAPTER XVII

THE BEGINNINGS OF REALISTIC EDUCATION . . . 240

The Relation of Realism to the Renaissance and the Reformation. The Nature of Realism. The Earlier Realism, Verbal and Social. The Earlier Realists. Rabelais. The Training of the Whole Man. The Informal Method. The Influence of Rabelais. Montaigne. His Aim, Means, Subjects, and Method of Education. The Effects of Montaigne's Theories. Mulcaster. Natural Education. Elementary Education. Higher Training. Education of Girls. Improvements in Teaching. Results of Mulcaster's Positions. Milton. His Definition of Education. His 'Academy.' Early Realism in Locke. His Aim, Means, Content, and Method of Education. Influence of Locke's *Thoughts*. The Effect of the Earlier Realism.

CHAPTER XVIII

SENSE REALISM IN EDUCATION 262

The Development of Realism. Bacon and his New Method. Solomon's House and the Pansophic Course. The Value of Bacon's Method. Ratich's Attempts at School Reform. His Extravagant Claims. His Realistic Methods. The Educational Influence of Ratich. The Education and Earliest Work of Comenius. The *Janua Linguarum*. The *Vestibulum, Atrium, Orbis Pictus*, and Other Janual Works. The *Didactica Magna*. Pansophia. The Threefold Aim of Education. Universal Education. The Four Periods in the School System. The College of Pansophia. Encyclopædic Course. The Mother School. The Vernacular School. The Latin School. The University. Method of Nature. Discipline. Effect of the Comenian Principles upon Education. Locke as a Sense Realist. Realistic Tendencies in the Elementary Schools. Secondary Schools. Universities.

CHAPTER XIX

EDUCATIONAL INFLUENCES OF PURITANISM, PIETISM, AND
RATIONALISM 296
    Reaction to the Conditions in Church and State. Puritanism and Its Contributions to Education. Results of Puritanism. Rise of the Pietists. Francke. His Institutions. Aim, Course, Methods, and Influence. Decline of Pietism. Rationalism in England and France. Locke's Disciplinary Theory. Effects of Locke's Educational Theories. Voltaire and the Encyclopedists. The Hardening of the Puritan, Pietistic, and Rationalistic Movements.

CHAPTER XX

THE PROGRESS BEFORE MODERN TIMES 315
    The Middle Ages. The Awakening. Preparation for Rousseau and the French Revolution. The Modern Spirit.

INDEX 319

A HISTORY OF EDUCATION

DURING THE MIDDLE AGES AND THE TRANSITION TO MODERN TIMES

PART I—THE MIDDLE AGES

CHAPTER I

THE PROBLEM OF THE MEDIÆVAL PERIOD

The Middle Ages as a Period of Assimilation. — A present-day historian tersely defines the 'problem' of *Civilization during the Middle Ages* as follows: —

> "To make out of the barbarized sixth century, stagnant and fragmentary, with little common life, without ideals or enthusiasms, the fifteenth century in full possession again of a common world civilization, keen, pushing, and enthusiastic."[1]

According to this interpretation, it was the office of the Middle Ages to enable the rude German hordes, who had everywhere taken possession of the decadent ancient world, to rise gradually to such a plane of intelligence and achievement that they might absorb the civilization of antiquity and become its carriers to modern times. Through the conquest of the Roman world by these barbarian tribes, the four factors which were destined to be the most influential in modern civilization — the Greek, the Roman, the Christian, and the German — came to meet in the early part of the sixth century and for a

The Middle Ages gradually fused the Greek, Roman, and Christian elements with the German,

[1] George Burton Adams, *op. cit.*, p. 11.

time to exist side by side. And it was the mission of the succeeding centuries to fuse these divergent elements into one organic whole.

But such a process was necessarily slow. Rome had absorbed and combined with her legal and political institutions the rich intellectual and æsthetic contributions of Greece. Also in becoming Christian she had institutionalized this religion and given it the form of a legal morality. The problem now was the assimilation of this culture with that of the German barbarians who had conquered Rome, and the uniting with the Greek, Roman, and Christian factors of the freer and more elastic institutions of these people. But Rome had been greatly sapped of her vitality and strength, and nearly a millennium passed before these diverse elements were blended.

<small>and in so doing regarded the Roman institutions as a completed system to be absolutely followed.</small>

Yet gradual as the movement was, it began almost immediately. While still flushed with their victories, the rough warriors must have found themselves in the presence and under the spell of Roman organization and culture. The government, wealth, art, and technical skill of ancient Rome were everywhere evidenced in the roads, bridges, buildings, and cities that challenged their interest and admiration. The concept of a universal empire as the only possible civil order had been impressed upon the Germans through long contact with it. They also found in the organization of the Catholic Church a visible enshrinement of this imperial idea, which spoke with authority and finality to all nations. Moreover, the classic literature and the Græco-Roman schools were still preserved, though in a diluted form, in the Christian educational institutions. The barbarians were inevitably impressed with a sense of the superiority of Roman institutions[1] and civilization, and they began, ofttimes unconsciously, to imitate and borrow from what must have appeared to them a completed and absolute system, divinely sanctioned.

---

[1] Not only did the Germans hold in mind as a goal of perfection the general imperial organization, but they even tried to retain the various offices and official titles.

The Middle Ages as a Period of Repression. — Consequently, the mediæval period was primarily one not of progress, but of absorption. The watchword was authority and the conformity of the individual to the model set, and there was a constant tendency to realize the ideals of life in concrete form. Therein appears both the weakness and the strength of the Middle Ages. It was only through the formation of the right social habits, or institutions, that the leavening of the barbarians was possible, but it was this crystallization through authority that made individualism and further ideals difficult. Little advance could be made until the social habits could be reshaped and new ideals tolerated. A machine is a most effective and economical instrument, but it permits no variation, originality, or advancement over the pattern. Hence Rashdall most aptly characterizes the situation in the Middle Ages, when he says: —

This resulted in an authoritative standard and a subordination of the individual to the model set, and progress was almost impossible until individualism was once more tolerated.

"Ideals pass into historic forces by embodying themselves in institutions. The power of embodying its ideals in institutions was the peculiar genius of the mediæval mind, as its most conspicuous defect lay in the corresponding tendency to materialize them."[1]

Assimilation and repression are thus the key to the Middle Ages, and until the bondage to authority, convention, and institutions was broken, progress was impossible. But, as will be seen, there grew up within mediævalism itself factors that, with the development of intelligence, were destined to lead to individualism and advancement. Slowly but surely, the repression was removed, and modern culture grew out of this fusion of German barbarism with Christianity and classical antiquity.

[1] *Universities in the Middle Ages*, Vol. I, p. 5.

CHAPTER II

MONASTICISM AND THE MONASTIC SCHOOLS

The mediæval Church became the guide, especially through its monastic schools.

IN all this mediæval assimilation, it was but natural that the Church should stand as the chief guide and schoolmaster of the Germanic hosts. Christianity had become the authoritative religion of the Roman world, and, through the complete organization of the Church with the Bishop of Rome as its head, its power became practically unlimited. Now while Christian culture and education had been greatly influenced by Græco-Roman learning, the Church had become very suspicious of this training, and in 529, by the decree of Justinian, had succeeded in having the pagan schools closed. This left Christian education without a rival, and, although the episcopal schools persisted to some extent, it tended to find its chief expression in the 'monastic,' or fourth type of Christian schools,[1] with their reversion to the 'otherworldly' ideal.

Monasticism arose as a reaction to the prevailing vice of Roman society.

Rise and History of Monasticism. — But to understand the *monastic schools*, which were so much wider and more enduring in range of influence than any Christian type which had preceded, it will be necessary to examine the movement and institution out of which they arose. *Monasticism* resulted in a time of moral decay from the desire of some within the Church for a deeper religious life. By the third century Roman society had become most corrupt. All hope of self-government had gone, class was arrayed against class, and the privileged orders reveled in luxury and depravity, while the rank

---

[1] For a brief account of the schools of Early Christianity, see Graves, *History of Education before the Middle Ages* (New York, 1909), pp. 278–296.

MONASTICISM AND THE MONASTIC SCHOOLS 5

and file were poor and oppressed. Religious enthusiasm likewise declined. Christianity was no longer confined to small extra-social groups meeting secretly, but was represented in all walks of society, and mingled with the world. It had become thoroughly secularized, and even the clergy had in many instances yielded to the prevailing worldliness and vice.[1] Under these circumstances there were Christians who felt that the only hope for salvation rested in fleeing from the world and its temptations and taking refuge in an isolated life of holy devotion.

Hence there grew up within Christianity that form of solitary living known as monasticism, with its 'asceticism,' or discipline of the body in the interest of the highest spiritual life.[2] Some of the elements of asceticism appeared in Christianity, through various sects, like the Therapeutæ, Gnostics, and Montanists, even during the first two centuries of its history, although it was not until the third century that any number of Christians adopted such a mode of living. As corruption increased in the Roman world, many abandoned their homes, or were driven from them by persecution. They withdrew farther and farther from society, until they reached the seclusion of the mountains, where they dwelt alone in caves. Thus these first Christian hermits were literally 'monks,'[3] and the dreary deserts and solitudes of lower Egypt naturally furnished them with a suitable dwelling-place. They pursued a life of prayer, contemplation, and repression of the body, even to the extent of practicing vigil and fasting, flagellation, exhaustive labor,

Many withdrew from society into the deserts of Egypt, where they led a life of asceticism and devotion.

---

[1] For a description of this decadence in its various phases, see Graves, *op. cit.*, pp. 234–235, 267, and 275–277.

[2] But long before Christianity, monasticism existed in many types of religion and philosophy and among a variety of races and peoples. Perhaps it appears earliest in India, with the Brahman self-torture, but among the Greeks, as early as the sixth century B.C., the Pythagoreans established a strict ascetic régime. Somewhat later, there were similar tendencies among the Cynics and the Stoics, and in Plato's emphasis upon the ideal life and meditation, especially as continued in Neoplatonism. There were also several ascetic sects among the Jews.

[3] The word is derived from the Greek *monos*, which signifies 'alone.'

6 A HISTORY OF EDUCATION

The first recluse was Paul, who was followed by Anthony and hosts of others.

and merciless exposure to heat and cold. Their food consisted mostly of bread and water, while oil, salt, and such fruits and vegetables as could easily be obtained, may occasionally have been used as luxuries. The first to court this life of isolation and repression was one Paul, who during the third century escaped from persecution into the Egyptian desert, and was generally regarded as the founder of the hermit life. He was followed by that Anthony who is reputed to have had so many encounters with 'the evil one,' and by hosts of others until the caves of Egypt were everywhere filled with recluses.

Before long, however, these monks began to live together, and the first monastery was founded by Pachomius about the middle of the fourth century.

The social instinct, however, still existed even in these anchorites, and before long the abodes of the more famous hermits were surrounded by the huts and dens of disciples. This led to the foundation of monasteries or common dwelling-houses, in which the monks lived apart in separate cells, but met for meals, prayers, communion, and counsel.[1] The first monastery was organized by Pachomius, about the middle of the fourth century, and was located on the island of Tabennæ in the Nile. The founder divided his fourteen hundred followers into bands of tens and hundreds, with an appropriate official over each group and with all finally subordinate to himself.[2] This form of monasticism was more humane than the solitary, and soon came to prevail. The influence of Pachomius was extended over all Egypt and into Syria and Palestine until there were some seven thousand monks living under his 'rule' or code.

This form of monasticism was extended into Europe

From the East this *cœnobitic* ('common life') monasticism was introduced into Greece by Basil, who had studied it in Egypt, Syria, and Palestine, and into Italy

---

[1] A good picture of this type of Egyptian monasticism can be formed by reading the description of Philammon's life in Abbot Pambo's *laura* at Scetis, given in Kingsley's *Hypatia*.

[2] He could not, however, have been known as *abbot* ('father'), as this term was not for some time restricted to the superior or head, but was applied to every monk.

MONASTICISM AND THE MONASTIC SCHOOLS 7

and Gaul by Athanasius during his flight from Alexandria to escape the Arian persecutions, and half a century later by Jerome, who came to Rome from his monastery in Bethlehem in order to evangelize. But monasticism in the West took on a very different character from that of the Orient or even from that in Greece. The passivity in living and the self-torture of the East could not appeal to the energetic people of the West and gave way to more active pursuits and milder discipline. The codes of Pachomius and Basil were replaced by those of St. Augustine and Cassian in the fifth century, and of Benedict in the sixth, and the monks turned to the cultivation of the soil, the preservation of literature, and teaching, under these rules. The discipline of Benedict, while based on that of his predecessors, was far broader and more practical, and had a wide range of influence. It was extended by his pupil, St. Maur, into Gaul, and in the eighth century was widely spread by Boniface, 'the apostle to the Germans.' *by Basil, Athanasius, and Jerome, and there, under Augustine, Cassian, and Benedict, it turned toward more active pursuits.*

Meanwhile, there were developing in Ireland a school of theology and a type of monasticism of quite a different kind. Britain had been Christianized while still a Roman province, but during the fifth century the country was reheathenized through its occupation by the Angles and Saxons. The Christianity there was crowded back into Ireland and parts of Wales, and, through its isolation from the rest of the Church, came to vary from that of Rome. Irish Christianity adopted a different time for Easter, and other peculiar ecclesiastical usages, and preserved a high development of learning for some time after it had been driven from the Continent. During the sixth century, through a fugitive monk called Columba,[1] Celtic Christianity spread as a *In Ireland a different type of monasticism arose, by the absorption of which into Roman Christianity, learning and progress were greatly stimulated.*

---

[1] According to Montalembert, O'Donnell, or 'Columba,' was condemned to exile as the result of a quarrel with his abbot and king over his making a copy of the Psalter surreptitiously. See *The Monks of the West*, Vol. II, pp. 15-24. He founded a monastery upon the west coast of Scotland, which became the prototype of many similar institutions.

8   A HISTORY OF EDUCATION

type through the southern part of Scotland and into Northumbria, and in the sixth and seventh centuries it was extended throughout Gaul. Before the arrival of Irish Christianity in northern England, however, Roman Catholicism and the Benedictine rule had been introduced into Kent and the southern kingdoms by a prior named Augustine, who, in 597, had been sent by the pope to evangelize England. Within a couple of generations the two types of Christianity came seriously into conflict, especially in Northumbria, until, through the king of that territory, Roman Catholicism was recognized as authoritative at the Council of Whitby in 664, and Celtic Christianity withdrew to Ireland or was absorbed by the Roman Church. An immense enthusiasm for the church, culture, and literature of Rome resulted from this merging of the rival organizations, and the monasteries of England, such as Wearmouth and Yarrow, became the great centers of learning for Europe.

The Benedictine 'rule' was generally adopted, but, as discipline grew lax, various reform orders of monks arose.

The discipline of Benedict continued largely to control the monasteries of Western Europe.[1] While each house remained independent, practically all adopted the 'rule' as Benedict himself wrote it, or in a modified form. But as the monastic lands and wealth increased, and the monks grew luxurious, and lax in their attention to religious duties, from time to time there sprang up new movements, which undertook to introduce reforms into the monastic system of living. Of such a nature were the efforts of Benedict of Aniane, the Cluniac monasteries,[2] Dunstan in England, St. Bruno, and the later orders known as Augustinians, Carthusians, Cistercians, Franciscans, and Dominicans.[3] Every succeeding foundation strove to outdo all the others in strictness,

---

[1] The popularity of the Benedictine rule was due in large part to Pope Gregory I (590–604), who, as a former monk of the order, gave it the benefit of his influence, and through the missionary, Augustine, another Benedictine, it received authoritative standing in England.

[2] For Cluny, Citeaux, Camaldoli, etc., as seats of reform of the Benedictine monasticism, see Milman's *Latin Christianity*, Vol. IV, pp. 228–236.

[3] See Chapter VIII.

but the 'rule' of each one had its ultimate basis in that of Benedict.

The Rule of Benedict. — Owing to the importance of the Benedictine code, it will be necessary to examine some of its provisions, and note their effect upon monastic institutions. The 'rule' consists of a prologue and seventy-three chapters, and deals with the organization, worship, discipline, admission, ordination, and other administrative functions of a monastery.[1] Benedict appreciated the temperament of the West and the needs of the times, and gave especial prominence to the doctrines of labor and of systematic reading. His forty-eighth chapter declares: — *The Benedictine 'rule' required at least seven hours of manual labor and two hours of reading;*

> "Idleness is the great enemy of the soul, therefore the monks should always be occupied, either in manual labor or in holy reading. The hours for these occupations should be arranged according to the seasons, as follows: From Easter to the first of October, the monks shall go to work at the first hour and labor until the fourth hour, and the time from the fourth to the sixth hour shall be spent in reading. After dinner, which comes at the sixth hour, they shall lie down and rest in silence; but any one who wishes may read, if he does it so as not to disturb any one else. Nones shall be observed a little earlier, about the middle of the eighth hour, and the monks shall go back to work, laboring until vespers."

These seven hours of labor might be increased in harvest time, if necessary, while in winter, from October to Lent, an extra hour was added to the two hours of reading, and during Lent still a fourth hour.

By the requirement of manual labor Benedict professedly intended to keep the robust and active monks from temptations and from brooding,[2] but it was eventually by this means also that the desperate material *the labor resulted in great material improvement, and the reading in the preservation of learning.*

[1] For the complete 'rule,' see Thatcher and McNeal, *Source Book for Mediæval History*, pp. 432-485.

[2] In Lecky we read that "a melancholy, leading to desperation, known to theologians under the name of 'acedia,' was not uncommon in monasteries. The frequent suicides of monks, sometimes to escape the world, sometimes through despair at their inability to quell the propensities of the body, sometimes through insanity produced by their mode of life, and by their dread of surrounding demons, were noticed by the early Church."

conditions, produced by the barbarian inroads, were largely reduced to law and order. Through the agency of the monasteries, swamps were drained, forests cleared, and the desert regions reclaimed; the peasants were trained in agriculture, and the various crafts and industries were preserved; the abandoned fields were repeopled, and the beginnings of cities formed anew. On the other hand, the requirement of daily reading proved the means of preserving some semblance of learning and reviving a literary education.

The Libraries, Multiplication of Manuscripts, and Original Writings of the Monasteries. — If the monks were to read, manuscripts had to be collected and reproduced. Hence the monasteries became the depositories of ancient literature and learning, and the interest in the collection and care of books increased as monasticism developed. Benedict, in the chapter from which we quoted above, gives some directions for the care of books. He even mentions a 'library,' but probably the books were not kept in a special room at first. They seem to have been placed in the cloister of the monastery, where they would be most accessible to the monks, and locked in presses when not in use; but before long a regular library room with seats and other conveniences for reading was arranged. The Cluniacs further appointed a special official to care for the library and the books, and the Carthusians and Cistercians even allowed outsiders to borrow books upon stated terms, and seem to have provided two sets of books, for lending and reference respectively. But the monastic libraries were very limited both in the number of the books and the character of their subject matter. The works in the average monastery were mostly religious in nature, as literature for its own sake was a conception unheard of in monastic times. Most libraries, too, contained but a few hundred volumes, although a few, like Fulda, St. Gall, and Croyland, came to have a thousand or two, and the Novalese in Italy, according to Montalembert, had risen to sixty-five hundred by the time of its de-

For the reading, manuscripts had to be collected and reproduced, and the library became a feature of each monastery.

struction in the tenth century. Nevertheless, the library became so important a feature of the monastic environment that in 1170 a sub-prior of Normandy voiced a general sentiment when he declared: *claustrum sine armario est quasi castrum sine armamentario* ('a monastery without a library is like a castle without an armory').

The multiplication of manuscripts for the sake of obtaining duplicates for the monks or for exchange with other houses soon became a part of the work of the monasteries.[1] Those who were especially skilled or were too weak or disabled to carry on rough toil, were allowed to put in their seven hours of labor in making copies of manuscripts. Others must also have undertaken it when the weather made it impossible to work outside, and in the convents that eventually arose for women the copying of manuscripts was the chief form of labor. Each monastery soon had a *scriptorium* ('writing-room') in one end of the building, and occasionally regular cells for copying were provided. While copies were multiplied mostly of the *Scripturæ Sacræ* ('sacred writings'),[2] the Christian Fathers, the missals, and breviaries, many of the Latin classics likewise helped to occupy the time of the monks, and were in this way preserved for the day of awakening. Although much of the copying may have been done automatically, with more regard for neatness and ornamentation than accuracy or meaning, it was intended that the content of the works should have its intellectual and moral influence upon the copyists. This multiplication and exchange of manuscripts by the monks must have been maintained upon rather a large scale. Until the cathedrals, palaces, and castles also came to collect manuscripts, and, through the art of printing, copies became more common, the monasteries were engaged in what might be termed a species of book-trade.

This resulted in the extensive copying of manuscripts, both sacred and secular, and a species of book-trade in the monasteries.

[1] It was begun at Viviers, Italy, in 539 by Cassiodorus, but the example was soon followed by all the Benedictine monasteries.
[2] This included not only the Scriptures, but all other works elucidating religious or ecclesiastical truths.

The monks also produced original writings, — religious, moral, and historical.

But the monasteries did not confine their efforts to copying the works of others. In fact, it has gradually come to be realized that the monks were the authors of a vast amount of original literature. While the subject matter is somewhat circumscribed, the quantity of monastic writings illustrates how absurd was the old notion of the 'Dark Ages.' Most of their productions were upon religious topics, such as commentaries upon the Scriptures or the Christian Fathers, The Lives of the Saints, and the sermons or moral tales called *Gesta Romanorum* ('Deeds of the Romans'),[1] but they also wrote histories of the Church, the monasteries, and the times. History, however, was not viewed in those days so much with reference to the facts as to the glory and advancement of the Church, and these accounts are consequently filled with superstition, inaccuracy, bias, and impossibility. They are, nevertheless, practically the only documents of the times that we possess. After making due allowance for the view-point of the writers, we shall get from them the best picture of the life, thought, and institutions of at least the earlier Middle Ages.

The requirement of reading necessitated the organization of schools in the monasteries,

Organization of the Monastic Education. — The life in the monasteries was a species of education in itself, and even in the 'rule' of Benedict there was no provision for anything more formal. However, since very early the monks were required to read, collect libraries, and copy manuscripts, it is not surprising that regular schools had arisen within the monasteries even a century before Benedict's time. And by the ninth century nearly all monastic houses had also schools for the children of the neighborhood, and, as time passed, many prescriptions concerning education were added to the Benedictine code. Literary education was at first recognized and then emphasized until all the monasteries of repute were also known for the learning and education maintained. Such, for example, were Monte Cassino, Bobbio, Pom-

[1] These *Gesta Romanorum* were merely popular tales (*fabliaux*) that had been given a moral twist.

posa, and Classe in Italy; Fulda, Reichenau, Hirschau, Gandersheim, Wissenbourg, and Hersfeld in Germany; St. Gall in Switzerland; Fontenelle, Fleury, Ferrières, Corbie, Tours, Toul, Cluny, and Bec in France; and Canterbury, York, Wearmouth and Yarrow, Glastonbury, St. Albans, Croyland, and Malmesbury in England; all of which furnished excellent advantages for the times. Many other monasteries, however, gave little or no attention to learning. The course may often have lasted eight or ten years, as boys of ten or even less were sometimes received into the monastic schools, and no one could become a regular member of the order before he was eighteen. Later, boys were also admitted who never expected to enter the order, although they were to be priests. These latter were called *externi* ('outsiders') in distinction to the *oblati* ('those offered'), who were preparing to become monks.

<small>and a course of from eight to ten years came about.</small>

The Three Ideals of the Monastic Education. — While some importance was thus attached to learning and intellectual development, the main aim of monastic education was the discipline and repression of the body. The training in all its aspects was primarily intended to make monks. It was a course in ascetic living, and its goal is summed up in the three ideals that appear in the usual oath of a monk before admission, of which the following is an example: —

<small>The chief purpose of monastic education was expressed in the ideals of obedience, chastity, and poverty.</small>

<small>"I, brother (name), a humble monk of the monastery of St. Denis in France, in the diocese of Paris, in the name of God, the Virgin Mary, St. Denis, St. Benedict, and all the saints, and of the abbot of this monastery, do promise to keep the vows of *obedience, chastity*, and *poverty*. I also promise, in the presence of witnesses, steadfastness and conversion of life, according to the rules of this monastery and the traditions of the holy fathers."</small>

These three ideals, — 'obedience, chastity, and poverty,' represented the various practices deemed necessary in monastic life. Each concept monasticism sought to defend by quotations from the Bible, and only by their joint practice and ingraining in the life of the individual was it believed that the soul could be purified and saved. 'Obedience' was felt to be an essential ideal for the training of a monk, as his superiors were held to be the representatives of God, and the effect of this submission upon the untamed Germans was most beneficial. By 'chastity' the monastics meant celibacy, and this was believed to be 'more blessed than marriage,' as one could accomplish so much more for religion if his attention were not distracted by family duties. Likewise, the monks felt that it would be difficult for one who was not wedded to 'poverty' to escape the hardening and debauching influences of the time.

Thus monastic education sought for the sake of salvation to oppose three of the fundamental obligations of the existing society, — allegiance to the state, care of the family, and economic provision for the future, and in this sense it might be regarded as anti-social. To come to such a conclusion would be, however, to view a mediæval institution from the modern point of view, as well as to ignore the tremendous contribution to social development made by these ideals. However unsuited they may seem at the present time, it was through them that the lives of the crude and ruthless warriors of the day were softened, and society was to a large extent reorganized upon a higher and more effective level.

The subject matter soon came to be the Græco-Roman Seven Liberal Arts,— **The Monastic Course of Study and the Seven Liberal Arts.** — The subject matter that was used by the monastic schools to carry out these ideals varied from time to time. In the first schools, founded by Cassian, the course was of an elementary and narrow sort, and was intended to prepare for only the bare duties of the monastic life. The embryo monks were required to learn to read, in order to study the Bible; to write, that they might copy the sacred books; and to calculate, for the sake of computing Church festivals. This limited training became even more formal and illiberal under the immediate successors of Cassian, but by the time of Benedict, the Christians, having succeeded in establishing their ideals, felt that the pagan culture was no longer threatening and began to introduce the Græco-

Roman learning into the course of study. By this time the pagan authors themselves had somewhat fallen into disuse, but practically none of the actual knowledge of the classical times had disappeared. It remained in that condensed and rather dry form known as the *Seven Liberal Arts*.

This canon of the proper studies, which was adopted by the monastic and other mediæval schools, is of so much importance as to demand a detailed account both of its origin and its content. It was a gradual evolution from Græco-Roman days, but became the especial topic for many treatises during the fifth and sixth centuries.[1] The discrimination of these liberal studies may be said to have begun with *Plato*, whose scheme of education included two groups of subjects, — the lower, consisting of gymnastics, musical practice, and letters, and the higher, made up of arithmetic, geometry, musical theory, and astronomy. These 'liberal' subjects, during the later days of Greece and the Roman Republic, gradually combined with the 'practical' studies of the sophists, — rhetoric and dialectic, and, after various changes, the pagan course settled down about the beginning of the Christian era into grammar (or literature), rhetoric, and dialectic, arithmetic, geometry, music, and astronomy. It is known, for example, that when the Roman *Varro* (116–27 B.C.) wrote upon the Hellenized school curriculum, he included all seven, although he added also medicine and architecture. *grammar, rhetoric, and dialectic, and arithmetic, geometry, music, and astronomy.*

While other writers of later Rome were not as definite in their conception of the liberal arts and omitted one or another of the subjects in their treatment, by the time of the decadence of Roman education, in the fourth century A.D., this canon of the Greek schools must have become fairly well fixed. The best illustration is found in the Latin writer, *Martianus Capella*, who in the early *This canon had become well fixed by the fourth century, and encyclopædic treatises were written by Capella, St. Augustine, Boethius, Cassiodorus, and Isidore.*

---

[1] An interesting and scholarly discussion of the subject is found in Abelson's *The Seven Liberal Arts* (New York, 1906), and a more detailed account of 'grammar' and 'rhetoric' in Paetow's *The Arts Course at Mediæval Universities* (Urbana, Illinois, 1910).

part of the fifth century produced a treatise upon the seven liberal arts, known as *De Nuptiis Philologiæ et Mercurii*. It is a dry allegorical account of the marriage of the god Mercury with the congenial maiden Philology, at which each of the seven bridesmaids, — *Grammatica, Dialectica, Rhetorica, Geometrica, Arithmetica, Astronomia,* and *Harmonia,* narrates her antecedents and describes the subject she represents. It was about this time that the Christians began to realize that this pagan course might be of service to them in the study of theology, and began themselves to write on the liberal arts. Even *St. Augustine* (354–430) justified these studies on the ground of 'despoiling the Egyptians,' and wrote treatises upon all of them, except astronomy. Thus he most fully influenced the Western world in accepting this curriculum, but a formulator of the liberal arts whose works were more widely read in the Middle Ages was the supposed Christian, *Boethius*[1] (481–525). He wrote especially upon logic and ethics, which made up the content of the mediæval 'dialectic,' and upon arithmetic, geometry, and music. A further contribution was made in the sixth century by *Cassiodorus*,[2] the founder, and later the head, of the monastery of Viviers, who in his *De Artibus et Disciplinis Liberalium Literarum* ('On the Liberal Arts and Sciences') first regularly used the term 'the *seven* liberal arts,' and justified this specific number by reference to the seven pillars of wisdom mentioned in Proverbs.[3] From this time on the seven liberal arts were recognized by the Christians as the orthodox secular studies preparatory to theology. With *Isidore* (566–636), the bishop of Seville, the term becomes definitely fixed, and the first three subjects are classed as the *trivium* and the other four as the *quad-*

---

[1] He was claimed as a Christian and his writings were much copied and used by the monastic schools, but while some of his expressions might be so interpreted, he was undoubtedly pagan in most of his conceptions.

[2] The early part of his activity was spent as chief counsellor to Theodoric, the Ostrogothic king, who had defeated Odoacer and taken possession of Italy. See also footnote, p. 11.

[3] Proverbs, IX, 1.

rivium. This distinction appeared in his *Etymologiæ* or *Origines*, an encyclopædic work, containing all the meager knowledge of the day, which he wrote for his monks and secular clergy. The first three of its twenty books treated the seven liberal arts, and the trivialities and absurdities they contain mark the retrogression in learning that had gradually come about in the successive treatises. However, from this time on the program of the seven liberal arts was traditional in mediæval education, and Isidore became the chief authority in the monastic schools.

But while at no time after the sixth century did the Church or the monastic schools show themselves seriously hostile to any of these secular studies, certain of the liberal arts were more emphasized at various periods, and the quality of instruction in some subjects varied at different times. The importance attached to a subject seems in each case to have been in keeping with the needs of the period. Up to the twelfth century, since an acquaintance with the Latin language and literature was absolutely necessary, and dialectic and mathematics were as yet but little developed, stress was laid upon the study of grammar and rhetoric, but, as will appear in the chapter on Scholasticism, in the later centuries of the Middle Ages, when cogency in thought and argument had become all important, dialectic was emphasized, and when mathematical knowledge came in with the Saracens, arithmetic, geometry, and astronomy were especially favored by the stronger minds. *Until the twelfth century, grammar and rhetoric were most prominent, but after that were forced aside by the development of dialectic and mathematics.*

It should also be remembered that while this curriculum was not a broad one, the scope was much wider than would be supposed from the mere names of the subjects. 'Grammar' was simply an introduction to literature, and, after gaining some facility in Latin through simple proverbs, epigrams, and fables, the pupils read some of the classic and Christian authors themselves.[1] The works most read seem to have been, *All subjects were much broader in content than would be supposed from the names.*

---

[1] Recent investigation has shown that the amount of classic literature was beyond the belief of the most enthusiastic mediævalists. See Specht, *Geschichte des Unterrichtswesens in Deutschland*, pp. 296-394.

on the one hand, first and foremost the Æneid of Vergil,[1] and then some of Terence, Horace, Statius, Lucan, Persius, and Juvenal; and on the other, Juvencus, Prudentius, and Sedulius. But little of the Greek literature, however, was known, except through the medium of translations.[2] 'Rhetoric,' which, in accordance with mediæval needs, was intended especially as an aid to writing official letters and drawing up legal documents, had to include also some knowledge of history and law.[3] While throughout the Middle Ages dialectic was similar to the formal logic of to-day, it paved the way in the later period for the problems of metaphysics. 'Arithmetic' consisted at first of little more than the calculation of Church festivals, but in the tenth century, with the introduction of columnal calculation, and later of the Arabic notation and symbols, the content was very greatly increased. Similarly, 'geometry,' which from the first included some knowledge of geography and geometrical concepts, was gradually enlarged to embrace the complete system of Euclid and all the existing knowledge of geography and surveying. Likewise, while 'astronomy' was at first limited to a practical knowledge of the courses of the planets and the changes of season, Ptolemy's treatise and Aristotle *On the Heavens* gradually found their way in through the Saracens, and, at the close of the Middle Ages, considerable mathematical

---

[1] During the Middle Ages Vergil was esteemed as the embodiment of wisdom, and, while the Christians tried to break from him as evil in doctrine, they seem to have been quite unable. Such features of his writings as were inconsistent with the thought and ethics of the age were harmonized by regarding them as allegorical. As his wisdom came to be considered more than human, legends grew up in which he figured as a prophet and magician. From such tales, when expanded and embellished, there sprang the material for various Old French *romans* and *fabliaux*. See Comparetti's *Vergil in the Middle Ages*.

[2] Greek was preserved somewhat longer in the British Isles, but probably not even Alcuin was much acquainted with the original literature. The pagan classics were generally distrusted by men who were absorbed in saving their souls.

[3] Later, this phase of rhetoric developed into a professional branch known as *ars dictaminis* or *dictamen prosaicum*, which, while short-lived, gave birth in Italy to the more specialized *ars notaria*, which was closely related to civil law. See Paetow, *The Arts Course*, Chapter III.

astronomy and physics were included. And although 'music' comprehended at the beginning only sacred compositions, in the end it covered a broad study of the history and theory of music. Thus, as the Middle Ages developed, while the content of the course of study in the monastic, as in the other, schools varied from time to time, it could at no period be considered really meager.

The Methods of Teaching and the Texts Used in the Monastic Schools. — So, too, in the matter of method, while the teachers of the monastic schools were far from attaining to modern theory, they seem to have possessed some pedagogical skill. Their interest in the art of instruction is also shown in the fact that, beside such general encyclopædic works as those of Capella, Boethius, Cassiodorus, and Isidore, a large number of texts upon each one of the liberal arts has survived.

In method the teachers showed considerable interest and skill, although dictation and memory had to be largely used.

The general method of teaching was that of question and answer. As an illustration of the drill of the times when applied to the first word of the Æneid, the following has been extracted from Priscian: —

"What part of speech is *arma ?*"   "A noun."
"Of what sort ?"   "Common."
"Of what class ?"   "Abstract."
"Of what gender ?"   "Neuter."
"Why neuter ?"   "Because all nouns whose plurals end in *a* are neuter."
"Why is not the singular used ?"   "Because this noun expresses many different things."

As copies of the various books were scarce, the instructor often resorted to dictation, explaining the meaning as he read, and the pupils took the passage down upon their tablets and committed it. The reading-books preparatory to the study of literature, many of which are still extant, were generally arranged by each teacher, and careful attention was given to the etymological and literary study of the authors to be read. There naturally was an unusually large number of commentaries upon Vergil.[1]

---

[1] See footnote 1 upon p. 18. Abelson speaks of these commentaries as divided into four groups, — literary, rhetorical, eulogistic, and allegorical.

Beside the encyclopædic writings on the liberal arts, various texts were produced upon single subjects.

As to texts, the leading works upon grammar, and those upon which most of the later treatises were based, were written by the Roman grammarians, Donatus (fourth century) and Priscian (sixth century). These texts were, however, poorly adapted to boys who learned Latin as a foreign language, and during the twelfth and thirteenth centuries there sprang up a series of grammars, of which the *Doctrinale* of Alexander of Villedieu, and the *Græcismus* of Eberhard of Bethune, were the most important.[1] The 'new' grammars devised a system of syntax, and, for the sake of memorizing, were often written in verse. As rhetoric was no longer concerned with declamation and panegyric, the rhetorical works of Cicero and Quintilian were rarely used as texts on the subject, although the writings of these authors were not infrequently referred to as themselves models of the best style. The various mediæval textbooks dealing with the art of prose writing, included rather a compendium of official letters, famous legal documents, and forms relating to daily life. The proper divisions of a letter or a document and the method of producing each part were also definitely described in the treatises.[2] The texts upon dialectic were in the earlier Middle Ages mostly confined to the encyclopædic writings on the liberal arts, but during the period of scholasticism, specific works on the various subjects were produced by nearly every writer of prominence. Dialectic was first based upon Latin translations of a few works of Aristotle, but toward the end of the twelfth century there came an influx of the 'new' Aristotle through the Moors, and soon all his works were in the possession of the Christians. After the tenth century there was also a large

---

[1] At the University of Paris the most remarkable grammarian was John Garland, whose chief works are *Clavis Compendii*, *Compendium Grammatice*, and *Accentuarius*.

[2] Alberich of Monte Cassino, in the latter half of the eleventh century, wrote a text on the new art, in which he taught the division of a letter into five parts, *salutatio, benevolentiae captatio, narratio, petitio, conclusio*. The art reached its height at Bologna with the famous master, Boncompagno.

number of texts upon arithmetic and geometry. In astronomy, besides the encyclopædic works, there were special editions and adaptations of the treatises of Ptolemy and Aristotle. The elaborate *De Musica* of Boethius lasted well into the day of universities, but several commentaries were also written during the ninth and tenth centuries by less known authorities.

How Monasticism Affected the Middle Ages and Civilization in General. — Much, then, is owed to the Christian monasteries for preserving and spreading humanity and culture. While we cannot always trust the unstinted praise of Montalembert, we may easily sympathize when he declares: —

<blockquote>
"To that unfortunate multitude condemned to labor and privation, which constitutes the immense majority of the human race, the monks have always been prodigal, not only of bread, but at the same time of a sympathy efficacious and indefatigable — a nourishment of the soul not less important than that of the body."
</blockquote>

Monasticism accomplished much for material progress and humanity,

Monasticism arose from a protest against vice and corruption, and pointed the way to a deeper religion and a nobler life. It tamed the spirits and refined the hearts and intellects of the German hordes. It cultivated the waste places and made "the deserts blossom as the rose." Through it barbarians acquired industrial skill and perceived the true dignity of labor. The poor, the hungry, and the sick found asylum and succor at the monastery door, and the weary traveller a hospice inside its halls. Monasticism preserved ancient culture and brought forth chronicles and religious works; it continued the classical schools and the traditions of education. It may not be that "without the monks we should have been as ignorant of our history as children," but we do have to rely upon them at present for many of our documents and sources of the Middle Ages, uncritical and superstitious though they were, and it is scarcely possible that without the monasteries and monastic schools the Latin and Greek manuscripts and learning would have survived and been available when the human spirit was at length aroused from its lethargy of a thousand years.

and for the preservation of learning and education.

22   A HISTORY OF EDUCATION

But it had periodic lapses from morality, piety, and industry, and was somewhat opposed to classical literature, and absolutely so to science and individualism.

Nevertheless, it must be admitted that monasticism was infected with many faults of the times. There were periodic lapses from its piety and morality, especially as the monasteries came to be wealthy, luxurious, and idle. While these times usually gave rise to new orders with additional strictness of living, carelessness in religion and industry, and even vice, often crept within the monastic walls. And in the matter of learning and education, although the amount of Græco-Latin culture retained and original works produced is now known to have been very much greater than was previously supposed, it is equally certain that monasticism was always somewhat hostile to classical literature as representing the temptations of the world and opposing the ascetic ideal, and at all times its rigid orthodoxy prevented every possibility of science and the development of individualism.

This is, of course, the secret of the unsparing criticism of such men as Voltaire, Gibbon, and Guizot, as far as it was not an outgrowth of their prejudices. Such wholesale condemnation is even more untenable for the historian than is the biased advocacy of Montalembert. The truth will, as usual, be found somewhere between the extremes. Perhaps the fairest picture is that given in the series of epigrams by a recent writer: —

> "Monasticism was the friend and foe of true religion. It was the patron of industry and the promoter of idleness. It was the pioneer in education and the teacher of superstition. It was the disburser of alms and a many-handed robber. It was the friend of human liberty and the abettor of tyranny. It was the champion of the common people and the defender of class privileges."[1]

All the criticisms in this estimate were probably true of certain monasteries during a considerable part of their existence and of almost all monasteries at particular periods, but in the main the merits cited are the more characteristic of this great institution. At any rate, in balancing these contradictions, the positive contributions of monasticism to the humanities and civiliza-

---

[1] Wishart, *Monks and Monasteries*, p. 389.

MONASTICISM AND THE MONASTIC SCHOOLS 23

tion must not be overlooked. While it may at times have retrograded, and did stand at every period in the way of actual progress, it was, after all, the chief means of enabling the Germans to keep alive and hand on to the modern world the light that had been kindled in them by their contact with antiquity.

SUPPLEMENTARY READING

I. SOURCES

ALEXANDER OF VILLEDIEU. *Das Doctrinale* (edited by Reichling in *Monumenta Germaniæ Pædagogica*, XII).
BACON, R. *Opera quædam hactenus inedita* (edited by Brewer).
BOETHIUS, A. M. T. S. *De Arithmetica, De Musica,* and *Interpretatio Euclidis Geometriæ.*
CAPELLA, M. *De Nuptiis Philologiæ et Mercurii.*
CASSIAN, J. *Institutio et Dialogi.*
CASSIODORUS, M. A. *De Artibus et de Disciplinis Liberalium Literarum.*
DONATUS, A. *Ars Grammatica.*
EBERHARD OF BETHUNE. *Græcismus* (edited by Wrobel in *Corpus Grammaticorum Medii Ævi*, Vol. I).
HENDERSON, E. F. *Historical Documents of the Middle Ages.* Bk. III, Nos. I and IV.
ISIDORE OF SEVILLE. *Etymologiæ.*
PRISCIAN. *Institutio de Arte Grammatica.*
ROBINSON, J. H. *Readings in European History.* Vol. I.
THATCHER AND MCNEAL. *A Source Book for Mediæval History.* Pp. 432–492.

II. AUTHORITIES

ABELSON, P. *The Seven Liberal Arts.*
CHURCH, R. W. *The Beginning of the Middle Ages.*
CLARK, J. W. *Libraries in the Mediæval and Renaissance Monasteries.*
COMPARETTI, D. *Vergil in the Middle Ages* (translated by Benecke).
ECKENSTEIN, L. *Woman under Monasticism.*
FEASEY, H. J. *Monasticism.*
HALLAM, H. *Europe during the Middle Ages.*
HARDY, R. S. *Eastern Monasticism.*
HEALY, J. *Insula Sanctorum et Doctorum;* or *Ireland's Ancient Schools and Scholars.*
HUNT, W. *The English Church* (597–1066). Chaps. VI, X, XVII, and XVIII.

HYDE, D. *A Literary History of Ireland.* Chaps. XIII–XVIII.
LAURIE, S. S. *Rise and Constitution of Universities.* Lectures II, IV, and V.
LECKY, W. E. H. *History of European Morals.* Chap. IV.
MILMAN, H. H. *The History of Latin Christianity.*
MONTALEMBERT, C. F. *The Monks of the West.*
PAETOW, L. J. *The Arts Course at the Medieval Universities with Special Reference to Grammar and Rhetoric* (in *University of Illinois Studies*, Vol. III, No. 7).
PARKER, H. *The Seven Liberal Arts.*
PUTNAM, G. H. *Books and Their Makers during the Middle Ages.*
SANDYS, J. E. *A History of Classical Scholarship.* Vol. I (sec. ed.).
SPECHT, F. A. *Geschichte des Unterrichtswesens in Deutschland.*
STANLEY, A. P. *History of the Eastern Church.*
TAYLOR, H. O. *Classical Heritage of the Middle Ages.*
VOIGT, E. *Das Erste Lesebuch des Triviums in den Kloster-und Stiftsschulen des Mittelalters.*
WISHART, A. W. *A Short History of Monks and Monasteries.*
WOODHOUSE, F. C. *Monasticism, Ancient and Modern.*
ZIMMER, H. *The Irish Element in Mediæval Culture.*

CHAPTER III

CHARLEMAGNE'S REVIVAL OF EDUCATION

WHILE the ecclesiastical organization was the main element, it was not the only means of furthering the assimilation that was going on in the Middle Ages. Although Rome had perished and the fragments of her dominions were in constant opposition and turmoil, occasionally the political factor had its effect upon mediæval civilization and education, especially as the idea of a universal empire had never entirely vanished.

Rise of the Franks and the Empire of Charlemagne. — For nearly three centuries after the fall of Rome, the inroads of the barbarians and the disintegration of the Roman civil organization, culture, and system of education went on. But by the eighth century conditions had settled somewhat, and a new social order and grouping about a Frankish king had come to pass. The 'Franks' consisted of a confederation of German tribes that alone had succeeded in establishing a permanent kingdom which was neither taken by other barbarian tribes nor reconquered by the Eastern emperor. By the middle of the sixth century, under the Merovingian kings, they had spread over what is now France, Belgium, Holland, and most of western Germany, and, through the rise of the more vigorous Carolingian dynasty in the seventh and eighth centuries, their control became even wider and the sovereignty more centralized. Karl Martel greatly strengthened the Frankish rule and the Carolingian dynasty by his repulse of the Saracens at Tours in 732. Two decades later, his son, Pippin the Short, consummated a family alliance with the pope, and, severely chastising the Lombards, who were threatening

The Franks alone of all the Germans established a permanent kingdom, and under the Carolingians centralized the sovereignty.

Rome, turned over a goodly strip of their land to the pontiff. Pippin's son, *Karl the Great* or *Charlemagne*[1] (742-814), deposed the troublesome dukes of Aquitaine and Bavaria, forced the Lombards to recognize him as their king, conquered the pagan Saxons, crowded the Saracens back of the Ebro, subdued the fierce Slavs and Bohemians, and generally completed the erection of Frankish supremacy into a single Christian empire.

This was recognized through the coronation of Charlemagne by the pope in 800.

This unification was recognized by the unexpected crowning of Charlemagne as Emperor of the Romans by the pope upon Christmas day, 800. And that act from the head of the Church Universal may fairly be regarded as a climax in the absorption of the Roman organization by the Germans, who thus, through the Franks, became the means of transmitting it as a basic element in modern society. Just as our religious inheritance from Rome was made possible through the organization of the Roman Catholic Church, so the heritage of Roman political and legal institutions has come to us through the establishment at this time of what was destined, when somewhat curtailed, to be known as the *Holy Roman Empire*.

Charlemagne strengthened his rule by abolishing the duchies, establishing margravates, sending out missi, forming a cabinet, and issuing capitularies.

Charlemagne's Improvements in Administration. — But Charlemagne readily saw the difficulty of holding together his wide and heterogeneous dominions, and his administration was as wisely conducted as his conquests. While still king of the Franks, he abolished the independent tribal duchies and divided them into districts under counts, responsible directly to the central government; and, as the hostile peoples were pushed back, he created military districts to prevent incursions and put *margraves*[2] ('counts of the border') in charge of them. As a check upon the counts and margraves, he sent out *missi dominici* ('royal commissioners'), who should report to him what was going on in the various districts. To assist in the central government, he had a council of

---
[1] At this time the Franks were all Germans, and the French form of the name is indefensible, except as the result of usage.
[2] I.e. *Mark* plus *Graf.*

nobles and ecclesiastics, with whose sanction he issued decrees called *capitularies* to all parts of his realm.

Charlemagne's Efforts to Improve Learning. — The great monarch, however, even before becoming emperor, had realized that a genuine unity of his people could be brought about only through the inner life by means of a common language, culture, and set of ideas. To produce this, he felt that a revival of learning was necessary, and sought to spread such of the Roman culture as had been preserved. By the latter half of the eighth century there had been a great loss in knowledge and education. The Gallic learning of the fifth and sixth centuries was disappearing, the copying of manuscripts had almost ceased, and the monastic and cathedral schools had been sadly disrupted. Charlemagne reveals the conditions of the times in writing the Abbot of Fulda: —

"We have frequently received letters from monks and in them have recognized correct sentiments, but an uncouth style and language. The sentiments inspired in them by their devotion to us they could not express correctly, because they had neglected the study of language. Therefore, we have begun to fear lest, just as the monks appear to have lost the art of writing, so also they may have lost the ability to understand the Holy Scriptures; and we all know that, though mistakes in words are dangerous, mistakes in understanding are still more so."

A similar lack of education seems to have prevailed among the 'secular'[1] clergy, the nobility, and most others who might have been expected to be trained, although the leading churchmen must still have had, beside their knowledge of ecclesiastical Latin, some acquaintance with the classical authors and the compilations of the seven liberal arts by Boethius, Cassiodorus, and Isidore. Evidently Charlemagne had a keen sense of the situation, and he made every effort to improve it. To assist him in his endeavors, he summoned the lead-

To improve learning, which had fallen into a desperate condition, Charlemagne engaged the most learned scholars of the day, — Peter of Pisa, Paul the Deacon, and especially the Saxon Alcuin.

[1] This term was used of the clergy, — priests, bishops, etc., given to parochial and other duties in society. They lived in the world (*sæculum*), as opposed to the monastic or 'regular' clergy, who lived according to rule (*regula*).

ing scholars of the day. His father's educational adviser, Peter of Pisa, was already with him, and through him he secured the services of Paul the Deacon, a prominent scholar of Lombardy. But more influential than either of these was *Alcuin* (735-800), whom Charlemagne called in 782 from the headship of the famous cathedral school at York to be his chief minister of education. This school had become, perhaps, the most prominent center in Europe, since, as we have noted,[1] learning had reached its height in England after it had largely vanished from the Continent, and Alcuin became the means of renewing the Græco-Roman training. Peter was growing very old and Paul was unpractical, and both of these refined Lombards were jealous of the Frankish supremacy and showed themselves out of sympathy with the rude and boorish warriors of Frankland. Neither objection held of Alcuin, for Anglo-Saxon interests were quite removed from the interference of the Franks, and Alcuin had, through a previous acquaintance, come to be a great admirer of Charlemagne and his achievements. Moreover, he was just enough older so that the impetuous monarch was willing to listen to his advice with grace. Through this English scholar, Charlemagne revived the monastic, cathedral, and parish schools,[2] and had a new higher institution, known as the *Palace School*, started at the head of his educational system.

Alcuin and the Palace School. — We may properly consider first the last named institution. It was soon organized at the court of the great king by Alcuin and the three teachers he had brought from York.[3] Charlemagne himself studied here under the Saxon educator, and with him his queen, his three sons and two daughters, his sister, son-in-law, and three cousins, and various

Alcuin organized the Palace School, at which he taught Charlemagne and his family and court,

---

[1] See pp. 7-8.
[2] For an account of these types of schools, see Graves, *History of Education before the Middle Ages*, pp. 281, 286, and 294.
[3] According to Maitre, this school had existed for several generations, but was given a new life by Alcuin.

prominent ecclesiastics and scholars of Frankland, including his biographer, Einhard. Alcuin must have found that a somewhat different mode of teaching was necessary with the adults from the formal one used with the more plastic minds. As in the monastic schools,[1] the plan for instructing the youth was the 'catechetical' method, in which a definite answer was arranged for each of a fixed set of questions. Usually the replies were learned and given by the pupil, although originally the teacher indicated the proper answers. This is shown in the following selection from *The Disputation of Pippin*, which is supposed to have taken place when that prince was about sixteen: —

but adapted his method according to the age of his pupils.

"PIPPIN. — 'What produces speech?' ALCUIN. — 'The tongue.'
P. — 'What is the tongue?' A. — 'The whip of the air.'
P. — 'What is air?' A. — 'The guardian of life.'
P. — 'What is life?' A. — 'The joy of the good, the sorrow of the evil, the expectation of death.'"

* * * * * * *

"P. — 'What is rain?' A. — 'The reservoir of the earth, the mother of fruits.'
P. — 'What is frost?' A. — 'A persecutor of plants, a destroyer of leaves, a fetter of the earth, a fountain of water.'
P. — 'What is snow?' A. — 'Dry water.'"[2]

But a more discursive method must have been employed in the Palace School with the older people, who could not memorize as rapidly and would not be as willing to regard the instructor as a final authority. Certainly the vigorous Charlemagne, with his eagerness and curiosity for learning, can hardly be thought of as tamely submitting to Alcuin without disputation and suggestion, and at times even attempts to prove that scholar inconsistent. Often he seems to have strained the patience of his tactful master, and occasionally led to a mild rebuke.

Among the subjects taught in the Palace School seem

---

[1] See p. 19.
[2] For the rest of the naïve metaphorical explanations of this colloquy, see *Alcuini Opera*, Migne, C. I., 975, seqq., quoted by Mombert, *Charles the Great*, pp. 244–245.

He there taught grammar, rhetoric, dialectic, arithmetic, astronomy, and theology. to have been grammar, including some study of the Latin poets and the writings of the Church Fathers, rhetoric, dialectic, arithmetic, astronomy, and theology, but Alcuin appears to have had but little command of the Greek learning, except in translation. Charlemagne had previously learned grammar from Peter of Pisa, and he now acquired from Alcuin the higher branches. According to Einhard, "he spoke foreign languages beside his own tongue, and was so proficient in Latin that he used it as easily as his own language. Greek he could understand better than he could speak. He was devoted to the liberal arts." This may be somewhat doubtful, but we may well believe the pathetic picture: "He tried to learn to write, keeping his tablets under the pillow of his couch to practice on in his leisure hours. But he never succeeded very well, because he began too late in life."

Charlemagne also issued capitularies to the abbots and bishops, and thus revived or established schools at the monasteries, cathedrals, and villages. **Educational Improvement in the Monastic and Other Schools.** — Nor did Charlemagne limit his endeavors to educating himself and his relatives and friends. Besides establishing the Palace School, he undertook to revive the monastic, cathedral, and parish schools. With the coöperation of Alcuin, he did everything within his power to increase facilities and improve standards. In 787 he issued an educational capitulary to the abbots of all the monasteries, of which the copy sent to Fulda has come down to us. After reproving the monks for their illiteracy in the words already quoted,[1] he writes: —

"Therefore, we urge you to be diligent in the pursuit of learning, and to strive with humble and devout minds to understand more fully the mysteries of the Holy Scriptures. For it is well known that the sacred writings contain many rhetorical figures, the spiritual meaning of which will be readily apprehended only by those who have been instructed in the study of letters. And let those men be chosen for this work who are able and willing to learn and who have the desire to teach others, and let them apply themselves with a zeal equaling the earnestness with which we recommend it to them."

[1] See quotation on p. 27.

CHARLEMAGNE'S REVIVAL OF EDUCATION

In apparently the same year that Charlemagne sent out this capitulary, it is stated that "he brought with him from Rome into Frankland masters in grammar and reckoning, and everywhere ordered the expansion of the study of letters." Two years later he wrote a more urgent capitulary to the abbots and bishops, in which he specified the subjects to be taught in the monastic and cathedral schools and the care to be taken in teaching them. Moreover, the *missi* of Charlemagne were instructed to see that the provisions of these capitularies and other educational efforts were carried out to the letter, and there is evidence for believing that the instructions were generally obeyed by the abbots and bishops. Schools seem to have been everywhere revived or established for the first time in the various monasteries, cathedrals, and villages, and the instruction at such places as Tours, Fulda, Corbie, Bec, Orleans, and Hirschau became famous. To insure this revival, according to the Monk of St. Gall, the monarch ordered that only those most interested in learning and education should be appointed to important dioceses and abbacies.

The Course of Study and the Organization in the Schools. — All the monastic and cathedral schools of Frankland thus came to offer at least a complete elementary course, and some added considerable work in higher education. Reading, writing, computation, singing, and the Scriptures were taught first, but, beyond this, instruction in grammar, rhetoric, and dialectic was often given, and in the more famous monasteries the *quadrivium* also appeared in the course. The schools in the villages, under the care of the parish priests, furnished only elementary subjects. In these schools, besides the rudiments, were taught the Lord's prayer, the creed, and the Psalms. *The elementary subjects were everywhere taught, and sometimes also the trivium and quadrivium.*

Tuition was free in all schools for those intending to become monks or priests, but for the higher work a small fee was sometimes paid by the laity. As a rule, elementary education was gratuitous and open to all. *Tuition was generally free, universal, and almost compulsory.*

This is shown to have been the case in the diocese of Orleans, if we may judge from the episcopal letter of Theodulf, which requires that "the priests hold schools in the towns and villages, and if any of the faithful wish to intrust their children to them for the learning of letters, let them not refuse to receive and teach such children. . . . And let them exact no price from the children for their teaching, nor receive anything from them, save what the parents may offer voluntarily and from affection." Indeed, Charlemagne almost makes elementary education compulsory by decreeing in his capitulary of 802 that "every one should send his son to study letters and that the child should remain at school with all diligence until he should become well instructed in learning."

The School of Alcuin at the Monastery of Tours.— After fourteen years of strenuous service, Alcuin was anxious to retire from the active headship of the school system, with its difficulties and discouragements. To this desire his royal master yielded and made him abbot of the monastery of St. Martin at Tours, the oldest and most wealthy[1] in Frankland. But even here his educational work did not cease. He soon established a model house of learning and education, whither there flocked to him the brightest youthful minds in the empire. As these rapidly became prominent as teachers and churchmen, Alcuin's influence came to be even wider than before, and the standard of learning in all the schools was greatly raised.

At this center he introduced the deepest learning in the Scriptures and liberal arts, and wrote a number of educational works, mostly along the lines laid down by Augustine, Cassiodorus, Isidore, and Baeda.[2] Further, through a large correspondence with kings and the higher clergy, during the eight years that intervened before his death, his influence was extended for several

In 796 Alcuin retired to the monastery of Tours, where he established a model monastic school,

and had a wide educational influence,

---

[1] The Archbishop of Toledo is known to have reproached Alcuin with being the master of twenty thousand slaves.
[2] See pp. 15–17 and 38.

generations and reached to lands beyond the Carolingian sway. Alcuin, however, was by nature conservative and timid, and with his retirement from the world and the near approach of death, he became decidedly set and narrow. His fear of the dialectic and the more advanced views of certain Irish scholars, "with their versatility in everything and their sure knowledge of nothing," who were drifting into Frankland, is almost ludicrous. He advises Theodulf, the new head of the Palace School, to hold to the 'old wine,' and urges the emperor to secure vigorous exponents of the old faith, lest the heresy spread. "You have by you," he writes, "the tomes of both secular learning and of the Church's wisdom, wherein the true answers will be found to all your inquiries." Similarly, he was inclined to counsel his pupils against the classic poets, even Vergil, his former favorite, saying: "The sacred poets are enough for you; you have no need to weaken your minds with the rank luxuriance of Vergil's verse." But while he became thus ascetic and hostile toward anything new, this is not remarkable under the circumstances, and he must be credited until the last with the highest ideals, the greatest energy, and even a certain breadth of vision. *but became set and narrow.*

Rabanus Maurus and Other Pupils of Alcuin. — While at the death of Alcuin practically all positions of educational importance were held by his pupils, the monastic school of Fulda was destined under *Rabanus Maurus* (776–856) to become the great center of learning. Rabanus was probably the most esteemed pupil of Alcuin,[1] and in many ways he was a man of broader gauge than his master. While he wrote even more prolifically than Alcuin upon grammar, language, and theology, he did not cling to the traditional subjects, and was not afraid to emphasize the new training in dialectic. Moreover, he enriched the formal study of grammar by a genuine training in literature, and advo- *Alcuin's pupil, Rabanus Maurus of Fulda, continued and advanced his educational ideals, content, and influence,*

---

[1] Alcuin gave him his surname, taking it from St. Maur, the most beloved disciple of Benedict.

cated the reading of the classic poets. Through his influence, too, the mathematical subjects of the curriculum were expanded into considerably more than the calculation of Church festivals, and he even made bold to ascribe all phenomena to natural laws, rather than to some mysterious cause. Thus he became a forerunner of the later movement of scholasticism.

while the Irish learning was added under the mastership of Joannes Scotus Erigena at the Palace School.

The pupils of Rabanus were even more numerous than those of Alcuin, and but few scholars or teachers of the next generation are not to be attributed to Fulda. However, the great scholar of East Frankland but continued the influence of his master in the West, and it would be difficult to separate the part played by each. Further, there was mingled with the Alcuinian growth the cross-fertilization of Irish learning. This came to Frankland especially through the mastership of *Joannes Scotus Erigena* (810–876)[1] at the Palace School in the middle of the ninth century. Thus during this century and the first half of the next, through the political tranquillity brought about by the Carolingians, there arose a marked revival in education. Most of the monasteries of the Continent and England for several generations enthusiastically supported schools and fostered learning. Curricula were expanded, and many famous scholars appeared. Theological discussions and other evidences of renewed intellectual activity sprang up. Owing to the weakness of Charlemagne's successors, the attacks of the Northmen, and the general disorder of the empire, learning gradually faded once more. But while the results of the revival are somewhat disappointing, intellectual stagnation never again prevailed. It is clear that even in the period of retrogression between the end of Charlemagne's influence and the greater activity of scholasticism, some educational traditions must have survived. Through the revival of the great Frankish monarch the classical learning was recalled to continental Europe from its insular asylum in the extreme West.

[1] See pp. 49–50 and 51.

SUPPLEMENTARY READING

I. Sources

ALCUIN. *Opera Omnia* (emendata cura et studio Frœbenii).
EINHARD. *Life of Charlemagne.*
HENDERSON, E. F. *Historical Documents of the Middle Ages.* Book II.
JAFFE, P. *Monumenta Alcuiniana* (*Bibliotheca Rerum Germanicarum*, VI).
RABANUS MAURUS. *Opera Omnia* (Migne, *Patrologia Latina*, CVII–CXII).
ROBINSON, J. H. *Readings in European History.* Vol. I, Chap. VII.
THATCHER AND MCNEAL. *A Source Book for Mediæval History.* Pp. 26–60.

II. Authorities

ABEL AND SIMSON. *Jahrbücher des Frankischen Reiches unter Karl den Grossen.* Band II.
ADAMS, G. B. *Civilization during the Middle Ages.* Chaps. VII and VIII.
ADAMSON, R. *Alcuin* (article in *Dictionary of National Biography*).
BARNARD, H. *German Teachers and Educators.*
DRANE, A. T. *Christian Schools and Scholars.* Chaps. V and VI.
GASKOIN, C. J. C. *Alcuin, His Life and His Work.*
HENDERSON, E. F. *A Short History of Germany.* Vol. I, Chap. II.
LAURIE, S. S. *Rise and Constitution of Universities.* Lect. III.
LORENZ, F. *Life of Alcuin* (translated by Jane Mary Slee).
MOMBERT, J. I. *A History of Charles the Great.*
MONNIER, F. *Alcuin et Charlemagne.*
MULLINGER, J. B. *The Schools of Charles the Great.*
TOWNSEND, W. J. *The Great Schoolmen of the Middle Ages.* Chap. II.
WEST, A. F. *Alcuin and the Rise of Christian Schools.*

CHAPTER IV

THE REVIVAL OF EDUCATION UNDER ALFRED

A WORK for education similar to Charlemagne's and possibly inspired by it was that of Alfred the Great (848–901), king of the West Saxons. It was, however, on a smaller scale, and was more personal and local in character. In Britain for several centuries there had been continual warfare between the various tribal kingdoms established by the Angles, Saxons, and Jutes, until in 827 all had been brought under the overlordship of Wessex. But a little later the Northmen, or 'Danes,' as they were called by the Anglo-Saxons, conquered all the country north of the Thames, and were prevented from extending their sway into Wessex only by Alfred, who had come to the throne in 871. This monarch, however, instead of attempting to reëstablish the supremacy of Wessex, devoted his energies to developing the realms that remained to him.

After improving the government of his country, Alfred of Wessex undertook a regeneration of educational conditions.

Alfred's Desire to Extend and Improve Education. — After the fashion of Charlemagne, Alfred improved the political administration of his country, displaying great breadth and sagacity, but his chief resemblance to the Frankish emperor rests on his interest in education. Just before his reign began, learning in England appears to have sadly retrograded since the days of Alcuin, and Wessex was probably the most ignorant kingdom in that land. But few lettered men were left, even in the more cultured towns. Alfred writes : —

"So general became the decay of learning in England that there were very few on this side of the Humber who could understand the Church service in English, or translate a letter from Latin into English; and I believe that there were not many beyond the Humber who could do these things. There were so few, in fact, that I cannot remember a single person south of the Thames when I came to the throne."

THE REVIVAL OF EDUCATION UNDER ALFRED

Alfred desired to lift this incubus of ignorance from his people. He expressed the wish "that all free-born youth now in England, who are rich enough to be able to devote themselves to it, be set to learn as long as they are not fit for any other occupation, until they are well able to read English writing; and those afterwards be taught more in the Latin language who are to continue learning, and be promoted to a higher rank."

The Establishment of Schools and the Importation of Educators. — To carry out this ideal, Alfred encouraged many schools at the monasteries. He also had the schools in general improved and increased in number, and personally supervised a Palace School for the education of his sons, "the children of almost all the nobility of the country, and many who were not noble." Here the pupils were taught reading and writing, both in Latin and Saxon, and acquired the Psalms, Saxon poetry and other literature, and some of the liberal arts.

However, with the exception of the Welsh bishop and chronicler, Asser, there were scarcely any men in the kingdom of sufficient education to aid him. But Asser tells us : —

"God at that time, as some relief to the king's anxiety, yielding to his complaint, sent certain lights to illuminate him, namely, Werfrith, bishop of the church of Worcester, . . . Plegmund, a Mercian by birth, archbishop of Canterbury; Ethelstan and Werwulf, his priests and chaplains, also Mercians by birth. These four had been invited from Mercia by King Alfred, who exalted them with many honors and powers in the kingdom of the West Saxons. . . . But the king's commendable desire could not be gratified even in this ; wherefore he sent messengers beyond the sea to Gaul, to procure teachers, and he invited from them Grimbald, priest and monk, a venerable man and good singer, adorned with every kind of ecclesiastical training and good morals, and most learned in the holy Scriptures. He also obtained John, priest and monk, a man of most energetic talents, and learned in all kinds of literary science and skilled in many other arts."

Thus, curiously enough, as Charlemagne had resorted to Lombardy and York, Alfred went to the Continent for men of reputation, to help in improving the schools. *Grimbald* was drawn from the Flemish monastery at

To make elementary education universal and afford some higher training, Alfred improved and increased the schools in general, and supervised a Palace School; and, beside certain Mercians, he summoned prominent educators from the Continent, such as Grimbald and John the Old Saxon.

St. Omer to become Abbot of Winchester, and *John the Old Saxon* was invited from Corbie to take charge of the new monastery and school established at Athelney.

He also translated the best books of the time.

Alfred's Personal Assistance to Learning and Education. — Of course old works were recovered and new texts were prepared for the work in the schools, but the most striking contribution to educational facilities was the translations made by Alfred himself. He attempted to open up to the pupils and the people at large the learning and information that had previously been confined to the clergy and nobility, and to that end rendered from Latin into English the best books of the time. For example, he translated into the vernacular the *Consolations of Philosophy* of Boethius, the *Universal History of the World*, compiled by Orosius, the *History of the Church in England*, written by Bæda, and the *Pastoral Charge* of Pope Gregory the Great.[1]

These works, chosen as the leading productions of the day, afford a concrete example of the lamentable way in which knowledge and culture had, through a lack of interest, declined since the day of Rome.[2] Fortunately, Alfred was an editor as well as a translator, and by abridging at times, expanding at others, and commenting throughout, he added a spice, enthusiasm, and intelligibility to each work that was entirely his own. Through him, too, the *Anglo-Saxon Chronicle* was compiled, in order that the people might become acquainted in the vernacular with the history of their own country.

Thus Alfred greatly increased the opportunities for schooling,

Significance of Alfred's Educational Work. — In these ways Alfred gave a new impulse to education among the West Saxons and elsewhere in England, very much as Charlemagne had upon the Continent. He greatly increased the opportunities for schooling, restored much

---

[1] Plummer undertakes to show to what extent each of these was the work of Alfred himself. See *Alfred the Great*, pp. 140–196.

[2] If Alfred had known Herodotus, Thucydides, Livy, and Tacitus, he would have preferred their works to the dreary compend of Orosius. So he would have found Plato, Aristotle, Seneca, and Epictetus preferable to the decadent philosophy of Boethius.

THE REVIVAL OF EDUCATION UNDER ALFRED 39

of the old learning, opened the best Latin works of the day to his people, and produced the first prose writings in England. He thus helped on the day of awakening, for, while the mediæval turmoil and narrowness ruled supreme for some centuries after his day, conditions in England were never as dark again.

and restored much of the old learning.

SUPPLEMENTARY READING

I. SOURCES

ASSER. *Annales Ælfredi* (translated by E. Conybeare).
CHEYNEY, E. P. *Readings in English History.* Chap. V, II.
GILES, J. A. *Six Old English Chroniclers.* Pp. 51-77.
STEVENSON, J. (Translator). *Anglo-Saxon Chronicle.*
THORPE, B. *Ancient Laws and Institutes of England* (edited by Plummer).

II. AUTHORITIES

ADAMS, G. B. *Civilization during the Middle Ages.* Chap. VIII.
BOWKER, A. (Editor). *Alfred the Great.* By Harrison, Oman, Earle, Pollock, and others.
CONYBEARE, E. *Alfred in the Chroniclers.*
GILES, J. A. *Life and Times of Alfred the Great.*
GREEN, J. R. *A Short History of the English People.* Chap. I.
GREEN, J. R. *The Conquest of England.* Chap. IV.
HUNT, W. *The English Church* (597-1066). Chap. XII.
MORLEY, H. *English Writers.* Vol. II, Chap. XII.
PAULI, R. *Life of Alfred the Great* (translated by Thorpe).
PLUMMER, C. *The Life and Times of Alfred the Great.* Especially Lectures V and VI.
RANSOME, C. *An Advanced History of England.* Chap. VI.
TRAILL, H. D. (Editor). *Social England.* Vol. I.
TURNER, S. *History of the Anglo-Saxons.* Especially Vol. IV, Bk. V.

CHAPTER V

THE MOHAMMEDAN LEARNING AND EDUCATION

The Rise of Moslemism and Its Absorption of Greek Culture.— One of the most important influences in awakening mediæval Europe was the revival of learning and education that came through the advent of the Moslems into Spain. In the early part of the seventh century, when Moslemism first appeared, one would hardly suppose that it could become a means of renewing education. The founder of this religion, *Muhammed*, or *Mohammed*, was almost illiterate, and the revelations that he claimed to have received were for nearly a generation handed down by tradition. The *Koran*, or sacred book of this faith, was not committed to writing until about 650. It appears to be a curious jumble of the Judaistic, Christian, and other religious elements with which Mohammed had become acquainted during his early travels.

As long as this religion was confined to the ignorant and unreflecting tribes of Arabia, it served its purpose without modification, but when it spread into Syria and other cultured lands,[1] it came in contact with Greek philosophy, and had to be interpreted in those terms, in order to appeal to the people there. Antioch, Edessa, Nisibis, and other places in Syria had become famous for the Greek learning cultivated by their catechetical schools. These schools had grown up during the third and fourth centuries through the expulsion from the Eastern Church of those who had amalgamated the

Moslemism, founded by Mohammed, who was almost illiterate,

became amalgamated with Greek learning in Syria,

---

[1] During the ten years that elapsed between Mohammed's famous *hegira* ('flight') from Mecca in 622, and his death, the whole of Arabia was converted, and under the *caliphs* ('representatives'), who immediately succeeded him as head of the religion, it was spread by the sword over Persia, Syria, and Egypt.

THE MOHAMMEDAN LEARNING AND EDUCATION 41

Greek philosophy with their Christianity.[1] The accession of the followers of Nestorius, whose Hellenized theology had in 431 been proscribed by the Council of Ephesus,[2] very greatly increased the importance of these cities, as intellectual centers. Here, from about the middle of the sixth century, the Nestorian Christians accumulated, in addition to the translations that were already there, a large range of the original Greek treatises on philosophy, science, and medicine. The works of Aristotle and Neoplatonism were especially sought, and, by the middle of the seventh century, when the Mohammedans came in contact with the Nestorians, these Christians had already become thoroughly imbued with the spirit of Hellenism. In order to make converts to Moslemism, a syncretism of this faith with Hellenism was necessary. Within a century, through the Nestorian scholars, the Mohammedans began to render into Arabic from the Syriac, or from the original Greek, the works of the great philosophers, mathematicians, and physicians. During the next two hundred years the movement continued to grow, and by the tenth century such Mohammedan cities as Damascus, Bagdad, Basra, and Kufa were renowned for their learning.

where the catechetical schools and Hellenized Christianity had taken refuge.

It was this interest in Greek learning that impelled the head of the Moslem religion, the caliph Almaimon, early in the ninth century to beg the emperor at Constantinople to allow Leo the mathematician to come to Bagdad, saying:

"Do not let diversity of religion or of country cause you to refuse my request. Do what friendship would concede to a friend. In return, I offer you a hundred weight of gold, a perpetual alliance and peace."

---

[1] An account of these catechetical schools is given in Graves, *History of Education before the Middle Ages*, Chap. XIV.

[2] Nestorius was Patriarch of Constantinople from 428 to 431, and his especial antagonist was the notorious Cyril, Patriarch of Alexandria, who was largely influenced by jealousy. For an account of this controversy, see Rainy, *The Ancient Catholic Church* (New York, 1902), pp. 376–392.

42   A HISTORY OF EDUCATION

Thus the thinkers in the Moslem schools of Syria undertook to root out the supernatural from the Moslem religion and to render its tenets more reasonable. A mysticism not unlike that of the Christian Gnostics resulted, and the Neoplatonism, as well as the Aristotelianism, of the Nestorians received a new lease of life.

The Syrian Moslems also absorbed learning from other people, and wrote treatises upon mathematics, medicine, philosophy, and theology; the chief of their works being the Encyclopædia of the Brothers of Sincerity.

The Brothers of Sincerity and their Scheme of Higher Education. — But besides the Greek science and philosophy, the Arabs absorbed similar matter from other peoples, such as the Hindu mathematical learning, and added many new ideas of their own. Among the Moslems arose such scholars as *Avicenna* (980–1037), who wrote many treatises on mathematics and philosophy, and a *System of Medicine* that was an authority for five centuries, and *Algazzali* (1058–1111), whose philosophical and theological productions were most numerous and influential. The combination of Moslemism with Greek philosophy was especially embodied in an *Encyclopædia*, or course of study, formulated about the year 1000. The resulting system was arranged at Basra by the Moslem society that called itself the *Brothers of Sincerity*. It presupposed an elementary training, and may thus be regarded as the higher education of the Mohammedans. It is composed of fifty-one treatises grouped under the four general heads of Propædeutics, Natural Science, Metaphysics, and Theology. These treatises deal at first with concrete subjects, and then with the more complicated problems of life, until the theories of divine law are reached. Under this last head there is given a dogmatic exposition of the Moslem faith, and in this feature the Encyclopædia differs radically from all Greek philosophy. Nevertheless, it is probably the best attempt at a harmonization of philosophy with revelation, and is the one complete educational system that the mediæval world affords.

But the masses of the Moslems were suspicious of

If the Brothers of Sincerity had succeeded in getting the Mohammedans generally to accept their scheme, modern civilization would probably have been hastened by several centuries. But the masses of the superstitious

THE MOHAMMEDAN LEARNING AND EDUCATION 43

and fatalistic Arabs were as suspicious as the mediæval Christians of the Greek learning, and toward the end of the eleventh century the Hellenic scholarship and education, and the rationalized theology of the Brothers of Sincerity were driven from the Orient. Fortunately, it was able to find refuge in the more liberal caliphates of Africa and Spain, where the Mohammedans had settled after their repulse from Frankland in the eighth century.[1] Here the Encyclopædia and other works had a large influence not only upon the Arabs of the West, who were known as Moors, but upon the later Jewish thinkers and the Christians. Among the Moorish writers was the celebrated *Averroës* (1126-1198), who undertook to unite the doctrines of Aristotle with those of Moslemism.[2] Throughout the Middle Ages he was the authoritative 'commentator' on the great philosopher.

<small>Greek learning, and the rationalized theology of the Brothers of Sincerity was driven from the Orient into Africa and Spain,</small>

The Moorish Colleges. — The stimulus thus given to higher education led to the founding of great schools at Cordova, Granada, Toledo, Seville, Alexandria, Cairo, and elsewhere by the Moors. At these places, during the eleventh century, when in the Christian schools of the East and West alike learning was at a very low ebb, the Mohammedans were teaching arithmetic, geometry, trigonometry, physics, astronomy, biology, medicine, surgery, logic, metaphysics, and jurisprudence. These Moorish institutions were *colleges* in the literal sense, for the students lived in them together with the professors. Through these colleges the highest spirit of culture and investigation flourished. The sciences were greatly advanced, Arabic[3] notation was introduced in place of the cumbersome Roman numerals, many inventions and discoveries were made, and practical achievements, like navigation, exploration, commerce, and industries, were

<small>where were founded the Moorish colleges, with their courses in mathematics, sciences, and philosophy.</small>

---

[1] Karl Martel had checked their advance by the battle of Tours in 732. See p. 25.

[2] For a most complete account of Arabic metaphysics, see Renan's *Averroës et l'Averroïsme*.

[3] It has long been called 'Arabic' from the source of its introduction into Europe, but the Arabs, of course, got it first from the Hindus.

developed. Hence Draper is naturally led "to deplore the systematic manner in which the literature of Europe has contrived to put out of sight our scientific obligations to the Mohammedans." And it was in the colleges of the Moors that the mediæval Christians afterward found a model for their universities. It would, indeed, be difficult to overestimate the remarkable influence of the Moorish development upon European civilization.

The Moslems also founded elementary schools, where the rudiments, religion, and elementary science were taught.

Elementary Education. — But the Mohammedans, both of the East and the West, did not limit themselves to higher education. Elementary schools for both boys and girls sprang up in practically all cities and towns that came under their influence. Children went to school at five. If they belonged to a poorer family, they remained only three years, when they went into some trade or industry, but children of the wealthy attended school until they were fourteen, and, wherever it was possible, they were encouraged to travel with a tutor. These elementary schools taught religion, reading, writing, grammar, versification, arithmetic, and geography. The chief reading-book was the Koran, but, as Draper shows, they must have taught geography by means of globes, while the Church doctrine of Rome and Constantinople was still asserting that the earth is flat.

The Moslem colleges and schools stimulated learning in the Christian schools, and introduced Aristotle into Christianity once more.

Stimulating Effect upon Europe of the Moslem Education. — These Mohammedan schools, especially the higher, naturally proved a great stimulus to education in the West. While learning had now largely disappeared from the Christian schools of the East, in those of Western Europe, through the example of the Moslems, it began to revive. By the middle of the twelfth century, Raymund, Archbishop of Toledo, had the chief Arabic treatises on philosophy translated into Castilian by a learned Jew, and then into Latin by the monks; while Frederick II, head of the Holy Roman Empire, had scholars render the works of the Aristotelian commentator, Averroës, into Latin. Such translations had, however, passed through several media, and, in consequence, were not at all accurate. Renan describes one

THE MOHAMMEDAN LEARNING AND EDUCATION 45

rendering of Averroës as "a Latin translation of a Hebrew translation of a commentary on an Arabic translation of a Syriac translation of a Greek text of Aristotle." But stimulated by this taste of the Greek learning, the Christians sought a more immediate version. Half a century later, when the Venetians took the city of Constantinople, and the works of Aristotle were recovered in the original, the Western world hastened to have translations made directly into Latin.

But during the thirteenth century the orthodox Mohammedans overwhelmed the Hellenized Moslemism and came to control even in Spain, and it was left to the Christian schools and the Jewish philosophers to continue the work of the Moslem scholars and institutions. Moslemism had returned to its primitive stage, but it had brought back learning, especially the works of Aristotle, to Christendom, and a worthy mission for progress was thereby performed. Thus the Græco-Roman learning, which had been driven out of Europe by orthodox Christianity, found its way back through the Mohammedans, and the circular process was complete. As the classical learning had been restored from the West during the revival of Charlemagne, it returned from its refuge in the East through the movement of the Saracens.[1]

After the orthodox Mohammedans came into control in Spain, Moslemism returned to its primitive stage, but it had brought learning back to Christianity.

SUPPLEMENTARY READING

I. SOURCES

BROTHERS OF SINCERITY. *Encyclopædia.*
LANE, E. W. *Selections from the Koran.*
MÜLLER, MAX. *Sacred Books of the East.* Vols. VI and IX.

II. AUTHORITIES

ADAMS, G. B. *Civilization during the Middle Ages.* Chap. XI.
ARNOLD, J. M. *Islam: Its History, Character, and Relation to Christianity.*
BOSWORTH-SMITH, R. *Mohammed and Mohammedanism.*

[1] The influence of the Moors and their scholarship will be more patent after a study of scholasticism and the universities. See Chapters VI and IX.

COPPÉE, H. *History of the Conquest of Spain by the Arab-Moors.*
    Especially Bk. X.
DAVIDSON, T. *The Brothers of Sincerity* (in *International Journal
    of Ethics*, July, 1898).
DRAPER, J. W. *History of the Intellectual Development of Europe.*
    Vol. I, Chaps. XI and XIII, and Vol. II, Chaps. II and IV.
FREEMAN, E. A. *History and Conquests of the Saracens.*
MUIR, W. *The Rise and Decline of Islam.*
NEALE, F. *Rise and Progress of Islam.*
SCOTT, S. P. *History of the Moorish Empire in Europe.*
STOBART, J. W. H. *Islam.*
WEIL, G. *Geschichte der Islamitischen Völker.*

CHAPTER VI

THE EDUCATIONAL TENDENCIES OF MYSTICISM AND SCHOLASTICISM

WE must now turn to a consideration of the mediæval philosophy and its effects upon education. Like most other periods of civilization, the Middle Ages made some attempt to formulate its attitude toward the problems of life. Its two chief methods have been generally known as 'mysticism' and 'scholasticism.' These methods were, in a way, opposed to each other. Mysticism, the earlier movement, was emotional and immediate, while scholasticism, which did not reach its height until toward the close of the Middle Ages, was rather intellectual and mediate in method. Yet the later mystics, in the end, borrowed the dialectic of the scholastics, while apparently most hostile to it, and, during the twelfth and thirteenth centuries the two methods coalesced. *The two mediæval methods of philosophy are known as 'mysticism' and 'scholasticism.'*

The Nature and Rise of Christian Mysticism. — The prior method, *mysticism*, may be described as an effort to grasp through intuition the ultimate reality or the Divine essence, and thus obtain direct communion with the highest. To the mystic, God is an experience, not an object of reason; and his religion stresses the realization of the Divine to such an extent that the individual shall lose himself therein, and all relations save that between himself and God become comparatively unreal. Mysticism is a life of contemplation and devout communion, and usually appears in history when a religion has begun to harden into formulæ and ceremonial, and constitutes a reaction of spirit against letter. Thus it arose in Christianity from much the same causes as monasticism, — the vice and corruption of the Roman world, the growing secularization of the Church, and the *Mysticism is the effort to hold direct communion with God.*

It arose in Christianity as a reaction of spirit against letter.

It appeared early, but it was upon the principles of Plotinus and the Pseudo-Dionysius that mediæval mysticism based its training.

demand for more immediate religious experiences. Most mystics were also monks, but mysticism constantly recurred without reference to monasticism and endured far beyond the monastic period.[1] Mysticism appeared in Christianity as early as the writings of the disciple John, the apostle Paul, and the first Christian Fathers, but it was upon the principles of Plotinus (205-270), who is generally regarded as the founder of Neoplatonism, and upon the procedure implied in certain mystical writings of the fifth century by the Pseudo-Dionysius,[2] that the mediæval mystics first based their training. These works developed a species of esoteric Christianity, of which the following summary of Dionysius may serve to give an idea: —

"All things have emanated from God, and the end of all is return to God. Such a deification is the consummation of the creature, that God may finally be all in all. The degree of real existence possessed by any being is the amount of God in that being — for God is the existence in all things. The more or less of God which the various creatures possess is determined by the proximity of their order to the center. The chain of being in the upper and invisible world through which the Divine Power diffuses itself in successive gradations is the Celestial Hierarchy. The Ecclesiastical Hierarchy is a corresponding series in the visible world. The (three) orders of Angelic natures and of priestly functionaries correspond to each other. The highest rank of the former receives illumination immediately from God. The lowest of the heavenly imparts divine light to the highest of the earthly hierarchy. Each order strives perpetually to approximate to that immediately above itself, so that all draw and are drawn towards the center — God."[3]

---

[1] Mysticism appeared, too, before the day of Christianity in the Brahmanic 'absorption' and the Buddhistic 'nihilism,' in the contemplative asceticism of the Essenes, in Plato's doctrine of the 'mystic vision' obtained only by speculation, in the esoteric 'knowledge' of the Gnostics, the ecstatic intuition and repudiation of the sensible and material in Neoplatonism, and in the syncretism that Philo makes of the Old Testament and the Platonic writings. See Graves, *History of Education before the Middle Ages*, pp. 78-79, 188-189, and 283-285.

[2] These forgeries were attributed to Dionysius the Areopagite, who was alleged to be a convert of the apostle Paul, and are an accommodation of the theosophy of Proclus to the claims of the ecclesiastical hierarchy. Read Inge's *Christian Mysticism*, Chaps. III and IV.

[3] Taken from Vaughn's *Hours with the Mystics*, pp. 113-115.

EDUCATIONAL TENDENCIES OF MYSTICISM 49

The Education in Mediæval Mysticism. — From such Neoplatonic doctrine did the mystics obtain their elaboration of the Platonic psychology and their educational practice. Gradually they came to hold that there are three aspects to the soul, — the lowest or *animal*, through which it is connected with the body; next, the *human*, by which it reasons; and finally, the *superhuman*, through which there is union with the divine intelligence. There are thus three degrees of intensity in soul experience, and the highest can be obtained only by withdrawal from the world of activity and sensation into that of thought, since pure existence, or God, can be reached and grasped only through the exclusion of sense. Hence the training of the mystics came to include three definite steps, and to consist in a most extreme type of discipline. First, during the stage of *purification*, one was to clear the way by getting rid of the impressions of sense; then, *illumination* might be obtained through a contest with the life within until good deeds were performed by habit; when finally, in the stage of *perfection*, one might, by viewing and assimilating, approximate to the life of God.

There were held to be three aspects to the soul,— animal, human, and superhuman, and three stages of training, — purification, illumination, and perfection.

The Development of Mysticism. — It can be seen that by the time this analysis of the soul and its training was made, the method of the first Christian mystics had been greatly changed. Logical gymnastics had come to be used to strengthen the mind for the mystic contemplation, and the immediacy of the religious experience had become reconciled with considerable discussion of the stages through which the soul had to pass in attaining a vision of the Divine. This transformation of mysticism was greatly advanced by *Joannes Scotus Erigena* (810–876), whom we have seen to have been instrumental in introducing dialectics and broader learning into Europe.[1] Erigena used the writings of the Pseudo-Dionysius as the basis of his own doctrines, but to a great extent rejected emanation and pantheism, and

Thus logical gymnastics came to be used to strengthen the mind for the mystic contemplation,

---

[1] See p. 34.

made more of an attempt to describe the intervening steps by which the soul reaches the Divine. Three centuries later, the monastic reformer *Bernard of Clairvaux* (1091-1153) went further in defining the three distinct stages through which reason passes in rising to its vision of the Divine, although he still held that more exalted than the highest of these is an ecstatic state, like that of St. Paul, by means of which one suddenly obtains a direct view. Even more minute distinctions were recognized, and a more systematic consideration of mysticism was made in the twelfth century by *Hugo and Richard of St. Victor*,[1] and in the thirteenth century by *Bonaventura*,[2] a student of these Victorine monks. Six divisions of the soul were distinguished, and as many stages in education devised.

The Character of Scholasticism. — This adoption of dialectics by mysticism shows how fully it had come to combine with the philosophic method known as *scholasticism*. The name of this later movement is derived from the term *doctor scholasticus*, which was applied during the mediæval period to the authorized teachers in a monastic or episcopal school, for it was among these 'schoolmen' that scholasticism started and developed. Like mysticism, it does not indicate any one set of doctrines, but is rather a general designation for the peculiar methods and tendencies of philosophic speculation that arose within the Church about the middle of the ninth century, came to their height in the twelfth and the thirteenth, and declined rapidly during the following century. The most striking characteristics of scholasticism are the narrowness of its field and the thoroughness with which it was worked.

The History of Scholastic Development. — Since it was

---

[1] St. Victor was an Augustinian monastery founded by William of Champeaux (see p. 80) at the beginning of the twelfth century, which became very influential in awakening piety. It grew very rich, and propagated similar foundations in Italy, England, Scotland, and Lower Saxony.

[2] For the further development of scholastic mysticism, see Inge's *Christian Mysticism*, pp. 140-148.

assumed that the Church was in possession of all final truth, which had come to it by Divine revelation, the aim of the schoolmen at first was to show how these doctrines were consistent with each other and in accordance with reason. In the earliest stages of scholasticism, however, even this naïve supposition that reason and dogma were in harmony did not prevent the Church from becoming suspicious of any attempt to explain its doctrines on the basis of reason. This is obvious in the attitude of the Church toward Erigena, who, though primarily a mystic, is generally accounted the first of the scholastics. His efforts to show that all true philosophy is identical with Church doctrine met with scant favor.[1] It was felt that faith was sufficient and did not stand in need of rational defense.

Its first aim was to show how the 'revealed' doctrines of the Church accorded with reason.

While in this attitude Erigena seems to have been in advance of his times,

But Erigena was simply a couple of centuries in advance of his time, for the same attitude in Anselm (1033–1109) met with the heartiest approval and probably led to his promotion in the Church. Anselm believed in the accord of reason with dogma, but held that faith must precede knowledge and that doubt as a preliminary step to belief could not be tolerated. His position is shown in the full title of his main work,— *Monologue of the Method in which One may Account for his Faith.* He makes among others the following explicit statements:—

Anselm was heartily approved for the same position later.

"I do not seek to know in order that I may believe, but I believe in order that I may know."

"The Christian ought to advance to knowledge through faith, not come to faith through knowledge."

"The proper order demands that we believe the deep things of Christian faith before we presume to reason about them."

If one is not successful in his attempts to understand, Anselm holds, let him desist and submit to the will of God as manifested in the doctrines of the Church. Such a failure, however, he did not deem likely, and he himself spent much time in elucidating the various dogmas,

[1] This conviction that faith and reason were in harmony is apparent as early as Clement in the Alexandrian school.

such as the Trinity and the Atonement, and became famous for his 'ontological' argument for the existence of God.[1]

With Anselm and Roscellinus began the dispute between the 'realists' and 'nominalists.'

With Anselm and his great opponent, *Roscelin* or *Roscellinus* (1050–1106), a canon of Compiègne, the dispute between the realists and nominalists became fixed, and divided the schoolmen into two camps. *Realism*, of which Anselm was the exponent, is based upon Neoplatonism, and that scholastic held with Plato that ideas are the only *real* existence and individual objects are merely *phenomena* ('appearances'). To the realists, therefore, universals or class names had real existence, and the more general a term the more real it was. Roscellinus and the subsequent adherents of *nominalism*, on the other hand, held that the class term is only a *name*, which can be used of a number of individual objects. The realists maintained that the senses are deceptive, and human experience is too limited to form the basis of an independent judgment. To them reason was reliable only as it supported revealed doctrine, and so realism became the orthodox position of the Church. Nominalism, on the contrary, implied the sufficiency of reason, and was, therefore, logically destructive of dogma. But Roscellinus was unconscious of the heresy in his position, and vigorously attacked Anselm's doctrines, particularly those concerning the Trinity.

'Nominalism' implied the sufficiency of reason and was thus heretical.

Roscellinus was martyred, but a great growth in the use of reason is apparent in the position of Abelard.

The martyrdom of Roscellinus in 1106 effectually suppressed nominalism for two centuries, but human reason had been given more scope and began to exercise itself in dialectic without consideration of any ser-

[1] The 'ontological' argument and his doctrine of the Trinity appear in the *Proslogion*, and his position on the Atonement in his *Cur Deus Homo*. He argued that God must exist because we all have the idea of a most perfect Being, and if this Being did not possess all possible qualities, including *existence*, another might be more perfect. This argument, which came originally from Augustine, was riddled by the monk Gaunilo, but it seems to have appealed to Descartes, Leibnitz, and other great philosophers, who have failed to distinguish between the idea of a thing and its objective reality. This distinction would not, of course, trouble a mediæval realist like Anselm, since to him the only realities were ideas.

vice to doctrine. A great growth in the use of reason is apparent in the position of *Pierre Abelard*[1] (1079-1142), the greatest of the schoolmen. Philosophically, Abelard held to *conceptualism*, and undertook to mediate between realism and nominalism. He held that, while a class term has no objective existence, it is not merely a sound or a word, out of all relation to individual objects, but an expression of a similarity of qualities in objects.[2] While his attitude in this matter of universals seems irenic, his inexorable logic led him to reverse the position of Anselm and the realists. He felt that the only justification of a doctrine is its reasonableness, that reason must precede faith, and that it is not sinful to doubt. Hence in the prologue to his chief work, the *Sic et Non* ('Yes and No'), he holds:—

His 'conceptualism' was irenic, but his Sic et Non advocated reason and investigation.

"Constant and frequent questioning is the first key to wisdom. ... For through doubting we are led to inquire, and by inquiry we perceive the truth. As the Truth Himself says: 'Seek and ye shall find, knock and it shall be opened unto you.' ... Now when a number of quotations from various writings are introduced they spur on the reader and allure him into seeking the truth in proportion as the authority of the writing itself is commended."

Accordingly, on each problem he presented a number of selections from the Scriptures and the Christian Fathers that were clearly in conflict with each other. He thus indicated that Christian doctrine was by no means a settled matter, and stimulated investigation in the place of an unthinking adherence to tradition and authority. The extent to which he dared to go in his endeavors in behalf of inquiry and reason is shown by the fundamental doctrines that he challenged in his *Sic et Non*. Among his questions are these:[3]—

"Should human faith be based on reason, or not?"
"Is God tripartite, or not?"
"Do the Divine Persons mutually differ, or not?"

[1] Also often Latinized as *Petrus Abelardus*.
[2] He even thought that the *name* might be said to have had *real* existence as a *concept* in the Divine mind before Creation took place.
[3] There were one hundred and fifty-eight questions in all.

"Is God the Father the cause of the Son, or not?"
"Can God be resisted, or not?"
"Does God know all things, or not?"
"Did man's first sin begin through the devil, or not?"
"Do we sometimes sin unwillingly, or not?"
"Does God punish the same sin both here and in the hereafter, or not?"

This rationalistic tendency spread through Moorish influences and the recovery of Aristotle, and scholastic thought was brought to a culmination with the work of a number of prominent schoolmen.

Abelard's own interpretations of the Trinity and other doctrines were decidedly rationalistic. His life was, therefore, filled with bitter opposition and persecution, but the tendency he fostered was destined to spread. This tendency was magnified by several movements of the times. By the contact of Europeans with the Greek philosophy through the Mohammedans in Spain, and more directly, in the thirteenth century, through the recovery of the Aristotelian Ethics, Physics, Metaphysics, and other works, the scholastic world was introduced to a mind of the highest order that did not devote itself exclusively to theology. In this way the development of the scholastic thought was brought to a culmination. When the Church saw that its whole system was threatened, and that it had failed to suppress the uprising by burning heretics and anathematizing Aristotle, it donned the Aristotelian armor itself and utilized the works of the Greek philosopher for its own defense. Through an authoritative interpretation, Aristotle himself was used as a means of suppressing reason. Reason thereafter was made identical with Aristotle, whose authority was not to be disputed. The inquiry was not as to what is rational, but what does Aristotle say on the subject. Thus were philosophy and theology once more allied, and during the thirteenth century scholasticism reached its zenith. Among the more prominent schoolmen of this period were *Alexander of Hales* (?–1245), the 'irrefragable' doctor; *Albertus Magnus* (1193–1280), the 'universal' doctor; *Bonaventura* (1221–1274),[1] the 'seraphic' doctor; *Thomas*

[1] Bonaventura has been seen (p. 50) to combine scholasticism with mysticism. While his pietistic tendencies made him a mystic, his analyses and classifications place him among the leading schoolmen.

EDUCATIONAL TENDENCIES OF SCHOLASTICISM 55

Aquinas (1225-1274), the 'angelic' doctor; *Duns Scotus* (1274-1308), the 'subtle' doctor; and *William of Occam* (1280-1347), the 'invincible' doctor.

Of all these *Aquinas* stands preëminent. Like his master, Albertus, he strove to support the tottering dogmas of the Church. It had become evident that faith and reason are not always in harmony. This, Aquinas held, does not imply a contradiction. Reason, as far as it can go, is in accord with faith, but truths have been revealed that are beyond the range of reason, and faith, through which one secures them, is the highest power of the mind. Hence, after the method of Aristotle, Aquinas reduced all existence to a hierarchy, making body subordinate to soul, matter to spirit, philosophy to theology, and the secular to the ecclesiastical. This position is obvious in his great treatise, *Summa Theologiæ* ('The Sum of Theology'), which has remained up to the present as the basis of orthodoxy in the Roman Catholic Church.[1] But the separation of revelation and reason becomes more marked from the position of *Duns Scotus* and *William of Occam* in the dispute with which scholasticism declined and came to a close.[2] While the disciples of Aquinas, who still inclined somewhat toward realism, maintained that the intellect of God is supreme and that his will is determined by his knowledge, they were opposed by the argument of Scotus and Occam that God must be a completely free will, for if his will is determined by an eternal truth above him, there is something superior to God. Hence with them truth and falsehood are established by the *fiat* of God, and ecclesiastical dogmas are not matters of reason, but purely of faith. As a result of this breach between

Of these Aquinas was preëminent, and his Summa Theologiæ is still the basis of Roman Catholic orthodoxy. The separation between revelation and reason made by Aquinas was increased by the dispute between the Thomists and the Scotists.

Two types of truth arose, with the tendency to emphasize that supported by reason.

---

[1] There were numerous *Summæ Theologiæ* written by various schoolmen. They did not represent the peculiar views of the author, but were intended to present in a systematized form the authoritative teaching of the Church.

[2] After the time of Aquinas scholasticism met with a marked and rapid decline. It descended into endless quibbles and trivialities. Such schoolmen as *Gerson* (1363-1429), who desired greater warmth and spiritual experience, leaned more toward mysticism.

revelation and reason, there arose two types of truth, and a tendency grew up to choose that type which was supported by reason.

The Tendency of Scholasticism.—Thus there is summed up in scholasticism a series of movements that tended to awaken the mediæval mind. Scholasticism began as an effort to vanquish heresy in the interest of the Church dogmas, which until then it had not generally been necessary to explain. At first it was held that faith must precede reason, and where reason was incapable of penetrating the mysteries of revealed doctrine, it must desist from its efforts. But the conviction was growing that human reason is reliable and that truth can be reached only through investigation. The complete revolution that this threatened was for a time averted, but a separation of the spheres of revealed and rational truth led to an emphasis of the truth which had reason on its side. The schoolmen were, then, throughout attempting to rationalize the teachings of the Church, and to present them in scientific form. As an education, scholasticism aimed also at furnishing a training in dialectic and an intellectual discipline that should make the student both keen and learned in the knowledge of the times.

Thus, throughout, scholasticism tended more and more to rationalize the Church doctrines.

Its Educational Organization and Content.—The schoolmen were generally identified with educational institutions of one sort or another. The origin of scholasticism, it has been indicated,[1] came through the teachers in the monastic and episcopal schools of the period, but the intellectual awakening bound up in the movement tended to bring about a development of those schools into universities, especially in the North of Europe. However, the rise of universities will require separate discussion, and the scholastic organization must be confined here to the monastic and episcopal schools. The course of study in these schools came, toward the close of the Middle Ages, to consist in the beliefs of the

Scholastic education was organized in the monastic and episcopal schools, and

---

[1] See p. 50.

EDUCATIONAL TENDENCIES OF SCHOLASTICISM   57

Church and the limited learning of the times arranged in a systematized form largely on the deductive basis of the Aristotelian logic. This knowledge could all be grouped under the head of philosophical theology. The great doctrines of the Church, — the Trinity, Atonement, Predestination, and other concepts, were taught, and all secular material, even the most abstract of philosophical problems, was dealt with from a theological point of view.

consisted in the limited learning of the times, systematized on the basis of the Aristotelian deduction.

The Method of Presentation. — Admirable illustrations of the way in which these doctrines were usually presented can be found in the *Sententiæ* ('Opinions') of *Peter the Lombard* (1100–1160),[1] a pupil of Abelard's and a teacher at Paris, and in the *Summa Theologiæ*, already mentioned as the chief work of Aquinas. These manuals, especially the *Sententiæ*,[2] were generally used as texts in the schools of the time. The work of Aquinas has four main parts, under each of which is grouped a number of problems. Every problem is concerned with some fundamental doctrine, and is further divided into several subtopics. After the problem has been stated, first the arguments and authorities for the various solutions other than the orthodox one are given and refuted in regular order, then the proper solution with its arguments is set forth, and finally, the different objections to it are answered in a similarly systematic way. The *Sententiæ* is likewise divided into four parts, and under each head Peter cites the arguments for the unorthodox side before drawing his conclusion.

Illustrations of this systemization are found in Peter the Lombard's Sententiæ and Aquinas' Summa Theologiæ.

This general method of presentation so current in scholastic times, with its formal deductions and finalities, seems decidedly dogmatic to us to-day. But there is little doubt but that, as a result of the influence of Abelard's *Sic et Non*, it was much more elastic than it would have been. While Abelard intended to arouse free inquiry and does not undertake in any place to do more than indicate the

This dogmatic method was more elastic than it would have been, through the influence of Abelard's Sic et Non.

---

[1] Peter was inspired by the enthusiasm and eloquence of Abelard, but did not abandon his own orthodoxy.

[2] Norton (*Mediæval Universities*, p. 77) indicates that there may have been several hundred commentaries written on this work.

solution that seems on the whole to be most satisfactory, the form at least of his method appears in practically every mediæval textbook after his day. While such a method as Abelard's may well be judged to be weak in yielding definite didactic results, it must have greatly assisted the cause of reason and the freedom of thought.

Scholasticism has generally been underestimated.

Scholasticism and Its Influence. — As a whole, the work of the schoolmen has been underestimated. From the time that scholasticism rang its own knell until the opening of the nineteenth century, it was never studied sympathetically or in historic perspective. In the years following its decline there was a tremendous reaction against it, and it was the habit of philosophers and scientists, especially those of the sixteenth and seventeenth centuries, to sneer at and condemn utterly its peculiar method and content. It was urged that it had ruined all spiritual realities by its extreme systemization of religion, that it dealt with mere abstractions, with a slavish adherence to Aristotle, and that it indulged in over-subtle distinctions and verbal quibbles, couched in the most absurd jargon.

It was too much systemized, but systemization is natural to reasoning beings, and this tendency did a great service for knowledge and accuracy in thinking.

But no movement can be fairly judged apart from its historic connections. Unless we consider the origin and environment of scholasticism, we are sure to do this tendency a grave injustice. It must be admitted that the schoolmen did reduce all the knowledge of the day to an extreme logical system, based upon the deductive method of Aristotle, which became a great obstacle to progress and the revival of learning. But since it is the nature of reasoning beings to analyze, compare, and classify, the schoolmen had to resort to some system, and the only available method was that of the great Greek philosopher. In this way, however, they also did a great service to knowledge. They found a confused mass of traditional and irrational doctrines and practices, and made them systematic, rational, and scientific, and greatly assisted accuracy in thinking. Moreover, the range of knowledge with which the scholastics were permitted to deal was exceedingly narrow. Unless they

The field was limited by the strict orthodoxy of

would subject themselves to persecution and martyrdom, they could defend only such theses as the Church held to be orthodox; and they were, therefore, obliged to exercise their keen analytic minds most intensively, and so divided, subdivided, and systematized their material beyond all measure. It is but natural under such circumstances that the spirit of religion should be crushed, and that more emphasis should be placed upon theories than experience.

Nor is it remarkable that the subject-matter with which the schoolmen dealt should seem to be mere metaphysical abstractions from which only formal principles could be derived. The value of the scholastic material and the completeness of its data were not scanned at all critically, but the scientific method had not been invented as yet, and scholasticism did much to make it possible. It may also be granted that the scholastic discussions not only did not seem to concern actual life in their content, but even appeared to have little validity in thought, and ofttimes consisted of mere argument over words and of extreme hair-splitting. But this does not indicate that they were altogether purposeless or as absurd as they seemed. For example, the celebrated inquiry of Aquinas as to the number of angels that could stand on the point of a needle contains more sense than appears on the surface, and is simply an attempt to present the nature of the Infinite in concrete form. The further censure of scholasticism for using a ridiculous and incomprehensible jargon is equally unfair. While the later schoolmen may have carried scientific terms to an extreme, as in the case of their classifying and their quibbling, they are not the only offenders, and the very invention of a technical language has contributed much to modern accuracy of terminology and the definition of truth since their day.

In fact, as a result of the terrific struggle to overcome the traditions, authority, and oppression of the Middle Ages, and with the necessity for ridding progress of all obstacles of outworn method and content, we have been

the Church, and the subject-matter was necessarily abstract; and, since the scientific method did not yet exist, the value and completeness of data were not critically considered.

But scholastic discussions were often not as absurd as they seem, and the criticism for using a jargon is unfair.

Scholasticism liberated philosophy from theology, unconsciously aided reason against authority, and produced subtle and acute minds.

blinded to the way in which scholasticism fulfilled its mission. The discussions of the schoolmen resulted in liberating philosophy from theology, and, without intending it perhaps, scholasticism aided the cause of human reason against authority. It greatly stimulated intellectual interests and for several centuries must have constituted the only real intellectual training. It produced the most subtle and acute minds of the age, made great intellects far more common in succeeding periods, and through its own development made the scholastic attitude impossible.

The Relations of Mysticism and Scholasticism to Education. — Thus, while both these mediæval trends of thought are of more importance to the history of philosophy than to the development of education, they are not without considerable educational significance. Neither one crystallized in a new educational institution, but both found some means of expression in the existing schools of the monasteries and cathedrals. The mystic training throughout proved the means of securing lofty and immediate religious experience, and was of great benefit to monastic education, especially in periods of stagnation or actual retrogression. Scholasticism brought about a tremendous intellectual activity and gave to the monastic and episcopal institutions a new life, which was to a large extent consummated in the universities that afterward arose. The awakening, mental and moral, produced by these two movements, helped to prepare the way for the Renaissance and the Reformation, and while not preserved in any special type of school, mysticism and scholasticism cannot be neglected in any account of education.

Both mysticism and scholasticism were of great benefit to mediæval education, and helped prepare the way for an intellectual awakening.

SUPPLEMENTARY READING

I. Sources

ABELARD. *Sic et Non.*
ANSELM. *Cur Deus Homo, Monologion,* and *Proslogion* (translated by Deane in the *Religion of Science Library*).
AQUINAS. *Summa Theologiæ* (translated by Rickaby).
BERNARD OF CLAIRVAUX. *De Consideratione, De Contemptu Mundi,* and *De Gradibus Humilitatis.*
BONAVENTURA. *Reductio Artium ad Theologiam.*
DIONYSIUS AREOPAGITICA. *De Cæli Hierarchia, De Ecclesiæ Hierarchia,* and *De Mystica Theologia.*
ERIGENA. *De Divisione Naturæ* and *De Prædestinatione.*
HUGO OF ST. VICTOR. *Didascalion* (see *Das Lehrbuch* in *Sammlung Pädagogischer Schriften, Band XXIII*), *De Sacramentis,* and *Eruditio Didascalica.*
PETER THE LOMBARD. *Sententiæ.*
PLOTINUS. *Enneades VI.*
RICHARD OF ST. VICTOR. *De Contemplatione.*

II. Authorities

CHURCH, R. W. *Saint Anselm.*
COMPAYRÉ, G. *Abelard.* Pt. I, Chaps. I and II.
DE WULF, M. *History of Mediæval Philosophy* (translated by Coffey).
DRANE, A. T. *Christian Schools and Scholars.* Pp. 170–217.
DRAPER, J. W. *Intellectual Development of Europe.* Vol. II, Chap. I.
EMERTON, E. *Mediæval Europe.* Chap. XIII.
ERDMANN, J. E. *The History of Philosophy* (translated by Hough). Vol. I, Pt. II.
HAURÉAU, B. *Histoire de la Philosophie Scholastique.*
INGE, W. R. *Christian Mysticism.*
INGE, W. R. *Personal Idealism and Mysticism.*
LA CROIX, P. *Science and Literature in the Middle Ages.* Pp. 47–53.
LAURIE, S. S. *Rise and Constitution of Universities.* Lects. V, VI, and IX.
MCCABE, J. *Abelard.*
MAURICE, F. D. *Mediæval Philosophy from the Fifth to the Fourteenth Century.*
MILMAN, H. H. *History of Latin Christianity.* Bk. XIV, Chap. III.
MULLINGER, J. B. *The Schools of Charles the Great.* Chap. V.
MULLINGER, J. B. *The University of Cambridge.* Chap. III.
OMAN, J. C. *The Mystics, Ascetics, and Saints of India.*

POOLE, R. L. *Illustrations of the History of Mediæval Thought.*
  Chaps. II–V and VIII.
RASHDALL, H. *Universities of Europe in the Middle Ages.* Vol.
  I, Chap. II.
RÉCÉJAC, E. *Essays on the Bases of Mystic Knowledge* (translated by Upton).
SCHMID, H. *Der Mysticismus in Seine Entstehungsperiode.*
STORRS, R. S. *Bernard of Clairvaux.*
TOWNSEND, W. J. *The Great Schoolmen of the Middle Ages.*
UEBERWEG, F. *History of Philosophy* (translated by Morris). II,
  Second Period.
WINDELBAND, W. *A History of Philosophy* (translated by Tufts).
  Part III.

CHAPTER VII

THE EDUCATION OF FEUDALISM AND CHIVALRY

The Origin of Feudalism. — Feudalism was an order of society and government which gradually grew up in the Middle Ages out of certain private relations. Feudal elements existed throughout the mediæval period alongside of the regular political organization, and when, under the successors of Charlemagne, the monarchy became weak and inadequate, society tended to fall back upon these relations as a means of control. In the unsettled conditions of the early Middle Ages, small landowners, and freemen lacking land altogether, came to depend upon some powerful neighbor for protection, and to seek from him a dependent tenure of land. In time these lords acquired a genuine sovereignty over their tenants, and were regarded as rulers as well as personal superiors. Taxes were paid them, and a system of private courts and legal fines grew up. The tenants went to war under the leadership of their lords, and military service on horseback became generally attached to the holding of land. Often the land was subdivided and lower orders of nobility thus arose. In this way, about the year 900, the feudal relations that had at first been private and subsidiary were, through lack of a strong central control, erected into a regular form of government.[1] This system was not disrupted until toward the close of the Middle Ages, when certain suzerains or overlords, who had been earlier chosen from their own number by the feudal nobles, succeeded in turning themselves into genuine sovereigns.

As the monarchy became weak, the dependence upon a powerful neighbor and the private sovereignty of feudalism grew into a regular form of government, and a gulf arose between nobility and peasantry.

[1] Adams (*Civilization during the Middle Ages*, pp. 194–217) gives a more definite and slightly different account of the way in which the Roman institutions of the *præcarium* and *patrocinium* were combined and adopted by the Franks, and of how, through the introduction of military service as a condition of land tenure, aided by grants of 'immunity' and by usurpation, the feudal relation of *jurisdictio* was instituted.

The serious business of the feudal noble was fighting, and to prepare him for this, mock battles were engaged in, which eventually degenerated into a pastime and pageant.

Hence, by the tenth century, there came to be a great social gulf between the nobility, who owned the land and lived in castles, and the peasantry, who tilled the soil and supported them. It is, of course, the life of the nobles that gives picturesqueness to the times. Their only serious business was fighting with spear, sword, or battle-axe, in their own quarrel or that of their feudal superior. These battles of the Middle Ages were conducted by companies of mailed knights charging on horseback, and consisted largely of feats of arms performed in personal combat. To prepare for this warfare, mock combats may have been occasionally engaged in as early as the ninth century. Within two centuries, however, these mimic encounters became organized into a definite species of pastime called a *tournament*, and, during the following centuries, they degenerated into mere pageants and were eventually carried to an absurd extreme.[1] When the knight was not engaged with war or the tournament, as he had few intellectual resources, he amused himself with hunting or hawking, or with feasting, drinking, and minstrelsy in the great hall of the castle.

Consequently, the good usage of feudal times, known as 'chivalry,' is divided into two periods,— that before the twelfth century being an 'heroic age,' and that afterward an 'age of courtesy.'

Chivalry and Its Development. — The good social usage of these times has been known ever since as *chivalry*,[2] and is as little susceptible of explanation as the code of manners of any other period. The best idea of it is obtained from the popular literature of that day, which deals almost entirely with the knight and his ideal behavior. While chivalry differed somewhat in different places and from time to time, it may in general be divided into two periods. Chivalry before the middle of the twelfth century may be considered that of the *heroic age*, during which the ideal knight was extraordinarily strong and brave, and was devoted to God, his country, and king. This crude but vigorous period, however, of which *Raoul de Cambrai* and the *Chanson*

---

[1] Scott's *Ivanhoe* furnishes us with a lively picture of these institutions, but the descriptions of this author must be taken with a grain of allowance.
[2] French *chevalerie* ('knighthood'), an abstract noun derived from *cheval* ('horse').

de Roland ('Song of Roland') are the typical expression, was succeeded by an *age of courtesy*. The characteristics of this later period appeared first in the wealthy nobility of southern France, and were largely the products of the stereotyped organization into which chivalry fell during the Crusades. The ideals and rules of chivalry became fixed and formal, and the art of horsemanship and the management of the lance and sword were developed and settled. Instead of the simple and natural relations growing out of primitive social conditions, we find gallantry, the graces of society, and romantic adventures as the chief ideals of the period. The lyrics of the Provençal *Troubadours* and the German *Minnesingers*, the longer narrative poems based upon the Arthurian legends, classical stories, and the German sagas, give expression to the artificiality and extravagance of this age, and the absurdities to which it went marked the dissolution of feudalism.

The Ideals of Chivalric Education. — It was out of this latter stage, however, that chivalric education arose. The ideals of knightly conduct and of education for the life of chivalry may be summed up under *service and obedience*. These manifestations of loyalty were to be rendered to God, as represented by the organized Church, to one's lord, or feudal superior, and to one's lady, whose favor the knight wore in battle or tournament. The three ruling motives of chivalry were, therefore, *religion*, *honor*, and *gallantry*. The feudal knight was expected to show reverence for his superiors and gentleness toward the weak and defenceless. He was to be brave and chivalrous in battle, to defend the Church and his religion, and to hold womankind in high esteem.

The Three Stages of Education Preparatory to Knighthood. — There may be said to have been three periods in the training of a knight. First, until the child was seven or eight, he was trained at home by his mother.[1]

Out of this latter arose chivalric education with its ideals of religion, honor, and gallantry.

Before knighthood a training was given the boy at home, and as 'page' and 'squire' at the castle of some lord.

[1] An ingenious, but rather tedious and uncritical reconstruction of the chivalric education can be found in Gautier's *Chivalry*, Chaps. V–XX, where, in the form of a story, he describes the life of a knight from birth to death.

During this stage he began his religious education, learned respect and politeness toward his elders and obedience to his superiors, and laid the foundation of rugged health and strength.

After this, it was the custom with the gentry from the highest to the lowest degree to place the boy in the castle of some secular lord or prominent churchman, to obtain a knightly training in 'courtesy.'[1] Usually the nobleman chosen was his father's feudal superior,[2] although, in the case of kings and great feudal princes, their sons were occasionally trained at their own palaces. The boy had now become a *page*,[3] and took his place among the inferior members of the household. The chief part of his training came through the performance of personal duties for his lord and lady. However, he also acquired from the lady the etiquette of love and honor, and learned chess and other games. In most cases, too, he was taught to play the harp and pipe, and to sing, to read and write, and to compose in verse. Occasionally he was given some knowledge of Latin, and, in England during the later period, of French. Outside the castle, the pages were trained in running, wrestling, and boxing, and those who had them in charge were further commissioned to "lerne them to ryde clenely and surely, to drawe them also to justes; to lerne them were their harneys."[4] Such training for the tournament was probably obtained by tilting at the ring or a dummy man known as the 'quintain.'

At fourteen or fifteen the youth passed to the grade of *squire*.[5] The squires of the house waited upon the lady, and with her they played chess, walked, hunted,

The 'page' performed personal duties for his lord and lady, learned games and 'courtesy' from the lady, and began his physical education.

The 'squire' especially served his lord, and attended him at the tournament or upon the battlefield;

---

[1] I.e., *curialitas*, or breeding at the *curia* ('court').
[2] This custom would seem to have arisen from the suzerain's originally taking his vassal's son as a hostage for the behavior of the father.
[3] *Page* ('assistant servant') was a late term, and a more common designation was *damoiseau* ('little lord') or *valet* ('little vassal').
[4] Furnivall, *Forewords*, ii, on *Early Education in England* in *The Babees Book*.
[5] *Squire* is a contraction of *esquire*, which comes from the Old French *esquier*, a development from the Latin *scutarius* ('a shield-bearer').

THE EDUCATION OF FEUDALISM AND CHIVALRY 67

and hawked. They also often carved, handed around the viands, served the wine, and presented water for the hands of the guests. But their chief service was to the knight. They not only made their lord's bed, helped him to dress, and slept near him at night, but groomed his horses and attended him upon the tournament ground or the actual battle-field. Usually the honor of performing the martial duties fell to the senior squire, who displayed the knight's banner, kept his armor and weapons in condition, made him ready for the fray, and furnished him with fresh lances or protected him with the shield in times of peril. Thus by practice the squire learned all the warlike arts, — to ride and handle shield, spear, and armor, and to joust and fight with the sword or battle-axe. Toward the close of this stage of his education the embryo knight also chose his lady-love. She was usually older than he and might be married or not, but to her he was to be ever devoted, — even after he married some one else. This accounts for the squire's expertness in verse-writing and dancing, as shown in Chaucer's description of him: — *he also chose his lady-love, and learned to write verses and dance.*

> "He could songs make, and well endite,
> Just and eke dance, and well pourtraie and write;
> So hote he loved, that by nighterdale (night time)
> He slept no more than doth the nightingale."[1]

Knighthood. — When the squire became twenty-one he was knighted. The final ceremony was preceded by many religious observances. After a season of fasting, purification, and prayer, the candidate entered the church in full armor, and spent a night in vigil and holy meditation.[2] In the morning he was shriven, and received the eucharist, and after presenting his sword to the priest, who blessed it upon the altar, he took a solemn oath "to defend the church, to attack the wicked, to respect the priesthood, to protect women and the *At twenty-one the squire was knighted with special religious ceremonies.*

---
[1] This is given as in the partially modernized quotation of Mills.
[2] Sometimes squires were knighted upon the field of battle, before they were of age, for some special act of valor.

poor, to preserve the country in tranquillity, and to shed his blood, even to its last drop, in behalf of his brethren." His sword was then returned and he was charged by the priest "to protect the widows and orphans, and to restore and preserve the desolate, to revenge the wronged, and to confirm the virtuous."[1] By so doing, it was promised, he would obtain everlasting joy. He then knelt before his lord, who laid his own sword upon the shoulder of the candidate and ordinarily addressed him thus: —

"In the name of God, of our Lady, of thy patron Saint, and of St. Michael and St. George, I dub thee knight; be brave, bold, and loyal."

Such was the preparatory training and the inauguration into knighthood. It can easily be seen that this chivalric education contained but little that was intellectual, though it afforded an excellent discipline in "the rudiments of love,[2] war, and religion."

Similarly, girls were instructed at the castle of some lord in domestic duties, manners, music, and the art of conversation.

Training of Women. — Girls were also educated during the régime of chivalry in the castle of some knight or lord. Their training consisted more exclusively in personal service, household duties, good manners, music, and pleasing conversation. In general, there was scarcely any intellectual element in it, save learning to say their prayers, play the harp, and sing various poems, although in the case of some maidens of the noblest birth, a little study of language and literature was made, and it was even said of the Earl of Warwick's daughter:

"She was thereto courteous, and free and wise,
And in the seven arts learned withouten miss."

These, however, must have been exceptional cases.

The Effects of Chivalric Education. — This chivalric training of the Middle Ages contains many anomalies

---

[1] Mills, *Chivalry*, pp. 48-54, gives a complete description of these inaugural ceremonies. A little different account is given by Froissart in the knighting of William IV, emperor of Germany.

[2] 'Love' is to be understood not only in the sense of devotion to the opposite sex (*par amours*), but also with the broader meaning of kindness and courtesy.

and contradictions. The elements in the mediæval knight were curiously mixed, and every virtue seems to have been balanced by a correlative vice. The knights were recklessly courageous in battle, but their anger, when aroused, was ungovernable, and their cruelty was extreme. There are several instances of a single knight, in a crisis, charging headlong upon an entire army, and there are many records of the most brutal slaughter of prisoners. Discretion, self-control, and mercy could not have been among the knightly virtues. A great self-respect and a disdain for petty meannesses were also supposed to characterize the true knight, but these too often reacted into an overweening pride and a tenacious insistence upon his own rights. The feudal claims of his inferiors and servants were scrupulously observed by every knight, but the persons themselves were generally regarded with scorn and contempt. There was no such duty as courtesy to one's subjects, and the most crying fault of chivalry was the tendency to regard all inferiors merely as ministers to one's pleasure. So, too, although great respect for womanhood was held to be essential to the knightly conduct, if the women were beneath a certain rank, no such consideration was expected, and the chivalrous convention was quite compatible with the laxest conversation and morals. Moreover, while the knights were rated largely according to their ideas of liberality and hospitality, the result was a great love of display and an extravagance beyond measure. The general notion of 'liberality' was to have a vast army of retainers wearing one's 'livery,'[1] and to excel all others in pomp and splendor. The Earl of Cornwall boasted of having entertained thirty thousand guests, and even after a most liberal allowance is made in the estimate, it is easy to see that 'hospitality' and wastefulness were sometimes synonymous.

This anomalous education of chivalry produced courage and cruelty, self-respect and pride, respect for women and gross immorality, liberality and extravagance, honor and bad faith.

---

[1] Livery may originally have had reference to the 'allowance' (*liberatura* or *liberatio*) of cloth or rations that were parcelled out to every member of the household. See Ransome, *History of England*, p. 383; Stubbs, *Constitutional History*, III, p. 547 and note.

No wonder, then, that Richard the Lion-hearted, the very type of late chivalry, should frankly admit that his 'three daughters' were pride, rapacity, and luxury. As for the knightly word of honor, so much vaunted, it would, if accompanied by certain forms, be held sacred under trying circumstances, but should these forms be omitted, a decided breach of good faith was not infrequent. There was often a complete disregard for the most solemn agreements. Hence it was that William of Normandy seems to have had little hope of holding King Harold to his promise, except for the holy relics by which he had sworn.

<small>Upon the whole, it refined the times and counteracted 'otherworldliness.'</small>
As a whole, however, the chivalric training had a beneficial effect upon the society of the times. It was not all militarism, parade, convention, and deception. It helped to organize and refine the turmoil and barbarism of mediæval Europe, and was an effective instrument in raising the position of women. To this extent chivalry was a healthful discipline for mediævalism. And incidentally there flowed from it a happy consequence. While this peculiar training was often extravagant, artificial, and 'worldly,' by that very tendency it did much to counteract the 'otherworldly' ideal of monasticism and the general asceticism of the period. It encouraged an activity in earthly affairs and a frank enjoyment of this life. In this way it gave rise to the first distinctive literature since Græco-Roman days. The virile narratives of the heroic age and the beautiful lyrics of the age of courtesy alike have lasted long after the dissolution of the society that produced them. Chivalry itself became fixed and conventional, but it had done its work for civilization.

THE EDUCATION OF FEUDALISM AND CHIVALRY 71

SUPPLEMENTARY READING

I. Sources

CHEYNEY, E. P. *Documents Illustrative of Feudalism.* (*Translations and Reprints*, Vol. IV, No. 3.)
FROISSART, J. *Chronicles* (translated by Bourchier and Berners).
FURNIVALL, F. J. (Editor). *The Babees Book* (including *The Book of Curteisie, Boke of Nurture, Boke of Kerynge, The Booke of Demeanor*, etc.).
MALORY, T. *Morte D'Arthur.*

II. Authorities

ADAMS, G. B. *Civilization during the Middle Ages.* Chaps. IX and XI.
BULFINCH, T. *Age of Chivalry.*
CORNISH, F. W. *Chivalry.*
CUTTS, E. L. *Scenes and Characters of the Middle Ages.* The Knights, Chaps. IV, VIII, and IX.
EMERTON, E. *Introduction to the Middle Ages.* Chap. XV.
FURNIVALL, F. J. *Early Education in England* (in *The Babees Book*).
GAUTIER, L. *Chivalry* (translated by H. Frith).
GUIZOT, F. *The History of Civilization.* Vol. IV, Lect. 6.
HENDERSON, E. W. *A Short History of Germany.* Vol. I, Chap. V.
LACROIX, P. *Military and Religious Life in the Middle Ages.* Feudalism, The Crusaders, and Chivalry.
MARTIN, H. *Histoire de France.* Vol. III.
MILLS, C. *The History of Chivalry.* Vol. I, Chaps. I–V, and Vol. II, Chap. VII.
ROUND, J. H. *Feudal England.*
SCHULZ, A. *Das Höfische Leben zur Zeit der Minnesinger.*
SCOTT, W. *Essay on Chivalry.*

CHAPTER VIII

THE EDUCATIONAL WORK OF THE FRIARS

<small>The friars combated the heretics that had arisen as a protest to ecclesiastical abuses.</small>

The Purpose of the Friars. — A large contribution to the development of scholasticism in its later stages was made through the monastic orders known as the *mendicant friars*.[1] These orders did not, like the earlier monks, spend their time in prayer and solitary contemplation, but mingled with the world. They endeavored to combat by peaceful methods the *Albigenses* and *Waldenses*, two groups of heretics that had sprung up in the twelfth century as a protest against the shocking abuses in the Church.[2] The friars made it their business to wander about among the people, living on charity, to set an example of piety and self-sacrifice, defend and propagate the orthodox faith, and awaken the people to renewed spirituality. To command the situation and make converts among all classes, they obtained an excellent training in theology, philosophy, and debating, and strove to communicate the proper education to others. With this purpose in view, they endeavored to control education and train the intellectual leaders of the times.

Their Organization and Methods. — The *Franciscans*, or 'gray friars,' were originally followers of Francesco Bernardone of Assisi, who had abandoned a life of luxury to minister to the poor and sick. The *Rule of St. Francis* commanded: —

---

[1] *Friar* is derived from the Latin *frater*.
[2] This seems to have been the deliberate purpose of Dominic in organizing his order. He was a Spanish monk, who had gone with his bishop among the Albigenses to dissuade them from their heresies. Francesco, however, had in mind only an imitation of Christ's life, and the conversion of heretics was incidental with the Franciscans.

"The brothers shall appropriate nothing to themselves, neither a house, nor a place, nor anything; but as pilgrims and strangers in this world, in poverty and humility serving God, they shall confidently go seeking for alms."

The order was authorized by the pope in 1212. The *Dominicans*, or 'black friars,' were instituted by a priest of noble birth named Dominic de Guzman, and in 1217 the pope sanctioned the order.[1] The Dominicans were carefully trained in the higher studies, and especially sought to direct the policy of the universities and other educational institutions. "Hence," says Rashdall, "the headquarters of the Dominicans in Italy were fixed at Bologna, in France at Paris, where a colony was established from their first foundation in 1217: in England their first convent was at Oxford. These central houses from the first assumed the form of Colleges: and a Dominican convent ere long was established in every important University town." Thus these friars secured members with the highest theological education of the age and eventually obtained a large share in the control of the theological teaching of the universities everywhere. They stood for a stanch support of all Church doctrines, and included such well-known schoolmen as Albertus Magnus and his even greater pupil, Thomas Aquinas.

The Dominicans especially sought to control education. While the Franciscans tended to remain more democratic and less intellectual, yet they found it necessary to make converts at the universities and to have their members trained in theology.

The Franciscans tended to remain more democratic and less intellectual. They devoted their lives to the relief and training of the poor and needy, but while some did not believe in the higher learning, they, too, soon found it necessary to make converts at the universities and have their members given a training in theology. In 1230, the Franciscans first founded a convent at Paris and before long they became almost as active intellectually as the Dominicans. Many Franciscans were well educated, and among the members of the order were such distinguished scholastics as Alexander of Hales, Bonaventura, Duns Scotus, and William of Occam.

[1] A good brief account of the rise of the friars can be found in Wishart's *Monks and Monasteries*, Chap. V.

Rashdall also tells us:—

> "Other mendicant orders — Carmelites, Austin Friars, and others of less importance — likewise established convents at Paris and sent novices to the Theological Schools, but they played a comparatively small part in the life of the University."

Their Influence upon Education and Progress. — Hence the friars did much for education. They gave their members a far broader training than monks generally received and among them were found many intellectual and educational leaders. They also instructed the people both informally in virtue and doctrine, and through their control of the universities and other institutions. While the origin and aim of the two great orders were so similar, each has been stamped with the personality and genius of its founder. The defense of orthodoxy remained the main purpose of the Dominicans, and preservation of the lines laid down by their early masters is apparent in all their later philosophy and teaching. On the other hand, the Franciscans have ever been the authors of new social, philosophical, and theological movements. While at first they were united in their efforts, a rivalry soon sprang up between the two organizations, which is reflected in the controversy of Duns and Occam with the followers of Aquinas.[1] But this opposition in theology and philosophy was a healthful thing for the times, since it tended to arouse discussion and break up all settled authority. It has even been declared that "the intellectual history of Europe for the next two hundred years is intimately bound up with the divergent theological tendencies of the two great Orders of S. Dominic and S. Francis." Moreover, when orders of such standing as the two sets of friars were often accused of heresy by each other, the common man could not well be blamed for following the dictates of reason and refusing to conform to ecclesiastical dogma in every detail.

Nevertheless, the defense of orthodoxy remained the main purpose of the Dominicans, and social and theological advancement that of the Franciscans. The rivalry between the two orders tended to arouse discussion and disrupt authority.

[1] See p. 55.

SUPPLEMENTARY READING

I. Sources

HENDERSON, E. F. *Historical Documents of the Middle Ages.* Bk. III, No. VIII.

II. Authorities

CUTTS, E. L. *Scenes and Characters of the Middle Ages. The Monks,* Chap. V.
DRANE, A. T. *History of St. Dominic.*
DRAPER, J. W. *Intellectual Development of Europe.* Vol. II, Chap. II.
JESSOPP, A. *The Coming of the Friars.*
LITTLE, A. G. *Educational Organization of the Mendicant Friars in England* (Royal Historical Society, New Series, Vol. VIII).
LITTLE, A. G. *The Grey Friars in Oxford* (Oxford Historical Society, Vol. XX).
MACDONELL, A. *The Sons of St. Francis.*
MILMAN, H. H. *History of Latin Christianity.* Bk. IX, Chaps. IX and X.
MULLINGER, J. B. *The University of Cambridge.* Chaps. I, III, and V.
OLIPHANT, MRS. M. O. *Saint Francis of Assisi.*
RASHDALL, H. *Universities of Europe in the Middle Ages.* Vol. I, pp. 251–253 and 362–392, and Vol. II, pp. 376–386.
SABATIER, P. *Life of St. Francis.*

CHAPTER IX

THE MEDIÆVAL UNIVERSITIES

Universities were in general a product of all that was best in the Middle Ages, but no two sprang from exactly the same causes.

General Causes of the Rise of Universities. — In discussing scholasticism and the friars, we have already had occasion to anticipate a description of the mediæval universities. These were the product of what was highest and best in the Middle Ages, and their growth is necessarily bound up with all the history and contributions of the times. The development of universities is intimately connected with that of the Empire, the Church and papacy, the older schools, and many other institutions of mediæval days. They arose from the old cathedral and monastic schools, and were brought into prominence through the broadening influences of the later Middle Ages. The contact with Arabic science and culture and Greek philosophy through the Crusades and the Moors in Spain, the interest in dialectic and theological discussions, with its development of scholasticism, the wider horizon produced through a knowledge of the Orient and of different customs and traditions, the reaction from 'otherworldliness' resulting from the ideals of chivalry and the growth of cities and wealth, the consequent emphasis upon secular interests and knowledge, all played a part in creating the intellectual atmosphere that was necessary for the growth of these organizations. The mediæval scholars eagerly scanned the liberal and professional courses of the Moorish colleges at Cordova, Granada, Seville, and Alexandria, and new groups of studies, broader methods, and, above all, great teachers, began rapidly to appear. Students crowded to the seats of learning at the old schools, and before long these institutions had come to be known as 'universities.'

The History and Purpose of the Universities. — Such were the general factors in the evolution of all the mediæval universities, but while all were more or less the product of the influences named, no two sprang from exactly the same set of causes.

The oldest of the universities was that at *Salerno*, near Naples. This organization seems to have been simply a school of medicine, and Rashdall attributes its origin primarily to the survival of the old Greek medical works in this part of the peninsula.[1] While other cities of southwestern Italy were interested in medicine, Salerno in particular became the center of medical study because of its reputation as a health resort, gained chiefly from its mild climate, but partly also from the mineral springs there. Greek medical writings were translated into Latin by the sixth century, and from the early part of the eleventh century Salerno seems itself to have been productive of medical works. By the middle of the century the revival of medicine was well under way and Salerno was known as the leading place for medical study. A great impulse was given the school by a converted Jew called *Constantinus Africanus*, who had wandered through India, Babylonia, and Egypt, and everywhere studied medicine. He had fled to Salerno from Carthage, and during the latter half of the eleventh century compiled and translated Hippocrates and various other Greek and Arabic authorities on medicine. Salerno was further assisted by the visit of Robert, Duke of Normandy, who came there in 1099, after the first Crusade, to be cured of a wound, and, with his returning knights, spread the fame of the school to all parts of Europe. Salerno, however, was never chartered as a regular university, and it was not until 1231 that it received any official recognition. Frederick II at that time gave it the monopoly for medical training in his realms in place of the school of medicine at the Uni-

Salerno early became the seat of a medical school, because of the survival of the old Greek medical works, the salubrity of the place, and the work of Constantinus, but it was never chartered as a regular university, and did not become a model for other universities.

[1] Laurie and Mullinger give more prominence to the influence of the Saracen medical writers than does Rashdall, who bases his conclusions upon Daremberg and Renzi, the authorities on the history of medicine.

versity of Naples, which he had created some seven years earlier. But this organization never became, like Bologna and Paris, a model for the foundation of later universities. It is, therefore, of less consequence in the development of universities, and by the fourteenth century it had met with a permanent decline.

The interest of southern Italy in medicine was paralleled by the attention to Roman law in the north of the peninsula. Amid all the changes that had come from the various conquests by Goths, Lombards, and Franks, the cities of northern Italy had never altogether lost their independence. This was especially true of the Lombard cities, which in the end expelled the counts or bishops that had for a time attempted to rule them, and even prevented the German emperors from ever making their nominal sway over them a real one. In undertaking to defend their independence, these cities made an especial study of Roman Law, in order to present some special charter, grant, or edict from the old Roman emperors upon which their claims might be founded. A knowledge of the Roman civil law had never altogether died out in northern Italy, but this struggle for independence caused an enthusiastic revival of the study.[1] There were several centers renowned for their pursuit of this subject, but early in the twelfth century *Bologna* became preëminent. This city, which had hitherto been known for its school of liberal arts, was now made famous by the lectures upon law of one Irnerius. For the first time the entire *Corpus Juris Civilis* ('Body of Civil Law'), a compilation of Roman law made by eminent jurists in the sixth century by order of the emperor Justinian, was collected and critically discussed. This expansion of the subject required the separation of civil law from rhetoric, of which it had previously been a branch, and forced stu-

Bologna became famous as a school of civil law through the struggle of the north Italian cities for independence and through the lectures of Irnerius,

---

[1] The former conclusion that the study of Roman jurisprudence was caused by the discovery of the *Pandects* of Justinian through the capture of Amalfi by Pisa in 1135 has since 1831 been shown by Savigny to be out of keeping with the natural evolution of events.

dents who would study it to give it their entire attention. The law students thus became differentiated from those in liberal arts, and Bologna came to be known as a great school of civil law.

But this city was destined to become also the seat of the study of canon law. Influenced by the scientific treatment of the *Corpus Juris Civilis*, a monk of Bologna, named *Gratian*, was impelled to furnish the Church with a code no less systematic and complete. Accordingly, he undertook in 1142 to harmonize all edicts, legislation, and statements of popes, councils, Church fathers, and Christian emperors in a convenient textbook upon canon law. This work, known as the *Decretum Gratiani* ('The Decree of Gratian'),[1] was organized after the plan of Abelard's *Sic et Non*, and gave the authorities upon both sides of each mooted point in ecclesiastical law. It was almost immediately recognized as the authority upon the subject, and Gratian became nearly as important in the development of Bologna and other universities as Irnerius. Canon law was made a separate study from theology, of which it had previously been a part, and attracted a large number of students.

and as a school of canon law through the *Decretum* of Gratian.

Thus the school at Bologna was greatly enlarged in its work, and was chartered as a university by Frederick Barbarossa in 1158, probably as a recognition of the services of its masters in support of his imperial claims. By the beginning of the thirteenth century, its fame had become widespread, and it is estimated that there were about five thousand students in attendance.[2] There had been a course in liberal arts for a long time at Bologna, and, besides the civil and canon law, medicine was added in 1316, and theology in 1360, although these subjects never became very prominent.

In 1158 it was chartered as a university by Frederick Barbarossa, and other courses were eventually added.

---

[1] After various additions had been made, it was generally known in the fifteenth century as *Corpus Juris Canonici*.
[2] Odofredus, the jurist, states that there were ten thousand students, but Rashdall holds that an allowance of at least one half must be made for the mediæval tendency to exaggerate.

80   A HISTORY OF EDUCATION

The University of Paris grew out of the cathedral school of Notre Dame, especially when under Abelard,

The development of the universities in France and England is not as easy to trace as in Italy, but they seem to have been more directly the product of the special interest in dialectic and scholasticism that appeared in this part of Europe. Of all the organizations north of the Alps the first foundation was that at *Paris*, which was by far the most famous of all mediæval universities. This university grew out of the cathedral school of Notre Dame, which had acquired considerable reputation by the earliest part of the twelfth century under the headship of *William of Champeaux*. But the intellectual movement was more largely developed by the brilliant and attractive *Abelard*,[1] who taught in Paris at various periods between 1108 and 1139. While well under thirty, Abelard had defeated both his chief masters, Roscellinus, the nominalist, and William of Champeaux, who was an extreme realist. In 1117 he succeeded to the position from which he had driven William in humiliation, and, through his eloquence, versatility, tact, and great intellectual endowment, drew thousands of students to Paris from all nations. McCabe estimates "that a pope, nineteen cardinals, and more than fifty bishops and archbishops were at one time among his pupils." He lectured especially upon dialectic and theology, and greatly stimulated free discussion and the liberation of reason. His successor was his pupil, *Peter the Lombard*, who became the author of the great mediæval textbook upon theology entitled *Sententiæ*.

and was first chartered by Louis VII in 1180.

Thus Abelard became the progenitor of the university, although it was not until almost a generation after his death that it could really have been organized. It was first formally recognized by the king, Louis VII, in 1180, and eighteen years later it had its privileges substantially increased by Pope Celestine III, but it was only in 1200, after canon law and medicine had been added to the liberal arts and theology, that it received complete recognition by the act of Philip Augustus.

[1] See pp. 53 f.

As we have seen, Salerno failed to reproduce its type, but Bologna, and even more Paris, became the mother of universities, for many other institutions were organized after their general plans. At Bologna the students, who were usually mature men, and, as a result of their political environment, very independent, had entire charge of the government of the university. They selected the masters and determined the fees, length of term, and time of beginning. But in Paris, where the students were younger, the government was in the hands of the masters. Consequently, new foundations in the North, where Paris was the type, usually became 'master-universities,' while those of the South were 'student-universities.' The universities that arose in Italy, France (with the exception of Paris), Spain, and Portugal, were patterned after Bologna, and those which grew up in England, Scotland, Germany, Sweden, and Denmark, followed Paris. But besides the universities that grew gradually, or sprang up rapidly as a result of migration from other organizations, sovereigns or ecclesiastics not infrequently started new institutions full-fledged, in order to produce more lawyers and other learned men or to propagate the Catholic faith.

Bologna, the 'student-university,' became the pattern for numerous universities in the South; and Paris, the 'master-university,' for those in the North.

Thus during the thirteenth and fourteenth centuries it became fashionable for the authorities, civil and ecclesiastical, to charter existing organizations or to found new ones. In England, Oxford began in the second half of the twelfth, and Cambridge at the beginning of the thirteenth century, although their first recognition by charter cannot easily be ascertained. Of the Italian universities, Naples was, as we have noted, established by imperial decree in 1224, Padua arose two years earlier through emigration from Bologna, and Arezzo grew up about the same time, although not recognized until 1355. The universities of Palencia, Salamanca, and Valladolid in Spain and that of Lisbon in Portugal were also founded during the thirteenth century. The next foundation in France after Paris was that made by Pope Gregory IX at Toulouse in

During the thirteenth and fourteenth centuries, universities sprang up throughout Europe, and by the Renaissance there were at least seventy-nine of them.

1233, and this was followed by Montpellier later in the century and by a number of others during the next century. The first German university, that of Prague, was not instituted until 1348, but, before the close of the century, Vienna, Erfurt, Heidelberg, and Cologne had sprung up, and twice as many more appeared within the next hundred years. By the time the Renaissance was well started, at least seventy-nine [1] universities were in existence in the different countries of Europe. All of these foundations were not permanent, however, for some thirty have, in the course of time, become extinct, and those which remain are much changed in character and course. Naturally enough from their origin, all the universities came to be located, not like the old monasteries in remote places, but in the centers of population.

Sovereigns and popes granted many privileges to the universities, such as direct protection and special courts,

Privileges Granted to Universities.—From the time of the earliest official recognition of the universities, a large variety of exemptions, immunities, and other special privileges were conferred upon the organizations, or upon their masters and students, by popes, emperors, kings, feudal lords, and municipalities. The universities were in many instances taken under the immediate protection of the sovereign, and were allowed to have special courts of their own, independent of civil jurisdiction, and complete autonomy in all their internal affairs. Both these privileges are granted in the document known as the *Habita*[2] of Frederick I, or 'Barbarossa.' This emperor, in 1158, for the benefit of the students of Bologna, issued the following general edict:—

"We, from our piety, have granted these privileges to all scholars who travel for the sake of study, and especially to the professors of divine and sacred laws; namely, that they may go in safety to the places in which the studies are carried on, both they themselves and their messengers, and may dwell there in security. For we think it fitting that, during good behavior, those should enjoy our approval

---

[1] There may have been others, of which the records have disappeared.
[2] *Habita* is the first word in the charter. The document is sometimes called the *Authentic Habita*, since it was placed by Pertz among the *authentica* or *originalia instrumenta*.

and protection, who, by their learning, enlighten the world, and mold the life of our subjects to the obedience of God, and of us, his minister. . . . Therefore, we declare by this general and perpetual law that hereafter no one shall be so rash as to inflict any injury on scholars, or to impose any fine upon them on account of an offense committed in their former province. And let it be known to violators of this decree, and to local rulers at the time who have neglected to punish such violations, that a fourfold restitution of property shall be exacted from all who are guilty, and that the brand of infamy shall be affixed to them by the law, and they shall be forever deprived of their offices.

"Moreover, if any one shall presume to bring a suit against the scholars on any ground, the choice in the matter shall be given to the scholars, who may summon the accusers to appear before their professors or the bishop of the city, to whom we have given jurisdiction in these circumstances. But if, indeed, the accuser shall attempt to take the scholar before another judge, even if his cause be most just, he shall lose his suit because of such attempt."

The provisions of the *Habita* were repeated for various universities by other monarchs. Perhaps the most sweeping protection and immunity were contained in the edict of Philip Augustus, by which all citizens of Paris who saw any one striking a student were required to seize the offender and deliver him to the judge, and the provost of the city and all judges were commanded to hand over the cases of the student criminals to the ecclesiastical authority.

These privileges seem to have been suggested in the first place by provisions made by the Roman emperors for students in the old universities. Similarly, there were conferred upon masters and students other general privileges with which the emperors had favored the philosophers, rhetoricians, and grammarians of the pagan schools.[1] Persons connected with the mediæval universities were relieved from all taxation, and, except in times of emergency, from military service. Rupert I, in founding the University of Heidelberg, makes the following grant to masters and students: —

exemption from taxation,

"When they come to the said institution, while they remain there, and also when they return from it to their homes, they may freely

[1] See Graves, *A History of Education before the Middle Ages*, pp. 265–266.

84   A HISTORY OF EDUCATION

carry with them, throughout all the lands subject to us, all things which they need while pursuing their studies, and all the goods necessary for their support, without any duty, levy, imposts, tolls, excises, or other exactions, whatever."

Similarly, before this, teachers and scholars were declared at Paris to be exempt from "*tallia*,[1] customs, and personal taxes, in coming or going," and the charter of Leipzig in the next century relieved the property of that organization of "all *losunge*,[1] exactions, contributions, *steura*,[1] and taxes, and from the control of the citizens." These exemptions applied not only to the corporation, students, and masters, but often to the bell-ringers, booksellers, bookbinders, parchment makers, illuminators, messengers, and others serving in a more or less menial capacity.

the right to license masters, and the right to suspend lectures and migrate.

The universities had also certain recognized privileges that had originated as customs with the early universities, but were specially granted by the civil or ecclesiastical authorities as a formality to institutions already exercising these rights, or to new universities that wished to be on a par with them. Such was the *jus ubique docendi*, or the right of a university to license masters to lecture anywhere without further examination, and the *cessatio*, or privilege of suspending lectures, when university rights were infringed. In the latter case, unless the wrongs were immediately redressed, the suspension was followed by an emigration of the university to another town. This could easily be done in mediæval days when universities did not have any buildings of their own and there was no need of expensive libraries, laboratories, and other equipment. So, in 1209, Cambridge got its first real start through an exodus from Oxford. Sometimes a special invitation would be issued to a university exercising the *cessatio* to come to another country. Thus the University of Oxford in 1229 met

[1] Taxes whose purpose is not exactly known. From *tallia* probably the feudal *taille* was developed, and from *steura* the Modern German *Steuer* must be derived. See Ducange, *Glossarium Mediæ et Infimæ Latinitatis*. The piling up of synonyms with little or no distinction seems to be common in legal documents at all ages.

THE MEDIÆVAL UNIVERSITIES   85

with its most substantial increase through King Henry III, who promised the striking masters and scholars of Paris —

"If it shall be your pleasure to transfer yourselves to our kingdom of England and to remain there to study, we will for this purpose assign to you cities, boroughs, towns, whatsoever you may wish to select, and in every fitting way will cause you to rejoice in a state of liberty and tranquillity."[1]

There were, of course, a number of less important privileges that were peculiar to the various localities, but those mentioned were generally held by all the universities. Through such special rights the universities obtained a great power and became very independent. Soon the liberty allowed to students degenerated into recklessness and license. The students seemed to have become dissipated and quarrelsome. Clashes were common not only with the townspeople, but even among themselves. Each nation was at times unsparing in its abuse of the others. We are informed, for instance, through the mutual recriminations of the students at Paris, that there were among them many drunkards, spendthrifts, fops, gluttons, bullies, roués, and adventurers.[2] After all allowance is made for the prejudice and exaggeration of the various nations, it is evident that the students had to some extent become uncleanly, bad-mannered, and immoral. This is especially seen in the life of the so-called *wandering students*. This class arose from the freer life consequent upon the decline of monasticism and from the sanctioning of migratory habits by the example of the friars. Like these orders, the students begged their way, as they wandered from university to university. They became rollicking, indolent, shiftless, and even vicious, and many found the life so attractive that they made it permanent and organized a

These privileges led to license, especially in the case of the 'wandering students.'

---

[1] The full text is translated in Norton's *Readings on Mediæval Universities*, pp. 95–96. See also Rashdall, *Universities in the Middle Ages*, Vol. II, pp. 392 and 546.
[2] See the description in Jacques de Vitry's *Historia Occidentalis*, Lib. II, c. 7, translated in Munro, *Translations and Reprints*, Vol. II, No. 3.

mock 'order' or gild of wandering students known as *Goliardi*[1] or *vagantes*.[2] The one compensating feature of this degeneracy was the production of jovial Latin and German songs to voice their frank appreciation of forbidden pleasures, and their protest against restraint and the formalism and corruption of the Church. Various collections of these songs have come down to us.[3] The following translation of the *Song of the Open Road*, in which every couplet was followed by an imitation of a bugle call, will afford some idea of the recklessness and exuberance of this vagabond student life: —

> "We in our wandering,
>   Blithesome and squandering,
> Eat to satiety,
>   Drink to propriety;
> Laugh till our sides we split,
>   Rags on our hides we fit;
> Craft's in the bone of us,
>   Fear 'tis unknown of us;
> Brother catholical,
>   Man apostolical,
> Say what you will have done,
>   What you ask 'twill be done!
> Folk, fear the toss of the
>   Horns of philosophy!
> Here comes a quadruple,[4]
>   Spoiler and prodigal!
> As the Pope bade us do,
>   Brother to brother's true:
> Brother, best friend adieu!
>   Now I must part from you!
> Tara, tantara, teino!"

'University' originally signified a 'company'

Organization of the Universities. — From its historical origin the nature of the mediæval university was similar

---

[1] The word 'is probably derived from the French *gaillard* ('gay'). The similarity of the term to *Golias* ('Goliath') seems to have suggested their taking him as a patron saint.

[2] In the latter part of the thirteenth century there grew up a type of younger wandering students known as *scholares vagantes*, who learned the elements from wandering masters in search of a school. They were also sometimes accompanied by still younger boys, known as *ABC shooters*.

[3] See especially Symonds, *Wine, Women, and Song*, or the reprints in Mosher, *Mediæval Latin Students' Songs*.

[4] The *quadrivium*, of which they thus bid honest people beware.

THE MEDIÆVAL UNIVERSITIES 87

to that of the gilds. This is shown in its complete name, — *Universitas Magistrorum et Scholarium* ('the body of masters and scholars'). The term *universitas* did not imply originally, as often claimed since, an institution where 'everything' is taught, but it was used of any legal corporation, and only in the lapse of time was it limited, without qualifying words, to a particular body.[1] It signified a company of persons that had assembled for study, and, like any other gild, had organized for the sake of protection, since they were in a town where they were regarded as strangers. Thus it did not refer to a place or school at all, but to the teachers and scholars. When it was desired to express the abstract notion of an academic institution, *studium generale* was the phrase used. This indicated a school or place where students from all parts of civilization were received, and was contrasted with a *studium particulare*, which taught only a few from the neighborhood.

of students and teachers, and when the school or its seat was intended, 'studium generale' was used.

The students of each *studium generale* naturally grouped themselves according to the part of the world from which they came, and the charters were sometimes conferred upon the *nationes* ('nations') separately, as these organizations had usually preceded the formation of the university. The nations, however, soon began to combine for the sake of obtaining greater privileges and power. By the early part of the thirteenth century, the students of Bologna had merged their organizations into two bodies, — the *universitas citramontanorum* ('Cisalpine corporation'), composed of seventeen nations, and the *universitas ultramontanorum* ('Transalpine corporation'), made up of eighteen; but not for some three centuries were these two united. The University of Paris included the four nations of France, Picardy, Normandy, and England.[2] Every year each nation chose its chief, who was called the

University students were usually grouped by their 'nations,'

and each nation chose a 'consiliarius' to represent it.

---

[1] During the fourteenth century the word *universitas* came to be used alone of the institution of learning.
[2] In later centuries England was replaced by Germany.

consiliarius ('councilor').¹ It was his duty to represent the nation, guard its rights, and control the conduct of its members.

Each 'faculty,' which originally meant a department of knowledge, soon elected its own 'dean,' and the deans and 'consiliarii' elected the 'rector.'

On the side of the masters, the university became organized into *faculties*. The word *facultas* was originally used of a special department of knowledge, and then applied to a body of masters teaching a particular range of subjects. Hence there arose the four faculties of arts, law, medicine, and theology, or even five, where law was divided into civil and canon.² But few universities, however, had the four faculties, and those they possessed were very unequal in strength. Even at its height Paris had no faculty of civil law, while in theology it shared what was practically a monopoly with the English universities. Law was in most universities the leading faculty. Each faculty came to elect a *decanus* ('dean') as its representative in the university organization. The deans, together with the councilors of the student bodies, elected the rector, or head of the university. This officer, however, had only such powers as were delegated to him. In the South the rector was usually a student, but in the North, where the masters controlled, he was generally chosen from the faculty of arts.

The Courses of Study. — The content of the courses offered by each faculty differed greatly in the various universities, and was somewhat modified from time to time even in the same university. However, during the thirteenth century it came in each case to be rather definitely fixed by papal decree or university legislation, and practically no departure from the course laid down was allowed.³ For the course in arts, which occupied

The course in 'arts' included the seven liberal arts and some of the treatises of Aristotle;

---
[1] In Paris he was known as the *procurator*; in Oxford and Cambridge as *procurator* or *proctor*, or sometimes in Cambridge as *rector*.

[2] Paetow (*Arts Course at Mediæval Universities*, pp. 55-58 and 81-84) has shown that there were separate faculties and distinct degrees in 'grammar' from those in 'arts,' and that Bologna had a separate faculty in *ars notaria*, if not in *ars dictaminis*, which conferred the degree of *doctor notariæ*.

[3] A clear and comprehensive treatment of the university courses is found in Norton's *Mediæval Universities* (Cambridge, 1909), pp. 37-80.

some six years, the compendia and texts on the liberal arts already referred to,[1] Donatus and Priscian, and Alexander of Villedieu and Eberhard of Bethune[2] on grammar, Boethius on rhetoric, dialectic, arithmetic, and music, Alberich and Boncompagno on *ars dictaminis*,[3] Euclid on geometry, Ptolemy on astronomy, and other standard works, were in general use, but they were enriched during this period by the additions of the Arabic treatises on mathematics and dialectic and many other new texts. The course in arts also included many of the works of Aristotle. Some of his logical treatises had been previously known, and during the thirteenth century the rest of the *Organon*, and the *Ethics, Politics, Poetics*, and *Rhetoric*, and his works upon natural science, came to be translated either from the Arabic or the original and used as texts. Thus in 1215 the following course in arts was prescribed for Paris by Robert de Courçon: —

"The treatises of Aristotle on logic, both old and new, and the two Priscians[4] are to be read in the regular course. On feast-days nothing is to be read except philosophy, rhetoric, *quadrivialia*, the Barbarisms,[5] the Ethics, and the Topics.[6] The books of Aristotle on Metaphysics or Natural Philosophy, or the abridgments of these works, are not to be read."[7]

But this 'liberal' course did not contain any of the modern studies, such as history or modern languages and literatures, and it devoted little attention to Roman classics, and, outside of Aristotle, none at all to Greek. Moreover, probably at no university were all the works mentioned in use, but rather there were different selections made in each institution.

The course in law generally consisted of two parts, —

[1] See pp. 14–21.
[2] See p. 20.
[3] See p. 18, footnote 3, and p. 88, footnote 2.
[4] The first sixteen books of Priscian's grammar were known as the *major*, and the last two as the *minor*.
[5] The third book of Donatus, *Ars Major*.
[6] A logical treatise of Boethius.
[7] The Church was at this time still a trifle distrustful of Aristotle.

civil and canon.¹ In the former, the *Corpus Juris Civilis* was the authorized text. This work now included the *Code*, or compilation of imperial edicts, the *Digest*² of opinions of Roman jurists, and the *Institutes*, which was an introductory text for students. The official treatise for the study of canon law was the *Decretum Gratiani*. That consisted of three parts on ecclesiastical offices, the administration of canon law, and the ritual and sacraments, respectively.

in medicine, works of Hippocrates, Galen, Avicenna, Isaac, and Nicolaus;

In the faculty of medicine were included the Greek treatises by Hippocrates (c. 460–375, B.C.) and Galen (c. 130–200, A.D.), together with the works of certain Saracen, Jewish, and Salernitan physicians. The chief of these latter treatises seem to have been the medical *Canon* of Avicenna,³ the *Liber Febrium* and *Liber Dietarum* written by Isaac Judæus, and the *Antidotarium* by Nicolaus of Salerno.⁴

and in theology, Peter the Lombard's Sententiæ and the Bible.

The students of theology put most of their time upon the four books of Peter the Lombard's *Sententiæ*, although the Bible was studied incidentally. This neglect of the Scriptures for the scholastic theology and the traditions of the Church, which was so characteristic of the Middle Ages, is thus stigmatized by the advanced thinker, Roger ('Friar') Bacon (1214–1294): —

" Although the principal study of the theologian ought to be in the text of Scripture, in the last fifty years theologians have been principally occupied with questions in tractates and *Summæ*, — horse-loads composed by many, — and not at all with the most holy text of God. And accordingly, theologians give a readier reception to a treatise of scholastic questions than they do to one about the text of Scripture."⁵

The Methods of Study. — The training of a mediæval

¹ See pp. 78 f.
² Sometimes called *Pandects*.
³ See p. 42 for Avicenna.
⁴ For the details of a general course in medicine, see Rashdall, *Universities in the Middle Ages*, Vol. II, Pt. I, p. 123; for that of Paris, Munro, *Mediæval Student*, pp. 16–17; for that of Oxford, Rashdall, *op. cit.*, Vol. II, Pt. II, pp. 780 and 454 f.
⁵ See Brewer's translation of Bacon's *Compendium Studii Theologiæ*.

student consisted not only in acquiring the subjects mentioned, but in learning to debate upon them. The acquisition of the subject matter was accomplished through lectures, which consisted in reading and explaining the textbook under consideration. This was rendered necessary by the scarcity of manuscripts, which had to be used until the invention of printing, and the difficulty in purchasing or renting copies of them. Each work consisted of a text and commentaries upon it. The glosses, which had often grown to such proportions as completely to overshadow the original, consisted of explanatory notes, summaries, cross-references, and objections to the author's statements.[1] To these the teacher might add a commentary of his own as he read. Odofredus, the jurist, thus describes his procedure at Bologna: —

The texts, with their glosses, were read and explained by the lecturers, and taken down without investigation by the students.

"First, I shall give you summaries of each chapter before I proceed to the text ; secondly, I shall give you as clear and explicit a statement as I can of the purport of each Law (included in the chapter) ; thirdly, I shall read the text with a view to correcting it ; fourthly, I shall briefly repeat the contents of the Law ; fifthly, I shall solve apparent contradictions, adding any general principles of Law (to be extracted from the passage), and any distinctions or subtle and useful problems arising out of the Law with their solutions."[2]

The master must often have had to read the passage repeatedly, in order that all might grasp it, and he ordinarily read slowly enough for the student to treat his commentary as a dictation. There was always considerable objection to rapid reading, and even university regulations were made against a master's lecturing so fast as not to permit of full notes. Naturally, such a method afforded little freedom in thinking. There could be no real investigation, but simply a slavish following of the text and lecture. The whole exercise was carried on in Latin, which had to be learned by the student before coming to the university.

The training in debate was furnished by means of

---

[1] An excellent illustration is given in the selection from Gratian in Norton's *Mediæval Universities*, pp. 59–75.
[2] See Rashdall, *Universities*, Vol. I, pp. 219–220.

A training in debate was also furnished by means of formal disputations between students.

formal disputations, in which one student, or group of students, was pitted against another. In these contests, which also were conducted in Latin, not only were authorities cited, but the debaters might add arguments of their own. Sometimes a single person might exercise himself by arguing both sides of the question and coming to a judgment for one side or the other. This debating had been instituted to afford some acuteness and vigor of intellect, and, compared with the memorizing of lectures, it served its purpose well, but by the close of the fifteenth century it had gone to such an extreme as to be no longer reputable. The aim came to be to win and to secure applause without regard to truth or consistency.

Upon passing the examination at the end, a student became a 'master' or 'doctor';

Degrees. — After three to seven years of study and training, the student was examined on his ability to dispute and define. If he passed, he was admitted to the grade of *master*, *doctor*, or *professor*. The taking of this degree signified that the candidate had, as in the gilds and other mediæval organizations, passed through the stages of 'apprentice' and 'journeyman,' and presented his 'masterpiece.'[1] He was now ready to practice the craft of teaching and to compete with the other masters for students. The degrees 'master' and 'doctor' seem to have been originally about on a par with each other.[2] The master's examination, which gave the license to teach anywhere, was private and most formal, while that for the doctorate was public and mostly a ceremonial. As soon as a candidate was successful in the one, he immediately proceeded to the other, upon which occasion he received both the license to teach and the doctor's degree.[3] Accompanied by friends and fellow-

---

[1] See p. 97. So the German universities still use *Arbeit* of the academic 'masterpiece,' — the doctoral dissertation.
[2] A fuller discussion of these synonyms is found in Rashdall, *Universities*, Vol. I, pp. 21–22.
[3] The German universities to-day combine the two, and at the completion of his course, create the candidate *philosophiæ doctor et artium magister*. But the master's degree has now generally come to be inferior to the doctorate, as in France and America.

students and preceded by a trumpeter, he marched to the cathedral in state. There, after a speech and a formal defense of some thesis against picked opponents, he was presented to the archdeacon of the diocese, who conferred the degree upon him with a formula not unlike that used on similar occasions in modern universities.[1]

The baccalaureate, or bachelor's degree, was at first not a real degree, but simply permission to become a candidate for the license. During the thirteenth century, however, it came to be sought as an honor by many not intending to teach, and after the lapse of two centuries it became generally recognized as a separate degree.

the baccalaureate was at first simply permission to enter.

The Value of the University Education and Its Effect upon Civilization. — The defects in the training of the mediæval universities are obvious. The content of their course of study was meager, fixed, and formal. It leaned toward dogmatism and disputation, and dealt entirely with books, without a genuine desire for the discovery of facts or the revelation of truth. It neglected completely the real literature of the classical age, and cared little for developing the imagination and the æsthetic side of life. Similarly, the methods of teaching were stereotyped and authoritative. They permitted little that savored of investigation or thinking.

The university course was meager, fixed, and formal, and the methods were stereotyped;

These, however, were the general faults of the Middle Ages, and the universities were evidently the product of the growing tendencies to break through them and burst the fetters of the intellect. Despite their adherence to dogmatism and their seeming opposition to investigation, they did much to foster intellectual development. They were the greatest encouragement to subtlety, industry, and thoroughness, and their tendency toward speculation was primarily responsible for the modern spirit of inquiry and rationality. The activity they nurtured made possible such minds as those of Dante, Petrarch, Boccaccio, and Erasmus in intellectual and literary lines; Wyclif, Huss, and Luther in the theological and ecclesiastical field; and

but these were the general faults of the Middle Ages, and the universities did much to foster intellectual development, and to make great minds possible.

[1] For the form used at Bologna, see Rashdall, *Universities*, Vol. II, pp. 734–735.

Friar Bacon, Copernicus, Galileo, and Francis Bacon in the realm of realism and science.

They were also of immediate assistance in moderating absolutism. Even as an institution the universities were of immediate assistance in promoting freedom of discussion and advancing democracy. They became the representatives of secular and popular interest, and moderated greatly the power of the papacy and absolute sovereignty. They were regarded by all classes as a court of arbitration, and to them were referred disputes between the civil and ecclesiastical powers. Paris, through its location, numbers, and government, was especially powerful. When appealed to by the king, Philip VI, it compelled the pope, John XXII, to retract his judgment and humbly apologize, and the same institution, half a century later, was most instrumental in forcing the abdication of John XXIII and Benedict XII, and thus closing the scandalous papal schism.[1] The influence of the universities liberalized all mediæval institutions, and aided greatly in advancing the cause of individualism and carrying forward the torch of civilization and progress.

SUPPLEMENTARY READING

I. Sources

DENIFLE, H. *Die Statuten der Juristen-Universität Bologna, 1317-1347.*

DENIFLE, H., AND CHATELAIN, A. *Chartularium Universitatis Parisiensis.*

HENDERSON, E. F. *Select Historical Documents of the Middle Ages.* Pp. 262–266.

MUNRO, D. C. *The Mediæval Student (Translations and Reprints,* Vol. II, No. 3).

NORTON, A. O. *Readings in the History of Education. Mediæval Universities.*

OGG, F. A. *Source Book of Mediæval History.* Chap. XXI.

ROBINSON, J. H. *Readings in European History.* Vol. I, Chap. XIX, IV.

SCHMELLER, J. A. *Carmina Burana* (third edition).

SYMONDS, J. A. *Wine, Women, and Song.*

---

[1] See D'Achery, *Spicilegium,* I, pp. 777 f.

II. AUTHORITIES

ABELSON, P. *The Seven Liberal Arts.*
BARNARD, H. *An Account of Universities (National Education,* Pt. III).
BRESSLAU, H. *Handbuch der Urkundenlehre für Deutschland und Italien.*
COMPAYRÉ, G. *Abelard and the Origin and Early History of Universities.*
DENIFLE, P. H. *Die Entstehung der Universitäten des Mittelalters bis 1400.*
DRANE, A. T. *Christian Schools and Scholars.* Pp. 366-475.
EMERTON, E. *Mediæval Europe.* Chap. XIII.
FOURNIER, P. J. M. *Les statuts et privilèges des Universités francaises.*
GIESEBRECHT, W. *Die Vaganten oder Goliardi und ihre Lieder.*
HASKINS, C. H. *The Life of a Mediæval Student (American Historical Review,* 1897-1898).
HASKINS, C. H. *The University of Paris in the Sermons of the Thirteenth Century (American Historical Review,* 1904, pp. 1-27).
JESSOPP, A. *The Coming of the Friars.* Chap. VI.
JOURDAIN, C. M. G. *Histoire de l'Université de Paris.*
KAUFMANN, G. *Die Geschichte der deutschen Universitäten.*
LAURIE, S. S. *The Rise and Early Constitution of Universities.*
LYTE, H. C. M. *A History of the University of Oxford.* Chaps. I-VI.
MULLINGER, J. B. *University of Cambridge.*
MULLINGER, J. B. *Universities (Encyclopædia Britannica).*
NEWMAN, J. H. *Historical Sketches.* Vol. III, Chaps. XIV-XVI.
PAETOW, L. J. *The Arts Course at Medieval Universities (The University of Illinois Studies.* Vol. III, No. 7).
PARKER, J. *The Early History of Oxford.*
PAULSEN, F. *The German Universities* (translated by Thilly and Elwang).
RASHDALL, H. *The Universities of Europe in the Middle Ages.*
SAVIGNY, F. *Geschichte des Römischen Rechts im Mittelalter.*
SHELDON, H. D. *Student Life and Customs.*
WALDEN, H. *On the Origin of Universities and Academic Degrees.*
WOODWARD, W. H. (Editor). *Mediæval Schools and Universities.*

CHAPTER X

THE DEVELOPMENT OF CITIES AND NEW SCHOOLS

The Crusades gave a great impulse to commerce, manufactures, and industries,

The Rise of Commerce and Cities. — An important influence upon civilization and education during the later Middle Ages was that produced by the *increase in commerce*. Foreign trade had never died out since Roman days, despite the injuries wrought by the barbarian invasions, as the nobles had always need of luxuries and the Church of articles of utility in its services. But the demand for vessels and transports during the Crusades, and the desire for the precious stones, silks, perfumes, drugs, spices, and porcelain from the Orient afterward, gave a tremendous impulse to commercial activity. Thus communication between the states of Europe was greatly facilitated, new commercial routes and new regions were opened, geographical knowledge was increased, navigation was developed, maritime and mercantile affairs were organized, manufactures and industries were enlarged, currency was increased, and forms of credit were improved. All this tended toward a larger intellectual view and a partial dissipation of provincialism and intolerance.

and thus contributed to the growth of cities

The most important consequence of this industrial awakening was the rise and *growth of cities*. The old Roman towns of Italy and Gaul revived and grew rapidly in size and wealth, and new cities sprang up around the manorial estates and monasteries as manufactures, trade, and commerce increased. The people in these cities rebelled against the rule of their lords and either expelled them altogether or secured from them for a monetary consideration a charter conferring more liberal rights and privileges. For example, a charter granted by Henry of Troyes in 1175, stipulated as follows: —

"All persons living in the said city shall pay each year twelve deniers and a measure of oats as the price of his domicile; and if he wishes to have a portion of ground or of meadow, he shall pay four deniers rent an acre. The inhabitants of said town shall not be forced to make war nor go on any expedition, unless I myself am at their head. I grant them besides the right to have six magistrates, who shall administer the common affairs of the town. No lord, cavalier, or other shall take from the town any of its inhabitants for any reason."

As manufactures and trade developed, the merchants and other citizens grew rapidly in wealth and importance, and before long the *burgher class* had a recognized position by the side of the clergy and nobility. The burghers became educated, and were soon appealed to for counsel by the kings.

and the development of a burgher class.

The Gild, Burgher, and Chantry Schools. — But besides the general organization of the towns, separate craft gilds had also been established, to prevent any one who had not been regularly approved from practising the trade he represented. Under the gild system, one had to spend from three to ten years learning his craft, first as an *apprentice* with no wages, and later as a *journeyman*, working for the public only through his *master*. The number of apprentices was limited, and the craft otherwise regulated and protected. The masons of Paris, for instance, had to observe these regulations: —

'Gilds' for each craft were also established, and a species of industrial training grew up, which was followed by 'gild schools.'

"No one shall have more than one apprentice in his trade, and if he has an apprentice, he shall engage him for not less than six years' service, but of course he may engage him for a longer term of service and for more money, if he is able to do so. If he engage him for less than six years, he shall be fined twenty sous. The mason, however, may take another apprentice as soon as the first apprentice shall have completed five years."

In this way there had grown up a species of *industrial education* with three definite stages in its organization. Before long, too, the gilds developed a formal means of education, which has ever since been known as the *gild schools*.

A famous foundation of this sort is recorded in the report of Edward VI's commissioner, who tells us concerning the city of Worcester: —

98 A HISTORY OF EDUCATION

"There hath byn tyme owt of mynde, a ffree scole kept within the said citie, in a grete halle belongyng to the said Guylde, called Trinite Hall; the scholemaster whereof for the tyme beyng hath hade yerely, for his stypend, ten pounds; whereof was paid, owt of the revenues of the said landes, by the Master and Stewards of the said Guylde for the tyme beyng, vi *li*., xiii *s*., iii *d*.; And the resydewe of the said stypend was collected and gathered of the denocioun and benyvolence of the brothers and systers of the said Guylde."[1]

Although the gilds demanded a new type of instruction, their schools were still taught by the clergy,—usually the priests who had been retained to perform the necessary religious offices for the members of the organizations concerned. The gild schools were generally elementary in character, but they not infrequently afforded some secondary instruction. While most of the work was in the vernacular, courses in Latin and other higher subjects were also afforded, and some of these gild schools, like *Merchant Taylors'* of London, have endured and attained to great repute as secondary institutions.

As the gild organizations merged with those of the towns, the gild schools were absorbed in the burgher schools, which sometimes came to embrace also other institutions.

But as the gild organizations gradually merged with those of the towns, the gild schools were generally absorbed in the institutions known as the *burgher schools*. Another type of institution that came into prominence toward the close of the Middle Ages and was also sometimes united with the burgher schools, was the *chantry school*. These chantry organizations arose out of bequests by wealthy persons to support priests who should 'chant' masses for the repose of their souls, for when the priests were not engaged in this religious duty, they were required to do some teaching. In this way all the various schools within a town were often combined, and many new foundations of a similar nature were made. These burgher schools were largely controlled and supported by the public authorities, although still generally taught by priests. They came to represent the interests of the merchant and artisan classes, and gave instruction in subjects of more practical value than had any of the schools hitherto. Such institutions sprang up everywhere

These burgher schools paved the way for secularization in education.

[1] Quoted from Toulmin Smith's *Ordinances of English Guilds* by Monroe, *Thomas Platter*, p. 17.

THE DEVELOPMENT OF CITIES AND NEW SCHOOLS

during the later Middle Ages, and while they were still inspected by the clergy, and the Church struggled hard to bring them under her control, the number of lay teachers in them gradually increased, and thus paved the way for the secularization of education that took place during the Reformation.

SUPPLEMENTARY READING

I. SOURCES

CHEYNEY, E. P. *English Towns and Gilds* (*Translations and Reprints*, Vol. II, No. 1).
GROSS, C. *The Gild Merchant.*
JONES, G. *Studies in European History.* VIII and IX.
SMITH, T. *English Gilds.*
ZELLER, B. (Editor). *L'Histoire de France racontée par les Contemporains.*
ZELLER, B. *Mœurs et Institutions du XIII Siècle.*

II. AUTHORITIES

ADAMS, G. B. *Civilization during the Middle Ages.* Chaps. X–XII.
ASHLEY, W. J. *An Introduction to English Economic History and Theory.*
CUNNINGHAM, W. *The Growth of English Industry and Commerce.*
CUNNINGHAM, W. *Essay on Western Civilization in its Economic Aspects.* Mediæval and Modern Times. Chap. III.
CUTTS, E. L. *Scenes and Characters of the Middle Ages.* The Merchants. Chaps. III and VI.
DRAPER, J. W. *History of the Intellectual Development of Europe.* Vol. II, Chaps. IV and V.
GUIZOT, F. *The History of Civilization.* Lects. VII and VIII.
KRIEGK, G. L. *Deutsches Bürgerthum in Mittelalter.*
MONROE, P. *Thomas Platter and the Educational Revival of the Sixteenth Century.* Pp. 3–18.
WILDA, W. E. *Das Gildenwesen im Mittelalter.*
WILKEN, F. *Geschichte der Kreuzzüge.*

CHAPTER XI

THE PASSING OF THE MIDDLE AGES

The Holy Roman Empire was disrupted in its struggle with the papacy largely through feudalism, but feudalism was itself undermined by the Crusades and other new forces, and national patriotism began to arise.

The Growth of National Spirit. — It can now be seen that a new spirit had begun to creep into European civilization. Even before scholasticism had come to its height, or the universities were well under way, it would seem that the Middle Ages were passing. The struggle between a world-wide political power and a universal spiritual organization was drawing to a close through the downfall of the former. Frederick II, ruler of the Holy Roman Empire, was in 1245 deposed by Innocent IV, head of the Imperial Church of Rome, although the civil monarch continued the struggle until his death five years later. This victory of the Church over the Empire had largely been aided by the growth of feudalism, which had worked itself out to a logical conclusion and split the Empire into fragments. For centuries afterward the emperors were mere figureheads, elected in each case because of their very weakness politically. But feudalism and the Church were themselves being undermined by new economic and political forces. The Crusades, which had continued upon a large scale during most of the twelfth century and in a smaller and more spasmodic way for another hundred years, while a failure from the standpoints of religious or military achievement, had very important results upon civilization. Thousands of crusaders were overcome by the rigors of the journey or butchered by hostile peoples before reaching the Orient, and the leaders became more absorbed in opposing their fellow-Christians of the East or in outwitting each other than in overcoming the Turks. But this very sharing of dangers by all nations and by all classes of people tended to level social distinctions and to bind Christendom together in a common purpose. It made evident their common needs and desires. The old nobility and the former allegiances were largely ruined, and the universal claims of the Church were greatly broken. The inherent weakness of feudalism began to appear, and national monarchies and national patriotism arose in the place of this mediæval order of society. The degeneracy of the papacy also promoted the culture of a national spirit.

The Development of Vernacular Literature. — In many other ways marked changes in the mediæval ideas and habits became evident. The break-up of the old authority and repression was apparent not only in new political institutions, but also in the altered æsthetic productions of the times. A literature of the people was beginning to arise. Before the eleventh century the written literature of Europe, since it dealt mostly with ecclesiastical and learned subjects, was usually in Latin, although there seem to have been songs, poems, and stories that were passed down in the vernacular, and, in England, the *Story of Beowulf* and other prose and poetry were actually written down. But with the eleventh century a large popular literature was rapidly appearing in the national languages that had now been well developed. The earliest form of these writings is found in the heroic poems of France. These deal with national themes of a semi-historical character, such as the deeds of Charlemagne and his knights, especially with the Saracen foe, and are known as the *chansons de geste*. Thus, during the eleventh and twelfth centuries appeared such productions of the *Trouvères*, or poets of Northern France, as the *Chanson de Roland*, *Aymeri de Narbonne*, and *Raoul de Cambrai*.[1] But in the latter half of the twelfth and during the thirteenth century, when the fervor of the Crusades was at its height, and the later and more artificial forms of

A new type of literature, written in the vernacular, also began to develop.

---

[1] See pp. 64 f.

chivalry held sway, there arose another type of poems, consisting of accounts of knightly adventures, with love and extravagant devotion to women as the central theme. The spirit of this later period is first displayed in the lyrics of the *Troubadours*.[1] These poets belonged to Southern France, where were the greatest wealth and luxury, but their songs were soon imitated by the bards of England and Germany. In the last named country the poets were known as *Minnesingers*, because they sang of love.[2] At this time, too, were composed the narrative poems based on the stories of King Arthur and his knights, the search for the Holy Grail, classical tales concerning the Trojan heroes, Alexander, Cæsar, and others, and the German sagas, of which the best example is, perhaps, the *Niebelungenlied* ('Song of the Niebelungs'). Sometimes these themes were combined, as in the famous *Parsifal* of Wolfram von Eschenbach, where the Arthurian legends are united with that of the Holy Grail. During this period also were produced short tales in verse known as *fabliaux*. They were intended only to amuse, and were broadly humorous, and at times even obscene.[3] German, as well as Latin, productions adapted to the spirit of the times, are also found in the rollicking songs of the wandering students, which, like the *fabliaux*, satirized the monks and priests, and the constraint of the times, and voiced their joy in riotous and illicit pleasure.[4]

All this literature shows what change was taking place in the spirit of the age and in the type of audience for which it was written. These interesting and amusing, although at times coarse and vulgar, productions were

---

[1] See p. 65.
[2] The Middle High German *Minne* signifies 'love.' The most famous of the Minnesingers were Walther von der Vogelweide and Wolfram von Eschenbach.
[3] They were soon recast in prose, and became the basis of Boccaccio's *Decameron*, Margaret of Navarre's *Heptameron*, some of Chaucer's *Canterbury Tales*, and even of a number of indecent stories of the present day.
[4] See p. 86.

clearly intended for the people of the town and tavern, which did not exist until the later Middle Ages. Yet they savor of the protest against the uniformity and absolutism still prevailing, and illustrate the progress toward the individualism of the Renaissance.

Mediæval Art. — With the development of cities, wealth, and a new literature, art also began to appear, although painting consisted mostly of *illuminations* in religious and secular books, illustrative of the text or for the purpose of decoration. It contained very many symbols and was done according to stereotyped rules. Sculpture was also carried on, but was largely subordinate to architecture, which was the chief art of the Middle Ages. Hence the works of the sculptor were mainly *decorations* upon pillars, altars, pulpits, choir screens, and clergy seats. These still appear in those beautiful cathedrals of the later Middle Ages, with their delicate towers, flying buttresses, exquisite windows, and massive pillars, which have not been equaled in modern architecture. By the thirteenth century secular buildings, especially gild and town halls, of a similar finish and beauty, began to be constructed. *Art also appeared, especially in works of architecture. While most art was shown in the cathedrals and their decorations, by the thirteenth century secular buildings began to be constructed.*

Summary of the Middle Ages. — This development in the spirit of politics, literature, and art, while not affecting educational ideals, institutions, and practices directly, is an indication of the intellectual activity of the times. However the earlier period may be characterized, the thirteenth century cannot be said to be altogether lacking in the development of culture, and under no circumstances can it be regarded as the 'Dark Ages.' But, as we intimated at the outset of our study,[1] during the early part of the Middle Ages there was a general fading of the literature, culture, and institutions of Greece and Rome. Between the fifth and eighth centuries, with the inroads of the uncouth German tribes, there had come about an increasing decline of Roman civilization. The Roman buildings, art treasures, libraries, and systems of

---

[1] See Chapter I.

education had been mostly destroyed or lost, and even the magnificent Roman roads, which had so facilitated commerce and communication, were permitted to fall into disuse and decay. Civil order was largely ruined, and a class of people came into control who were too untrained for classic learning and culture to continue.

and in order to enable the Germans to absorb them, an authoritative standard was necessary.

But barbarous as the Germans were, they were destined to absorb the Græco-Roman civilization and the Christian ideals, and, amalgamating them with their own institutions, to pass them on to modern times. To stop the decay and bring these mediæval people up to the level of the past, it was necessary to set an authoritative standard and repress all variation on the part of the individual. The human intellect was confined to narrow limits, and all efforts to obtain truth by investigation were discouraged.

But the periodic rebellions against this system gradually weakened the bonds of absolutism,

Yet such bondage of the human spirit was unnatural, and the fetters upon individualism were bound to be broken. Throughout the Middle Ages there were periodic tendencies to rebel against the system. In fact, mediævalism contained within itself the germ of its own emancipation. During the eighth century, as the barbarians began to settle down and re-group themselves under Frankish kings, there came about a new order, culminating in the Carolingian revival of education. While conditions were never as desperate again after this advance, the disruption of Charlemagne's empire, the hardening of the feudal system, various civil wars, and the isolation of many parts of Europe, led before long to another decline.

and, through a variety of factors, there arose that great awakening of the human spirit known as the Renaissance.

However, the bonds of absolutism and feudalism were gradually weakened, national monarchies and a secular spirit began to arise, and by the twelfth and thirteenth centuries a new revival, material and intellectual, had begun to appear. Several developments gave evidence of the expansion within, and helped to produce it. The worldly appeal of chivalry, the broadening of horizon produced by contact with the Moors, and through the Crusades, together with the growth of cities, gilds, commerce, wealth, and luxury, the development of literature and art, and, above everything, the emancipation of thought and reason through the discussions of scholasticism and the foundation of universities, — all helped by accumulation to make the last two centuries of the Middle Ages a period of increased activity and progress. And from this there was destined shortly to arise a great awakening of the human spirit and that revival of classic culture known as the *Renaissance*.

PART II — THE TRANSITION TO MODERN TIMES

CHAPTER XII

THE RENAISSANCE AND HUMANISTIC EDUCATION

The mediæval repression and uniformity were breaking almost from the start, but not until the latter half of the fourteenth century was it apparent that these tendencies were giving way to a renewed individualism.

The General Tendencies of the Renaissance. — A study of the Middle Ages has revealed how restricted and stereotyped intellectual activity had become, and how largely the cultural products of Greece and Rome had disappeared. Equally obvious were the efforts of the human spirit to burst through its confinement and uniformity, and attain to some freedom of expression and a renewed individualism. The repression was slowly breaking almost from the time it was formed, but while there was a definite revival during the latter part of the eighth and the first half of the ninth centuries, and one much more marked in the twelfth and thirteenth, it was not until the latter half of the fourteenth century that the movement made itself really felt.

At that time the transition was greatly accelerated, and it became evident that the dormant period had at length given way to the dawn. There appeared a general intellectual and cultural progress that began to free men from their bondage to ecclesiasticism and induce them to look at the world about them. The absolute adherence to an 'otherworldly' ideal that was characteristic of early Christianity and monasticism, the suspicion of the Latin and Greek classics, the restriction of learning, the reception of the teachings of the Church without investigation, and the basing of all reasoning upon deductions therefrom were by this time rapidly disappearing. Such tendencies were clearly being replaced by a genuine joy in the life of this world, a broader field

THE RENAISSANCE AND HUMANISTIC EDUCATION 107

of knowledge and thought, and a desire to reason and deal with all ideas more critically. Uniformity and repression through authority were clearly giving way to renewed and enlarged ideals of individualism. The purpose of education was gradually coming to be no longer an attempt to adapt the individual to a fixed system, but to produce a differentiation of social activities and to encourage a realization of the individual in society. The days of mere absorption and assimilation were passing.

The Renaissance and the Revival of Learning.— This tremendous widening of the intellectual, æsthetic, and social horizon is generally known as the *Renaissance* ('new birth'). Such a description, although it is now well fixed in historical terminology, may appear too strong. It seems to imply a long interval of hibernation during the mediæval period from which there had at length come an awakening. Whereas, we have seen that the Middle Ages, while largely fixed and limited in their intellectual scope, certainly possessed considerable activity of their own, and the expanded outlook of the revival can be traced back to economic, political, and social factors that gradually arose during this very period of restriction. Yet, if the rapidity of the emancipation that resulted from these forces and the difference in the viewpoint of the two periods be taken into account, the term 'Renaissance' will seem more appropriate. It may be taken to indicate that the spirit of the Græco-Roman development had returned, and that possibility of expression was granted to the individual once more. Hence the new era may well be viewed as "a re-birth of emotions and faculties long dormant, an awakening of man to a new consciousness of life and of the world in which he lives, and of the problems which life and the world present for the thinking mind to solve, and to a consciousness also of the power of the mind to deal with these problems." [1]

The Middle Ages had considerable activity of their own, but the rapidity of emancipation justifies the term Renaissance, or 'new birth.'

But this period is also properly known as a *Revival*

---

[1] Adams, *Civilization during the Middle Ages*, p. 365.

of Learning. The awakening preceded the recovery of classical literature and learning, but intellectual freedom was very greatly heightened and forwarded thereby.¹ The only food at hand that could satisfy the intellectual craving of the times was the literature and culture of the classical peoples. The discovery that the writings of the ancient world were filled with a genuine vitality and virility, and that the old authors had dealt with world problems in a profound and masterly fashion, and with far more vision than had ever been possible for the restricted mediævalists, gave rise to an eager desire and enthusiasm for the classics that went beyond all bounds. As we have seen,² a knowledge of classical literature had never altogether disappeared, and various works had been preserved by the monks and others. To search out the manuscripts of the Latin and Greek writers, the monasteries, cathedrals, and castles were now ransacked from end to end. The manuscripts found were rapidly multiplied, and the greatest pains were taken to secure the correct form of every passage. The texts of the different manuscripts were carefully compared and revised in the light of history. Thus, besides the recovery of old knowledge, a better method of criticism and a development of the critical judgment were produced that were quite impossible under the scholastic system of the Middle Ages.

Margin note: While the recovery of classical literature did not cause the Renaissance, it greatly heightened it, and the period, with its ardent search for manuscripts, may well be considered a 'Revival of Learning.'

Humanism and the Humanists. — Because of their emphasis upon the beauty of this world and upon human affairs, rather than upon the life to come, the devotees of the new movement were generally called *humanists*, and in later times the intellectual phase of the Renaissance became known as *humanism*.³ The new learning

Margin note: The movement, because of its emphasis upon human affairs, became known as 'humanism' and its devotees as 'humanists.'

---

[1] The old statement that the Renaissance was caused by the accidental recovery of classical works, or, still worse, by the Greek teachers taking refuge in Italy after the conquest of Constantinople in 1453, shows an ignorance of the social movements in the Middle Ages.

[2] See p. 15 and footnote on p. 17.

[3] Of course the development of painting and sculpture, and the progress of discovery, during the Renaissance were fully as remarkable as the revival in literature, but they have little place here. Painting began in the

was regarded as that which taught mankind how to live most fittingly. So when he has discussed this type of education, the youthful enthusiast of Ferrara writes at the close of his treatise [1]: — " Learning and training in virtue are peculiar to man; therefore our forefathers called them *humanitas*, the pursuits, the activities, proper to mankind." These humanistic scholars were not the first to read the works of classical Latin, as this interest had been kept alive throughout the Middle Ages, but they were the first to reject the hard and narrow 'otherworldliness' of mediævalism and to find through the classics a joy in living and an inspiration to achievement in this life. With the revival of these classical models, the humanists began to produce a literature of their own, such as had not existed since the palmiest days of Rome. Poetry, drama, and romances flourished, and the new motives eventually resulted also in the beginning of historical and social writings. Through the humanists and their works the spirit of modern times was ushered in.

fourteenth century, but did not come to its height until the latter part of the fifteenth century with such masters as Fra Angelico and Botticelli in Florence and the Van Eycks in Holland, and in the sixteenth with Raphael, Michael Angelo, and Leonardo da Vinci in Rome, Andrea del Sarto in Florence, Titian in Venice, and Holbein and Dürer in Germany. Later came the Flemish Rubens and Van Dyck, the Dutch Rembrandt, and the Spanish Velasquez.

[1] B. Guarino in his *De Ordine Docendi et Studendi*.

CHAPTER XIII

THE HUMANISTIC EDUCATION IN ITALY

The movement first became evident in Italy, because of the closeness of the Italians to the papacy,

Causes of the Awakening in Italy.—This general tendency toward an awakening was apparent throughout Western Europe, but it first became evident in Italy. There were several special reasons why this part of the country should be the foremost to feel an intellectual quickening. They are mostly connected with the fact that Italy was at this time the natural center of activity. This holds true of the political and commercial spheres even more than of the religious, but one main source of the early restiveness in the Italian peninsula appears in the fact that the seat of the Church was at Rome. The Italians were almost too close to the papacy to have the respect for that organization which was held by the rest of Christendom. They felt that the days of the pope as a great international authority above all secular powers had passed. The pontiff was clearly no longer interested, as in the time of the Cluniac popes, in insisting upon a spiritual supremacy that should include all nations, but was engaged with local Italian politics. He was attempting to maintain himself as a petty temporal ruler or to secure some small principality for his nephews or other relatives. It appeared that the large revenues that still came rolling in from all parts of Europe were being expended to increase the papal possessions or promote some small Italian war. Hence the people of Italy came to regard the Church merely as a great business organization, and became rather skeptical about the divine institution and authority of the pope. They began to think for themselves outside the scholastic system.

The chief factor, however, in producing mental alertness and early development in Italy was the political circumstances of her mediæval history. This country was a regular storm center for civic and interstate quarrels.¹ In the first place, Italy never became a unified nation, but remained to a large degree a series of independent city-states. This was due to the fact that the country was legally a part of the Holy Roman Empire under the rule of the king of the Germans, who was never able to make his control effective there. In the early period there was a count over each city who was supposed to represent the emperor, but was really a sort of feudal lord. Within the cities, however, the rule of the counts was soon disputed by the bishops, whose jurisdictions often coincided with those of the counts, and, as the bishops were generally supported by the people, the counts were eventually expelled. But the bishops, too, before long fell under the suspicion of the cities, which then gradually (1000-1100) took over the sovereign rights into their own hands and chose their officials by ballot. However, only a few of the influential families were allowed to have any voice in the government, and the other classes were constantly striving for representation. There was also a continual struggle between the higher and lower gilds, and between the great lords, who, after the decay of feudalism, had come into the cities from their castles.² Disgusted with this party strife and confusion, most of the cities at length allowed the government to slip into the hands of some usurper. Usually these despots concealed at first the real nature of the government by a misleading title, and by having their powers voted them anew each year,³

the continual turmoil in politics,

---

¹ A good account of the political situation and the part it played in developing individualism is given in Burckhardt, *The Renaissance in Italy*, Parts I and II.

² This was the underlying cause of the strife in Italian cities between the Guelphs and the Ghibellines. It was not so much that one party favored the pope and the other the emperor, as the historic opposition of two great families to each other and their seizure of this pretext as a basis of party differences.

³ Such was the case with the *podesta, capitano del popolo,* and other similar offices in the various cities. Sometimes, however, as with Francesco Sforza at Milan, the government was seized by a *condottiere*, or leader of mercenary troops, who had been employed by the city.

but the dictatorship generally became permanent (1250–1450), and the hereditary rule was vested in certain families.

Hence, throughout its mediæval history Italy had undergone constant turmoil in politics. There were continual struggles with the emperor, conflicts between the several cities, and civil strife in the cities themselves. One result of this political unrest was that the citizens were kept constantly on the outlook for their own safety and interests, and their wits were greatly sharpened.[1] Even the exile, into which one party or another was constantly forced, had the effect of broadening their vision and bringing out the greatest possibilities within them. And so, where birth counted for little, and ability and energy might at any time win control, these cities of Italy became very democratic and independent. Individualism was greatly heightened and a natural opening afforded for the Renaissance.

the commercial activity,

But there was yet another important factor in the intellectual development of Italy. This is found in the commercial intercourse of the Italian cities with other countries, which, for various physiographic and historic reasons, had become extraordinarily active. The coastline and harborage of Italy are, in proportion to the area of the country, the greatest of any in Europe, and during the Crusades the Italian cities obtained the most extensive trade relations that had ever been known. Venice, Genoa, and a few other ports of Italy for a time controlled the commerce of the world, and through these channels unprecedented wealth and luxury poured into the lap of Europe. This commercial activity and contact with different traditions had a remarkable intellectual effect, and tended to open the minds of the Italians, break up their old conceptions, free them of prejudice, and increase their thirst for learning.

and the survival of the classics in Italy.

It should be noted, furthermore, that the ghost of the classic ages still haunted its old home. A knowledge

[1] This intellectual alertness was in many instances heightened by the necessity of drawing up or modifying the constitution of the city.

of the Latin tongue had never ceased to exist in Italy, and many manuscripts of the Latin and Greek authors had been preserved.[1] The influence of the old writers during the Renaissance was due to what had long been known rather than to the discovery of a great deal that was new. There was needed in Italy only an intellectual quickening sufficient to shake off the thraldom to the Church and produce an appreciation of classical literature and culture in order to bring back this spirit of the past into real pulsating life.

In this way, from a combination of a variety of forces, there becomes more and more evident in Italy a remarkable widening of the intellectual, æsthetic, and social horizon. Authority began to give way to independence and reason, and the individual burst his mediæval bonds and obtained faith in himself. "In the Middle Ages," declares Burckhardt, "human consciousness lay dreaming or half awake beneath a common veil. The veil was woven of faith, illusion, and childish prepossession, through which the world and history were seen clad in strange hues. Man was conscious of himself only as member of a race, people, party, family, or corporation —only through some general category. In Italy this veil first melted into air; man became a spiritual *individual*, and recognized himself as such. In the same way the Greek had once distinguished himself from the barbarian. At the close of the thirteenth century Italy began to swarm with *individuality;* the charm laid upon human personality was dissolved; and a thousand figures meet us, each in its own special shape and dress."

Thus there was a return to the ideals of individualism that existed in the classical civilization, and men of many-sided development appeared once more. "When this impulse to the highest individual development," adds the authority quoted, "was combined with a powerful and varied nature, which had mastered all the

These various factors produced a return to individualism and account for the appearance of 'many-sided' men.

[1] There were also occasionally anachronistic revivals of the Roman senate and other features of the ancient government. See the revolts of Crescentius and of Arnold of Brescia.

elements of the culture of the age, then arose the 'all-sided man' — *l' uomo universale* — who belonged to Italy alone. Men there were of encyclopaedic knowledge in many countries during the Middle Ages, for this knowledge was not confined within narrow limits. . . . But in Italy, at the time of the Renaissance, we find artists who in every branch created new and perfect works, and who also made the greatest impression as men. Others, outside the arts they practiced, were masters of a vast circle of spiritual interests." There is not space here to describe the work of every one of these 'all-sided' men, but some of them are of such importance to the history of culture and education, as theorists or practical men, that some mention of them cannot be omitted.

The earliest humanist was Petrarch, who emphasized the present, self-development, and individualism, and vigorously opposed the mediæval traditions and institutions.

Petrarch and His Influence. — Probably the man who should stand as the earliest[1] great humanist was *Francesco Petrarca* (1304-1374), or *Petrarch*, as he is commonly called. In him we find the very embodiment of the Renaissance spirit.[2] He completely repudiates the 'otherworldly' ideal of mediævalism, and is keenly aware of the beauties and the joy of this life. He emphasizes the present and the opportunities for self-development in this world. In him appear the modern desire for personal fame, and an aggressive faith in his own ability to gain it. There is evident in him at all times a marked individualism and an abhorrence of an appeal to authority. He does not hesitate to attack the most hoary of traditions, and to rely upon observation, investigation, and reason. Hence he strongly reacts

[1] The world-renowned *Dante*, who belonged to the generation before Petrarch, can hardly, despite his modern independence and individualistic tendencies, be considered a real humanist. The picture of the future life that is portrayed in the *Divina Commedia* and his theology in general are thoroughly mediæval, and his interest in Vergil, Homer, and other classical writers, who appear in his great epic, was not unknown in other works of the Middle Ages. Monroe regards Dante's *Il Convito* as the natural link between the mediæval period and the awakening.

[2] See the interpretation of Petrarch in Adams, *Civilization during the Middle Ages*, pp. 375-377.

from scholasticism, and objects to the absolute dependence upon Aristotle, who had so fully become the philosopher of the Church. He says:—

"I believe that Aristotle was a great man, and that he knew much; yet he was but a man, and therefore something, nay, many things, may have escaped him. I am confident, beyond a doubt, that he was in error all his life, not only as regards small matters, where a mistake counts for little, but in the most weighty questions, where his supreme interests were involved."[1]

Likewise, Petrarch's impatience with the conservatism and narrowness of the universities, which he stamps as 'nests of gloomy ignorance,' is vented in such tirades as the following:—

"The youth ascends the platform mumbling nobody knows what. The elders applaud, the bells ring, the trumpets blare, the degree is conferred, and he descends a wise man who went up a fool."[2]

Consequently, he feels a kinship with the thinkers and writers of the past age, when independence, æsthetic culture, and breadth were given more scope, and holds that their works must be recovered before their spirit can be continued. This led to a tremendous enthusiasm for the Latin classics, and, while Petrarch had been bred to the law, much of his life was spent in restoring ancient culture. He devoted himself during his extensive travels largely to collecting manuscripts of the old Latin writers, which had previously been widely scattered, and endeavoring to repair in them the ravages of time. He likewise inspired every one he met with a desire to gather and study the works of the classic authors. *He felt a kinship with the past and endeavored to restore ancient culture.*

Petrarch's own works, too, whether literary, critical, or ethical, are naturally filled with the classic spirit. Besides the beautiful sonnets, ballads, and other lyrics that appear in his *Canzoniere* ('Collection of Songs'), *His classical spirit was shown in his Epistolæ, De Viris Illustribus, and Africa.*

[1] Petrarch, *De Sui Ipsius et Multorum Ignorantia* in *Opera* (1581), pp. 1042–1043.
[2] See Mullinger, *A History of the University of Cambridge*, Vol. I, p. 382, note 2.

for which he is especially known to literature, he wrote a large number of Latin works, which, while now little mentioned, had the greatest effect upon the times. Among other writings, he produced several collections of *Epistolæ* ('Letters'), a work of erudition called *De Viris Illustribus* ('On Famous Men'), and an epic poem on Scipio Africanus known as *Africa*. Some of his letters were indited to Cicero, Homer, and other classical persons as if they were still living.

He visited many Italian cities and spread the Renaissance spirit.

The climax of his career was reached at the age of thirty-six. In that year he was invited by both the University of Rome and the University of Paris to become their poet laureate. He chose to be honored by the former institution, and on Easter of 1341 he was publicly crowned with a laurel wreath on the Capitol at Rome. After this, he visited many Italian cities, and was received in honor by all. He did much to spread the Renaissance spirit, and became the literary and scholastic progenitor of a multitude that proved greater than he. But, as a modern authority has said, "if he was, before many generations, excelled in more than one respect, it was only as the discoverer of the New World would ere long have had to give way before the knowledge of a schoolboy."[1] Thus, in the words of Renan, Petrarch was 'the first modern man.'[2]

Among those inspired by Petrarch was Boccaccio, who wrote in the classical spirit and devoted most of his life to classic culture.

Among the younger scholars and literary men around Petrarch was *Giovanni Boccaccio* (1313–1375). While a great admirer and correspondent of the elder humanist, Boccaccio never met him until the brief visit of Petrarch to Florence in 1350.[3] Before this the youthful poet[4] had resided at the court of Naples, where literary men were numerous, and had already displayed his admiration for the ancients, advanced far in his classical studies,

---

[1] Voigt, *Die Wiederbelebung des classischen Alterthums*, Vol. I, p. 22, quoted by Robinson and Rolfe, *Petrarch*, pp. 8–9.
[2] Renan, *Averroës*, p. 328.
[3] See Petrarcha, *Epistolæ de Rebus Familiaribus*, XXI, 15, and *Epistolæ de Rebus Senilibus*, V, 3.
[4] Cf. the final phrase of the epitaph he wrote for himself, — *studium fuit alma poesis*.

THE HUMANISTIC EDUCATION IN ITALY

and produced in Italian a number of important romances, tales, and poems with classical allusions, of which the most famous is his *Decamerone* ('Ten-Day Book'). But in Florence he developed, through the influence of Petrarch, a perfect passion for the ancient writers, and devoted most of the rest of his life to classical culture. He obtained a wide knowledge of the Latin writers, and searched out, preserved, and had copied as many ancient manuscripts as possible. So keen was his interest in the classics, that, upon visiting the library at Monte Cassino and finding it neglected and badly mutilated, he is said by a pupil to have been moved to tears.[1]

A younger humanist enthused through Petrarch's work was *Gasparino da Barzizza* (1370–1431). Barzizza earned a larger reputation for scholarship than either Petrarch or Boccaccio. He became a great collector of the manuscripts of Cicero, and was the first to approach the study of that author in a critical and analytic spirit. He treated Latin as a living tongue and did not hesitate to modify the standard vocabulary and style of Cicero for the purposes of his day.

Barzizza, the most scholarly of early humanists, was also enthused by Petrarch.

The Development of Greek Scholarship. — Numerous other humanists were descended from the *coterie* of Petrarch, but with all this revival of Latin literature, for some time there was little done with the Greek. During the Middle Ages that language had almost disappeared in Europe, and the greatest Greek authors were accessible only through Latin translations.[2] Even the authoritative philosopher of the Church, Aristotle, was known simply through a small and unimportant part of his writings. Of Homer there existed in Latin the merest summary of the *Iliad*, written by Silius Italicus, for even the translation of Livius Andronicus had been

---

[1] See Benvenuto on Dante, *Paradiso*, XXII, 74 f., quoted in full by Sandys, *Classical Scholarship*, Vol. II, p. 13.

[2] Where the names of Greek poets or philosophers are cited in mediæval writers, it is to be assumed that this knowledge comes at second hand from the Latin versions.

lost. The other great writers, — historians, poets, and orators, had fared even worse.

Attempts were made by Petrarch, Boccaccio, and others to learn Greek.

But a knowledge of the Greek language and literature still persisted in the Eastern empire, and the humanists of Italy were, through the works of the Latin authors, constantly directed back to the writings of the Greeks, and became eager to read them in the original. Attempts were made by several humanists to learn Greek. Greece and Constantinople were frequently visited, and active efforts made to secure copies of the Greek authors. Petrarch had begun Greek under Barlaam, a Calabrian Greek, who had been sent as an envoy from Constantinople, but his study of the language had been interrupted. Later, when a friend [1] sent him a copy of Homer, Petrarch pathetically wrote: —

"Thy Homer is dumb to me, while I most certainly am deaf to him. Nevertheless, I am delighted at the very sight of him." [2]

In the same letter he thanks his friend also for a manuscript of Plato, and, in an epistle to Boccaccio, urged that scholar to translate the Homer into Latin.[3] Boccaccio had been able to secure the guidance of a pupil of Barlaam named Leonzio Pilato, and had thus become the first humanist to gain any real knowledge of the Greek language. At the request of Petrarch, Pilato and Boccaccio made a translation of the Iliad and Odyssey. While this version was in wretched Latin, it gave all of Homer to the humanists, and greatly encouraged the study of the Greek authors.

Thus, before the close of the fourteenth century, teachers of Greek often came to be invited to Italy. In 1453 Constantinople fell into the hands of the Turks, and the Greek scholars fled to Italy, carrying with them many treasures of literature. No labor or expense was spared in discovering and copying these manuscripts, or in multiplying translations of the Greek authors. In this way, by the second half of the fifteenth century, a

---

[1] Nicolaus Syocerus, another envoy from Constantinople.
[2] See *Epistolæ Variæ*, XX, p. 998.
[3] *Epistolæ De Rebus Senilibus*, VI, p. 807.

sufficient number of the Greek, as well as of the Latin, classics was secured to lay the foundations of modern scholarship. Not until then did texts of the authors and works on inflection and syntax become common and simple enough to make Greek learning a part of the training of every educated man.

Chrysoloras and His Pupils. — The first great man of learning to settle in Italy and teach Greek was *Manuel Chrysoloras* (1350–1415). When sent to Venice by the Eastern emperor in 1393 to implore aid against the Turks, he was besieged by the young Italian scholars to give them Greek lessons during his stay. Three years later, he was invited to the professorship of Greek, which the influence of Boccaccio had established at Florence for Pilato, and readily accepted. With shorter or longer intervals of absence, for sixteen years he taught here and in Pavia, Venice, Milan, Padua, and Rome. He started schools in various cities, made a series of translations of Greek authors, and composed a work on Greek grammar called *Erotemata* ('Questions'), which long remained the basis of Greek instruction for the Italians. From his efforts sprang several generations of scholars, who made the great works of Greek literature known throughout Europe. So, just as the revival of classical Latin had been started by Petrarch, a second impulse was given the Renaissance through the instruction of Chrysoloras in Greek.

<small>but not until 1396, when Chrysoloras settled in Italy, did the Greek classics become generally known.</small>

Among the first Italian pupils of Chrysoloras was *Niccolo de' Niccoli* (1364–1437), who was instrumental in inducing the Signory of Florence to call that scholar to the university. Niccoli acted as literary minister to Cosimo de' Medici,[1] and advised him in his purchase of manuscripts and his distribution of financial assistance to scholars. His biographer[2] tells us that "if he heard of any book in Greek or Latin not to be had in Florence, he spared no cost in getting it; the number of the Latin

<small>Among the pupils of Chrysoloras were Niccolo de' Niccoli, the literary minister to Cosimo de' Medici;</small>

---

[1] See p. 122.
[2] Vespasian, *Vita di Niccolo*, p. 473.

books which Florence owes entirely to his generosity cannot be reckoned." And he allowed any one who wished, to consult or borrow his books or discuss them with him. Before his death, he had collected or copied with his own hand some eight hundred volumes, and bequeathed them for public use to the library of San Marco.[1]

Bruni, author of De Studiis et Literis;

Another well-known pupil of Chrysoloras was *Leonardo Bruni* (1369-1444).[2] He had previously been a student of civil law, but upon the arrival of Chrysoloras he declared to himself that "there are in every city scores of doctors of civil laws; but should this single and unique teacher of Greek be removed, thou wilt find no one to instruct thee." As a result, Bruni began to study under Chrysoloras. He became devoted to Greek literature, and made excellent translations of Homer, Plato, Aristotle, Demosthenes, Plutarch, and other Greek writers. He also left works of his own composition, including a treatise on humanistic education called *De Studiis et Literis* (' On the Study of Literature ').

Guarino, who trained a number of brilliant humanists, including Vittorino, and opened a court school at Ferrara,

Guarino da Verona[3] (1374-1460), however, was the most famous humanist to study under Chrysoloras. For five years he was in the home of that scholar at Constantinople, after Chrysoloras had first returned from Italy. In 1408 the young humanist came back, and, through the influence of Bruni, started a private school of classics at Florence under the patronage of Niccoli and other prominent citizens. When the University of Florence was reopened four years later, he was appointed to the professorship of Greek previously held by Chrysoloras. Here and at Venice and Padua he trained in Greek a number of brilliant young scholars, including Vittorino. In middle life, Guarino undertook the training of Leonello, son of Niccolo d'Este, the Marquis of

---

[1] Half of the volumes were placed in the Marcian collection, but the other half were kept by Cosimo for the Medicean library. See Symonds, *The Revival of Learning*, pp. 173-174.

[2] Sometimes called *d'Arezzo* or *Aretino* from his birthplace.

[3] He was usually known as *da Verona* or *Veronese* from his birthplace, but he was also called *Guarino dei Guarini*.

Ferrara, but was allowed to receive other youths into the school. Thus a species of court school was founded which was continued even after a university was opened at Ferrara, and Guarino was made one of the professors. From Guarino's teaching came many distinguished and scholarly humanists. Among them was his son, the brilliant *Battista Guarino* (1434-1513), who succeeded to his chair at Ferrara and continued his methods. This younger Guarino at twenty-five wrote a well-known treatise on humanistic education called *De Ordine Docendi et Studendi* ('On the Method of Teaching and Studying').

where he was succeeded by his son, Battista;

Other famous humanists to feel the influence of Chrysoloras were *Braccolini Poggio* (1380-1459), who, through the patronage of Niccoli, was rivaled only by Guarino as a finder of manuscripts, and *Francesco Filelfo* (1398-1481), who had been trained in Latin by Barzizza, and in turn had among his pupils the two great humanist popes, Nicholas V and Pius II. But probably the most remarkable pupil of Chrysoloras was *Pietro Paolo Vergerio* (1349-1420), or *Vergerius*. Although already one of the most learned scholars of the day, he did not disdain at fifty years of age to sit with the youths at the feet of the great Byzantine scholar. A few years after studying with Chrysoloras he wrote the most widely read treatise on the humanistic education, *De Ingenuis Moribus et Studiis Liberalibus* ('On Noble Character and Liberal Studies').

and Poggio, Filelfo, and the learned Vergerio.

The City Tyrants as Humanists and Founders of Education. — Thus during the fifteenth century there appeared a host of famous humanists, skilled both in Latin and Greek. A powerful support to the efforts of these scholars resulted from the rivalry of the Italian cities. The tyrant in control of each place was keenly aware of his usurpation and the illegitimacy of his title, and had to rely largely upon city pride to maintain his power. "With his thirst of fame and his passion for monumental works, it was talent, not birth, which he needed. In the company of the poet and scholar, he felt himself

The city tyrants fostered humanism to add luster to their rule.

in a new position, almost, indeed, in possession of a new legitimacy."[1] In order to appeal to a people of intellectual acumen and classical enthusiasm, he was forced to do everything possible to propagate the humanistic movement and make his city illustrious.

Gian Galeazzo Visconti founded a library and university; Cosimo de' Medici supported humanistic scholars, established a 'Platonic Academy,' and founded the Medicean library; and Lorenzo de' Medici procured manuscripts and maintained scholars and artists.

Perhaps the most typical examples of these humanist princes are found among the Visconti at Milan and the Medici at Florence. The former extended their power over northern Italy and culminated with the brilliant, though corrupt, *Gian Galeazzo Visconti* (1378-1402). He founded a library at Pavia, reorganized the university at Piacenza, and was generally a liberal patron of art, literature, and scholarship. The Medici showed a similar interest in humanism, and made their power secure in this way even more than through political ability. *Cosimo de' Medici* (1389-1464), the first to rule Florence and the founder of the dynasty, sympathized greatly with scholars, and, through Niccoli, furnished them with the means of forwarding their ambitions.[2] It was in his time that Gemisthos Pletho was induced to come from Greece and establish the Platonic Academy in Florence. Cosimo also projected a great public library, and within two years had forty-five authors in two hundred volumes copied from libraries at Milan, Bologna, and elsewhere. These books formed the nucleus of the famous *Medicean library*, which its founder left with a collection of some eight thousand volumes.[3] Cosimo had a worthy successor in his grandson, *Lorenzo de' Medici* (1448-1492), ordinarily known as *il Magnifico* ('the Magnificent'). Lorenzo was a model prince, humanist, and public benefactor. He encouraged Greek learning and twice sent an agent to Greece to procure manuscripts. To give luster to his rule, he gathered about him and maintained a famous

[1] Burckhardt, *The Civilization of the Renaissance in Italy*, p. 9.
[2] See pp. 119 f.
[3] See Vespasiano, *Vita di Cosimo*, cc. XII, seqq.
This library, also called the *Laurentian* from its proximity to the Church of San Lorenzo, to-day contains about twelve thousand manuscripts, many of which are important and valuable to classical scholars.

circle of humanists and artists, including Politian, Mirandola, da Vinci, and Michael Angelo.

But, besides the Visconti and the Medici, *Federigo da Montefeltro,* who had assumed the title of Duke of Urbino, *Francesco da Carrara,* Lord of Padua, *Niccolo d' Este,* Marquis of Ferrara, *Alfonso of Naples,* and other princes later showed a like activity in forwarding the new learning and culture, and in attracting scholars to their courts. The humanists would otherwise have found it difficult to maintain themselves, as they were not for some time encouraged to teach in the universities, and could not hope to make a living from writing books. Their only prospect lay in the patronage of one of the princes, who were able to use both their private resources and the funds of their cities.

The Court School at Mantua and Vittorino da Feltre. — In some instances these court circles promoted the new learning informally, but often, where a scholar had been taken into the family of a prince as a private tutor, children of the neighboring aristocracy were associated and a regular school was started. *Court schools* of this sort soon existed at Florence, Venice, Padua, Pavia, Verona, Ferrara, and several other cities. The most famous of these schools was that organized by *Vittorino da Feltre*[1] (1378-1446) at Mantua.

<small>Schools grew up at the courts of these tyrants.</small>

Vittorino had been trained at Padua in the very home of Barzizza, the greatest of living Latinists, and under the influence of the humanistic ideas[2] and example of Vergerius. When he had obtained his degree, he remained in Padua and studied mathematics under the ablest of private masters. In 1415, after staying in Padua as student and teacher for nearly a score of years, he took up Greek with Guarino in Venice. Five years later he returned to Padua, where he received

<small>The best known of these schools was that established by the Marquis of Mantua under the mastership of the famous humanistic scholar, Vittorino da Feltre.</small>

---

[1] His name was really *Vittore dai Rambaldoni,* but he was generally known as *da Feltre* from the town of his birth. Feltre was in northeast Italy, near Venice.

[2] For the treatise of Vergerius on humanistic education, see pp. 121 and 131 f.

pupils in his own house and looked after their morals as well as instructed them in the humanities. Thus when he was called at forty-five to found a school for the children of *Gianfrancesco Gonzaga*, Marquis of Mantua, Vittorino had received the best possible education of the times in Latin, Greek, and mathematics, and had greatly distinguished himself as a teacher and a man of piety. The marquis wished to secure a leading humanist to add luster to his court, and, failing to induce Guarino, turned to the other great light, whom Guarino himself had recommended. Vittorino disliked courts and the morals of court life, but finally replied: —

"I accept the appointment, on this understanding only, that you require from me nothing which shall be in any way unworthy of either of us: and I will continue to serve you as long as your own life shall command respect."

These conditions were granted and were abided by until the day of Vittorino's death, twenty-three years later. The marquis and his wife allowed him to shape the school exactly as he wished, and granted him support and sympathy in every move.

The school was located in the most pleasant surroundings, and the pupils were under the immediate supervision of Vittorino.

The location of the school was ideal. It occupied a former pleasure-house situated on a little eminence in the park surrounding the palace. The building was large and dignified, and most handsomely proportioned. Inside, the rooms were high, and the corridors broad, although, to give the place a studious atmosphere, Vittorino had stripped it of its sumptuous furnishings. The beautiful meadows surrounding furnished an ample and attractive playground. By an adaptation of the former name, Vittorino most happily called the school *La Casa Giocosa* ('The Pleasant House').[1] Vittorino and the princes lived in the schoolhouse, and scions of the leading Mantuan families, together with the sons of Vittorino's personal friends[2] and promising boys of every de-

[1] This was simply a play upon the former name of *La Casa Zoyosa* ('House of Pleasure').
[2] Among others were the sons of such distinguished scholars as Guarino, Poggio, and Filelfo.

gree,[1] who were received into the school at his request, dwelt near enough to be under his immediate supervision. He was most strict in his selection of masters and of attendants, that the morals of the pupils might be of the highest. Likewise, the 'father of his scholars,' as Vittorino held himself to be, looked out for their food, clothing, and health, and shared in their games, interests, and pleasures. It was the intention of Vittorino to secure for his pupils that harmonious development of mind, body, and morals that the old Greeks had known as a 'liberal education.' He emphasized the practical and social side of the individual's efficiency, and wished to prepare his pupils for a life of activity and service, and not merely to create rhetoricians and pedants. As a pupil of his put it, his desire was to educate young men "who should serve God and state in whatever position they should be called upon to occupy."   *He aimed at a harmonious development of mind, body, and morals;*

To accomplish this, Vittorino felt that the best subjects were those connected with the grammatical and literary study of the Greek and Roman writers. The pupils learned to converse in Latin from the beginning, and there were games with letters for the youngest and simple exercises to train them in clear articulation and proper accent and emphasis. Also, before the boys were ten, they were drilled in memorizing and reciting with intelligence the easier portions of classic authors. This elocutionary work, which was increased in length and difficulty as the boys grew older, gave them an excellent grasp of vocabulary, rhythm, and style.   *by means of a broad study of the classics,*

As they advanced, the pupils read a variety of Latin writers, and soon took up Greek. They then carried on a study of the Hellenic poets, orators, and historians, and continued those of Rome. The Church Fathers, both Latin and Greek, were also studied. Thus every class

---

[1] Each pupil paid in proportion to his means; the poorest, of whom there were sometimes as many as seventy, were not only taught free, but even clothed and boarded without charge.

of subject matter was obtained from the classical and patristic writers, and even the study of the seven liberal arts was retained, although with a different relative importance and a new interpretation as to content. The mathematical subjects were especially enlarged in scope, and taught in connection with drawing, mensuration, surveying, and other applications. Because of the lack of books, the teaching was carried on largely by dictation. The works of Guarino and Chrysoloras gave the pupils some command of inflections, but their knowledge of vocabulary, idiom, and syntax had to be acquired inductively. The master usually dictated the vocabulary and inflections of the passage, then translated and explained it, commented on the style, and drew moral lessons from the subject matter. There was, further, a careful drill in Latin and Greek composition and in translating from Latin into Greek.

As we have noted, physical and moral education were insisted upon quite as fully as intellectual. Vittorino introduced especially fencing, wrestling, dancing, ball-playing, running, and leaping, in all of which he was himself an expert. The purpose of these, however, was to aid and stimulate the mental powers. Likewise, he believed that there could be no true education without religion, and both by precept and example inculcated piety, reverence, and religious observances. As it has been pointed out, the Christian authors, especially Augustine, were largely read, but Vittorino believed that truth and moral beauty could be derived also from the classic writings. The use of dictation enabled him to expurgate at will, and throughout he chose the passages to be read with reference to character building.

But the general method of Vittorino was the most notable feature of his school. He was completely absorbed in his pupils. He carefully studied their ability, interests, and the career contemplated by each. He has been quoted as saying : —

"We are not to expect that every boy will display the same tastes or the same degree of mental capacity; and, whatever our own predilection may be, we recognize that we must follow Nature's lead. Now she has endowed no one with aptitude for all kinds of knowledge, very few, indeed, have talent in three or four directions, but every one has received some gift, if only we can discover it."

On the basis of this conception, Vittorino selected the studies and method best suited to each intelligence, and thus inaugurated a thoroughly elastic course for the school. Under such circumstances, it is not remarkable that the discipline of the school was mild, and corporal punishment was almost unknown. The appellation of 'Pleasant House' must have seemed to the pupils to be no misnomer.

Thus Vittorino's was the most potent influence upon the educational practice of the times. He introduced the wider curriculum and brought out the real spirit and individualism of the classics. He saw the important relation of the physical to the mental, the necessity for moral and religious elements in education, and carried out the Greek ideal of harmonious development. Intuitively, he anticipated much of modern pedagogical theory, especially in his regard for the personality of the student. Questions of aim, content, and method that were in a state of flux when he began his work at Mantua were definitely settled before his death. Vittorino naturally made a profound impression upon all his contemporaries and pupils, and educated a large number of distinguished ecclesiastics, statesmen, scholars, teachers, and rulers. Well might his successor, Platina, declare that "the death of this man was a bitter grief not merely to a single state, but to all Greece and Italy."

Vittorino thus broadened the curriculum, revived the Greek 'harmonious development,' and anticipated much in modern theory. He made a profound impression on the times.

The Relation of the Court Schools to the Universities. — Such were the court school at Mantua and the educational work of the greatest schoolmaster of the early Renaissance. The description has been given somewhat in detail, because the training of the Mantuan school is broadly typical of that at the other court schools, and of the Renaissance education in general. The school of Guarino at Ferrara,[1] for instance, differed

The Mantuan school was typical of many other court schools.

---

[1] See pp. 120 f.

slightly in aim and curriculum, but it made use very largely of the Greek and Latin literature, and recognized the importance of physical and moral, as well as intellectual, training in the making of a well-rounded man.

These court schools, while taking pupils very early, often retained them until they were twenty-one, and covered as much, if not more, ground than the arts course of the universities. They were, in a way, competitors of the older institutions. A student might, for the sake of a degree, go from a court school to the university, but, as a rule, if what he wished were a general course,[1] he would be satisfied with the greater prestige that came from being a pupil of one of the distinguished humanists that the court schools were generally able to retain at their head.

<small>These schools soon rivaled or supplemented the universities, which gradually took up the new learning.</small>

In fact, the want of hospitality, if not the actual hostility, of universities to the new learning, often stimulated the growth of court schools. At Mantua there was no university, and the court school remained independent, while the school of Guarino, necessarily from the connection of that scholar, always had close relations with the University of Ferrara, but in many instances where the university was especially conservative, a court school was set up by its side as a professed rival. Gradually, however, the new learning crept into all the universities, and the classical literature of the Greeks and Romans largely took the place of the former grammar, rhetoric, and dialectic. Before the close of the fifteenth century, Florence, Padua, Pavia, Milan, Ferrara, Rome, and other cities had admitted the humanities to their universities, and the other university seats were not long in following their example.

Attitude of the Humanists toward the Church. — It would seem that some of the humanists were able to combine the pagan culture with their Christian principles. Such was the case with Vergerius, Bruni, Guarino,

---

[1] If he desired a professional training in law, medicine, or theology, he would, of course, be obliged to go to a university.

and Vittorino, who sought to use the ancient learning, together with the Christian writers, as a means of teaching morals. But the implications of humanism were logically destructive of Church dogma and tradition, if not of all Christianity. With some humanists the new learning really resulted in a revival of paganism and a repudiation of the Church. This seems to have been true at least of Poggio and Filelfo, and partially so of Valla, who were inclined to substitute humanism for Catholic allegiance. *Valla* (1407–1457),[1] who was the most learned of the humanists and the first great critical scholar in the modern sense, even went so far in his opposition as to deny the apostolic origin of the *Symbolum Apostolicum* ('Apostles' Creed'), to declare the *Constantini Donatio* ('Donation of Constantine')[2] a forgery, and, in his *Adnotationes*, to subject Jerome's *Vulgate* translation of the New Testament to a critical comparison with the Greek original.

Some of the humanists repudiated the Church and revived paganism; Valla, most learned of humanists, was far-reaching in his criticism.

But very few ventured to attack the doctrines of the Church so directly, or to give vent to the skepticism they felt. The majority were genuinely indifferent, or stayed in outward conformity to the dogmas, with a complete irreligion within.[3] In fact, many who were enthusiastic supporters of the new learning and were of pagan disposition attained to places of great prominence in the Church. Two pupils of the skeptical Filelfo even came to the papal throne as *Nicholas V* (1398–1455) and *Pius II* (1405–1464). The former, when only a monk, went deeply into debt to secure manuscripts of the classical authors, but was given financial assistance by Cosimo de' Medici. After his elevation he used the

Most humanists, however, remained in outward conformity, and some, like Nicholas V and Pius II, even became very prominent in the Church.

---

[1] *Lorenzo della Valle*, generally known as *Laurentius Valla*, was for a short time a pupil of Vittorino at Mantua, and became an itinerant professor of philosophy and classics at Pavia, Milan, Genoa, Ferrara, Mantua, and Naples.
[2] This was a document by which the emperor Constantine was alleged to have given the pope temporal power over Italy, in return for a miraculous cure from leprosy.
[3] On this phase of the revival, see especially Owen's *Skeptics of the Italian Renaissance*.

K

money that came in from the papal jubilee of 1450 to make the collection from which the Vatican library sprang,[1] and was obviously more interested in classical works and scholarship than in theology and the Church. So Pius II, while still *Ænea Silvio*, or *Æneas Sylvius*, wrote a treatise on the humanistic training known as *De Liberorum Educatione* ('On the Education of Children'). He was also the author of many poems, novels, comedies, orations, and letters in the classical style, although, upon his election to the pontificate, he abandoned the humanists and his former liberalism.

Bembo was probably the most devoted humanist among churchmen.

The most extreme devotion to humanism in a church official, however, is exhibited in the case of the papal secretary, *Pietro Bembo* (1470–1547). He was accomplished, amiable, and worldly, and while a collector of classical books and manuscripts and an author of many works, slavishly imitated Cicero in all his style and completely reverted to paganism. He used *Jupiter Maximus* as the designation of God the Father, *Apollo* for Christ, and *divi* to indicate the saints,[2] and warned his colleague Sadoleto to "avoid the Epistles of Paul, lest the style of the Apostle should spoil his taste." Bembo was, however, only typical of the degenerate humanism of the times. He was the literary ruler at the brilliant court of *Leo X* (1513–1521), who, though pope, was a true son of his father, Lorenzo the Magnificent, in his love of art, ancient literature, and paganism. Humanism had now hardened into a formalism, and the prevailing tendency had come to be that known as 'Ciceronianism.'

The 'liberal education' of the ancients became the ideal of the humanistic training.

Ideals of the Humanistic Education. — But during its height Italian humanism evidently tended to encourage personal development and individual expression rather than authority. From our study of the various Italian humanists and their work, it has been possible to see how different were the ideals from those of the medi-

---

[1] See Vespasiano, *Vita di Niccolo V*, cc. XXV, seqq.
[2] It is probably Bembo at whom Erasmus is tilting in his *Dialogus Ciceronianus*, when he satirizes the paganized description of Christian conceptions. See Miss Scott's translation, pp. 66–71.

æval period. Life was no longer viewed in prescribed and formal fashion, and education had a far wider outlook than merely on its ecclesiastical and theological sides. The 'otherworldly' ideal had given way to the Græco-Roman aim of securing as much satisfaction as possible out of this life. The isolation of the monk, the contemplation of the mystic, and the discussions of the schoolmen were being abandoned, and there was a marked tendency to return to the conception of a 'liberal education' portrayed by Plato, Aristotle, Cicero, and others of the ancients.

The various educational treatises of the times by such men as Vergerius, Bruni, Barbaro, Æneas Sylvius, Battista Guarino, Vegio, and Porcia, and the pedagogical procedure of the great schoolmasters, Guarino da Verona and Vittorino da Feltre, alike show a remarkable agreement in respect to this aim of education. They all hold to the ideal of a well-rounded man, fitted for the society in which he is living and adapted to its institutions. They advocate complete development of the individual, mentally, physically, and morally. Vergerius, for example, recommends "that education which calls forth, trains, and develops those highest gifts of body and of mind which ennoble men, and which are rightly judged to rank next in dignity to virtue only."[1] This was certainly the practice of Vittorino and the Mantuan school.

The humanistic theory and practice held to the complete development of the individual, mentally, physically, and morally,

At the same time, the practical side of this individual development was duly emphasized. The humanists felt that culture and breadth of view were not ends in themselves, but were to be developed for the sake of citizenship or efficiency in statecraft. Thus Æneas Sylvius quotes Cicero as reproaching Sextus Pompey for too great devotion to abstract studies, and declares:—

which included social efficiency,

"His reason was that the true praise of men lies in *doing*, and that, consequently, all ingenious trifling, however harmless in itself, which withdraws our energies from fruitful activity, is unworthy of the true citizen."[2]

[1] *De Ingenuis Moribus*, § 3.
[2] *De Liberorum Educatione*, § 8.

Again, Vittorino alludes to this sentiment of Cicero in consoling his friend, Ambrogio, for his want of leisure for study, resulting from administrative duties. A similar view is attributed by Vergerius to Aristotle.[1]

and even personal distinction. This practical view, however, while it included a desire for personal distinction and the modern notion of individual reputation and glory, did not limit itself to mere material success, and nothing is more decried than sordidness and pleasure-seeking. "For to a vulgar temper," says Vergerius, "gain and pleasure are the one aim of existence, to a lofty nature, moral worth and fame."[2]

This was thought to be obtained through a broad study of the classics, **The Content of the Humanistic Education.** — This loftiness of purpose, breadth of view, and efficiency, the humanists believed, is to be obtained primarily through the ancient literatures. "The foundations of all true learning must be laid in the sound and thorough knowledge of Latin," writes Bruni.[3] To this he would probably have added, with Battista Guarino: "I wish now to indicate a second mark of an educated man, which is at least of equal importance; namely, familiarity with the language and literature of Greece. . . . Without a knowledge of Greek, Latin scholarship itself is, in any real sense, impossible."[4]

But while the value in these classic languages did not consist merely of a drill in grammar, this subject was regarded as very essential, simply because it was a key to unlock the literature. "To attain this essential knowledge," Bruni claims, "we must never relax our careful attention to the grammar of the language,"[3] while Æneas Sylvius calls grammar "the portal to all knowledge whatsoever."[5] In every case, however, a wide range of reading in the literature was recommended. Cicero, Vergil, Livy, Sallust, Curtius, Horace, Quintilian, Statius, Ovid, Terence, and Juvenal on the one hand, and, on the other, Homer, Hesiod, Theocritus,

---

[1] *Op. cit.*, § 4. [3] *De Studiis*, § 1. [5] *Op. cit.*, § 5.
[2] *Op. cit.*, § 3. [4] *De Ordine Docendi*, § 3.

THE HUMANISTIC EDUCATION IN ITALY 133

Plato, Aristotle, and the dramatists and historians, seem to have been generally used in the humanistic course. "That high standard of education to which I referred at the outset," says Bruni, "is only to be reached by one who has seen many things and read much. Poet, orator, historian, and the rest, all must be studied, each must contribute a share. Our learning thus becomes full, ready, varied, and elegant, available for action or discourse in all subjects."[1]

This material was held to be valuable also for moral and religious training, as well as intellectual and æsthetic, and Bruni adds: "None have more claim than the subjects and authors which treat of religion and of our duties in the world; and it is because they assist and illustrate these supreme studies that I press upon your attention the works of the most approved poets, historians, and orators of the past." The works of the Christian Fathers, both Latin and Greek, the Bible, creed, Lord's Prayer, and Hymn to the Virgin were likewise to be read for this purpose, together with the works of the pagan writers. *the Christian Fathers, and religious works,*

Thus the mediæval rhetoric and dialectic gave way to an absorption in the classic writers and a study of the languages and literatures of ancient Greece and Rome. But besides the classical and Christian literature, there seems to have been some room in this broad course for mathematics, natural philosophy, and astronomy, and, to some extent, for music, singing, and dancing. Oratory, history, and ethics were taught from the works of the classic authors themselves. *and of mathematics, science, and music;*

The physical side was nurtured by various exercises, which were partly an inheritance from the court training of chivalry and partly a revival of the æsthetic ideals of the Greeks. "It will thus," declares Æneas Sylvius to the young prince, "be an essential part of your education that you be taught the use of the bow, of the sling, and of the spear; that you drive, ride, leap, and swim. These are honorable accomplishments in every *and through certain physical exercises inherited from chivalry and the Greeks.*

---

[1] *Op. cit.,* last section.

one, and therefore not unworthy of the educator's care."¹

This course was adapted to the ability and interest of each pupil, and the discipline was mild.

Method of the Humanistic Teachers. — Thus the curriculum of the humanistic education contained a wide range of elements, — intellectual, æsthetic, moral, and physical. But it was not expected that every one should study thoroughly all subjects, and, as we have seen in the practice of Vittorino,² the course was largely adapted to the ability and interest of each pupil. Of the various 'disciplines' Vergerius declares : —

"It must not be supposed that a liberal education requires acquaintance with them all, for a thorough mastery of even one of them might fairly be the achievement of a lifetime. Most of us, too, must learn to be content with modest capacity as with modest fortune. Perhaps we do wisely to pursue that study which we find most suited to our intelligence and our tastes, though it is true that we cannot rightly understand one subject unless we can perceive its relation to the rest. The choice of studies will depend to some extent upon the character of individual minds. For whilst one boy seizes rapidly the point of which he is in search and states it ably, another, working far more slowly, has yet the sounder judgment and so detects the weak spot in his rival's conclusions. The former, perhaps, will succeed in poetry, or in the abstract sciences ; the latter in real studies and practical pursuits." ³

It has already been shown, in the case of Vittorino, how this study of the disposition of each pupil and close personal contact stimulated the interest and obviated in the humanistic training ⁴ the need of brutal discipline. While emulation was occasionally appealed to, corporal punishment was practically unknown.

This education was largely institutionalized at first in the court schools, but

Organization of the Humanistic Education. — These educational aims, studies, and methods of humanism were carried out informally in the guidance of the home before the boy went to school. From earliest infancy, mothers⁵ undertook to train the character, manners,

---

¹ *Op. cit.*, § 2. ³ *De Ingenuis Moribus*, § 4.
² See pp. 123-127. ⁴ See pp. 126 f.
⁵ During the Italian Renaissance girls, as well as boys, were often carefully educated, and we have several instances of noted women humanists. To one of these, the daughter of the Duke of Urbino, Bruni dedicated his treatise *On the Study of Literature.*

speech, and physique of their children according to the highest humanistic standards. But, as we have found in viewing the history of humanism,[1] these ideals first took on a genuine institutional form in the schools founded at the courts of the city despots. These court schools were sometimes connected with the universities, and gradually the universities themselves, after something of a struggle, admitted the new learning to their curriculum, where it speedily thrived and multiplied. Humanistic education in Italy thus became completely organized. *was eventually admitted to the universities.*

Decadence of the Italian Humanism and the Rise of Ciceronianism. — Toward the close of the fifteenth century, however, this liberal education of the humanists in Italy began to be fixed and formal. Until the death of Nicholas V, the ideals, content, and meaning of this training were constantly expanding, but through the latter half of the century there was a gradual narrowing and hardening, and during the early years of the sixteenth century the degeneration became complete. This was the age of the purists. It began with the formal and pretentious artificialities of Valla,[2] especially as crystallized in his book on *Elegantiæ Latinæ* ('Elegancies of Latin'), and reached its height under the dictatorship of Bembo and the Medicean pope, Leo X.[3] *At the close of the fifteenth century, humanism became fixed and formal, and the æsthetic and social elements were replaced by a drill in grammar.*

As the subject matter became institutionalized, the literature of the Greeks and Romans failed more and more to be interpreted in terms of life. Instead of giving understanding and meaning to certain activities suitable for mankind, the study of the humanities became an end in itself. The aim of education came to be a mastery of ancient literature and of the preliminary training in grammar, and emphasis was placed upon the form rather than the content of the classical writings. The æsthetic, moral, social, and physical elements were gradually read out of education, and the humanistic training became simply a preparation for the formal life of the times.

[1] See pp. 123 and 127 f.   [2] See p. 129.   [3] See p. 130.

In the course of study, grammatical drill was more and more emphasized as a means of formal discipline. Etymological and syntactical scholarship received almost exclusive attention, and was supplemented only by a rhetorical and stylistic study of Latin authors, such as Plautus, Terence, Vergil, Ovid, and especially Cicero. In fact, before long the course was limited almost entirely to the last-named writer, and the new learning fell into that decadent state afterward called *Ciceronianism*. It consisted in an attempt to teach a perfect style with Cicero as a model, and to give one a conversational knowledge of Ciceronian Latin. The structure, metaphors, and vocabulary of all Latin writing had to be copied from the phrases of Cicero, and the literature of the day became little more than a sequence of model passages from that author. The humanistic curriculum thus lapsed into a formalism almost as barren as that of the schoolmen, except that Cicero, rather than Aristotle, became the authority.

This decadent stage is known as 'Ciceronianism,' from the almost exclusive study of the phrases, forms, and figures of Cicero.

To acquire the diction of this writer, the pupil was required to make a long and careful study of his works. In the satire of Erasmus on *Ciceronianism*, the devotee brags that he has read no other author for seven years. He declares that he "has compiled an alphabetical lexicon of Cicero, so huge that two strong carriers well saddled could scarcely carry it upon their backs; a second volume even larger than this, in which are arranged alphabetically the phrases peculiar to Cicero; and a third, in which have been gathered all the metrical feet with which Cicero ever begins or ends his periods, and their subdivisions, the rhythms which he uses in between, and the cadences which he chooses for each kind of sentence, so that no little point could escape." The Ciceronian in his dialogue further holds that one whose style is pure will not use any grammatical form whatsoever not in Cicero, saying: —

"There is no exception. A Ciceronian he will not be in whose books there is found a single little word which he cannot show in the writings of Cicero; and a man's whole vocabulary I deem as spurious as a counterfeit coin, if there is in it even a single word which has not the stamp of the Ciceronian die; for to Cicero alone, as the prince of eloquence, it has been given by the gods above to stamp the coin of Roman speech." [1]

This is, of course, an exaggeration of the Ciceronian tendency, but the pupil apparently was ordinarily expected to commit lists of Ciceronian words, phrases, introductions, and perorations, and to indite letters, make conversations, and construct orations in the Ciceronian style. All textbooks of the period seem to have been arranged with these objects in view. The boys were taught formal grammar upon the basis of Cicero, as if their minds worked like those of an adult. Fine grammatical distinctions of as subtle an order as the quibbles of the scholastic dialectic came to be made, and memory rather than reason became the basis of acquisition. Such methods, sadly lacking in the power to stimulate interest, were inevitably accompanied by corporal punishment, which was inflicted quite as unsparingly to produce conformity to the stereotyped course as to insure proper conduct. Hence, by the early part of the sixteenth century, the humanistic education of Italy had become almost as 'cribbed, cabined, and confined,' and fully as formal, as that of the days of scholasticism. The interest in life and its opportunities, and the pursuit of self-culture in the broad sense, seem for the most part to have gone to seed.

The methods were lacking in interest, and were accompanied by corporal punishment.

Italian humanism, however, had at its best been largely individual and personal, and had looked more to the joy in living than to social improvement and the advancement of morals. The desire for liberty of expression and an immortality in this world, and the enthusiasm for pagan culture that are patent in the life and writings of early humanists, like Petrarch and Boccaccio, are found to have degenerated eventually into license, immorality, paganism, and sacrilege, with a consequent neglect of

[1] The whole of the *Dialogus Ciceronianus* should be read. The excellent translation recently made (New York, 1908) by Izora Scott, from which the passages above have been taken, makes this an easy matter for English readers.

all things religious. Thus the humanistic movement in Italy became formal and crystallized, and subversive of all real progress. It had largely defeated its own ends, and the mission of humanism to refine the manners and morals, to purify religion, and advance society, was left for the achievement of other countries than the states of Italy.

SUPPLEMENTARY READING

I. Sources

NORTON, A. O. *Readings in the History of Education.* Chapters on The Renaissance.
OGG, F. A. *A Source Book of Mediæval History.* Chap. XXVI
PRENDILACQUA, F. *Intorno alla vita di Vittorino da Feltre.*
ROBINSON, J. H. *Readings in European History.* Vol. I, Chap. XXII.
ROBINSON, J. H., AND ROLFE, H. W. *Petrarch. A Selection from His Correspondence.*
SCOTT, IZORA (Translator). *Ciceronianus by Desiderius Erasmus.*
VESPASIANO DA BISTICCI. *Vite di Uomini Illustri del Secolo XV* (edited by Mai and Bartoli).
WHITCOMB, M. *A Literary Source Book of the Italian Renaissance.*
WOODWARD, W. H. *Vittorino da Feltre.* (Includes a translation of *De Ingenuis Moribus* of Vergerius, *De Studiis et Literis* of Bruni, *De Liberorum Educatione* of Æneas Sylvius, and *De Ordine Docendi et Studendi* of Battista Guarino.)

II. Authorities

ACTON, LORD (Editor). *The Cambridge Modern History.* Chap. XVI by Jebb and Chap. XVII by James.
ADAMS, G. B. *Civilization during the Middle Ages.* Chap. XV.
BARNARD, H. *The Renaissance in Italy.* (*American Journal of Education*, Vol. VII, pp. 413-460).
BURCKHARDT, J. *The Civilization of the Renaissance in Italy* (translated by Middlemore).
DRANE, A. T. *Christian Schools and Scholars.* Chap. II.
DRAPER, J. W. *History of Intellectual Development in Europe.* Vol. II, Chaps. II-VI.
FARRAR, F. W. (Editor). *Essays on a Liberal Education.* Essay I, §§ IV-V.
GUIZOT, F. *History of Civilization.* Vol. I, Lect. X.
JEBB, R. C. *Humanism in Education.*
LAURIE, S. S. *Educational Opinion since the Renaissance.* Chaps. I-II.

MONROE, P. *Text-book in the History of Education.* Chap. VI.
MULLINGER, J. B. *A History of the University of Cambridge.*
 Vol. I.
OWEN, J. *The Skeptics of the Italian Renaissance.*
SANDYS, J. E. *A History of Classical Scholarship.* Vol. II, Bk. I.
SCHAFF, P. *The Renaissance.*
SYMONDS, J. A. *A Short History of the Renaissance in Italy.*
 Chaps. III–IV and VII–XI.
SYMONDS, J. A. *Giovanni Boccaccio.*
SYMONDS, J. A. *Renaissance in Italy. The Revival of Learning.*
THURBER, C. H. *Vittorino da Feltre* (*The School Review*, Vol.
 VII, pp. 295–300).
VOIGT, G. *Die Wiederlebung des Classischen Alterthums.*
WOODWARD, W. H. *Vittorino da Feltre and Other Humanist
 Educators.*
WOODWARD, W. H. *Education during the Renaissance.*

CHAPTER XIV

THE HUMANISTIC EDUCATION OF THE NORTH

The Spread and Character of Humanism in the Northern Countries. — Until almost the end of the fifteenth century the Renaissance was largely confined to Italy. In the Northern countries sporadic humanists appeared here and there by the middle of the century, but the movement could not have been at all general. But the introduction of printing gave the humanists a new means of preserving the classical learning and of extending its sphere of influence. This art, invented in Germany about 1450, was brought into Italy some fifteen years later by pupils of Johann Fust, and spread through France, Switzerland, the Netherlands, Spain, England, and a dozen less important states before the close of the century. In 1472 an edition of Vergil was struck off in Florence, and after this the multiplication of all texts was rapid and continuous.

Through the invention of printing, humanism spread into France, the Teutonic countries, England, and elsewhere in the North,

As a result, the revival of learning and the renewed spirit of independence and criticism could not be limited to a single country. The Renaissance and the classic literature leaped the Alps, and made their way first into France, and then into the Teutonic countries, England, and elsewhere. At first, humanistic scholars wandered into the North, soon others were invited in large numbers by patrons of learning, and, at length, students from the Northern countries thronged into Italy for instruction. Toward the close of the fifteenth century the humanists outside the peninsula became very numerous, and the movement, during the sixteenth century, after it had lost its vitality in Italy, came to its height in the Northern lands, and did not sink into a formalism until the very end of the century.

But the character and effects of the Renaissance and humanism in the North differed greatly from those in the country of their origin. The peoples of the North, especially those of Germanic stock, were naturally more religious than the brilliant and mercurial Italians. With them the Renaissance led less to a desire for personal development, self-realization, and individual achievement, and took on more of a social and moral color. With the great Italian educators, it was, indeed, felt that the humanistic training should lead to symmetrical development and social efficiency, but largely for the sake of the individual's happiness and fame. Whereas the prime purpose of humanism in the North became the improvement of society, morally and religiously, and much less attention was paid to the physical, intellectual, and æsthetic elements in education. The classical revival here pointed the way to obtaining a new and more exalted meaning from the Scriptures. Through the revival of Greek, Northern scholars, especially the Germans and the English, sought to get away from the ecclesiastical doctrines and traditions, and turn back to the essence of Christianity by studying the New Testament in the original. This suggested a similar insight into the Old Testament, and an interest in Hebrew also was thereby aroused. In consequence, to most people in the North a renewed study of the Bible became as important a feature of humanism as an appreciation of the classics, and the purer religious and theological conceptions that eventually resulted mark the Reformation as a logical accompaniment of the Renaissance. Thus the Northern humanism was at the same time both broader and narrower than that of Italy. But this can best be understood by a more detailed account of the movement in the various countries of the North and a study of the more prominent figures in each case.

The Development of Humanism in France. — It was but natural that the first of the Northern states to take up the new scholarship should be France. During the days of scholasticism this country had been the great

where it took on more of a social and moral color.

Northern scholars sought an insight into the New Testament by studying it in the original Greek, and this suggested a study of Hebrew for the Old Testament.

France, which had, during the scholastic period, been the intellec-

142   A HISTORY OF EDUCATION

tual center of Europe, was naturally the first to take hold of the new learning, and was especially stimulated by the expeditions of Charles VIII and Louis XII.

intellectual center of Europe, and had yielded its position only as the humanistic enthusiasm swept over Italy. Before the middle of the fifteenth century it began to take hold of the new learning. By 1458 a professorship of Greek was established at the University of Paris and occupied by a certain Gregorio of Tiferno, and a dozen years later it was filled by a native Spartan named Hermonymus. The humanistic movement, however, was especially stimulated in France through the expedition into Italy of Charles VIII in 1494 and that of Louis XII some four years later. The former monarch claimed to have inherited the kingdom of Naples among other possessions, and, in his efforts to secure it, temporarily occupied Florence and Rome. His successor also claimed Milan through his grandmother, who was a member of the Visconti family, and seized this city as well as Naples (1498–1500). While these undertakings of France had no immediate political results, for Charles was soon glad to escape from Italy, and the more able Louis sold his title to Naples and was driven out of Milan, yet a lasting impression was thereby made upon the art and literature of the North. The French had come into direct contact with humanism at its sources, — Milan, Florence, Rome, and Naples, and their admiration was challenged by the evidences of classical culture, intellectual activity, modernness, and individualism that they met there. They were incited to recover their lost prestige, and, from the end of the fifteenth century, the French scholars and printers, in their struggles to further humanistic ideals, became the foremost in Europe.

The universities were conservative, but under Francis I arose many humanistic educators.

Budæus and His Treatise. — Owing to the narrowness and conservatism of the universities, which existed in spite of the chair of Greek at Paris, the new learning met at first with formidable opposition. Happily, it found an influential patron in the youthful Francis I (1515–1547), who succeeded Louis XII. Under his protection, many prominent humanistic scholars and educators appeared. Among these the most doughty

THE HUMANISTIC EDUCATION OF THE NORTH   143

champion of the ancient classics was found in *Guillaume Budé* or *Budæus* (1468–1540). He read widely, translated, and taught the Greek and Latin authors. He also produced a treatise on humanistic education, which he entitled *De l'Institution du Prince* ('On the Instruction of the Prince'), and dedicated it to the young king, Francis.[1] This work was intended to be propagandist and inspirational rather than instructive, and contains much that is trite, but it accomplished a great deal for classical training. "Every man," writes Budæus, "even if a king, should be devoted to philology." By that he means all liberal learning or 'humanities,' which is so called because, without it, man would become a mere animal. This training, he holds, can be obtained only through Latin and Greek, especially the latter, about which he is most enthusiastic. Shortly after writing this treatise, Budæus was appointed royal librarian. He then began earnestly to collect classical manuscripts, and assisted in the foundation of the famous humanistic press of the Estiennes. Later, he succeeded in getting the king to complete his plans for a great humanistic institution of learning, and the College of France, with its chairs of Greek, Hebrew, and Latin, was established. Thus by the time of his death, France was fairly committed to humanistic training.

Budæus wrote a humanistic treatise and collected many classical manuscripts.

Corderius as Schoolmaster and Author. — Another enthusiast on the classical learning was *Mathurin Cordier* (1479–1564), or *Maturinus Corderius*, as he is more commonly called. He had a successful teaching experience and displayed a strong advocacy of the humanistic education at various colleges in Paris and Bordeaux. When well along in life, he listened to a call from his old pupil, Calvin, who was now administering the affairs of Geneva, and went to that city to organize and teach in the reformed schools of Switzerland. Among his early writings is a book on Latin inflections and syntax called *De Corrupti Sermonis Emendatione Libellus* ('A

Corderius taught and advocated the humanistic education in France and Switzerland, and wrote De

---

[1] So Vergerius, Bruni, Æneas Sylvius, and B. Guarino had addressed their treatises to scions of royalty or the nobility.

Emendatione and Colloquia upon the study of Latin.

Little Book for the Amendment of Corrupt Speech '), which was intended to improve Latin style in the French schools. In Switzerland he wrote four books of *Colloquia* ('Colloquies'), with the purpose of training boys, by means of conversations on timely topics, to speak Latin with facility. The *De Emendatione* taught Latin through the medium of French, making a simultaneous study of both languages, but from his *Colloquies*, which give an excellent picture of the school life of the times, and from accounts of the curricula in Switzerland, it is seen that he must have changed his plan of teaching after he came to Switzerland. Here, it would seem, Latin had scarcely been the traditional means of instruction, and to raise the tone of scholarship, it was necessary to require Latin to be spoken at all times. The *Colloquia* came in the latter part of the sixteenth century to have the widest circulation of any textbook, and was translated into English and other languages.

The Collège de Guyenne was reorganized on a humanistic basis, and is typical of the schools in the French cities generally during the sixteenth century.

The Collège de Guyenne and Other Schools. — Gradually all the schools of France began to respond to the new training. It would hardly be possible or desirable to describe many of them, but the *Collège de Guyenne* at the seaport of Bordeaux, which was one of the first to feel the humanistic impulse, may well be considered in detail. The reorganization of this institution had been undertaken by the humanistic educator, Gouvéa, and the staff of the school always included several distinguished scholars, such as Corderius and Vinet. From the latter we have a description of the actual course and administration there in vogue. According to him, "this school was especially intended for learning Latin," but it also included other subjects in its course. It consisted of ten classes in secondary work, and two years more in philosophy, which partially overlapped the faculty of arts in the university. Latin and religion were taught throughout the grammar school, and Greek, mathematics, rhetoric, and declamation could be taken in the last three or four classes. The course in philosophy consisted largely of the Aristotelian works on logic and

THE HUMANISTIC EDUCATION OF THE NORTH 145

natural science. The methods employed in the school seem to have been admirable for the times. The pupils were introduced to the rudiments of Latin through the vernacular, and developmental methods and enlivening disputations were used. Naturally severe punishments seem not to have been needed. Probably the general conditions at this college of Bordeaux were typical of the humanistic schools everywhere in French cities during the sixteenth century.

Classical Studies in the German Universities. — By this time humanism had also spread through the Teutonic countries. Even the German universities had begun to respond to the humanistic influences. While the University of Paris was for a generation the center of the new learning, as early as the middle of the fifteenth century, wandering teachers of the classics began to visit the higher institutions in the German states and left their impress upon them. In 1494 Erfurt established a professorship of Poetry and Eloquence, which covered the field of classic literature, and within a short time the university had been completely reformed upon a humanistic basis. So Leipzig, in 1519, under the great Duke George, introduced more polished translations of Aristotle to replace those of the old schoolmen, and lectures were given on Cicero, Quintilian, Vergil, and Greek authors. Many other university centers, — Heidelberg, Tübingen, Ingoldstadt, and Vienna were similarly transformed, and a number of new universities were humanistic from their foundation. Such were Wittenberg, which was started as early as 1502, and Marburg, Königsberg, and Jena, which were founded nearer the middle of the century.[1] And before the close of the first quarter of the sixteenth century, humanism had prevailed in practically all of the German universities.

The German universities established chairs of classics, and new humanistic universities were founded.

The Hieronymian Schools. — But probably the earliest and most influential factor in German humanism ap-

The Hieronymian schools.

[1] Much of this remodeling and extension was due to the influence of Melanchthon. See pp. 156 f.

L

peared in the education furnished by the religious order known as the *Brethren of the Common Lot* or the *Hieronymians*.[1] Most of the first leaders in humanism were connected with this brotherhood either as members or pupils. The order was founded in 1376 by *Geert Groot* (1340-1384) at Deventer, Holland, and was composed of pious men devoted to industry, learning, and popular education. They maintained themselves by copying manuscripts, and gave instruction to the poor. In some places they founded schools and superintended all the classes; in others they acted as assistants in schools already existing. Naturally they at first stressed instruction in the Bible and the vernacular, and taught reading, writing, singing, and conversation in ecclesiastical Latin. But as the Italian influence began to be felt in the upper countries, although the Hieronymians still held to their moral and religious motives, they broadened the course by the addition of humanistic elements. They retained their Christian training, but added the classic literature and Hebrew. While the education they offered was generally elementary and secondary, and consisted mostly of Latin and Greek, it included rhetoric and theology in the higher classes, and the Brethren often expanded the course so that in several instances it covered the work of the faculty of arts in a university. Before the opening of the Renaissance in the North they had established a chain of forty-five houses, extending through the Netherlands, the German states, and France, and within a generation this number had trebled. The Brethren were in control of the famous institutions at Deventer, Zwolle, Liège, Louvain, Mechlin, Cambrai, and Valenciennes, and founded the Collège de Montaigu in connection with the University of Paris. Before the close of the sixteenth century, there were two thousand students in attendance at Deventer, and several hundred at ten or a dozen other of the Hieronymian institutions. The constant visits of

---

[1] The order was sometimes known from its patron saints, Jerome and Gregory, as the Hieronymian or Gregorian.

THE HUMANISTIC EDUCATION OF THE NORTH 147

members of the order to Italy and the frequent change of their teachers brought about an interchange of knowledge, which silently molded public opinion and exerted a tremendous influence for humanism and higher ideals. The Hieronymian schools, especially those at Deventer and Zwolle, became recognized centers of intellectual interests and humanism. They were visited by wandering scholars, and the pupils that were trained there strengthened the new learning as teachers in the universities and schools throughout the Netherlands and Germany.

Wessel, Agricola, Reuchlin, and Hegius. — The first educator of importance to introduce humanism into these schools seems to have been *Johann Wessel* (1420–1489). He had received his first schooling at Zwolle, and after studying and teaching the classics and Hebrew in Cologne, Paris, Florence, and Rome, returned to his early school as an instructor. His interest was in teaching even more than in scholarship, and he held that "the scholar is known by his ability to teach." He had, in consequence, a marked influence upon humanistic education, and sent out a number of distinguished pupils. Among those influenced by him while at Paris were *Rudolphus Agricola*[1] (1443–1485) and *Johann Reuchlin* (1455–1522). Agricola studied later in Pavia, Ferrara, and elsewhere in Italy, and after absorbing all the best influences of the Renaissance, returned as a humanistic missionary to his own 'barbarous, unlearned, and uncultured' people. At Heidelberg and Worms he lectured on the classics, and while he could never be induced to tie himself down to the routine of a single institution, he showed at all times a genuine interest in good schools. Toward the close of his life he wrote a humanistic treatise, *De Formando Studio* ('On the Regulation of Study'), and he was regarded by all the other humanists as the most potent influence in introducing the study

Wessel introduced humanism into the Hieronymian schools.

Agricola lectured on the classics, and wrote a humanistic treatise.

---

[1] He is best known by this Latinized form of his name, but he was originally *Roelof Huysman* ('farmer'). This tendency for educators to translate their names became one of the formal marks of humanism.

of classics into the North. Erasmus in particular declares that he was *inter Græcos Græcissimus, inter Latinos Latinissimus.* Reuchlin, the friend of Agricola, had a somewhat similar influence, but gave more attention to Hebrew. After studying at Paris with Wessel and at other humanistic centers, he taught Latin, Greek, and Hebrew at the Universities of Heidelberg, Ingoldstadt, and Tübingen. He prepared a Latin lexicon, many editions of Greek classics, and a combined grammar and lexicon of the Hebrew language, to which he applied the words of Horace, —*exegi monumentum ære perennius* ('I have raised a monument more lasting than bronze'). Alexander Hegius (1433-1498), for a whole generation the head of the school at Deventer, was also connected with Agricola. Although ten years older, he studied Greek under him, and modestly said: "I learnt from him all I know or men suppose me to know." Hegius introduced many reforms in texts and methods, and wrote a treatise, *De Utilitate Linguæ Græcæ* ('On the Utility of the Greek Language'). During his time there graduated from Deventer a large number of leading humanistic scholars and teachers, including Erasmus, the most famous humanist of the North.

The Work of Jakob Wimpfeling. — But before endeavoring to do justice to the work of that brilliant cosmopolitan scholar, Erasmus, we must first consider the influence of *Jakob Wimpfeling*[1] (1450-1528), who was an earlier product of the Hieronymian education. He was educated in the school of Schlettstadt in Alsace, which was an offshoot of Deventer, and became the means of training several humanists of reputation. He obtained further education at the humanistic universities of Basel, Erfurt, and Heidelberg, and became a professor, dean of the faculty of arts, and finally for two years rector, in the last named institution. He lectured upon the classical authors and St. Jerome, and wrote a number of treatises upon education. Of these the most

---

[1] Also less properly written *Wimpheling* or *Wympfeling.*

prominent are *Isidoneus Germanicus* ('An Introductory Book for Germans'), which was the first educational treatise in the Northern humanistic period, and deals with the proper curriculum and methods, as well as deeper educational principles and problems; and *Adolescentia* ('Youth'), which advocates moral principles by means of selections from the Bible and the classics, and makes an attempt to analyze the mental processes of the child. He also embodied his theories in several textbooks. Wimpfeling's humanism was of a broad but religious type. While he sought to stress the content rather than the form of the classics, and recommended a wide selection of Greek and Latin authors, he held to the social and moral aim in their study. "Of what use," he asks, "are all the books in the world, the most learned writings, the profoundest researches, if they only minister to the vainglory of their authors, and do not, or cannot, advance the good of mankind? . . . What profits all our learning, if our character be not correspondingly noble, all our industry without piety, all our knowing without love of our neighbor, all our wisdom without humility, all our studying, if we are not kind and charitable?" However, while a true reformer, like Erasmus he never broke from the Church. He had a great influence upon humanism and his pupils, and, because of his prominence, he was frequently called upon by educators and rulers for advice concerning their schools. Hence he has sometimes shared with the Protestant Melanchthon the title of *Germaniæ præceptor*('the teacher of Germany').

He recommended a wide selection of classic authors, but held to the social and moral aim. While a true reformer, he never broke from the Church.

Erasmus, the Leader in Humanistic Education. — Desiderius Erasmus [1] (1467–1536), while still a pupil at Deventer, exhibited remarkable ability in the new learning, and when he was only eight his greatness is said to have been prophesied by Agricola while on a visit to Hegius. After leaving Deventer, Erasmus furthered his knowledge of Latin and Greek at the Collège de Montaigu

After studying classics at Deventer, Paris, Oxford, and various Italian centers, Erasmus occupied the chair of

---

[1] His name was originally *Geert Geerts* ('Gerard, the son of Gerard'), but he turned *Geert*, which means 'well-beloved,' into its Latin and Greek equivalents, respectively. See note on p. 147.

150   A HISTORY OF EDUCATION

divinity at Cambridge and lectured gratuitously on Greek.

at Paris, where in 1499 he met a number of English students, and was by them induced to visit Oxford. Here he became acquainted with Colet and More, and studied under Grocyn and Linacre. Afterward he insisted that no one need go to Italy, if he could learn of Linacre, adding: "To me any one who is truly learned is an Italian, even if born among savages." Yet Erasmus could not help sighing for the Mecca of all devoted humanists, and, after struggling with poverty in the North for seven years, he at length found it possible to visit the ancient libraries, meet the learned men, and pursue the study of Greek at Venice, Florence, Padua, Bologna, and Rome. In 1510, he returned to England, and for four years occupied the chair of divinity at Cambridge. During this period he also lectured gratuitously upon Greek, and afforded Colet much help in establishing his school at St. Paul's. Three years later he undertook the project of a new humanistic college at Louvain, but in 1422, when the Reformation controversies began, he retired to Basel. In this home of humanism and the printing art, he found time to edit, translate, and produce works of his own until his death.

He made great contributions to humanism and social reform, and believed in purifying by the removal of ignorance rather than by a division of the Church.

Thus Erasmus traveled widely, met all the prominent scholars of his day, and made great contributions to humanism and social reform. While he was bitterly opposed to the corruption and obscurantism of ecclesiastics, he believed, like Wimpfeling, that the remedy lay, not in a division of the Church, but in the study of classics and the Church Fathers and in the general removal of ignorance. Accordingly, he gave much time to improving the facilities for humanistic education. He helped Colet and Lily with their Latin Grammar,[1] translated into Latin the Greek grammar of Theodore of Gaza, wrote a work on Latin composition, known as *De Copia Verborum et Rerum*, and an elementary textbook of Latin conversations on topics of the day, called *Colloquia*, translated or edited a large number of the Greek and Latin classics, and, through his *Adagia* ('Adages'), made the

[1] See p. 170.

THE HUMANISTIC EDUCATION OF THE NORTH 151

sayings of the ancients familiar to all. Similarly, he produced an edition of Valla's *Adnotationes* on the New Testament, edited the New Testament and translated it into Latin, and popularized the Gospels, and Jerome and other Christian Fathers through paraphrases. Better known, however, is the direct work which Erasmus performed in undertaking to reform the foibles and abuses of his times by means of satires. The *Adagia*, which was nominally a compilation of proverbs, maxims, and witty sayings, was really intended to expose ecclesiastical abuses, and the *Colloquia*, although in the form of a textbook, was a terrible arraignment of prevailing conditions in education, religion, and society, while his *Encomium Moriæ* ('Praise of Folly') mercilessly scored the absurdities of monks and priests. In his *Dialogus Ciceronianus* ('Dialogue on Ciceronianism'),[1] as has been pointed out, he turns to a different theme. Here he ridicules the narrower tendency of humanism by having its advocate explain his system of education and translate the Christian creed into the heavy pagan conceptions of Cicero.

To reform abuses, he wrote satires,— Adagia, Colloquia, Encomium Moriæ, and Dialogus Ciceronianus.

Erasmus also made positive contributions to educational theory, and, besides his references to the subject in the *Colloquia* and *Ciceronianus*, he wrote *De Pueris Statim ac Liberaliter Instituendis* ('On the Liberal Education of Children from the Beginning'), *De Ratione Studii* ('On the Right Method of Study'), *De Civilitate Morum Puerilium* ('On Courtesy of Manners in Boys'), and other treatises. His statement of the aim of education is best given in the *De Civilitate*, where he says:—

He also produced educational treatises,— Colloquia, Ciceronianus, De Pueris, De Ratione, and De Civilitate.

> "The first and most important part is that the youthful mind may absorb the seeds of piety; next, that it may love and thoroughly learn the liberal arts; third, that it may be prepared for the duties of life; and fourth, that it may from the earliest years be straightway accustomed to the rudiments of good manners."

These ideals,— piety, learning, moral duty, and manners, which he repeatedly approaches elsewhere from different angles, are connected each with the other, and together stand for all that goes to make up social

His educational aim was a combination of piety, learning, morals, and manners.

[1] See pp. 136 f.

efficiency. The religious is not looked upon as something distinct from the rest of training, for in the plan of Erasmus, all that illumines the individual is held to elevate him and the social order of which he is a part. Accordingly, Erasmus appears everywhere to believe in universal education, — education for the poor as well as the rich, for women as for men, and holds that the amount and kind of education should be based upon ability rather than upon wealth, birth, or sex. In the *De Pueris* he shows that education should start in infancy, and that children should be trained by their mothers in health, habits, and control until they are six or seven years of age. The elements of reading, writing, and drawing, and some knowledge of familiar objects and animals, should also be given them at this time by methods as informal as possible. He advises the use of stories, pictures, games, and object teaching rather than mere memory, and, with a belief in such appeals to interest, he naturally feels that "teaching by beating is not a liberal education, and the schoolmaster should not indulge in too strong and too frequent language of blame."

At seven the boy's education is to be taken over by his father, or, in case that is impossible, by a tutor or a day school. Now he is to be given a thorough humanistic training in the Scriptures, the Christian Fathers, and the classics. The Greek and Latin authors that should be read and the methods of teaching the classics are detailed in the *De Ratione*. These subjects, Erasmus believes, present all that is needed as a standard of living or for a reformation of society, but he maintains that a sufficient range must be had to get fully into their spirit. Grammar, too, is to be studied only as a necessary gate to literature and the content of the classical writers. At the outset of the *De Ratione*, Erasmus says:

"But I must make my conviction clear that, whilst a knowledge of the rules of accidence and syntax is most necessary to every student, still they should be as few, as simple, and as carefully framed as possible. I have no patience with the stupidity of the average teacher of grammar, who wastes precious years in hammering rules into children's heads. For it is not by learning rules that we acquire the power of speaking a language, but by daily intercourse with those accustomed to express themselves with exactness and refinement, and by the copious reading of the best authors. Upon this latter point we do well to choose such works as are not only sound models of style, but are instructive by reason of their subject matter. . . . Some proficiency of expression being thus attained, the student devotes his attention to the *content* of ancient literatures. It is true, of course, that in reading an author for purposes of vocabulary and style the student cannot fail to gather something beside. But I have in mind much more than this when I speak of studying 'content.' For I affirm that with slight qualification the whole of attainable knowledge lies inclosed within the literary monuments of ancient Greece. This great inheritance I will compare to a limpid spring of whose undefiled waters it behooves all who truly thirst to drink and be restored."

Therefore, he holds that mythology, geography, agriculture, architecture, military tactics, natural history, astronomy, history, music, and other subjects, must be studied for the sake of the light they throw upon classical writers. Informal methods are also to be continued during this stage. A vocabulary is first to be acquired through objects and conversation, and even when formal grammar is taken up, he holds that it should never be an end in itself.

Hence the humanism of Erasmus is of the broader sort. It involves a grasp of ideas and content, and is not confined to a mere study of language and form, and the methods of acquisition appeal to interest. But while both his ideals and his practical suggestions in education seem remarkable for the day, they must have been largely typical of the Hieronymian schools and of Northern humanism in general. It simply represents the culmination of the union between the biblical training of the Brethren and the new education in the classics.

The humanism of Erasmus is of the broad type.

The Fürstenschulen and the Gymnasien. — It can thus be seen what a profound effect the Hieronymian schools had upon education, and how greatly those who had studied in them influenced the universities and other educational institutions. But there were other schools

154 A HISTORY OF EDUCATION

that were even more directly the outgrowth of humanism in the North than the Hieronymian. The cathedral, burgher, and other city schools offered accommodations scarcely sufficient for their own locality, and, as they had to furnish both elementary and secondary education at the same time, their course was necessarily limited. Therefore, to meet the demand for well-prepared officials in church and state, Duke Moritz of Saxony in 1543 opened a public boarding-school in two of his cities, where the more brilliant sons of native citizens might be fitted at public expense for the university and ecclesiastical and civil leadership. Moritz afterward added to the number of these schools, and his example was followed by the heads of other Protestant states of Germany, although these state schools were never very numerous. They became, because of their origin, generally known as *Fürstenschulen* ('princes' schools'), but, since their endowment came largely from the monasteries, which had been secularized in the Protestant states, they were often popularly referred to as *Klosterschulen* ('cloistral schools').[1] While their foundation came about in a different way, they greatly resembled the 'court schools'[2] of Italy in general aim and course of study. Since their chief purpose was to produce leaders, temporal and spiritual, a comprehensive program of humanistic studies almost equivalent to that of the universities, was furnished.

'Fürstenschulen,' endowed largely from the secularized monasteries, were started by the Protestant princes to produce leaders.

The 'Gymnasien' grew out of the cathedral and upper burgher schools, and were under the control of the cities.

A more typical and lasting institutional development of the Renaissance in the North, however, was the set of schools known as *Gymnasien*. They grew largely out of the old cathedral and upper burgher schools, and from the beginning differed from both the *Fürstenschulen* and the Hieronymian schools in being under the control of the cities and in not being boarding-schools. This tendency to establish humanistic schools for the benefit of the municipality, rather than for state and church,

---

[1] They were also called *Landesschulen*. See Russell's *German Higher Schools*, pp. 38, 98, 140, 144, and 196–198.
[2] See pp. 123 and 127 f.

grew rapidly in the German states, and the *Fürstenschulen* were afterward merged in the system, although their course was somewhat beyond that of the former Latin schools of the cities. Some of the oldest and most important of these institutions for the nobility, Meissen (1543), Pforta (1543), Grimma (1550), and Rossleben (1554), while remaining boarding-schools, are classed among the leading gymnasia to-day. The Hieronymian schools also in most cases became *Gymnasien*, but some of them came under the control of the Jesuits.

The organization and curriculum of these municipal humanistic schools were slowly developed during the first half of the sixteenth century. They substituted the Latin, and later also the Greek, classical literature for the grammar, rhetoric, and mediæval Latin of the old courses, and eventually replaced the dialectic with mathematics. As peculiar to the Germanic humanism, the Greek of the New Testament and Hebrew were often added. The burgher school at Nuremberg in 1495 was the first to add 'poetry,' or classical literature, to its course, and the other higher schools of the various cities soon took up the subject. But the most definite shaping of the gymnasial idea was effected through the organization of the Latin school at Eisleben in 1525, and of the system in Saxony three years later, after the plan of Melanchthon, and through the foundation of the Strasburg gymnasium in 1538 by Sturm. The public influence of these two men was so wide that a separate treatment of their work is required.

The curriculum.

Melanchthon and His Organization of Schools. — Through Reuchlin, his scholarly great-uncle, *Philip Melanchthon*[1] (1497–1560) had, by the time he was seventeen, obtained a thorough training not only in Greek, Latin, Hebrew, and biblical exegesis, but in logic, mathematics, history, law, and medicine. He had

The early life and education of Melanchthon.

[1] He was known as *Schwartzerd* ('black earth') until, in recognition of humanistic attainments most remarkable for a boy, Reuchlin translated his surname into Greek.

been very influential in reviving humanism at the Universities of Heidelberg and Tübingen, while a student there, and was already considered one of the most learned scholars of the day. In 1518, when the Elector of Saxony asked Reuchlin to recommend a young scholar to teach Greek at the University of Wittenberg, the great humanist wrote in reply: —

"Melanchthon will come, and he will be an honor to the university. For I know no one among the Germans who excels him, save Erasmus of Rotterdam, and he is more properly a Hollander."

As soon as he had delivered his inaugural address, Melanchthon became one of the most popular lecturers the institution had known, and Luther, who was now well established there, declared that "all students of theology are clamoring to learn Greek."

His lectures at Wittenberg upon theology and the classics, and his work in furthering humanistic education.

Through his association with Luther, Melanchthon was soon turned toward theology, and lectured on New Testament, Old Testament, and dogmatics as well as the Greek and Latin classics. But while he is generally known to history for theological works and his part in the Reformation, his influence upon the education of the times was probably even greater. Except that it was limited to Germany, his work in furthering humanistic education was similar to that of Erasmus. Not only did Melanchthon renew and extend humanism at Wittenberg, as he had previously done at the other universities with which he had been connected, but through him several new universities were founded on a humanistic basis. He also wrote Greek and Latin grammars, and produced editions of various classics, and clear and well-arranged school books upon rhetoric, dialectic, ethics, history, physics, and other subjects. The esteem in which he was held at the university and his great interest in his students gave him a peculiar power equalled by very few teachers. Hence his influence was largely extended throughout Germany by means of his pupils, among whom were many of the most renowned schoolmasters[1]

His large influence.

[1] Such, for example, were Camerarius, Trotzendorf, and Neander. It has even been said that every great rector, except Sturm, had been a pupil

THE HUMANISTIC EDUCATION OF THE NORTH 157

of the following generation. Likewise, the advice of Melanchthon was sought personally or through correspondence by princes, magistrates, and educators, and his genius for organization, methods, and texts was felt everywhere in his native land. Small wonder, then, that by the time of his death there was scarcely a city in all the German states which had not been touched by his influence, or that he has ever since been by common consent referred to as *Germaniæ præceptor*.

The influence of Melanchthon upon the *Gymnasien* came through his educational recommendations to the Elector of Saxony in 1528. He had three years previously, at the request of the Count of Mansfeld, organized a school at Eisleben, and in 1526 had assisted in the foundation of an *Obereschule* ('higher school') at Nuremberg. His success as an organizer led in 1527 to his appointment as *Schulvisitant* for Saxony, and the next year his *Schulplan*, contained in the *Visitationsbuch*, was enacted into law. The Latin schools, which were thereby established in every town and village of the electorate, were to be divided into three classes, as had been the school organized by Melanchthon at Eisleben, but his former plan was somewhat simplified as the result of experience. "The first class," he advised, "should consist of those children who are learning to read; the second class of those who have learned to read, and are now ready to go into grammar; while when these children have been well trained in grammar, those among them who have made the greatest proficiency should be taken out and formed into the third class." In the elementary class the children first learned to read and write from a Latin primer prepared by Melanchthon, which contained the alphabet, the Lutheran creed, the Lord's prayer, and other prayers. They then read from the *Grammar* of Donatus and the *Precepts* of Cato, memorized Latin words, and were taught music. In the next grade they were trained in

His appointment as 'Schulvisitant' for Saxony and his Schulplan.

His division of the schools into three classes.

of Melanchthon's, while Sturm was among those who went to him for counsel.

etymology, syntax, and prosody, and read first from such easy works as the *Fables* of Æsop, the *Pædology* of Mosellanus, and the *Colloquies* of Erasmus, and later from the comedies of Plautus and Terence. More specific attention was also given to the Scriptures, the Lord's prayer, the creed, the Commandments, the Psalms, the Proverbs, the Gospels, and the Epistles. The youths who were selected for the highest class read Vergil, Ovid, and Cicero, and were given a more thorough training in grammar, especially prosody, and in logic and rhetoric. The pupils of the two upper grades were also practiced constantly in Latin composition, and were required to converse in Latin almost exclusively.

From these institutions the humanistic Gymnasien sprang.

These institutions of Saxony were thus intended chiefly to fit boys for the university, and were rather narrow in ideals and course. They were literally 'Latin' schools, for no Greek or Hebrew appears anywhere in the course; much less the vernacular, mathematics, science, or history. Nevertheless, it was from these municipal secondary schools, when the course had been somewhat modified and expanded, that the *Gymnasien* sprang. A generation later the general plan in a modified form was copied by the duchy of Würtemberg, and other states followed the example until the 'gymnasium' became the chief type of school in the German system.

Sturm's Gymnasium at Strasburg. — But an educator who gave a greater impulse to the foundation of *Gymnasien*, and, as a practical schoolmaster, had more influence upon their course, was *Johann Sturm* (1507-1589). This man was the organizer, and for forty-five years the rector, of the famous classical school or gymnasium at Strasburg. He had received a humanistic training at the Hieronymian school at Liège and at the Universities of Louvain and Paris. By the time of his call to Strasburg, at thirty-one years of age, he had a large reputation as a classical scholar and a private teacher of Greek and Latin.

The ideals of Sturm's

Sturm had a definite set of ideals for his school, which he states as follows: —

THE HUMANISTIC EDUCATION OF THE NORTH 159

"A wise and persuasive piety should be the aim of our studies. But were all pious, then the student should be distinguished from him who is unlettered by scientific culture and the art of speaking. Hence, knowledge and purity and eloquence of diction should become the aim of scholarship, and toward its attainment both teachers and pupils should sedulously bend every effort."

school,— piety, knowledge, and eloquence.

In other words, as Sturm puts it more tersely elsewhere, "the end to be accomplished by teaching is threefold, and includes piety, knowledge, and eloquence." 'Piety' he believed to be cultivated mainly through the catechism and creed, while 'knowledge' with him consisted chiefly in an acquaintance with the Latin and some of the Greek literature, and 'eloquence' meant the ability to speak and write Latin readily and elegantly, so that it might be used as a medium of intercourse in the outside world. Hence his ideals, which seem to have been practically those of his contemporaries, except that they were more clearly expressed, were more restricted than those of Erasmus, or possibly even of Melanchthon.

To attain these educational ends, Sturm worked out a gymnasial organization of ten classes,[1] upon which the pupils entered at six or seven years of age. This was to be followed by a university course for five years more. The content of the course in the gymnasium, which alone concerns us here, is well known from the sketch given in his *Best Method of Opening an Institution of Learning*, published at the founding of the school, from the *Classic Letters* of instruction written to the teachers of the various classes in 1565, and from the records of a general examination of the school, which took place still thirteen years later. As these three documents agree in all essentials, it would seem that there was little change in the curriculum during the management of Sturm.[2] For 'piety,' the Lutheran

Its organization into ten classes, to be followed by a university course of five years.

The curriculum in the ten classes.

---

[1] In his original plan he had only nine classes, but, from the *Classic Letters* and the examination records, it would seem that this number was increased to ten.

[2] The course is given in full by classes in Barnard's *German Teachers and Educators*, pp. 196–208.

catechism was studied in German for three years, and in Latin for three years longer. The *Sunday Sermons* were read in the fourth and fifth years, and the *Letters* of Jerome also in the fifth year, while the *Epistles* of Paul were carefully studied from the sixth year through the rest of the course. On the 'knowledge' and 'eloquence' side, Latin grammar was begun immediately and the drill continued for four years, during which the pupil passed gradually from memorizing lists of words used in everyday life and reading dialogues that embodied them to the translation of Cicero and the easier Latin poets. In the fourth year exercises in style were begun, and this was accompanied by a grammatical and literary study of Cicero, Vergil, Plautus, Terence, Martial, Horace, Sallust, and other authors, together with letter writing, declamation, disputation, and the acting of plays. Greek was begun in the fifth year, and after three years of grammatical training, Demosthenes, the dramatists, Homer, and Thucydides were undertaken.

While other authors than Cicero were read, the object of this training clearly was to acquire an ability to read, write, and speak Ciceronian Latin. Words, phrases, and expressions from Cicero's works were carefully committed to memory, and the main emphasis throughout was upon form, with little regard for content. The Latin and Greek were largely regarded as an end in themselves. The last three grades made a little study of rhetoric, and the highest included a little logic, astronomy, and geometry, but otherwise there were no studies besides the classics and religion. The mother tongue was neglected, no mention was made of geography, history, or natural sciences, and but little of mathematics, and there was no connection indicated between the school and the world outside. Under these circumstances, it would be surprising if the chief educational methods were not those of imitation and memory.

Sturm shows the formal- Obviously, toward the close of the sixteenth century, humanism had come to be about as formal and narrow in Germany as in Italy. Sturm would have made as good a subject for the satire of Erasmus as Bembo or any other of the Italian Ciceronians. Yet his gymnasium was an enormous success, and profoundly influenced not only the education of his own times, but of the next three centuries. Students flocked into Strasburg by thousands, among them many youthful noblemen and princes, and Sturm seems to have trained most of the leading educators of the next generation. His pupils became the headmasters of all the most prominent schools and organized many new institutions of repute beside.[1] Moreover, through his wide correspondence and personal advice to sovereigns and others, and through his textbooks, the course of study formulated by Sturm became a model not only for Germany, but, in a sense, for the rest of Europe. Even more than Melanchthon's recommendations, Sturm's practice affected the code introduced into Würtemberg by Duke Christopher in 1559, and the reorganization in Saxony by Elector Augustus I in 1580. Since his day, mathematics, modern languages, and the natural sciences have somewhat mitigated the amount of classics prescribed, and in many instances Hebrew has also been added, but otherwise the humanistic *Gymnasien* are essentially the same as in the day of their originator, Johann Sturm.

ism in Northern humanism toward the close of the sixteenth century.

The influence of Sturm.

The Early Humanistic Movement in England. — In its northward march, humanism came also into England, and in this country effected profound changes. Here learning had sunk into scholasticism and inactivity, but a revival was started early in the fifteenth century through the efforts of *Humphrey, Duke of Gloucester.* This noble patron of learning gathered about himself practically all the native scholars of the period, and brought from Italy several of the younger humanists, who translated the classics and introduced the spirit of the Renaissance. He also afforded financial assistance to the work of the older Italian humanists, who could not be induced to

The efforts of Humphrey, Duke of Gloucester.

---
[1] Sturm himself founded schools at Lauingen, Trasbach, and Hornbach; his pupil Schenck at Augsburg; and his pupil Crusius at Meminger.

come to England, gave a large number of Greek and Latin books and manuscripts to Oxford, where he had studied, and in every way encouraged reforms in the education of the times. Æneas Sylvius,[1] in writing to the Bishop of Chichester in 1444 concerning the humanistic awakening in England, declares: —

"For this advance all gratitude is due to the illustrious Duke of Gloucester, who zealously received polite learning into your kingdom. I hear that he cultivates poets and venerates orators; hence many Englishmen now turn out really eloquent. For as are the princes, so are the people; servants progress through imitating their masters."

Oxford scholars visited Italian centers of humanism.

Greek at Oxford. — As the result of the impetus thus afforded, by the middle of the fifteenth century many former students of Oxford began to visit the various centers in Italy and obtain the inspiration of humanism at first hand. Through them the number of manuscripts, translations, and classical scholars in England was greatly increased, but for a generation the influence of these innovators was not seriously felt upon education. Toward the end of the century, however, there migrated to Italy a new group of Oxford men, who succeeded in their united effort to advance humanistic training in England. This movement began in earnest with the labors of the three friends, Grocyn, Linacre, and Latimer, who had gone to Florence about 1488, and undertook to introduce Greek into education upon their return home.

Greek was introduced into education in England through the visit of Grocyn.

William Grocyn (1442-1519), after the visit to Italy, became the first lecturer on Greek at Oxford,[2] where he found the excellent library donated by Duke Humphrey of great service. He also lectured upon the Pseudo-Dionysius and began his work in Bible criticism, but left few works, as, like most humanists of his period, he disliked publicity. *Thomas Linacre* (1460-1524), while in Italy, became interested in Aristotle, and was led to the study

Linacre,

---
[1] See p. 130.
[2] Erasmus declares that Grocyn had taught Greek before going to Italy, but if so, it could not have been with any degree of influence.

THE HUMANISTIC EDUCATION OF THE NORTH 163

of natural science and medicine at Padua, where he was also a professor for a time. But he had become well versed in classics, rhetoric, and dialectic, as well as in his chosen specialty, and while lecturing on medicine at Oxford, he also taught Greek and Latin, and assisted Grocyn in training Erasmus, More, and Colet. So versatile a scholar was he that it was doubted whether he were "a better Latinist or Grecian, a better grammarian or physician," and Erasmus wrote Latimer that with Linacre as his teacher he had found no need of going to Italy.[1] His correspondence with humanists in all lands was very extensive, and he had everywhere a great influence. *William Latimer* (1460–1545), the last of the Oxford trio, attained less distinction as a scholar, largely because of his extreme modesty. He was, however, a deep student of Greek, and, according to Erasmus, a man of eminent learning. When once the work of these Oxonians was well under way, English scholars in increasing numbers were stimulated to seek a training at the Italian centers, and returned to spread the gospel of humanism.[2]

and Latimer.

Greek at Cambridge. — Humanism did not reach Cambridge, however, until the close of the fifteenth century, but with the progress of the sixteenth that university rapidly overtook its sister institution. The development of humanistic education appeared at Cambridge first through *Bishop Fisher*, who became Chancellor of the University in 1504. Through him the Countess of Richmond, mother of Henry VII, was induced to found and endow three humanistic colleges for the university. He also encouraged *Erasmus*, while a professor of divinity at Cambridge, 1510–1514, to lecture upon Greek as a labor of love. Among the pupils of Erasmus was *Richard Croke,* who afterward lectured upon Greek in Cologne, Louvain, Leipzig, and other places, and in 1519

Through Bishop Fisher, Erasmus was induced to lecture on Greek at Cambridge, and he was succeeded by Croke, Smith, Cheke, and Ascham.

---

[1] See p. 150. Erasmus also includes Tunstall in this declaration.
[2] This movement was greatly assisted by the quieter conditions that began to settle upon England under the strong hand of the Tudors. Peace and the liberal arts flourished together.

returned to Cambridge to teach the subject. While for a time after this, Hellenic learning was suppressed at Cambridge by Wolsey, out of opposition to Fisher, in 1533 *Sir Thomas Smith* gave lectures upon it, and seven years later one of the new *regius* ('royal') professorships was founded for Greek, and *Sir John Cheke* (1514-1557) became the first incumbent. Cheke succeeded in promoting the subject more than any who had preceded him, not by advocating it loudly, but through reading the Greek authors with select pupils and covering as much ground as possible. Like most Northern humanists, he also used his Greek for the interpretation of the New Testament, and produced a translation of the Gospel of Matthew. However, within four years he was appointed Latin tutor to Prince Edward, and was succeeded in the chair at Cambridge by his pupil and contemporary, *Roger Ascham* (1515-1568). Four years later Ascham, too, resigned, in order to become the tutor in Greek and Latin to Princess Elizabeth. The influence of Ascham, however, extended far beyond the university, and lasted long after his death through the posthumous publication of his work called *The Scholemaster*. Of this we must speak more fully later on.[1]

More and Wolsey persuaded the king to support the humanists.

Humanistic Influences at the Court. — A more powerful source of influence than the progressive scholars of the universities in developing humanism in England was that found at the royal court. Here the humanistic training possessed, in addition to the royal tutors Cheke and Ascham, an especially stanch supporter in *Sir Thomas More* (1478-1535), and through him in *Cardinal Wolsey*, and even the king, Henry VIII. When Greek and New Testament exegesis were being violently opposed in Oxford by a group of scholastics and heresy-hunters,[2] these subjects would probably have been rooted out, had it not been for More and his standing with the king. That statesman finally wrote the university authorities a

[1] See pp. 166 f.
[2] This was the party of 'Trojans,' so-called from their war upon the Greeks.

letter, censuring the conservatives and declaring that, if they did not desist, the institution would lose the goodwill of the king, of its patron, Cardinal Wolsey, and of its chancellor, Archbishop Warham. This speedily silenced the opposition.

The humanists of the court also made positive contributions to classical education. More himself had been educated at Oxford. He learned Greek under Grocyn and Linacre, and, during his career at the bar and in politics, continued his studies in the classics. In 1516 he wrote in Latin his *Utopia*, which was the story of an imaginary commonwealth whose manners, laws, education, and other conditions might be a model for England. With the Utopians education was depicted as universal and covering a wide range of subjects, and when they heard of the Greek learning, they made haste to acquire this also. [sidenote: More and his *Utopia*.]

Elyot's *Governour*. — Sir Thomas Elyot (1490–1546) was another government official to write on the humanistic education. His father had been a member of the group about More, and while he himself had not been at either of the universities, he had grown up in the atmosphere of the classics and had the benefit of Linacre's instruction. Even during his activities in officialdom and diplomacy, he found time to indulge his love of classics and literary work. In middle life he retired entirely from public life, to devote himself to translation and educational writing, and published, among other humanistic works, *The Boke named the Governour*. This treatise described the education of boys for statesmanship, which he held to consist especially in a training in Greek and Latin literature, and maintained: "Grammar being but an introduction to the understanding of authors, if it be made too long or exquisite [*i.e.* elaborate] to the learner, it in a manner mortifieth his courage. And by that time he come to the most sweet and pleasant reading of old authors, the sparkes of fervent desire of learning is extinct with the burden of grammar."[1] [sidenote: The *Governour* of Sir Thomas Elyot held the classics to be the best training for statesmanship.]

[1] A good account of *The Governour* can be found in Woodward's *Education during the Renaissance*, Chapter XIII, 1.

166   A HISTORY OF EDUCATION

Vives, the Spanish humanist, was brought to England by Wolsey.

Educational Works of Vives. — Contemporaneously with Elyot, Wolsey brought to England the Spanish scholar, *Juan Luis Vives* (1492-1540), who had been a friend of Budæus and Erasmus. Vives had been given a humanistic education in Valencia, Paris, and Louvain, and had lectured upon classical subjects at the last-named place. In England he gave lectures upon the humanities at Oxford, wrote a manual upon the rudiments for Princess Mary, and dedicated his work upon Christian education to the queen. Both these and his chief treatise, *De Tradendis Disciplinis* ('On the Transmission of Learning'), which, with several other educational works, he wrote after leaving England, insist strongly upon religion and classics as the main content of education, although, more than any other Northern humanist, the proud Castilian finds an educational value in his native language.

The Scholemaster of Ascham recommends the teaching of Latin and Greek by 'double translation.'

Ascham's *Scholemaster* and the Teaching of Latin. — But the best known treatise on education written by any English humanist was *The Scholemaster* of Ascham, already mentioned.[1] This book was produced by request after a conversation in which Ascham had taken strong ground against the severity of school discipline then in vogue, and declared it unnecessary if the proper course of instruction were provided. As its name implies, the work deals purely with the formal education of the school. It is not altogether original, but is based largely upon the principles of the best classical writers on education, — Plato, Aristotle, Cicero, and Quintilian, and the works of the leading Northern humanists, such as Budæus, Erasmus, Sturm, and Elyot. The method of teaching and learning Latin and Greek is especially treated in *The Scholemaster*. As soon as the rudiments of Latin have been acquired, Ascham recommends that the student begin with his famous method of 'double translation.'[2] His plan is as follows : —

[1] See p. 164.
[2] There is some reason to believe that Ascham took this method from his old teacher, Cheke, who used it in tutoring Prince Edward.

THE HUMANISTIC EDUCATION OF THE NORTH 167

"The childe must take a paper booke, and sitting in some place, where no man shall prompe him, by him selfe, let him translate into Englishe his former lesson. Then shewing it to his master, let the master take from him his latin booke, and pausing an houre, at the least, than let the childe translate his own Englishe into latin againe, in an other paper booke. When the childe bringeth it, turned into latin, the master must compare it with Tullies booke, and laie them both togither."

In this way the pupil can be taught grammar in connection with his reading and much more pleasantly than by means of abstract rules. "For whan the Master shall compare *Tullies* booke with his Scholers translation, let the Master, at the first, lead and teach his Scholer, to joyne the Rewles of his Grammer booke, with the examples of his present lesson, untill the Scholer, by him selfe, be hable to fetch out of his Grammer, everie Rewle, for everie Example." Greek he advises to be taught in a similar way. By this method he declares that his royal pupil, Elizabeth, "hath atteyned to soch a perfite understanding in both the tonges [*i. e.* Latin and Greek] as they be fewe in nomber in both the universities or els where in England comparable with her maiestie." He then passes some severe criticisms upon the schools of the day for their inefficiency and want of economy. Their chief error consists in using translation only of the single sort and in hobbying constantly upon grammar. Their discipline, he feels, is naturally very harsh and brutal, when such dull methods are employed. With the appeal to interest that he has proposed, there will be no need of corporal punishment. In the second book, which is of little importance here, *The Scholemaster* treats of style, or "the ready way to the Latin tong."

John Colet and His School at St. Paul's. — The humanistic changes in English education and sentiment were not, however, limited to the universities, the court, or the theorists. Of far greater importance than the enriched curriculum of the universities or the broader ideals of the times was the effect of humanism upon the schools of England. The most important factor in bringing about the enlarged purpose and curriculum was the foundation of St. Paul's School in 1509[1] by *John Colet* (1466–1519). Colet had studied at Oxford under Grocyn and Linacre, and had Erasmus as his closest friend. He then spent three or four years in Italy, where he was especially attracted by Neoplatonism and Bible criticism. Upon returning to England, he lectured gratuitously at Oxford upon the Pauline Epistles from the standpoint of the author's social environment, and upon the Pseudo-Dionysius. He referred to humanistic rather than scholastic authorities, and his lectures attracted not only the students of the university, but many prominent churchmen from outside. In 1505, having been made Dean of St. Paul's Cathedral in London, he started in earnest upon a campaign of reform. With the aid of Grocyn and Erasmus, he opened lectures upon divinity, especially the Epistles of Paul, in which he strove to replace ecclesiastical traditions with a purer Testament. This naturally aroused the opposition of some of his conservative superiors. As Erasmus wrote to a friend: "The Dean had never stood right with the Bishop, who was a very rigid Scotist, and the more jealous of the Dean, because his lectures and sermons were chiefly employed in opening the sense of the Scriptures, which being in the new way of learning, was called *heresy*."

But persecution only made Colet the more determined in the cause of humanism, purer religion, and the advancement of humanity, and he decided to devote most of the fortune left him by his father to establish a humanistic school in St. Paul's Churchyard, dedicated to 'the child Jesus.' Our best description of this school also comes from his friend Erasmus, who tells us: —

"He added dwelling-houses for the two masters, and to them allotted ample salaries, that they might teach a certain number of boys free, and for the sake of charity. He divided the school into

[1] The date of the foundation of St. Paul's is variously placed between 1508 and 1512 by different authorities.

THE HUMANISTIC EDUCATION OF THE NORTH   169

four apartments. The first was for catechumens, or the children to be instructed in the principles of religion, where no child is to be admitted that cannot read and write; the second, for the lower boys, to be taught by the second master or usher; the third, for the upper forms, under the headmaster. . . . The fourth or last apartment is a little chapel for divine service. . . . They are not to admit all boys, of course, but to choose them in accordance with their parts and capacities. The wise and sagacious founder saw that the greatest hopes and happiness of the commonwealth were in the training up of children to good letters and true religion."

Apparently Colet would have liked to secure Erasmus as 'hygh Maister' of his school, and such an appointment would surely have met his requirement of "a man hoole in body, honest and vertuouse and lernyd in the good and clene laten litterature and also in greke." But *William Lily* (1466–1529), whom Colet had previously met at Oxford and now made headmaster, had been well trained in classics at Oxford, Paris, Rome, and Greece, and must have filled the office well. *John Ritwyse*, whom Erasmus selected for the school, while at Cambridge, was appointed 'surmaister' or usher. {William Lily became the first headmaster.}

As we might expect from Colet's personality and education, the character of the school was of the Northern humanistic type, and combined religious training with a study of the classics. Its prospective patrons were informed: "If youre chylde can rede & wryte laten and englyshe suffycyently, so that he be able to rede and write his own lessons, then he shal be admytted into the scole for a scholer." And for the pupils of the school Colet prescribed: —

"I wolde they were taught all way in goode litterature both laten and greke, and goode auctours suych as have the veray Romayne eliquence joyned withe wysdome, specially Cristyn auctours that wrote theyre wysdome with clene and chaste laten other in verse or in prose, for my entent is by thys scole specially to incresse knowlege and worshipping of god and oure lorde Criste Jesu and good Cristen lyff and maners in the Children. And for that entent I will the Chyldren lerne ffirst aboue all the Cathechyzon in englyshe, and after, the accidence that I made or some other yf eny be better to the purpose to induce children more spedely to laten spech. And thanne Institutum Christiani homines which that lernyd Erasmus made at my request and the boke called Copia[1] of the same Erasmus."

Lily's Grammar.

The textbook on 'accidence' to which Colet refers in the foregoing quotation as his own production, was sent with large additions by him to 'Maister Lilye' for corrections and improvements, and, after further revision by Erasmus, it became the basis of the celebrated *Lily's Grammar*. This work was not only in use at St. Paul's, but in various editions remained the standard textbook in England for three centuries.

The English secondary schools, taking St. Paul's as a model, were humanistic,

Humanism in the English Grammar Schools. — St. Paul's School thus played an important part in shaping not only English education, but the humanistic tendencies in the North. It trained a long list of brilliant scholars, literati, clergy, and statesmen, and was the immediate model for a host of other grammar schools. There were in existence at the time St. Paul's was founded some three hundred secondary schools of various types, and those which survived the general dissolution of ecclesiastical foundations by Henry VIII and Edward VI were remodeled on the new humanistic basis.[2] These schools had come down from the Middle Ages and had been established throughout the country in connection with the cathedrals, monasteries, colleges, collegiate churches, and gilds, or in some cases upon an independent foundation. Their chief purpose had been training young men for the priesthood, and their curriculum was usually of the mediæval monastic type. These soon felt the influence of the Renaissance and the example of St. Paul's School. New schools were also established in accordance with the humanistic ideals.

[1] I.e. *De Copia Verborum et Rerum*, a work on Latin composition which Erasmus had dedicated to St. Paul's. See p. 150.
[2] Leach (*English Grammar Schools at the Reformation*) has shown through the records of the Chantries Commission that it is a moderate estimate to place the number of 'grammar' schools before the Reformation at three hundred. Grammar schools were, therefore, an old institution in England, and did not begin with the Reformation, so that Edward VI may, by his Chantries Act of 1548, be more properly considered a 'spoiler of schools' than a founder.

THE HUMANISTIC EDUCATION OF THE NORTH 171

But the humanism of the schools in England, as in Italy and Germany, soon degenerated into the narrower and more formal sort. The purpose of humanistic education became not so much a real training in literature as a practical command of Latin as the means of culture in all ages. The Roman and Greek literatures were treated not so much as ends in themselves as storehouses of adequate and eloquent expression that was needed by all. The legal, medical, and clerical professions all required a ready acquaintance with Latin, and it was a necessity in travel and international communication. The educators of the times did not belittle the literary aspect, but felt that such an understanding of the authors would be limited to the intellectual genius, whereas Latin conversation, and an adaptation of classical terms and phrases to the communication of ideas, was perfectly feasible for all.

but the humanism soon became narrow and formal,

Accordingly, the training of the grammar schools in the later sixteenth and the seventeenth centuries became one of dictionaries, grammars, and phrase-books. The study of grammar and rhetoric completely displaced the mediæval dialectic, and, in the place of the former disputations, the pupils were exercised in writing Latin themes, verses, and orations in the style of different classical authors. A large range of writers was employed, so that standards for variety and accuracy might be afforded the students. Expressions and selections were culled from the authors, especially Cicero and Terence, and treasured in note-books. Books of *Colloquies*, such as those of Erasmus, Vives, and Corderius, were also used to give a training in Latin conversation and to purge away all tendencies toward mediæval barbarisms. The methods became, therefore, largely *memoriter* and passive, although some exercise of judgment and taste was required of the pupils in making the proper selections, and in analyzing paragraphs, sentences, phrases, and words.

Brinsley's Description of Formalism in the Grammar Schools. — The formalism into which the grammar

172   A HISTORY OF EDUCATION

as shown in Brinsley's Grammar Schoole.

schools of England had thus fallen in the seventeenth century is depicted in a work by *John Brinsley* (1587-1665) called *Ludus literarius: or the Grammar Schoole.* This book, in which "two schoolmasters discourse concerning their functions," was intended to accomplish a reform of the conditions. It indicates that when Latin was once begun, the vernacular, arithmetic, and other subjects were neglected, and the time was entirely devoted to the drill of inflecting, parsing, and construing a fixed set of texts and authors. The standard grammar of Lily was memorized by the pupils, and references to it glibly repeated, with little understanding of their meaning. A Latin theme had to be ground out each week, and all conversation was fashioned upon some phrase-book like the *Colloquies* of Corderius. The Greek in the course was small and exceedingly elementary. The school hours were long, and the discipline, very naturally, was severe and irrational.

Some modifications have been made, but the English grammar schools in principle remain the same to-day.

English Grammar and Public Schools To-day. — While, of course, reforms have since been made in all these directions, the organization and the humanistic character of the course and the organization of the English grammar school have been preserved in principle even to this day. Considerable enlargement and modification of the curriculum have been effected through the addition of mathematics, modern languages, and sciences, and a 'modern' course has been established by the side of the old one, but the classics are still the emphasized feature, and, to a large degree, the drill methods prevail. In the earliest grammar schools boys were admitted at seven or eight, and passed through eight classes, whereas the number of classes, or 'forms,' is now six, and the pupil enters at twelve, but if the 'preparatory school,' which is usually an integral part of the organization, is considered, the pupils enter and graduate at almost the same age now as in the sixteenth century.

It was, however, originally intended that the grammar schools should be open to rich and poor alike and that the endowment should be sufficient to obviate the need

THE HUMANISTIC EDUCATION OF THE NORTH 173

of fees, but, because of the great increase in expenses, necessary and unnecessary, there is little possibility now of any one in the lower classes attending a grammar school. Similarly, a distinction has come to be drawn between 'grammar' and 'public' schools, although it is not a very clear one. As a rule, a 'public' school has a more aristocratic patronage and greater wealth, but it would be difficult to decide just what schools should fall in this class. Nine great public schools were recognized by the royal commission headed by Lord Clarendon in 1864, — Winchester (founded in 1387), Eton (1441), St. Paul's (1509), Shrewsbury (1551), Westminster (1560), Rugby (1567), Harrow (1571), Merchant Taylors' (1575), and Charterhouse (1609). Other old schools, like Christ's Hospital (1553), and Dulwich (1619), are generally admitted, as are also some of the stronger foundations of Queen Victoria's reign, — Cheltenham (1841), Marlborough (1843), Rossall (1844), Wellington (1853), Haileybury (1862), and Clifton (1862). The Public School Year Book recognizes more than twenty other schools that may be ranked as 'public' schools, and many others claim this dignity that would not be so considered outside of the immediate locality.

The great 'public' schools.

The Grammar Schools of America. — It was after these 'grammar' schools of the mother country that the first secondary schools in America were modeled and named. In many instances the fathers of the American colonies, such as Roger Williams, William Penn, John Davenport, Theophilus Eaton, and Edward Hopkins, had been educated in the grammar schools of England, and naturally sought to transplant these institutions to their new home. The Boston Latin[1] School was founded as early as 1635, and other towns of Massachusetts — Charlestown, Ipswich, Salem, Dorchester, Newbury, Cambridge, and Roxbury — followed the example before the middle

The first secondary schools of the American colonies were modeled and named after the English grammar schools, but the hold of humanism was afterward more readily loosened.

---

[1] Of course 'grammar' is used in the sense of 'Latin grammar,' and the schools were known either as 'grammar' or 'Latin' schools. They were also sometimes called 'free' schools.

of the century. Similarly, the towns of Connecticut, Rhode Island, New York, and Pennsylvania, and the counties of Virginia and Maryland, had in many cases founded grammar schools before the close of the century. After the act of 1647 by the General Court of Massachusetts, whereby it was ordered that "where any towne shall increase to ye number of 100 families or householders, they shall set up a gramer schoole," these borrowed secondary institutions were generally made compulsory in the various communities through the colonial legislatures. The American grammar schools, like their prototypes, were secondary and sustained no real relation to the elementary schools. They were intended to prepare pupils for college, although often the college had not yet been established, and, like the colleges, their ideal was "the service of God in church and commonwealth," the chief form of which was the Christian ministry. Hence their course, which covered only seven years, consisted chiefly in reading the classics and the New Testament, and used among its texts the *Grammar* of Lily and the *Colloquies* of Corderius. The course, like that of the English grammar schools, was, however, not as barren as it appeared, since ethics, history, and other subjects were studied through the medium of the classic authors. Moreover, educational traditions were, of course, more flexible in the United States, and the hold of the narrower humanism upon secondary education was more readily loosened during the subsequent stages of the 'academy' and the 'high school.' Nevertheless, even in America formal classical training remained confused with liberal education, and, with little modification, lasted well into the nineteenth century.

The aim of humanistic education in the North was more social, moral, and religious, and less literary and æsthetic.

The Aim of Humanistic Education in the North. — After this extended survey of the Renaissance and humanistic education in the various European countries north of Italy, it can easily be seen that these movements took on rather a different color here from what they did in the peninsula that gave them birth. While the humanism of the North was narrower in not concerning itself so much with self-culture, personal development, and the opportunities of life in all directions, it had a wider vision through interesting itself in society as a whole and in endeavoring to advance morality and religion everywhere. It took less account of the literary and æsthetic aspects of education, but it sought to remove the abuses of Church and State by abolishing ignorance and superstition. If not as broad, it was at least deeper than the self-centered movement of the South. It was democratic and social in its trend, where the Italian Renaissance was more aristocratic and individual.

In consequence, most of the humanists of the North were also religious or social reformers, and in Germany, France, and England humanism passed over into the Reformation. Erasmus differed from Luther only in believing that education would eventually effect the desired changes. So Melanchthon is ranked as a reformer, but he was fully as much a humanist, while the great humanistic educator, Sturm, was in hearty sympathy with the Reformation. Lefèvre and others gave the first impulse to French Protestantism through their translation of the Bible. Colet endeavored to dethrone dogma and tradition through a better interpretation of St. Paul.

The Northern Educational Organization. — Hence the educational institutions of the North, such as the universities, *collèges*, Hieronymian schools, *Fürstenschulen*, *Gymnasien*, and grammar schools, became the seats of moral development. Until the time of the Jesuit institutions, the typical humanistic schools were usually supported by the Reformation cities and were under Reformation leaders, and the chief educational influence of the Reformation, as will be seen, appeared in the foundation of humanistic schools and universities under the cities and states. Thus the two movements were generally fused in the institutions of education. *The educational institutions of the North fused the Renaissance and the Reformation.*

The Course of Study. — As in Italy, the curriculum of these humanistic foundations consisted mostly in the mastery of Latin and Greek, but the renewal of Greek meant a key to the New Testament and the abolition of irrational tradition rather than the revelation of a new joy in living. The Italian Renaissance re-created the liberal education of Plato and Aristotle, Cicero and Quintilian, but the movement in its Northern spread found in the classics a means of religious reform, and later, a new interpretation of theology.

The Formalization of Humanistic Education. — With the rise of the Reformation, however, the humanistic movement in the North seems to have completed its mission. By the middle of the sixteenth century the spirit of criticism, investigation, and intellectual activity had begun to abate, and by the opening of the seventeenth century, humanistic education in the North, as in Italy, had become almost as formal as education in mediæval times, except that literary and linguistic subjects had replaced dialectic and theology. In the study of the classics, all emphasis was placed upon grammar, linguistics, and style. Form was preferred to content, and methods became *memoriter* and imitative, with the inevitable accompaniment of brutal discipline. Thus in Italy and the North, the attempts of the Renaissance to break up uniformity of life and thought, to overthrow authority and repression in Church and State, and to allow some latitude of expression to the individual, had hardened into a new type of formalism, and a new awakening was needed to revivify education and society in general.

SUPPLEMENTARY READING

I. Sources

ALLEN, P. S. *The Letters of Rudolph Agricola.*
ASCHAM, R. *The Scholemaster* (Arbor Reprint).
BRINSLEY, J. *Ludus Literarius: or the Grammar Schoole.*
BUDÉ, G. *De l'Institution du Prince.*
CHALONER, T. (Editor). *Moriae Laudatio of Erasmus.*
ELYOT, T. *The Boke named the Governour.*
FREUNDGEN, J. (Editor). *Wimphelings Pädagogischer Schriften.*

THE HUMANISTIC EDUCATION OF THE NORTH 177

HOOLE, C. (Editor). *The School Colloquies of Corderius.*
MELANCHTHON, P. *De Corrigendis Studiis.*
MONROE, P. *Thomas Platter* (contains Platter's *Autobiography*).
NICHOLS, F. M. *The Epistles of Erasmus.*
NORTON, A. O. *Readings in the History of Education.* Chapters on the Renaissance.
PATER, W. *The Praise of Folly, Colloquies, and Educational Writings of Erasmus.*
SCOTT, I. *A Translation of Erasmus' Ciceronianus* (with Introduction by P. Monroe).
STURM, J. *De Literarum Ludis Recte Aperiendis Liber.*
TAVERNER, R. *Proverbes or Adagies of Erasmus.*
VIVES, J. L. *De Disciplinis Libri XX.*
WHITCOMB, M. *Select Colloquies of Erasmus.*
WHITCOMB, M. *Source Book of the German Renaissance.*
WOODWARD, W. H. *Erasmus concerning Education* (contains the treatises, *De Ratione* and *De Pueris*).

II. AUTHORITIES

ACTON, LORD. *The Cambridge Modern History.* Vol. I, Chaps. XIII, XVI, and XVII, and Vol. II, Chap. XIX.
ADAMS, G. B. *Civilization during the Middle Ages.* Chap. XV.
BARNARD, H. *English Pedagogy.* First Series, pp. 21-76, and Second Series, pp. 1-176, and 401-405.
BARNARD, H. *German Teachers and Educators.* II-V.
BARNARD, H. *The American Journal of Education.* Vol. IV, No. X, §§ VIII and IX; No. XI, § VII; and No. XII, § XI.
BRODRICK, G. C. *A History of the University of Oxford.* Chap. VII.
BROWN, E. E. *The Making of Our Middle Schools.* Chaps. II-VII.
DRUMMOND, R. B. *Erasmus, his Life and Character.*
EGGLESTON, E. *The Transit of Civilization from England to America in the Seventeenth Century.*
EINSTEIN, L. *The Italian Renaissance in England.* Chap. I.
EMERTON, E. *Desiderius Erasmus of Rotterdam.*
FROUDE, J. A. *Life and Letters of Erasmus.*
JEBB, R. *Erasmus.*
JOHNSON, J. N. *The Life of Thomas Linacre.*
KNIGHT, S. *The Life of Dr. John Colet.*
KÜCKELHAHN, L. *Johannes Sturm, Strassburgs Erster Schulrector.*
LAURIE, S. S. *Educational Opinion from the Renaissance.* Chaps. III-V and VII.
LEACH, A. F. *English Schools at the Reformation.*
LUPTON, J. H. *Life of John Colet, D.D.*
LYTE, H. C. M. *History of the University of Oxford.* Chaps. XII-XVI.
MONROE, P. *Thomas Platter.* Pp. 39-75.
MULLINGER, J. B. *The University of Cambridge.* Chap. IV.

NOHLE, F. *History of the German School System.* (Report of U. S. Commissioner of Education, 1897-98, Vol. I, pp. 26-44.)
PAULSEN, F. *The German Universities* (translated by Thilly and Elwang). Chap. II, § I.
PUTNAM, G. H. *Books and their Makers.* Vol. I, pp. 317-347.
QUICK, R. H. *Educational Reformers.* Chaps. III and VII.
RICHARD, J. W. *Philip Melanchthon.* Pp. 125-141.
RUSSELL, J. E. *German Higher Schools.* Chaps. II-IV.
SANDYS, J. E. *Harvard Lectures on the Revival of Learning.*
SANDYS, J. E. *History of Classical Scholarship.* Vol. II, Chaps. VIII and X.
SEEBOHM, F. *The Oxford Reformers, John Colet, Erasmus, and Thomas More.*
STAUNTON, H. *The Great Schools of England.*
WATSON, F. *Maturinus Corderius.* (*The School Review*, Vol. XII, Nos. 4, 7, and 9.)
WATSON, F. *Notices of Some Early English Writers on Education.* (Report of U. S. Commissioner of Education, 1902, Vol. I, pp. 481-509.)
WATSON, F. *The English Grammar Schools to 1660.*
WOODWARD, W. H. *Erasmus concerning Education.*
WOODWARD, W. H. *Education during the Renaissance.* Chaps. V-VIII, X-XI, and XIII.

CHAPTER XV

EDUCATIONAL INFLUENCES OF THE PROTESTANTS

General Causes of the Reformation. — The revolt of the Protestants from the Catholic Church, a movement generally known as the 'Reformation,'[1] may be regarded largely as an outgrowth of the Renaissance. It began to appear as the humanism of the North reached its height in the early part of the sixteenth century. The opposition to repressive authority that was characteristic of the age was felt in the case of ecclesiastical, as of cultural, educational, and social matters, but the Church stubbornly resisted the efforts toward reformation and emancipation in doctrine and ritual. The transformation was, therefore, not effected gradually and quietly, but came to pass through force. The immense wealth, large numbers, and trained intellects of the supporters of the ecclesiastical institutions made it possible for a long time to thwart the spirit of the age, and the result was revolution rather than evolution.

For several centuries there had been those within the Church who had earnestly striven to purify it of various abuses, and when peaceful measures had failed, serious rebellions had, upon some occasions, ensued. In the thirteenth century there occurred the uprisings of the Albigenses and Waldenses, which were in the one case crushed by the tortures of the Inquisition, and in the other kept in isolation until the Waldenses had merged with the later reformers.[2]

There had been previous attempts to revolt from the Church, as in the case of the Albigenses and Waldenses,

---

[1] This description is somewhat unfair. The endeavor to purify the Church existed before the time of any separation, and such men as Wimpfeling, Erasmus, and Montaigne were as true reformers as Luther, Zwingli, and Calvin, although bitterly opposed to any division in Catholic Christianity.

[2] These early heretics of southern France differed somewhat in position. The Waldenses, or followers of Peter *Waldo* of Lyons, imitated the simple life of Christ and the early Christians, but refused to accept the doctrines

A century and a half afterward, reaction to the extravagance, corruption, and nepotism of the papal court, especially while at Avignon (1305-1377), had brought sympathy and substance to the revolt of John Wyclif (1320-1384). But while this leader had been protected from the wrath of the Church by a division of political parties in England, and died peaceably, great efforts had been made to exterminate his followers, the 'Lollards.' However, through the marriage of Richard II to Anne of Bohemia, the Bohemian students had become generally acquainted with the works of Wyclif, and the reform movement had been spread throughout that country by Johann Huss (1369-1415) and others. While Huss had been burned as a heretic, and his followers held in check by persecution, the Hussite feeling had never altogether died out. Similarly, the Councils of Pisa (1409) and Constance (1414), which were held to decide who really was pope and to bring about a general reformation 'in head and members,' were, while peaceful, an organized opposition to supreme authority and traditional abuses.

of Wyclif and Huss, and of the Councils of Pisa and Constance,

None of these attempts achieved anything permanent, but during the sixteenth century, as the result of the social and intellectual conditions of the times, there arose a series of revolts against the papal authority that resulted in the establishment of a church or set of churches outside of Catholic Christianity. While each revolt had some peculiarities of its own, there were underlying them all certain general causes that indicated their connection with the Renaissance. It has been seen in the foregoing chapter how the humanistic revival, with its tendencies toward individualism, had, in the more pious countries of the North, taken on a moral and religious aspect, and had resulted in efforts to secure a more accurate translation of the Scriptures, without regard to the traditions

but nothing permanent resulted.

Owing, however, to the humanistic revival of the North and other conditions, there arose in

and practices of the Church, and would not obey the sinful clergy. The Albigenses, on the other hand, completely rejected Christianity, and held that the Old Testament Jehovah, whom the Church worshiped, was the evil power of the universe. These latter were named from *Albi*, a town in the south of France, where their influence was centered. See p. 72.

and dogmas of the Church. At the same time that ecclesiastical pomp and ceremony had come to such a height, there was present in the sixteenth century an evident tendency to consider theology unnecessarily complicated and to react toward a simpler faith. Many were seeking to read the Bible for themselves and to stress repentance rather than the outward forms of religion. This had led to a freedom of discussion and a criticism of the conduct of monks, priests, and theologians, and of other abuses in the Church. Moreover, outside of Italy, the national sentiment that had arisen produced a feeling against the secular powers exercised in each country by the pope.

the sixteenth century a series of revolts that established churches outside of Catholic Christianity.

Causes of Luther's Revolt. — Such were the sentiments and conditions of the times that will explain the success of the reformers in general. Their main support grew out of the spirit of the day. But to understand the Reformation and its effect upon education, it will be necessary to study briefly the situation and the character of the leader in each revolt. The acts of *Martin Luther* (1483–1546), the earliest and most prominent reformer, first engage our attention. Luther's attitude did not grow primarily out of the Renaissance, but was rather the result of his spiritual struggles. Anxiety for his soul's welfare drove him at twenty-two to enter an Augustinian monastery near the humanistic University of Erfurt, where he had been studying. Here, despite all fasting, vigils, and penance, he found himself harassed by doubts concerning his salvation, until at last he decided to rely upon the Divine mercy toward those who truly repent rather than upon mere outward 'good works.'[1] But there was an intellectual, as well as a moral, side to Luther's nature, so that he was not satisfied until, on the basis of Augustine's writings, he worked out his 'justification by faith' into a logical and systematic theory. This doctrine he defended and taught tenaciously, especially after he was

Luther, harassed by spiritual struggles, formulated his 'justification by faith.'

---

[1] To the extent that the Protestant Reformation made an immediate knowledge of God possible for each individual soul, the movement may be regarded as an outgrowth of mysticism. See p. 47.

transferred to a theological professorship at the University of Wittenberg. He attacked Aristotle and the schoolmen with great vigor, appealing to primitive Christianity and the right of free thought, and in this way his movement becomes identified in spirit with the Renaissance.

He challenged Tetzel to a debate on the value of 'indulgences.'

In 1517, when a Dominican friar named Tetzel came to Wittenberg to sell 'indulgences' and made claims that seemed to emphasize outward forms and contravene 'justification by faith,'[1] Luther felt logically bound to challenge him to a debate, and nailed ninety-five theses concerning the value of indulgences to the church door at Wittenberg. This was a common university custom, and apparently he had no idea of breaking from the Church. He hardly supposed that his disputation, which was written in Latin and was in scholastic form, would be read by any save scholars.[2] Yet within a fortnight all Germany, and at the end of a month all Christendom, were acquainted with his declarations and probably recognized their significance more clearly than he.

After his contest with Eck, realizing that he was in conflict with the Church, and feeling the humanistic and individualistic tendencies of the times, he attacked the

However, after his contest with Dr. Eck, two years later, in which he was led to deny the authority of both pope and council to determine the belief of the individual, Luther must have realized that he was in open conflict with the whole organization of the Church. But being of an obstinate temperament, and feeling that he was supported by the humanistic and individualistic tendencies of the times, he gradually grew more overt, and attacked the church doctrines and the papacy in popular pamphlets. In 1520 he was excommunicated by the pope, but burnt the 'bull,' and the following

---

[1] It is a popular belief among Protestants that an 'indulgence' is a forgiveness of sin before its commission, or even a license to commit it, but this has no foundation, and did not constitute Luther's objection to the doctrine. He felt that it stressed penance rather than penitence, and was, therefore, superfluous. For Tetzel's *Sermon on Indulgences*, see Robinson and Whitcomb, *Early Reformation in Germany*, pp. 9-11.

[2] A translation of these theses will be found in any good source book covering the Reformation. See Robinson's *Readings*, Vol. II, pp. 58-62, or Robinson and Whitcomb, *Early Reformation in Germany*, pp. 11-19.

EDUCATIONAL INFLUENCES OF THE PROTESTANTS 183

year he was summoned by the emperor, Charles V, to appear before the Diet at Worms and answer for his heresies. At the trial he was simply asked whether certain writings were his, and was not allowed to defend his conclusions, and when he refused to retract unless he were refuted by the Scriptures, the diet declared him an outlaw.

Educational Features of Luther's Religious Works. — Since the thirteenth century it had been well understood that both the emperor and the decrees of the imperial diet had but little power, but since no one knew just how effective an edict like that of Worms might prove,[1] Luther was spirited away by his friends to a castle called 'the Wartburg.' The nine months spent in hiding gave him an opportunity, long desired, to awaken the minds and hearts of the common people by a translation of the Greek Testament into colloquial language. A dozen years later, in 1534, he had completed a translation of the entire Bible, and afterward revised it twice. There had been many vernacular translations before, but this was the first in modern High German, and it fixed a definite standard for the language. Its educational effect in getting the masses to read and reflect must have been very great. For the further instruction of the people, whom he found exceedingly ignorant, he produced, in 1529, two catechisms, one for adults and the other for children. And everywhere through the volumes of addresses, sermons, and letters that he has left are found allusions to the organization of education and sound pedagogical advice.

Luther's Chief Educational Works. — Many of the efforts of Luther in behalf of education, then, were evidently incidental to his religious and theological development. But he also made very early more direct

Side notes: papacy, and was condemned at the Diet of Worms.

While in hiding at the Wartburg, Luther translated the New Testament, and later the entire Bible, to get it before the masses. He also wrote two catechisms for the instruction of the people.

To improve education, he issued his *Letter to Mayors and Aldermen* and wrote his famous *Sermon*.

---

[1] The Diet of Worms was followed by a series of diets that attempted to enforce its findings. Little, however, could be done until the emperor returned from his foreign wars. Even then he was obliged, because of the interference of France and dissensions within his own ranks, to consent, in 1555, to the Peace of Augsburg, whereby each German state was allowed to choose between the Lutheran and Catholic confessions.

efforts to better the education of the times, which he could easily see was sadly deficient in organization, curriculum, methods, and discipline. Owing to the excesses of some of the other reformers and his various allies, and his own opposition to their acts,[1] he was obliged to depend more and more upon the secular powers and the civil government for assistance, and in 1524 he issued his *Letter to the Mayors and Aldermen of All Cities of Germany in behalf of Christian Schools*. This was followed half a dozen years later by his longest educational writing, the *Sermon on the Duty of Sending Children to School*. The school systems had been so closely connected with the Church that it seemed during the first few years of the German revolt as if all higher training would be destroyed, especially as some of the extremists among the reformers held that education was unnecessary for right faith.[1] But Luther insisted upon secondary, as well as elementary, training, and believed that this was not possible without the languages. Hence he adopted the humanistic education, and we find him working on school problems side by side with Melanchthon, the great representative of that tendency.

The Civic Aim of Education. — The purpose of education Luther everywhere holds to involve the promotion of the State's welfare quite as much as that of the Church. The schools were to make good citizens as well as religious men. In his *Letter* he claims: —

He held that education should prepare for citizenship,

"The highest welfare, safety, and power of a city consist in able, learned, wise, upright, and cultivated citizens, who can secure, pre-

[1] Luther was, of course, a revolutionary, and there was a tendency for all other discontented elements in the state, stirred by his success, to hasten to his standard, regardless of the nature of their own grievances. Such were *Carlstadt*, who believed in breaking up all the monasteries, and abandoning scholarship; the mystic *Anabaptists*, who taught that learning was as naught, and only through direct communication with God could anything be accomplished; the *knights*, like von Sickingen and von Hutten, who were jealous of the princes and prelates; and the *peasants*, who were impelled by oppression to indulge in anarchistic orgies. Luther was in great danger of being identified with anarchy and violence in general, and had to repudiate and vehemently oppose these allies, and depend wholly upon the princes for support.

serve, and utilize every treasure and advantage. . . . Though there were no soul, nor heaven, nor hell, but only the civil government, would not this require good schools and learned men more than do our spiritual interests? . . . For the establishment of the best schools everywhere, both for boys and girls, it is a sufficient consideration that society, for the maintenance of civil order and the proper regulation of the household, needs accomplished and well-trained men and women."

The Organization of Education by the State. — Educational institutions, he believes, should, on that account, be maintained at public expense for every one — rich and poor, high and low, boys and girls alike. Parents are, however, frequently too selfish, ignorant, or busy to look out for the schooling of their children, and "it will, therefore, be the duty of the mayors and councils to exercise the greatest care over the young." In his *Sermon* he even goes so far as to maintain: — [sidenote: and should be state-supported and compulsory.]

> "The civil authorities are under obligation to compel the people to send their children to school. . . . If the government can compel such citizens as are fit for military service to bear spear and rifle, to mount ramparts, and perform other martial duties in time of war; how much more has it a right to compel the people to send their children to school!"

This is the first hint since the Roman days of a system of education supported and controlled by the State, which before very long was destined to become general in Germany and then throughout the world.[1]

Industrial and Academic Training. — The most important innovation of Luther, however, was his desire to introduce schools in which the common people could be fitted for their occupations in life. He likewise wished to correlate the school more closely with the home. "My idea," he says on this matter, "is that boys should spend an hour or two a day in school, and the rest of [sidenote: He advocated education for occupation, and higher work for the brighter pupils.]

---

[1] This suggestion becomes an actuality in the organization of the schools of Saxony in 1528 by Luther's colleague, Melanchthon, at the request of the elector, Johann. See pp. 157 and 187. That was, of course, much more thoroughly a state system than the subsidization and partial control of the Roman schools by the emperor and was the forerunner of all state management. See Graves, *History of Education before the Middle Ages*, pp. 265-267.

the time work at home, learn some trade and do whatever is desired, so that study and work may go on together." But he does not limit education to an industrial training. He also plans a more academic course for "the brightest pupils, who give promise of becoming accomplished teachers, preachers, and workers."

Religious, Humanistic, and Other Content of Education.
— The chief study in the school, Luther very naturally holds, should be the Bible. "Where the Holy Scriptures are not the rule," he says, "I should advise no one to send his child." And again he declares: "The soul can do without everything except the Word of God." Next to the Scriptures he held the catechism to be necessary.[1] But the great reformer was also a humanist, and, like the other humanists of the North, recommends the ancient languages — Latin, Greek, and Hebrew — for the light they would throw upon the Scriptures and the patristic writers. He likewise approves of rhetoric and dialectic, which were very valuable subjects in those days of controversy, and he makes a decided advance in advocating history, natural science, vocal and instrumental music, and gymnastic exercises. History is advised, not only, as was common with the humanists, for the sake of illustrating moral truth, but also for the purpose of understanding social institutions. The study of nature had a bearing upon religion, and was intended to reveal "the wonders of Divine goodness and the omnipotence of God." He considered gymnastics of value both for the body and the soul, and music a means of "driving away all care and melancholy from the heart."

The Bible, catechism, ancient languages, rhetoric, dialectic, history, science, music, and gymnastics as the content of education.

Rationality in Method and Competency in Schoolmasters.
— The methods that Luther proposed were a decided advance upon those of the narrower humanism. They were to be less mechanical and *memoriter*, and to appeal more to interest and rationality. He would utilize the natural activity of children and not attempt to repress them, and

The natural activity of children was recognized, and concrete examples used; languages were taught by speaking.

[1] Hence the translation of the Bible and the preparation of catechisms may well be regarded as part of his educational work.

would make use of concrete examples, wherever possible. Languages he would teach less by grammar than by practice, since, "while printed words are dead, spoken words are living; on the printed page they are not so forcible as when uttered by the soul of man through the mouth." And it is his recognition of the need of proper method that leads him to comment upon the importance of the teacher's function as follows: —

"An industrious, pious schoolmaster or teacher, who faithfully trains and educates boys, can never be sufficiently recompensed. . . . Next to the ministry, it is the most useful, greatest, and best calling; and I am not sure which of the two is to be preferred. For it is hard to make old dogs docile and old rogues pious, yet that is what the ministry works at; but young trees, though some may break in pieces, are more easily bent and trained."

The Embodiment of Luther's Ideas in Schools by His Friends, Melanchthon and Sturm. — The organization, content, and method advocated by Luther in his *Letter*, *Sermon*, and other writings, were worked out in actual institutions by his friends and associates, especially Melanchthon. The year after the *Letter* was published, the Protestants were requested by the Count of Mansfeld to establish in Luther's native town of Eisleben an elementary and secondary school, which should put his educational theories into practice. This institution, as has been stated in the preceding chapter,[1] was established through *Philip Melanchthon* (1479–1560), and became a prototype of the *Gymnasien*. We have also noted how three years later, in 1528, Melanchthon was likewise engaged by Luther's protector, Johann, Elector of Saxony, to reorganize the schools of that state, and the plan he formulated was, after modifications, adopted in many other places. An account of the work of the humanist and reformer, *Johann Sturm* (1507–1589) at Strasburg, which, although on the basis of the decadent humanism, influenced all Europe, has likewise been given.[2]

Bugenhagen. — Many other institutions and school

<small>Luther's principles were institutionalized by Melanchthon and Sturm,</small>

[1] See p. 157.　　　[2] See pp. 158–161.

188   A HISTORY OF EDUCATION

by Bugenhagen in his orders to the cities and states of northern Germany,

systems, which have not been mentioned, were organized by the colleagues of Luther and Melanchthon. A noted humanist named *Johann Bugenhagen* (1485-1558) was in 1520 attracted by Luther to Wittenberg, and three years later became professor of theology there. He had previously taught in classical institutions, and from now on he was engaged in reorganizing the churches in the cities and states of northern Germany. In all these places, by his general 'church order' to each, he made ample provision for schools. Through his order for Hamburg in 1520, for instance, he organized a single Latin school with a rector and seven teachers, together with a German school for boys and one for girls in every parish. The curriculum of the Latin school, which taught Latin, Greek, Hebrew, dialectic, rhetoric, mathematics, catechism, and singing, would seem to have been taken directly from the Lutheran pattern. Eight years afterward the church order of Brunswick provided two classical schools, two vernacular schools for the boys, and four for the girls, so located in the city that all children could conveniently reach a school. Within half a dozen years, similar requirements were made in Lübeck, Minden, Göttingen, Soest, Bremen, Osnabrück, and other cities, and throughout some entire states of Germany, such as Holstein and Bugenhagen's native duchy of Pomerania;[1] and in 1537 the system of Hamburg was introduced into Denmark.

by Trotzendorf's monitorial school in Silesia,

Trotzendorf. — Another collaborator of Luther's, *Valentin Trotzendorf*[2] (1490-1556), made some very striking improvements in his school at Goldberg, Silesia. He reorganized this school in 1531 on the basis of the ideas of his teacher, Melanchthon, and during the quarter of a century that he was rector, it became very famous as a humanistic and religious institution. The aim and course of study were practically those of the reformers, but,

---

[1] From this duchy, Bugenhagen is sometimes called *Pomeranus* or *Dr. Pommer.*

[2] His real name was *Friedland,* but he was born in the village of Trotzendorf.

EDUCATIONAL INFLUENCES OF THE PROTESTANTS

in addition, he instituted a system of student government, after the plan of a Roman republic, which elected its own officers. As an outgrowth of this organization, he resorted to a species of monitorial method in teaching. The students in the higher classes instructed the younger pupils, and were thus given a training to become regular teachers.

Neander. — *Michael Neander*[1] (1525–1595), another pupil of Melanchthon, likewise conducted a successful Latin school after the plan of the reformers. He had already obtained some experience in a Latin school, when, upon the recommendation of Melanchthon, he was at twenty-five made rector of the cloistral school at Ilfeld in the Harz. Neander found his life work in building up this institution. He formulated a course of study running from the sixth to the eighteenth year of the pupil, and by the nature of this curriculum, he showed himself more liberal and daring than any other Northern schoolmaster. He even ventured, at the height of humanism, to question why Greek and Latin should be taught at all, and showed his true humanistic spirit by adding history, geography, science, and music to the course, and by reforming the methods of teaching grammar, rhetoric, and dialectic. He was forced to make texts for his own needs, and although he never had any assistant, he found time to publish thirty-nine books and prepare the manuscripts for some fourteen more. This school was considered by Melanchthon the best in the country, and its pupils from the beginning occupied most important positions in Church and State. Those who entered the university took precedence of all who were prepared elsewhere.

and by Neander's broad humanistic school at Ilfeld.

Causes of Zwingli's Revolt. — About the same time that Luther's breach with the Church was coming to a crisis, another successful, though less eventful, revolt was beginning in northern and central Switzerland under the leadership of *Ulrich*[2] *Zwingli* (1484–1531). His

---

[1] *Neander* is the Hellenized form of *Neumann*, which was his name originally.
[2] Perhaps more properly written *Huldreich*.

reforms were more directly the result of Northern humanism than of any such serious personal and spiritual struggles as those of Luther. Zwingli was born in a wealthy family, and had been able to obtain the most complete education that the times afforded. He learned from Erasmus and others that there was little basis in the Bible for the traditional theology, and became himself a deep student of essential Christianity as depicted in the New Testament. He read the accounts carefully in the original Greek, even committing the Epistles of Paul to memory, and began the study of Hebrew to get at the meaning of the Old Testament. After about a dozen years in the priesthood, he was chosen preacher for the Cathedral at Zürich, and in 1519 began his attack upon the dogmas and abuses of the Church. He denounced the sale of indulgences, and had a friar who was selling them driven out of Zürich. As many of the towns of Switzerland, including Zürich, were, by an old agreement, allowed to administer their own religious affairs, Zwingli was able, by securing the support of the town, to bring about a fairly peaceful revolution. He gradually dropped one tradition or form of the Church after another, until, within five years, he had abolished even the celebration of the mass. In the matter of the eucharist he went much farther than Luther and held that the ordinance was simply a commemoration of Christ's atoning death. Luther, in consequence, refused Christian fellowship to Zwingli, but since many adopted the latter's position, another complication was introduced among the reformers.

Zwingli's Educational Foundations and Treatise. — Zwingli made the extension of educational facilities a part of his reform. He founded a number of humanistic institutions, and introduced elementary schools into Switzerland. In 1523 he published in Latin his *Brief Treatise on the Christian Education of Youth*, which he translated into the Swiss dialect the following year.[1]

[1] The Latin title was *Praeceptiones pauculae, quo pacto ingenui adolescentes formandi sunt,* but as translated in the Swiss German it read

EDUCATIONAL INFLUENCES OF THE PROTESTANTS 191

In the plan outlined by this work, Zwingli arranged a systematic course on the Bible so that the material of the Gospels and Epistles was gradually developed. The classics and Hebrew were likewise advocated to bring out the true meaning of the Word. Similarly, he advised the study of Nature, as revealing the handiwork of the Almighty, and inculcating reverence and love. From the practical turn of his temperament, which he had in common with most reformers, he was led to recommend arithmetic, surveying, and music, and to propose almost a Greek palæstral course in running, jumping, putting the shot, and even wrestling.

The reforms of Zürich soon spread to the other towns, but were vigorously resisted with arms by the Catholic cantons, and, during the conflict that followed, Zwingli was slain at the battle of Kappel in the prime of life. His position was maintained by his successor in the cathedral, but his work was overshadowed and merged during the second generation of reformers in the more aggressive movement of Calvin. *[Zwingli was slain in battle, and his movement was merged in that of Calvin.]*

Causes of Calvin's Revolt.—*Jean Calvin*[1] (1509–1564) was among the French Protestants who were forced to flee from the persecutions of the king, Francis I, in 1535. Protestantism in France had begun through the influence of Northern humanism and the study of the Greek Testament. As a result of the keener insight thus obtained, many of the traditional forms were rejected, and a doctrine akin to the 'justification by faith' was preached there even before the time of Luther. But the revolt which started at Wittenberg must also have had some effect upon Calvin. That reformer had received an excellent legal and theological education, and had naturally a logical and judicial mind of great strength. Consequently, he did not content himself *[Calvin's revolt grew out of the study of the Greek Testament. He was the first Protestant to undertake a positive system of theology.]*

Leerbichlein (i.e. *Lehrbüchlein*) *wie man die Knaben christlich unterweysen und erziehen soll.* See Schmid, *Geschichte der Erziehung,* Vol. X, pp. 695 ff.

[1] *Calvin* is abbreviated from the Latinized form (*Calvinus*) of the original French, *Cauvin*.

with merely attacking Catholic doctrine, but was the first Protestant to undertake a positive system of theology, formulating among other doctrines that of 'predestination.' He based his position upon the infallibility of the Bible, rather than that of the pope and the Church.

At Geneva he worked out his theology, and established colleges, to the management of one of which he called Corderius.

Calvin's Encouragement of Education, and the Work of Corderius. — The call of Calvin from Basel, where he had first settled after leaving France, to reorganize the civil and religious administration of the city of Geneva, gave him an excellent opportunity for working out his doctrines. While he was much engrossed in religious disputes, he established *collèges* at Geneva and elsewhere, and in other ways undertook to found schools and promote education. He succeeded, too, in persuading his former teacher, *Maturinus Corderius* (1479–1564),[1] to come to Switzerland, and organize, administer, and teach in the reformed *collèges*. From 1546 to 1559 Corderius managed the institution at Lausanne, and for the last five years of his life, although past eighty, he taught in the *Collège de la Rive* in Geneva under the headmastership of another. From his two chief works, *De Emendatione* and *Colloquia*,[1] we learn the character of the course he favored and obtain a vivid account of the life and methods of the schoolmaster and pupils in his day. Clearly the ideal for education with Corderius was the *pietas literata* ('learned piety') of Melanchthon, Sturm, and the other Northern humanists. In the *De Emendatione*, after stating his purpose of developing a good French and Latin style in the pupils, he expresses the desire "that youths not only may be stirred to speaking Latin, but also stimulated to the leading of a noble life. For we have interspersed in the whole of this little work, as the opportunity offered, a number of exhortations to live a pious and Christian life." A similar attempt at moral and religious training, while teaching Latin, is made in the conversations upon everyday topics in the *Colloquia*. From this work, too, we may infer that in

The theory of Corderius, as shown in his De Emendatione and Colloquia.

---

[1] See pp. 143 f.

the Calvinist schools psalms were sung every day, public prayers were offered, selections from the Bible repeated, questions asked concerning the sermon, and other religious exercises urged upon the pupils.

The Collège at Geneva. — That humanistic and religious subjects made up the usual curriculum of the Calvinist *collèges*, we can easily perceive from the course of the *Collège de la Rive* at Geneva, which has been preserved to us in the 'constitution' of 1559.[1] In the seven classes of this school the pupils first learned their letters and how to form syllables, then they were taught reading and grammar from the French-Latin catechism, and finally they studied Vergil, Cicero, Ovid, Cæsar, Livy, and Latin composition. Greek was begun in the fourth year, and, beside such classical authors as Isocrates, Xenophon, Polybius, Homer, and Demosthenes, and the translation of Latin into Greek, they read the Gospels and Epistles in the original. In the higher classes, as in the other Reformation schools, they studied logic from such a text as Melanchthon's, rhetoric from the speeches of Cicero and Demosthenes, and elocution by the delivery of two original orations each month.

The Collège de la Rive, its seven classes, and the humanistic and religious subjects taught in each.

Spread of the Calvinist Education. — *Collèges* of the Calvinist type rapidly spread among the Huguenots of France, who by this means soon became far better educated than the rest of their countrymen. Also as Geneva became, about the time of Calvin, a city of refuge for all the oppressed, Protestants from many countries imbibed the religious and educational ideas of Calvin, and brought them back to their native lands. Thus Calvinism and a regard for a humanistic, religious, and universal education were carried not only through Switzerland, France, and Germany, but were taken up by the persecuted Netherlanders, the English Protestants of Mary's time, and the Scotch in the days of Mary, Queen of Scots, and, being also adopted by the English Puritans, found their way into America.

French, German, Dutch, English, and Scotch Protestants, fleeing to Geneva, bring back Calvinistic education with them.

---

[1] See Woodward's *Education during the Renaissance*, pp. 158 ff.

o

194 A HISTORY OF EDUCATION

Through John Knox free elementary schools were established in Scotland under parish control.

Knox and the Elementary Schools of Scotland. — But of all the men influenced by Calvin, probably his contemporary, *John Knox* (1505-1572), who headed the religious revolt in Scotland, was the most forceful, and did the most important work for education. It was largely through him that the first free elementary schools were established in Scotland under the control of the parishes, and education was freed from its bondage to feudalism, ecclesiasticism, and royalty. These schools were to give instruction in reading, writing, and religion, with the Bible as text, and they have done a wonderful work in raising the level of intelligence and morality in Scotland.[1] Through them, since they have not always stopped with elementary education,[2] the sons of even Scotch laborers and peasants have been able to rise to positions of the greatest dignity.

Henry VIII induced Parliament to make him head of the Church, and authorize him to receive the ecclesiastical payments.

Causes of Henry VIII's Revolt. — England also tended to break from the doctrines of the Church. This was somewhat the result of humanism, and possibly of the doctrines of Luther,[3] which had later spread into England, but the immediate cause of the breach was the attack made upon the Church by the king and government. Henry VIII (reigned 1509-1547), wanting a male heir, and being tired of his wife, attempted to secure a divorce through the pope. When the pope forbade his doing this, Henry took advantage of the independent political spirit of England and persuaded the country that the pope was interfering with their internal affairs. In 1533 the king induced Parliament to forbid all legal appeals to any authority outside the country, and then had his marriage set aside by the

---

[1] In the matter of free elementary education, Scotland preceded England by more than two centuries. In England, until 1870, education was furnished almost entirely through endowed 'grammar' or 'public' schools, private schools, or institutions maintained by religious or philanthropic societies.

[2] See pp. 199 f.

[3] It is not unlikely that Lollardism also furnished a congenial soil for individuality in interpreting the Scriptures. While the Lollards as an organized sect no longer existed, the spirit of Wyclif was still abroad in the land.

subservient court of Archbishop Cranmer. He further had himself recognized as head of the national church, and was given the right by Parliament to appoint all bishops and to receive the payments that were formerly made by English ecclesiastics to the pope.

The Effect of Royal Confiscations upon Education. — On the ground that the monks were practicing fraud and immorality, in 1536 Henry began to confiscate the monastic lands and property. Within a decade he suppressed over six hundred monasteries, ninety colleges, twenty-three hundred free chapels, and one hundred hospitals, and thereby secured an annual income of one hundred and fifty thousand pounds. About one half of the plunder thus secured Henry spent upon coast defenses and a new navy, and much of the remainder he distributed among his favorites and supporters. Very little of this money was spent for education, higher or secondary, to atone for the wholesale destruction of schools and colleges he had wrought. The effect upon education of the reign of his successor, Edward VI (1547–1553), was very similar.[1] It was formerly supposed that this latter monarch used the income which he secured from the monastic and chantry foundations in the cause of education. Leach has, however, shown that "never was a great reputation more easily gained and less deserved than that of King Edward VI as a founder of schools." Elementary and secondary schools were old institutions in England, and did not begin with the Reformation. There were in existence from the time of the Middle Ages schools upon cathedral, monastic, collegiate, hospital, gild, chantry, and independent foundations, and these were much more numerous before the Reformation than afterward. Prior to the reign of Henry VIII, even the smallest towns and villages would

He also confiscated the monastic lands and property, and spent little of the income for education. His successor, Edward VI, did not do much better.

[1] The basis of Edward's action was, however, quite different. "At the very time Henry was dissolving the Chantries he was prosecuting people for not believing in Purgatory. The Parliament of the Protector Somerset placed their action on religious grounds. They dissolved the Chantries because they condemned the objects of the Chantries." See Leach, *English Schools at the Reformation*, pp. 65 ff.

seem to have had elementary schools, and no boy would need to go a great distance for a 'grammar' school, whereas the small number of students at the close of the Reformation shows the effect of the legislation in the days of King Henry and his son.

Some schools were not destroyed, and a great many others were endowed by wealthy men during the days of the last Tudors and the first Stuarts. All these adopted the curriculum of the Northern humanism.

The Later Increase in Grammar Schools. — Of the three hundred 'grammar' schools that had probably come down from the Middle Ages, however, some, by the terms of the parliamentary acts, were not destroyed, and popular sentiment caused others to be refounded. And after the establishment of St. Paul's School by Dean Colet,[1] the number of 'grammar' schools was very largely added to, though by the philanthropy of wealthy men rather than out of the spoils of the monasteries. During the reign of Elizabeth (1558–1603) and of the first two Stuart kings (1603–1649) these foundations were greatly increased by grants of land and money. All of these schools, largely following the example of St. Paul's, adopted the Northern ideals of humanism,[2] and furnished a curriculum of classics and religious training. The latter became based, of course, upon the teachings of the Church of England. These schools were intended to be open to rich and poor alike, an ideal, as has been shown,[3] that was afterward lost sight of, and it was hoped that every parish might soon have one of these schools, and furnish preparation for the university to all boys of intelligence.

The Anglican Church remained midway, and the Puritans had to form their own type of education.

The Puritans and Their Education. — Despite his radical changes in the administration of the Church, Henry VIII made few departures from the old doctrines. He insisted upon the retention of transubstantiation, private masses, confession, and the celibacy of the clergy.[4] And although Edward VI and Elizabeth[5] greatly advanced Protestantism, the Anglican ritual remained

---

[1] See pp. 167–170.   [3] See pp. 172 f.
[2] See pp. 170 f.   [4] See footnote on p. 195.
[5] Mary, whose reign (1553–1558) came between those of these sovereigns, naturally sought to bring the English Church back to its allegiance to Rome.

EDUCATIONAL INFLUENCES OF THE PROTESTANTS 197

midway between Catholicism and the extreme Protestant position, and gradually a third party, composed of more radical Protestants, arose in England. These people later became known as the 'Puritans,' and were forced to Inaugurate a type of education and set of schools of their own. The period of their educational prominence can best be considered later on.[1]

The Aim of Protestant Education. — After this general review of the Reformation, it can be seen that, while other factors entered into the various revolts from the Church, each seems to have had a common element in the spirit that appeared in Northern humanism. The social and moral awakening of this Renaissance of the North furnished support for every reform of Church doctrine and practice that arose. Many came to feel that religion did not consist in a completed revelation, but in a progressive interpretation of the original teachings of Christianity. It depended less upon uncritical and obedient acceptance of dogma than upon the constant application of reason to the Scriptures. The Protestants, therefore, generally stressed not only the religious conception of education, but the idea of its universality, since they felt that every one should be intelligent enough to make his own interpretation. With nearly all of them, too, education was to be civil as well as religious. It must promote Christian beliefs and lead to church affiliation, they held, but it should exist quite as much for the sake of the State as of the Church. *Protestants held that a progressive interpretation of Christianity was needed, and that education should be religious, civil, and universal.*

The Foundation of Elementary Schools in Protestant Countries. — To accomplish this, the reformers, as a rule, desired to coöperate with the civil officials in matters of education, and to have the schools managed, and to some extent supported, by the State. It came to be felt that it was the duty of the civic authorities to insist that each child should obtain at least an elementary training, and in this way the modern tendency toward universal, free, and compulsory education began. Although at first the *The reformers coöperated with the civil officials, and insisted upon an elementary education for all.*

---

[1] See Chapter XIX, and *Milton* in Chapter XVII.

Protestant reaction from authority and the beaten path produced in many instances confusion, destruction of schools, and a depletion of educational facilities and a lowering of standards, it resulted eventually in the general foundation of elementary schools and the increase of education in most Protestant countries.

This is seen in Magdeburg, Eisleben, and the North German cities, and in Saxony, Würtemberg, and other states.

Elementary Education in the German States. — In Germany there were many illustrations of this spread of elementary education and civic control. These principles were, as has been evident,[1] most emphatically held by Luther and his colleagues, and the effect of their expression of them was widely felt. As an immediate result of his appeal to the magistrates,[2] in 1524 the city of Magdeburg united its parish schools under one management and adopted the Protestant ideals. So, in 1525, upon the request of the Count of Mansfeld, Melanchthon organized upon a Protestant basis the school at Eisleben, which included elementary as well as secondary work.[3] Similar ideals and organization appear in the provision for 'German' schools in the 'Church orders' sent out by Bugenhagen in 1520–1537 to the Protestant cities and states of North Germany.[4] A further step was taken in 1528, when Melanchthon was commissioned to draw up a plan for schools throughout the entire electorate of Saxony.[3] This, the first state school system in history, was followed by one in Würtemberg, where in 1559 Duke Christopher adopted a modification of the Saxon plan, which called for a religious and elementary training for the children of the common people in every village of the duchy. Brunswick in 1569, and Saxony in 1580, followed the lead of Würtemberg, and made new statutes to improve their school systems. Before the middle of the next century a number of other states of Germany, such as Weimar, Hessen-Darmstadt, Mecklenburg, Holstein, Hessen-Cassel, and Gotha, started elementary schools after an improved form of the organization in

---

[1] See pp. 184 f. and 187–189. [3] See pp. 157 and 187.
[2] See p. 184. [4] See p. 188.

Saxony and Würtemberg. Of these the most complete and systematic was that established in 1642 by Ernst 'the Pious,' Duke of Gotha, which became the basis of the present school system of Germany.

Equal opportunities for girls to secure elementary education were soon provided by the various German states, and both sexes were required by statute to attend school during certain years. As early as 1619 Weimar first insisted that all children, boys and girls alike, should be compelled to attend school from the sixth to the twelfth year; and when Duke Ernst adopted his system, he required every child in Gotha to enter at five and stay in school until he was well versed in religion and the rudiments. In spite of the decimation of population and the terrible havoc upon finance and education wrought by the Thirty Years' War (1618–1648), the institution of universal education continued its advance, and by the end of the eighteenth century practically every village throughout the German states had its *Volksschulen*. These institutions were under the direction of the pastor of each parish, and while actual conditions may often have been somewhat below the statutory level, every child not studying at a secondary school was in theory obliged, between the ages of six and thirteen, to attend one of these schools of the people.

Equal opportunities were soon provided for girls.

School Systems in Holland, Scotland, and the American Colonies. — But Germany was not the only country to feel the effect of the Reformation upon the foundation of elementary schools. Under the auspices of the Dutch Protestant movement, Holland made early provision for instruction in religion, reading, and writing. Notwithstanding the terrible persecutions of Spain and the Duke of Alva (1567–1573), this effort at universal training continued, and just as the Thirty Years' War began, the Synod of Dort, by a combination with the State authorities, required every parish to furnish elementary education for all. Similarly, as an outcome of the Reformation and the work of John Knox, it has been

Through the Synod of Dort, every parish in Holland had to furnish universal elementary education. The Scotch parliament made a similar requirement. By enactments in the

various colonies, America early established elementary schools.

seen¹ that Scotland also started elementary schools in the parishes. By 1616 a decree of the Privy Council compelled each parish to maintain a school, and this act was ratified by the Scotch parliament in 1633. A further step was taken in 1646, when the parliament enacted that there be "a Schoole founded, and a Schoole master appointed in every Parish," and further provided that if the parish should fail in this duty, the presbytery should have power to establish the school and compel the parish to maintain it. Half a century later this school system was given over more to the control of the State, but even then much of the old connection with the Church was apparent. Again, although England did not generally establish elementary schools after the breach with Rome, her colonies in America, through the schools required by the Dutch of their trading companies, and through the Puritans, who had absorbed Calvinist principles, almost from the first provided elementary education. During the seventeenth century the various colonies provided for a general system not only of 'grammar' schools, as shown in the last chapter, but also for instruction in the elements. This provision was made compulsory in 1647 by the famous act of the General Court of Massachusetts already mentioned,² which, after a most pious preamble, "ordered yt every towneship in this iurisdiction, after ye Lord hath increased you to ye number of 50 householders, shall then forthwith appoint one within their toune to teach all such children as shall resort to him to write and reade." Connecticut followed the example three years later, and before the close of the century, similar action was taken by New Hampshire, Pennsylvania, Maryland, and other colonies.

The secondary schools in the various Protestant countries

The Effect of Protestantism upon the Secondary Schools. — While the increase in elementary instruction under civil control was the most important educational outcome of the Reformation the effect of the movement

---

¹ See p. 194.   ² See p. 174.

was also evident in the secondary schools, whose ideals had been largely fixed by humanism. As the Reformation advanced, the Latin schools and *Gymnasien* of Germany, like the *Fürstenschulen,* came under the control of the princes and the State rather than the Church, and gradually became the backbone of the state school systems. Luther's *Letter* suggested the establishment of secondary schools,[1] as well as elementary, under the management of the civil authorities, and there was a speedy response not only in such cases as Eisleben and the cities under the influence of Bugenhagen, Trotzendorf, Neander, and Sturm, but in the provision made by the various school systems, already mentioned. The religious spirit, however, remained, and the direct management of education was simply transferred to Protestant ministers or leaders. The schools were still taught and inspected by representatives of the Church. The change came in the form of organization and the *personnel* of the administration. In England there was a similar transfer of management to the Protestant clergy. None of the grammar schools was outside ecclesiastical control, for, while these secondary institutions were not financed by the Church, their existence had to be authorized, and their teachers licensed by the bishop, and under whatever auspices they were organized, they were at any time liable to visitation from ecclesiastical authority. The one marked difference was that the Anglican Church had taken the place of the Roman, for the grammar schools were never organized, like the *Gymnasien*, into a system. Each school remained independent of the rest and of any national combination, under the close corporation established by Henry VIII or Edward VI, or by some wealthy founder. The Calvinistic *collèges*, being located for the most part in Catholic countries, were also not united into a national system, although their management was in each case in the hands of the Huguenots or other Calvinists. In Germany, however,

came under the control of the civil authorities and the Protestant clergy.

---

[1] See p. 184.

where the *collèges* approached the *Fürstenschulen* in character, they were absorbed into the system of *Gymnasien*. Again, the Scotch parish schools, while intended primarily for elementary education, often gave secondary instruction and fitted for higher work, especially as their teachers were usually university graduates.[1] Finally, the Puritans that had fled to America, since they were also Calvinists in their turn of mind, sought, as we saw in the previous chapter,[2] to vest the establishment and control of the grammar schools they had inherited from the mother country in the authorities of the state and the several towns.

The Organization of the Universities. — The universities, too, in Protestant countries, while remaining religious and Christian in spirit, in many instances during the sixteenth and seventeenth centuries withdrew from the control of Church and pope, and came under the State and temporal powers. Although still supported by the old foundations of monastic days, the German universities, together with the rest of the state, often followed the prince when he changed from the old creed to the new. Wittenberg, through its connection with Luther and Melanchthon, was the first German university to become Protestant, and the others, such as Marburg, Königsberg, Jena, Helmstadt, and Dorpat followed rapidly. Sometimes new Protestant universities, as in the case of Altdorf and Strasburg, were developed from the *Gymnasien*. The English universities, Oxford and Cambridge, went over to Protestantism with the national church. A few new colleges and *regius* professorships[3] were founded by Henry VIII and Edward VI, and additional support was later given by the State and the Church of England. In America, too, Harvard and other early colleges were closely connected with the various commonwealths and the Calvinistic or the Anglican communions.

The Studies of the Curricula. — Such was the effect of the Reformation upon the organization of education,

In many instances the universities turned Protestant, and new Protestant universities were developed.

[1] See pp. 194 and 199 f. [2] See pp. 173 f. [3] See p. 164.

elementary, secondary, and higher. Similarly, the course of study in the various Protestant institutions was, as might be expected, largely shaped by the political and ecclesiastical events of the times. In the elementary schools the curricula were primarily religious, and the staple subjects included, beside reading, writing, and some rude arithmetic, the Scriptures, the Lord's Prayer, the Ten Commandments, the Lutheran, Calvinist, or Anglican creed and catechism, and the hymns and sacred songs of the Protestant churches. The secondary schools and universities were, from their connection with the Renaissance in the North, largely humanistic and religious in their courses. Latin, Greek, and Hebrew were taught chiefly, that it might be possible to read the Bible and the Church Fathers in the original, and thus form a check upon the traditional interpretations, while instruction in the Latin catechism, creed, and prayer-book was given for the sake of success in theological contentions. Likewise, in the universities there were courses upon dialectic, mathematics, rhetoric, philosophy, and theology that would furnish a training in definition, argumentation, and forceful discussion with ecclesiastical opponents.

The curricula were religious and humanistic,

The Lapse into Formalism in Content and Method.— There was, however, always a tendency to lose sight of the real purpose of linguistic and religious studies, and to esteem these subjects as material for discipline rather than because of the value of their content. Thus the studies largely became an end in themselves and were deprived of almost all their vitality and strength. The curriculum of the institutions became fixed and stereotyped in nature, and education lapsed into a formalism but little superior to that of the mediæval scholastics. As in the later humanistic training, the methods of teaching came to stress the memory and logical activity. Hence, while the Protestants had nominally broken with tradition and resorted to reason as a guide, such a conception of the curriculum and of method necessarily tended to emphasize the importance of authority

but education soon lapsed into a formalism but little superior to that of scholasticism.

and the repression of the individual. The management and instruction of the schools, too, remained generally in the hands of the clergy, although these authorities were now Protestants instead of Catholics.

The Distrust of Reason and Individualism.—In this way, as the Protestant cause came to have a foundation of its own, the vitalizing tendency to rely upon reason rather than dogma hardened into a fresh distrust of rationality and individualism. Liberty of conscience was insisted upon during their revolt by Protestant leaders, but when once they met with some measure of success they felt it impossible to grant the same right to others that differed from them. While making his fight against the pope, Luther declared "that reason is the chief of all things, and among all that belongs to this life, the best, yea, a something divine," and even earlier he insisted that "surely what is contrary to reason is more contrary to God"; but when his position had become well established, he swung to the opposite extreme and held that "the more subtle and acute reason is, the more poisonous a beast it is, with many dragons' heads; it is against God and all his works." Hence he held that Zwingli's rational view of the eucharist placed him outside the pale of Christianity.[1] Henry VIII similarly took pride in presiding at the trial of one who held to this interpretation of Zwingli's, and argued in behalf of his death at the stake. In the same way, Calvin did actually sanction the burning of Servetus[2] for heresy, and this action was approved by Melanchthon, while Knox declared it a "pious and memorable example to all posterity."

Apparently all the other Protestant reformers were similarly inoculated with the spirit of the age, and bade farewell to 'reason' when their own doctrines and opinions were once well fixed. So various creeds were established as authoritative, and were enforced by the

---
[1] See p. 190.
[2] See *Complaint against Servetus* in Whitcomb, *Period of the Later Reformation*, II, pp. 12–16.

governments, wherever they were adopted. An improved statement of doctrine was regarded as the most important feature of religion, and the possibility of a religious life for others under any formulation than one's own was emphatically denied. The various Protestant sects became as intolerant of any opposing doctrine as ever Mother Church had been. The standard for estimating religion came to be theological formulations rather than life and conduct.

Under these conditions there was about as little liberality in the Protestant education as in that it sought to supplant. The schools of the reformers strove to propagate their new types of Christianity with little regard for open-mindedness and the search for truth. During the latter half of the sixteenth and the first half of the seventeenth century, despite the humanistic and religious material of the curriculum, there was a decided tendency to react from the individualism of the Renaissance and the early part of the Reformation. The Protestant Reformation had largely abandoned its mission.

SUPPLEMENTARY READING

I. SOURCES

BARNARD, H. *German Teachers and Educators* (VI on Luther gives a translation of his *Letter* and parts of his *Sermon*).
CHEYNEY, E. P. *Early Reformation Period in England* (Translations and Reprints, I, No. 1).
CHEYNEY, E. P. *England in the Time of Wycliffe*.
JACKSON, S. M. *Selections from the Writings of Zwingli*.
MICHELET, M. (Editor). *The Life of Luther Written by Himself* (translated by Hazlitt).
PAINTER, F. V. N. *Luther on Education* (contains *Letter to Mayors and Aldermen* and *Sermon on Duty of Sending Children to School*).
ROBINSON, J. H., AND WHITCOMB, M. *Period of the Early Reformation in Germany* (Translations and Reprints, II, No. 6).
ROBINSON, J. H. *Readings in European History*. Vol. II, Chaps. XXV–XXVII.
ROBINSON. J. H. *The Pre-Reformation Period*.
WHITCOMB, M. *Period of the Later Reformation* (Translations and Reprints, III, No. 3). II. The Geneva Reformation.

II. Authorities

ACTON, LORD. *The Cambridge Modern History.* The Reformation, Chaps. IV–VI and XIX.
ADAMS, G. B. *Civilization during the Middle Ages.* Chaps. XVI and XVII.
BARNARD, H. *American Journal of Pedagogy.* Vols. VI, 426–432; XI, 159–164; XVII, 165–175; XXVIII, 1–16.
BARNARD, H. *English Pedagogy.* Second Series, I–VI.
BARNARD, H. *German Teachers and Educators.* VI–IX.
BEARD, C. *Martin Luther and the Reformation.*
BEARD, C. *The Reformation of the Sixteenth Century in its Relation to Modern Thought and Knowledge* (Hibbert Lectures, 1883). Chaps. I–IV.
CREIGHTON, M. *History of the Papacy.* Vol. VI, Chaps. III, V, VII, and VIII.
DRAPER, J. W. *Intellectual Development of Europe.* Vol. II, Chaps. VI and VII.
FISHER, G. P. *The Reformation.* Chaps. I–X.
HAUSSER, L. *The Period of the Reformation* (translated by Sturge). Pts. I–VI.
HENDERSON, E. F. *A Short History of Germany.* Vol. I, Chaps. X–XV.
JACKSON, S. M. *Huldreich Zwingli.*
JACOBS, H. E. *Martin Luther.* Bk. II.
JANSSEN, J. *History of the German People at the Close of the Middle Ages.* Vols. III–X.
KOESTLIN, J. *Life of Luther.*
KURTZ, J. H. *Text-book in Church History* (translated by Bomberger). Vol. II, pp. 32–150.
LINDSAY, T. M. *A History of the Reformation.* Bks. II–V.
MERTZ, G. K. *Das Schulwesen der Deutschen Reformation.* Chaps. I–IV.
MŒLLER, W. *History of the Christian Church in the Middle Ages* (translated by Rutherfurd). Fourth Period.
NOHLE, E. *History of the German School System* (Report of the U.S. Commissioner of Education, 1897–98, Vol. I, Chap. I, § III, a).
PAINTER, F. V. N. *History of Education.* Pp. 135–154.
PAINTER, F. V. N. *Luther on Education.*
PASTOR, L. *History of the Popes* (edited by Kerr).
PAULSEN, F. *German Universities* (translated by Thilly and Elwang). Bk. I, Chap. II, § I; Bk. II, Chap. III.
POOLE, R. L. *Wycliffe and Movements for Reform.*
RUSSELL, J. E. *German Higher Schools.* Chaps. II–IV.
SCHAFF, P. *History of the Christian Church.* Vols. VI and VII.

SEEBOHM, F. *The Era of the Protestant Revolution.* Pt. II, Chaps. II–V ; Pt. III, Chaps. I–V.
WALKER, W. *John Calvin.*
WALKER, W. *The Reformation.* Chaps. III–VIII.
WATSON, F. *Maturinus Corderius (The School Review,* Vol. XII, Nos. 4, 7, and 9).

CHAPTER XVI

THE EDUCATION OF THE CATHOLICS

The Council of Trent and the Catholic Reaction.— Some time before Luther and the others revolted, there had been many reformers within the Church who wished to improve the character of the priesthood and purify its practices without changing the organization.[1] But this movement must have been greatly stimulated by the secession of the Protestants, and the Council of Trent was called in 1545 to rid the Church of abuses, as well as to repress heresy. A number of important reforms were made, but the spirit of the Council as a whole was reactionary. The chief consideration became a careful reaffirmation of the Catholic doctrines and administration, and the specific rejection of all Protestant principles.

<small>The efforts of the Catholics to crush the Protestant heresy resulted in a number of extended conflicts.</small>

Thereafter, the Catholics devoted their main efforts to crushing the Protestant heresy and recovering the ground they had lost. The result was a number of religious wars between Catholics and Protestants. These usually began within a single country, but tended to become international. Such were the civil wars in France, with the massacre of St. Bartholomew's Day (1562–1598); the uprising of the Dutch during their oppression by Philip II and the 'bloody' Duke of Alva and other governors (1567–1585); the disorders in England, culminating in the execution of Mary, Queen of Scots (1569–1587) and the attack of the Spanish Armada the next year; and finally, the ruinous series of

---

[1] For that reason it seems scarcely proper to refer to the Catholic attempts at reform as 'the Counter-Reformation,' thereby implying that this arose for the first time in response to the movements of the Protestants. See footnote 1 on p. 179.

national and international conflicts known as the 'Thirty Years' War' (1618-1648), in which Denmark, Sweden, France, and Spain, as well as Germany, all played a part, and through which progress in Europe was put back a hundred years.

Loyola and the Foundation of the Society of Jesus. — In these reactionary movements Philip II, with his terrible Spanish Inquisition, acted only as a destructive and suppressive agent, but a more effective and constructive instrument in advancing the interests of Catholicism was the religious organization known as the *Jesuits*. This order had been founded by *Ignatius de Loyola*[1] (1491-1556), a knight of the little Spanish kingdom of Navarre and a contemporary of Luther's. Loyola had been severely injured in the siege of Pampelona by the French in 1521, and while recovering in his father's castle he read the *Lives of the Saints*, and was inspired to do some service for God and the Church. He had at first gone on a pilgrimage to Jerusalem, but seeing that little could be accomplished without an education, he returned, and, although already thirty-three, entered the grammar school at Barcelona. Later he undertook a university training at Alcala and Salamanca. In 1534, while studying still further at Paris, Loyola had persuaded six[2] fellow-students to join with him in devoting themselves to missionary work and to maintaining the authority of the pope. Six years later, after considerable opposition, the new order had been recognized by Pope Paul III, and the *Societas Jesu* ('Society of Jesus'), as it was called,[3] had entered upon its campaign of converting the heathen and combating Protestantism. Many privileges, in the way of founding schools, teaching, and lecturing publicly, were added by subsequent popes, and

In this reaction the Inquisition was purely destructive, while the Jesuits were constructive in their aid to Catholicism.

Early life of Loyola, the founder of the Jesuits.

---

[1] He was called *de Loyola* from his ancestral estate, his original name being *Don Inigo Lopez de Recalde*.
[2] These were the pious and scholarly *Francisco de Xavier* ('Francis Xavier'), afterward canonized, *Laynez, Bobadilla, Faber, Salmeron,* and *Rodriguez*.
[3] The members gave their brotherhood this name even before it was sanctioned by the pontiff.

P

210   A HISTORY OF EDUCATION

after a varied career of nearly three centuries, the organization is still in existence, and is worthy of careful study as one of the most influential institutions in the history of education.

The Jesuit ideal was to extend Catholic organization throughout the world.

The Aim of the Jesuit Education. — The Jesuits sought to carry on their work of strengthening the pope and eliminating Protestant heresies in two ways. They strove through missionary labors to win back Protestant territory to its former allegiance and extend Catholic organization throughout the world, and by means of their schools to hold their converts and educate all peoples to submission. Protestant education was to be counteracted by the establishment of equally good or better Catholic facilities. Their educational ideal, therefore, has been to equip all youth, whether intending to enter the order or not, with principles and habits of life in harmony with morality, religion, and the teachings of the Catholic Church.

The *Constitution* was not published until 1558, and the *Ratio Studiorum* not until 1599.

The *Constitutiones* and the *Ratio Studiorum*. — The outline of the Jesuit organization was drafted by Loyola, with the assistance of *Diego Laynez*, the provincial of Italy, during the sixteen years that intervened between the pope's sanction of the order and the death of its founder. However, this *Constitutiones* ('Constitution') was not given its final revision and approval until two years later, under the generalship of Laynez. The *Ratio atque Institutio Studiorum Societatis Jesu* ('The Method and System of Studies of the Society of Jesus'), which was an expansion of Part Four of the *Constitution* and described the school administration in detail, was not published until 1599, when *Claudio Acquaviva* had become the general. This *Ratio Studiorum*, therefore, summed up the experience of the Jesuit schools during fully sixty years, and was worked over and revised by several important commissions before being presented as a permanent educational system for the order.

At the head of the organization is the 'general,'

Military Organization of the Jesuits. — In accordance with the *Constitution*, the organization of the schools and of the society at large has always been military in

THE EDUCATION OF THE CATHOLICS 211

type. After his change of life purpose, Loyola still had the instincts and habits of a soldier, and did not believe that any system could be effective, unless, like that of the army, it was based upon implicit obedience to one's official superiors. Hence, from the first, the Jesuits have had a stable and uniform organization. At the head of the order is the *general*,[1] who is elected for life and has unlimited powers. For the order, he is as the pope to the entire Church, — the vicar of God. "In him should Christ be honored as present in his person."[2] As the society spread, the countries that came under its control were divided into provinces. At the head of all the Jesuit interests, spiritual and educational, within each one of these districts is the *provincial*,[1] who is chosen by the general for three years. In each province, besides other Jesuit institutions, on the educational side, there are various colleges, whose presiding officer is usually known as the *rector*. The rector is appointed for three years by the general, but is directly responsible and reports to the provincial. Similarly, within each college are *prefects of studies*, immediately subordinate to the rector, but selected by the provincial. Under the constant inspection of the rector and the prefects are the *professors* or *preceptors*,[3] and each professor is assisted by one or more *monitors*, selected from the students. This series of official gradations, with its checks and balances, has kept the Jesuit teachers from any display of individualism and prevented any serious change in the established system since the beginning.

with unlimited powers; over each district is a 'provincial,' chosen by the general; at the head of each college is the 'rector,' appointed by the general, but responsible to the provincial; and under the 'rector' are 'prefects,' 'professors,' and 'monitors.'

The Lower and Upper Colleges of the Jesuits. — The Jesuits never engaged in elementary education. From the time the *Constitution* was formulated, their pupils had to know how to read and write before being admitted to any school. The Jesuits claimed that this

The Jesuit educational organization has consisted of a secondary course in the 'studia inferiora,'

---

[1] The full titles are *praepositus generalis* and *praepositus provincialis*.
[2] His power and influence are so great that he has often been denominated 'the black pope.'
[3] While these titles have varied from time to time, in general *professor* has been used in the upper classes, and *praeceptor* in the lower.

and a university course in the 'studia superiora.'

was necessary because their limited number of teachers did not warrant their offering a training in the rudiments. But it is barely possible that they were shrewd enough to perceive how much deeper an impression could be made upon boys during the adolescent stage. Moreover, when the Jesuits began their work, the public elementary school was just coming to be regarded as of importance, and the secondary education of the humanistic type was everywhere dominant. In consequence, the *Constitution* limited the Jesuit educational organization to *studia inferiora* ('lower colleges'), or schools with a gymnasial course, and *studia superiora* ('upper colleges'), which were to be of university grade.

The smaller Jesuit 'colleges,' of course, have furnished only the secondary work, and have been by far the more numerous. Boys are admitted to these lower colleges at from ten to fourteen years of age, and spend five or six years there. After finishing this secondary curriculum, the student spends two years in religious preparation before entering the higher work. During the university course, those who are in training for membership in the order are known as *scholastici*, while other students are ranked as *externi*. The full university course lasts seven or nine years, without counting the five or six years taken in the middle of it by most young Jesuits for teaching in the lower college. At the end of the university training, the students usually become either *coadjutores spirituales* ('spiritual assistants')[1] or *professi* ('professed').[2] The *coadjutores spirituales*, who make up the largest part of the order, take the three monastic vows of chastity, poverty, and obedience, and bind themselves to zealous preaching and teaching, especially the latter. The care of the colleges is in their hands. The *professi* take an additional oath to place themselves absolutely at the disposal of the pope and to travel continually on assigned missions, if neces-

The 'scholastici' and the 'externi';

the 'coadjutores' and the 'professi.'

---

[1] There are also *coadjutores temporales*, lay brothers who engage in secular pursuits outside of preaching and teaching.
[2] I.e. *professi quattuor votorum*.

THE EDUCATION OF THE CATHOLICS 213

sary. They are the aristocracy, and, under the general, the legislative body of the order, and from their number only can the general and provincials be selected. Hence a complete Jesuit training might take from twenty-one to twenty-three years, counting in the years of novitiate and teaching, and a 'professed' or 'coadjutor' member of the order might well be thirty-five years of age before completing his education.

Endowment and Administration of the Colleges. — Loyola was intensely practical in all his arrangements for maintaining the work of the order. He insisted early that no Jesuit college should be located where suitable provision could not be made for buildings and equipment, support of the professors, and a steady attendance, or where the social and political conditions were unfavorable to freedom of action. These regulations were extended and made more definite by his successors, and the Jesuits have been widely known for the generous gifts and bequests that have come into their hands, and for their wisdom of administration. They have steadfastly opposed any tuition fee or anything else that might interfere with their securing the ablest recruits possible. *Gratis accepistis, gratis date* ('freely ye have received, freely give') commanded the *Constitution*,[1] and while in some places colleges were founded especially for the nobility and princes, usually no social distinctions have been permitted, and the poor and lowly born have mingled indiscriminately with the aristocratic and wealthy.

<small>The Jesuit colleges have had to be suitably equipped and supported.</small>

<small>Tuition is free and no social distinctions have been permitted.</small>

The Humanistic Curriculum of the Lower Colleges. — The course of study in the Jesuit colleges was the natural product of the period in which they were started. In the lower school the curriculum was originally of the humanistic and religious type, and seems to have been somewhat modeled after that of the Hieronymian schools, and may also have been influenced by the ideas of Sturm.[2] Their humanism, at any rate, soon

<small>The course of the lower colleges was largely limited to speaking and writing Ciceronian Latin, but after 1832 some modern studies were added.</small>

[1] Pars IV, Cap. VII, n. 3.
[2] Some have claimed that Sturm copied the Jesuit system rather than

became of the narrower sort, and was limited largely to a drill in speaking and writing Ciceronian Latin. All study of the vernacular was forbidden, unless special permission was obtained from the provincial, and, except on a holiday, nothing but Latin could ever be spoken. The first three classes were devoted to a careful study of Latin grammar, and a little of Greek; in the fourth year, under the name of *humanitas*, a number of the Greek and Latin poets and historians were read; while the last class, to which two years were usually given, took up a rhetorical study of the classical authors. Only slight variations in the curriculum were allowed after 1599, until 1832, when there was a revision by which a little work in mathematics, the natural sciences, history, and geography was added. However, the classics remain to-day the largest element of the *studia inferiora*, and the course is still weighted with formalism.[1]

In the boarding colleges Christian instruction and religious observances were practiced.

Moral and Social Training. — The social, moral, and religious training has, however, from the first been considered very important. Boarding colleges, called *Convictus*, where the pupils could be constantly under the care of the Jesuit fathers, were established as early as the generalship of Laynez (1556–1565). In these institutions, Christian instruction, prayers, meditation, and all religious observances, such as daily mass and frequent confession, were in constant practice, and determined efforts were made to remove all vicious tendencies from the life of the youths. Moreover, the Jesuits, in spite of the formal character of their course, have shown themselves eminently wise and practical in worldly matters. Their pupils have ever been famous for their suavity and polished manners, and the facility

Suavity and good manners.

---

the reverse. Probably both systems were the product of the times, and each affected the other.

[1] This restriction, however, is not admitted by Hughes, who claims in his *Loyola* (p. 93): "As the new sciences came into vogue, they received at once the freedom of this city of intellect; and here they received it first."

with which they handle Latin, once the medium of intercourse between nations.

The Philosophical and Theological Courses in the Upper Colleges. — The curriculum of the upper colleges or universities of the Jesuits has regularly offered three years in philosophy, followed by a theological education of six years. The training in 'philosophy' now includes not only logic, metaphysics, psychology, ethics, and natural theology, but also work in algebra, geometry, trigonometry, analytics, calculus, and mechanics, and such natural sciences as physics, chemistry, geology, astronomy, and physiology, together with outside electives. This philosophical course leads to the degree of *Master of Arts*, if the student passes successfully in a public examination upon all the subjects. After the course in philosophy, most of the Jesuits teach in the lower colleges five or six years,[1] while they are still in large sympathy with youth. In the 'theological' course four years are devoted to a study of the Scriptures, Hebrew, and other Oriental languages that may throw light upon the Bible, together with church history, canon law, and electives, as well as theology proper. After this, there is offered a further training of two years, to review the work in philosophy and theology, and to prepare a thesis for public presentation. At the end of this course, the candidate for graduation defends his thesis and undergoes another public examination, and, if successful, is awarded the degree of *Doctor of Divinity*. The universities now also offer, in the place of theology, courses in law and medicine under faculties from outside the order, and this professional work leads to the appropriate degrees.

Excellence of the Jesuit Teaching. — The methods of teaching and the splendid qualification of the instructors were the most distinctive features of the Jesuit colleges. When one considers how little attention had up to that time been given to the preparation of teachers, the

[1] They ordinarily begin by teaching in the first class and advance regularly through the entire six years.

extent to which their system of pedagogy was from the first developed seems most remarkable. No one could become a teacher in the lower colleges who had not passed through the philosophical course and exhibited a singular degree of talent, while the professors in the universities had to complete the theological course of six years.

Instruction was imparted orally in the 'prælectio,' in which was given first the general meaning and then the detailed explanation.

The 'Prælectio.' — Although Jesuits have written a number of textbooks, instruction in the colleges, higher and lower, was generally imparted by the teacher orally, and memorized in the case of the pupils in the secondary work, or taken down in lecture notes by those in the universities. The form of instruction was the so-called *prælectio*, which, in the subjects of the lower colleges, meant an explanation of the passage being studied, or lectures upon the topic under consideration, in the case of the universities. This method of presentation consisted in giving: first, the general meaning of the whole passage or proposition; then, a more detailed explanation of the construction or the phraseology; next, similar thoughts or expressions in the works of other poets, historians, or philosophers; fourthly, informational comment upon the history, geography, and manners and customs, or other 'erudition' concerning the passage; then a study of the rhetorical figures, and of the propriety and rhythm of the words; and finally, the moral lesson to be drawn from the passage.

To fix the subject in the mind, short hours and brief lessons were assigned,

Tendency toward Memorizing. — Such a method as this obviously implied an exceedingly careful preparation on the part of the teacher, and a reliance almost entirely upon memory by the student. In fact, the greatest stress was, from the very nature of the Jesuit ideals, placed upon memorizing, even to the exclusion of reasoning. To fix the subjects firmly in the mind, short hours, few subjects, and brief lessons were found necessary. The lower colleges had a session of two hours and a half in the morning and two in the afternoon, and often a day's work was limited to three or four lines of a Latin author and was practically one continuous recitation. For this reason, too, the *Ratio Studiorum* insists: *pluribus diebus fere singula præcepta inculcanda sunt* ('usually each rule must be impressed for several days'). They hoped by means of such brief assignments to keep the health of both master and pupil at its maximum, and produce a concentration of attention. Loyola himself, in his endeavor to make up for lost time in his education, had grasped at too many subjects. Suffering thereby both in health and achievement, from the first he decided to limit the number of subjects and the length of the lessons in the Jesuit schools, and to organize the work with an eye to economy of effort.

Reviews. — Likewise, in the system of the Jesuits, reviews were always systematic and frequent, and the motto of the Jesuit method was *repetitio mater studiorum* ('repetition is the mother of studies'). Each day began with a review of the preceding day's work and closed with a review of the work just accomplished. Each week ended with a repetition of all that had been covered in that time. The last month of every year reviewed the course of the year, except in the three lowest classes, where the whole last half of the year was a repetition of the first half.[1] The students also obtained a complete review of the secondary course after their philosophical training by teaching in the *studia inferiora*, and the work in philosophy and theology was reviewed during the last two years of the theological course.

and regular reviews were held each day, week, month, and year.

Emulation as a Stimulus to Interest. — So, while the curriculum of the Jesuit colleges was not very broad in scope, it was most thorough and systematic. However, because of the emphasis upon memorizing, it would be difficult to account for the amount of interest displayed by the pupils of the Jesuits and the pleasantness of their schools, were it not for some other features of their methods whereby an indirect interest is aroused. The chief element in this borrowed interest comes from emu-

---

[1] The brightest boys could, on that account, be advanced every half-year and could accomplish the work of all three grades in eighteen months.

lation. As Ribadeneira, the friend and biographer of Loyola, tells us: —

"Many means are devised, and exercises employed, to stimulate the minds of the young, — assiduous disputation, various trials of genius, prizes offered for excellence in talent and industry. These prerogatives and testimonies of virtue vehemently arouse the mind of the students, awake them even when sleeping, and when they are aroused and running on with a good will, impel them and spur them on faster."[1]

Decuriones,' 'æmuli,' 'disputationes,' 'concertatio,' and 'academiæ,' as the means of obtaining interest.

Among the devices used to promote this rivalry was the appointment of the most able and responsible pupils as *decuriones*. These student officers, after reciting the lesson themselves to the teacher, heard the others in groups known as *decuriæ* ('squads'). Besides this stimulus, the pupils were arranged in pairs as *æmuli* ('rivals'), whose business it was to check on the conduct and studies of each other, and thus keep up their interest and energy. In addition to this constant rivalry of individuals, public *disputationes* between two sides were engaged in each week. The sides were sometimes known as 'Rome' and 'Carthage,' and much zest was shown in the work. From the lowest classes upward the form of 'disputation' called *concertatio* was employed. This consisted in a debate upon the grammatical, rhetorical, poetical, and historical features of the lesson. Usually the prefects and teachers served as judges, and prizes and half holidays were awarded the victorious side or any one who especially distinguished himself. Similarly, discussions of a higher type upon humanistic, dialectic, and philosophical subjects were conducted by the more brilliant students in voluntary societies known as *academiæ*. Poems, speeches, dialogues, and declamations all formed part of the program, and membership in these associations was a much coveted honor.

Corporal punishment was infrequent, and when in-

Infrequency of Corporal Punishment. — In this way, despite the ever present authority and the tremendous memory grind, the Jesuit schools had little occasion to appeal to corporal punishment or severe discipline.

[1] *Bollandists*, July, tome VII, nn. 376-377.

They showed a decided advance over the harshness of their times. The pupils even in the early days were led and not driven, and the Jesuits were masters of kindness and tact. In the sixteenth century, Bader, the Provincial of Upper Germany, said: —

flicted, it was by some one outside the order, and only as a check upon bad conduct.

"Let not the Prefects consider their authority to consist in this, that the students are on hand in obedience to their nod, their every word, or their very look; but in this, that the boys love them, approach them with confidence, and make their difficulties known. . . . The pupils should be led to see that penalties are necessary and are prompted by affection; and let it be the most grievous rebuke or penalty for them to know that they have offended the Prefect."

Occasionally a *corrector*, usually from outside the order, had to be engaged for some of the more refractory pupils, but even in that case punishment was never inflicted for poor standing in studies, but only as a check upon bad conduct.

Estimate of the Jesuit Schools. — The Jesuit education, then, seems to have been in advance of that in most schools at the time of its foundation. It had the advantage of being organized upon a systematic and thorough basis, and was administered by a set of splendidly trained teachers through the best methods that were known in that day. The schools were interesting and pleasant, and were open without money and without price to all who had the ability and desire for that type of education. The Jesuits, too, were devoted to their duty, and were wedded to their ideals of self-denial, poverty, obedience, and fealty to the pope. They were indefatigable in their efforts to advance mankind spiritually and intellectually, and to promote the cause of Catholicism.

The Jesuit education was systematic and thorough, the teachers were well trained, the schools were interesting and pleasant, and the Jesuits were devoted to duty.

The chief criticism that might be made of their schools rests in their insistence upon absolute authority and the consequent opposition to individuality. The Jesuits consistently observed the caution of the *Ratio Studiorum*: —

"Also in things which contain no danger for creed and faith, nobody shall introduce new questions on any important topic, nor an opinion, without sufficient authority or without permission of his superiors; nor shall any one teach anything against the doctrines of the Church Fathers and the commonly accepted system of school doctrines; but everybody shall follow the approved teachers and the doctrines accepted and taught in Catholic academies."

But the Jesuits held to authority, memorizing, rivalry, passivity, and opposition to investigation.

With such an ideal, it would be impossible to develop education in keeping with the varying spirit and demands of the times, and if progress is held to be in any measure dependent upon the toleration of individualism, the Jesuit system of courses, subjects, and methods would seem to have been too uniform and fixed. It depended very largely upon memory and appeal to interest through a system of rivalry, honors, and rewards. It cultivated a passive and reproductive attitude in the pupil, and, while there were always some scientists and thinkers among the Jesuits, their course of study logically tended to discourage investigation and independence. The results of such an education are likely to incline toward the stereotyped and mechanical.

The schools grew tremendously and spread throughout the world, and the Jesuits trained most of the great minds of the period.

Effects of the Jesuit Education. — Nevertheless, the Jesuits furnished the most effective education during the latter half of the sixteenth, the entire seventeenth, and the early part of the eighteenth, centuries. The growth of their schools was phenomenal. When Loyola died, although he had at first thought of limiting the order to sixty members, there were already one hundred colleges, and the Jesuit educators had penetrated Ireland, Scotland, Hindustan, Japan, China, and Abyssinia, as well as Europe. Under Acquaviva the number of colleges and universities had grown to be three hundred and seventy-two, and a century and a half after the death of Loyola, there were seven hundred and sixty-nine institutions spread throughout the world. The lowest number of students in attendance at any of these colleges during the seventeenth century was about three hundred, and in several of the larger centers there were between one and two thousand. Paris had nearly fourteen thousand at the fourteen colleges within its borders, and the college at Clermont is said to have run up to three thousand. At a modest estimate, there must have been some two hundred thousand students in the Jesuit colleges, when the education of the order was at its height. Hence it came about that the Jesuits trained most of the great minds of the times, Protestant as well as Catholic. The graduates of their schools seem to have become prominent in every important activity of life. Nearly three thousand noted authors in all countries, including such men as Tasso, Calderon, Corneille, Molière, Bossuet, and Diderot, were pupils of the Jesuits; and they everywhere trained men of affairs, like the noted general and statesman, Don Juan of Austria, General Tilly, Cardinal Richelieu, and the Duc de Luxembourg, marshal of France.

By the middle of the eighteenth century, however, the ideals and content of education were greatly changed, and the Jesuits failed to change their course so as to meet the new conditions. As a result, the training, being anachronistic, came to lack efficiency. Moreover, the Jesuits themselves, who had at first rejected all preferment or influence in the Church or State, had become powerful and ambitious. They deteriorated into a great political machine, and interpreted their abbreviated motto, A. M. D. G., *ad maiorem Dei gloriam* ('for the greater glory of God'), as meaning the advancement of the Church and the interests of their own order. While it is not likely that they went so far as always to claim that "the end justifies the means," or indulged systematically in the other forms of casuistry of which they have been accused, their ethical ideals certainly became less strict. They seem to have been indulgent toward many forms of moral abuse when committed in the interest of the order, and they quarreled frequently and arbitrarily with different bishops, governments, and universities, and with the Dominicans and other monastic orders. Finally, after they had been banished from nearly every country of Europe, in 1773 the pope himself, Clement XIV, "recognizing that the members of this society have not a little troubled the Christian commonwealth,

But they failed to change the content of education in keeping with the times, and came to lack efficiency, and deteriorated into a political machine.

and that for the welfare of Christendom, it were better that the order should disappear," dissolved the Society of Jesus. The individual members became missionaries or settled down individually as educators in the various dioceses. Forty years later the order was restored by Pius VII, but, owing to the development of educational ideals and organization, their work has never since become relatively as effective or held as important a place in education.

Subsequent orders were influenced to make education part of their work. One important result of the Jesuit interest in education and of their care in crystallizing their ideas in institutions is the effect they have had upon subsequent orders in making education an integral part of their work. The Dominicans, and, in a less degree, the Franciscans, had given some attention to education, but they had sought to make their influence felt through the existing schools and universities, and had not spread institutions of their own throughout the world. But after the foundation of the Jesuits, education of the diffusive sort became the rule with the orders, and was adopted by the Oratorians, Jansenists, Piarists, Christian Brothers, the Protestant Pietists, and many other religious societies.

The Oratorians became a teaching order in France in 1611. **The Establishment and Results of the Oratorian Schools.** — However, some of the later teaching orders organized within the Catholic Church were quite opposed in their education to the Jesuit principles of absolute authority and memorizing. Of these the earliest was the *Oratory of Jesus*, which held to the rationalistic philosophy of Descartes, and advocated the primacy of reason rather than memory. It had been started in Italy[1] during the sixteenth century as a monastic order, though with no vows beyond those of the secular priesthood, but in 1611 an independent organization was, through Pierre (later Cardinal) de Bérulle, effected in France, where it became a teaching order. Its members established a

---

[1] The founder was St. Philip Neri. The order took on a new life in England during the nineteenth century through (Cardinal) John Henry Newman.

set of secondary schools, and devoted themselves to the training of parish priests. The *Oratorians*, therefore, departed from the somewhat mechanical and ostentatious training of the Jesuits, and were much nearer the deeper education of the Port Royalists, to whom they became very friendly. Their course permitted a greater liberty and latitude on the theological side than did that of the Jesuits, and they emphasized the vernacular, modern languages, history, geography, natural sciences, and philosophy. In consequence of the interest aroused in this subject matter, the Oratorians found little need in their instruction of resorting to corporal punishment, and believed that praise, threats, and rewards furnished sufficient means of discipline.

<small>They emphasized the vernacular, modern languages, history, geography, natural sciences, and philosophy.</small>

While the Oratorians naturally came under the suspicion of the Jesuits and others who held to authority and the traditional curriculum, they were, from the first, very successful in their educational work. Almost immediately they had a large number of schools under their control, including the well-known college at Juilly, founded in 1638. Many noted teachers also came from this organization. Such were Lamy, who published a *Treatise on the Sciences* in 1683, Thomassin, who, during the years 1681-1690, produced a series of *Methods* for the study of languages, literature, and philosophy. Among other members of the order were Malebranche, Mascaron, Massillon, Lecointe, and Lelong. When the Jesuits were disbanded in 1773, the Oratorians obtained charge of secondary education in France, and while they were themselves dissolved later, they were reorganized in 1852, and have always been of some importance as an educational order.

<small>They had a number of schools under their control, and educated many noted teachers.</small>

The Jansenists and Their Doctrines. — Another teaching congregation within the Church, much more opposed to the principles of the Jesuits, was that known as the *Jansenists*, or *Gentlemen of Port Royal*. The doctrines of this order were formulated in 1621 by *Cornelius Jansen* (1585-1638), a professor in the University of Louvain and afterward Bishop of Ypres, but were more sedulously propagated throughout France by his friend, Jean Duvergier de Hauranne (1581–1643), more often called by the name of his monastery, 'Saint-Cyran.' In France, the Cistercian convent of *Port Royal des Champs* at Chevreuse near Versailles became known as the center of Jansenism.[1] While this order was bitterly condemned by the Jesuits and occasionally pronounced against by various popes, the members persisted in calling themselves Catholics and for about a century succeeded in doing their work within the Church. They were opposed, however, to the prevailing doctrines of penance and confession, and, appealing, as Luther had, to the Scriptures and St. Augustine, they professed to be bringing the Church back to its original principles. Like the Oratorians, they had adopted the philosophy of Descartes and held to the development of reason. They were also not unlike Calvin in denying the freedom of the will and claiming that only a few can be saved. Humanity was regarded by them as naturally corrupt, except as it is properly watched and guided. Evil, they felt, could be eliminated only by moral and religious, not to say ascetic, surroundings.

<small>The Jansenists adopted the philosophy of Descartes, but held to the natural corruption of humanity.</small>

The 'Little Schools' of the Port Royalists. — Because of this harsh and rather pessimistic belief, they desired to increase the number of the elect by removing what few children they could from the temptations of the world and suitably preparing them to resist the assaults of the devil. In 1643 they started a school on this basis in the convent at Port Royal, which had been vacated by the nuns, and similar institutions quickly sprang up in the vicinity and then spread through Paris. With the idea of carrying out their purpose of careful oversight, these schools usually took only twenty to twenty-five pupils, and each master had under him five or six boys whom he never allowed out of his immediate su-

<small>They, therefore, founded 'little schools' at Port Royal and elsewhere, to save as many children as possible.</small>

---

[1] This was partly due to the influence of its abbess, Mère Angelique, who was a sister of Antoine Arnauld, professor of theology at the Sorbonne and an ardent Jansenist, and partly to Saint-Cyran himself, who was spiritual adviser to the Cistercian nuns of Port Royal.

pervision day or night.¹ For this reason, and in order that they might not seem to be competing with the universities, as the Jesuits were, the Port Royalists called their institutions *petites écoles* ('little schools'). They took in children at nine or ten, before they could be seriously contaminated, and usually kept them through the impressionable period of adolescence. From the beginning, however, Saint-Cyran made it understood:

> "If the children turned out intractable and unwilling to submit to the discipline under which I wished them to live in this house, it should be in my power to dismiss them without those from whom I had received them bearing me any ill-will for it."

The Port Royal Curriculum and Texts. — Since the Port Royalists held that character was of more importance than knowledge, and reason was to be developed rather than memory, these 'little schools' sought to impart an education that should be sound and lasting rather than brilliant and superficial. Unlike the Jesuits and other educators of the times, they did not start the children with Latin, but with the vernacular, since this was within their comprehension. As, however, French contained no literature suitable to pupils of an early age, translations of Latin works, after proper modification and editing, were put in the hands of the children. The pupils read versions of the *Fables* of Phædrus, the *Comedies* of Terence, and the *Letters* of Cicero, and thus obtained a pleasant introduction to literature. As soon as they possessed a feeling for good works and desired to read them, they began the study of Latin through a minimum grammar written in French, and soon took up the Latin authors themselves, rendering them into the vernacular. Greek literature was treated in similar fashion. In order that the reason might be trained, the older pupils were also taught logic and geometry. The course of study, however, was mostly literary, and had

Reason, rather than memory, was developed; they began with the vernacular, and taught Latin and Greek through the medium of French, and used logic and geometry to train the reason.

---

¹ In discussing the origin of the first 'little school,' Saint-Cyran tells us: "I only intended to build it for six children, whom I would have chosen throughout the city of Paris, as it might please God that I should meet with them."

The Port Royal Grammar, the Port Royal Logic, and the Elements of Geometry.

no regard for science or original investigation. It paid little attention to physical training. Port Royal sought to present the education of the past most effectively, but did not see beyond it. The textbooks of the 'little schools' seem to have been largely written by *Antoine Arnauld* (1612–1694).[1] The *Port Royal Grammar* was produced by him with the aid of *Claude Lancelot* (1615–1695), while *Pierre Nicole* (1625–1695) collaborated with him on the *Port Royal Logic*, which was for the most part a polemic in favor of Descartes' principles against the scholastic type of philosophy. He also wrote an *Elements of Geometry*, which so pleased *Blaise Pascal* (1623–1662) that he abandoned a similar work of his own.

Reading was taught phonetically.

The Phonetic Method, the Neglect of Emulation, and the Spirit of Piety. — The methods of the Port Royal schools introduced innovations as striking as their curriculum. They departed from the usual plan of teaching their pupils to read by means of the alphabet and spelling, and declared: —

"It seems, then, that the most natural way would be, that those who are teaching to read should, at first, only teach the children to know their letters by their value in pronunciation; and that thus, to teach to read in Latin, for example, they should give the same name *e* to simple *e*, *ae*, and *oe*, because they are pronounced in the same way; and the same to *i* and *y*; and also to *o* and *au*, as they are now pronounced in France. Let the consonants also only be named by their natural sound, simply adding *e* mute, which is necessary in order to pronounce them. Let those which have several sounds, as *c*, *g*, *t*, and *s*, be named by the most natural and usual sound. And then they would be taught to pronounce separately, and without spelling, the syllables, *ce*, *ci*, *ge*, *tia*, *tie*, and *tii*. These are the most general observations on this new method of teaching to read."

This idea had been originated by Pascal and introduced at Port Royal through his younger sister, Jacqueline, who was in charge of the girls there. It was included by Arnauld and Lancelot in their grammar, from which the quotation above is taken.

Quite as revolutionary as this phonetic method in

---

[1] See footnote on p. 224.

THE EDUCATION OF THE CATHOLICS 227

reading was the refusal of the Port Royalists to permit the use of emulation and prizes in their schools. They rightly claimed that such an interest is extrinsic, and that the only true rival of any pupil is his own higher self, but their exclusion of rivalry resulted, on the whole, in indifference, and lagging attention. They were never able to secure the energy, earnestness, and pleasing environment of the Jesuit colleges. They did, however, succeed in inculcating a general spirit of piety without the formal teaching of either doctrine or morals. They held that piety comes rather through atmosphere and surroundings than by direct instruction. Saint-Cyran thought no pains too great to secure pious and fitting teachers, and when obtained, he enjoined them "to speak little, put up with much, pray still more."

No rivalry was permitted, and the schools lacked the earnestness and pleasantness of the Jesuit colleges.

Piety was cultivated without being formally taught.

The Closing of the 'Little Schools.' — The 'little schools' of the Port Royalists were allowed to exist but for a brief while. The first one was not opened until 1643, and by 1661 they were all closed by the order of Louis XIV through the influence of the Jesuits.[1] But this victory of the Jesuits cost them more dearly than any defeat they ever sustained. Not only did it lose them sympathy, but it gave the Jansenists occasion and opportunity to issue tracts against Jesuitism that have given it unpleasant notoriety ever since. The *Lettres Provinciales* ('Provincial Letters') and the *Pensées* ('Thoughts') of Pascal have proved the most terrible arraignment the Jesuits have ever received.

The Jesuits persuaded Louis XIV to close the Port Royalist schools, and thereby fell into great notoriety.

While the Gentlemen of Port Royal were thus forced to cease their formal work as schoolmasters, they became educators in a larger sense, and produced a great variety of writings upon their system of thought and training. Besides the textbooks already mentioned, Arnauld published the *Regulation of Studies in the Humanities*, which describes the literary instruction of the Port Royalists after some modification as the result of experience. Lancelot also published his *Methods* for

The Port Royalists then became educators in a wider sense and wrote many treatises upon education.

[1] See Cadet, *Port Royal Education*, pp. 58 ff., for a discussion of the jealousy of the Jesuits.

the study of language, literature, and philosophy; and Nicole, by whose works Madame de Sévigné was so largely influenced, contributed *The Education of a Prince.* Varet wrote a work on *Christian Education.* Coustel produced his *Rules for the Education of Children*, and many other Jansenists of the time published treatises embodying the Port Royal education. The Jansenistic principles were also applied to the education of women by *Jacqueline Pascal*, who had written out *The Regulations for the Girls' School at Port Royal.*

Rollin and his Treatise on Studies. — Later on *Charles Rollin* (1661–1741), who had twice been rector of the University of Paris, summarized in his *Traité des Études* ('Treatise on Studies') the reforms that had been wrought in the university and the lower schools through replacing the formal and dogmatic education of the Jesuits with the Jansenistic methods and rational philosophy. Thus, although their schools had to be abandoned, the Port Royalists continued to teach by means of messages to the people at large, and their new ideas upon classical and literary education have affected France and many other countries ever since that time.

La Salle and the Christian Brethren. — The Jansenists and Oratorians were, however, like the Jesuits, engrossed with secondary and higher education, and gave little heed to the education of all the people in the rudiments. The Protestants, it has been seen, began early to be interested in universal elementary education, and during the seventeenth century many Protestant countries established systems of elementary schools.[1] But not much was undertaken by the Catholics until toward the close of the century, although a few attempts were made before this.

'Catechism' schools, the Piarists, and the Brethren of St. Charles. — There were 'catechism' schools founded at the churches; the Council of Trent indorsed them, and the great Jesuit, Canisius, wrote a manual for their especial use. More noteworthy was the organization started by the order known as *Patres Piarum Scholarum* ('Fathers of the Pious Schools'), or *Piarists*, which was

[1] See pp. 197–200.

founded at Rome in 1617 by José Calasanzio, and authorized by Pope Gregory XV in 1621, for affording a public education in religion and the rudiments; and that of the *Congregation of the Brethren of St. Charles*, organized at Lyons in 1666 by Charles Démia for the elementary instruction of poor children. But, upon the whole, little advance was made. The few elementary schools that had come into existence were weakened by quarrels of the authorities, the teachers were often without intellect or moral fitness, and the curriculum was not clearly distinguished from that of the secondary schools. However, in 1684, *Jean Baptiste de la Salle* (1651–1719), probably influenced somewhat by the example of Démia, founded the *Institute of the Brethren of the Christian Schools*.[1] This order was destined, with little or no resources, to do almost as large a work for elementary education in France and other Catholic countries as the Jesuits did for secondary training. But owing to the determined opposition of the clergy, and the teachers of the schools already established, the Christian Brethren were not recognized by the pope until nearly forty years after their organization.

La Salle founded the Christian Brethren to conduct elementary schools.

The Religious and Repressive Aim of La Salle. — La Salle was a priest with a delicate constitution, but an almost superhuman energy and consecration.[2] He had secured his own education only by a most heroic struggle, and turned his attention to the instruction of the poor with unabated zeal. He became intensely devout and ascetic, and made his life one of constant self-sacrifice and devotion to the education of the lowly. The *Rule* of his society declared: —

La Salle was devout and ascetic,

"The spirit of the Institute consists in a burning zeal for the instruction of children, that they may be brought up in the fear and

---

[1] "For a name they chose that of 'Frères des Écoles Chrétiennes,' Brothers of Christian Schools, which was probably soon abbreviated into the well-known title of 'Frères Chrétiens,' or Christian Brothers, so familiar to us." See Wilson, *The Christian Brothers*, Chap. VII.

[2] English readers will find an interesting and sympathetic account of La Salle's life in Wilson, *op. cit.*, Chaps. II–III, VI–IX, and XII–XVII.

love of God, and led to preserve their innocence where they have not already lost it; to keep them from sin, and to instil into their minds a great horror of evil, and everything that might rob them of their purity. In order to maintain and abide in this spirit, the Brothers of the Society shall labor continually by prayer, by teaching, by vigilance, and by their own good example in the school, to promote the salvation of the children entrusted to them by bringing them up in a truly Christian spirit, that is to say, according to the rules of the Holy Gospel."

and his character appears in the religious and repressive nature of his schools.

The religious and repressive nature of his educational aim was evident everywhere in his schools. There was scarcely a moment in the day when some of the pupils were not kneeling in prayer, and mass, confession, spiritual reading, and sacred singing were also practiced at all hours;[1] and both teacher and pupils were required always to be quiet in their actions. In order that the necessity of speaking might be removed as far as possible, La Salle invented a system of signs, and in other ways endeavored to suppress all noise and restrain every evidence of freedom. This was, of course, out of keeping with the best possibilities for progress, but was a natural reaction from the noisy schools of the times.

The type of school and seminary at Rheims spread to Paris and elsewhere.

The Institutions of the Christian Brethren and *The Conduct of Schools*. — The first school of this type was established by La Salle himself at Rheims in 1679, before the foundation of the order. A decade later, under the Christian Brothers, schools of this type soon spread through Paris and the rest of France. In 1685, in order to secure suitable teachers, he opened a seminary for schoolmasters at Rheims, and a little later also one at Paris, with which he connected a practice school. These normal schools likewise spread to different centers. In addition, he founded a technical school for boys at St. Yon, near Rouen, and another at Paris, and this type of instruction also increased rapidly. In all these schools of the Christian Brothers, tuition was free.

Technical school at St. Yon.

[1] Mrs. Wilson outlines the time-table of the school day on pages 129–131 of *The Christian Brothers*. Four hours would seem to be allotted to prayer and religious exercises, and probably six hours more on Sunday were given to Divine service and catechetical study.

The plan of the elementary schools of the order was worked out during the first generation of their existence, and was crystallized in a system of definite rules. This was published in 1720,[1] under the title of *Conduite à l'usage des Écoles Chrétiennes*, and is usually known in English as the *Conduct of Schools*. The code was quite as uniform and repressive as the *Ratio Studiorum* of the Jesuits, but changes and revisions, to adapt the rules to the spirit of the times, have been more often allowed.

Conduct of Schools describes the plan of the order.

The Curriculum, Method, and Discipline of the Elementary Schools. — The course of study in the schools of the Christian Brethren was generally limited to the rudiments. A training in religion, good manners,[2] reading, writing, and arithmetic made up the main curriculum. A little elementary Latin, however, was taught in the higher grades through the medium of the vernacular, as in the Port Royal schools. The technical schools furnished, besides, work in manual training and in industrial and commercial pursuits.

Training in religion, good manners, reading, writing, and arithmetic.

Manual training.

From the beginning, the Christian Brothers taught by the 'simultaneous' method. By this was meant the division of the school into classes rather than the instruction of each pupil individually. This seems a perfectly natural procedure now, but at that time, when even the Jesuit masters had each pupil recite separately, it was a great advance in educational economy.

The 'simultaneous' method.

The normal schools started by La Salle also contributed much to advancing the efficiency of teaching. For the first time, teachers of ability and training were made possible for the elementary schools. According to an account of the times,[3] the elementary teachers just before La Salle's day consisted of sextons, retired soldiers, innkeepers, old-clothes men, wig-makers, masons, cooks, and

Improvement in teachers.

---

[1] La Salle must have drawn up the *Conduct* about 1695, but after retiring from the headship of the order, he revised it carefully, and it was printed for the first time the year after his death.

[2] La Salle considered a training in politeness so important for Christian culture, that he wrote a special manual for his schools called *Les Règles de la Bienséance et de la Civilité Chrétienne*.

[3] See Victor Plessier, *Histoire d'une École Gratuite*.

others who had failed in their own employment, and ignorance and immorality alike were characteristic of the class. Contrasted with such persons, it can be seen how superior were the teachers in La Salle's schools.

Mechanical, memoriter, and repressive methods, and the ferule and rod and espionage.

Nevertheless, the 'simultaneous' method soon became mechanical, *memoriter*, and repressive, and resulted in a lack of incentive on the part of the pupil. In consequence, interest and control had to be secured by means of frequent penances and severe corporal punishment. Reprimand was occasionally used, and even expulsion, although only as a last resort. The official instruments of correction — the ferule and the rod — are carefully described in the second part of the *Conduct of Studies*, which treats of discipline. Here also are specified the exact offenses that are to be punished, and the number of blows to be administered for each misdeed. Espionage and tale-bearing likewise had to be encouraged for the maintenance of order.

Rapid growth and spread of the Christian Brothers' schools, and the extension of their scope.

The Educational Results of the Christian Brothers. — The schools of the Christian Brothers, however, met with a rapid growth. By the time of La Salle's death, the number of houses belonging to the brethren had grown to be twenty-seven and the membership of the society had become two hundred and seventy-four. Before the close of the eighteenth century, there had been a further increase to one hundred and twenty-two schools and over eight hundred brothers, so that facilities were furnished for thirty-six thousand pupils. During the nineteenth century, in spite of vicissitude and persecution, the brethren and their institutions were diffused over all the states of Europe and America, amid Catholics and Protestants alike, and the scope of their labors and instruction was very greatly extended. While great changes in the curriculum and method of these schools have taken place from time to time, they are still predominantly ascetic in their tone. There is, nevertheless, much to admire in the history and system of the Christian Brothers and in the wonderful work they have done for elementary education among the Catholics.

Catholic Education of Girls. — Likewise, before the close of the seventeenth century, some attempt was made by Catholic writers and educators to provide for the training of women, but the suggestions made were generally conservative and unsatisfactory. Even *Jacqueline Pascal* (1625–1661) in her *Regulations* seems to have been very austere and to have applied the Port Royal methods to the education of girls in a much less satisfactory way than did the writers on the training of boys.[1] The *Letters* of the Marquise de Sévigné[2] (1626–1696) to her daughter show that she was much interested in education, but she formulated no definite system. The educational work of the *Marquise de Maintenon* (1635–1719), who bore such an intimate relation to Louis XIV, was likewise unfruitful. While at first breaking from the convent idea in the school she had founded at St. Cyr, and endeavoring to give a fairly broad and literary course, she later reverted to the ascetic ideal, although it was tempered by her desire to fit the girls for society and motherhood, as well as for the veil. Her *Letters and Conversations on the Education of Girls* and her *Counsels to Young Women Who Enter Society*, however, are filled with good sense and sound pedagogy.

Austere methods of Jacqueline Pascal; the Letters of Marquise de Sévigné; and the institution of Marquise de Maintenon at St. Cyr.

The Educational Aim, Course, and Method of Fénelon. — These works were probably produced while the marquise was under the influence of *François Fénelon*[3] (1651–1715), who was one of the greatest theorists that has ever dealt with the education of women. His writings have not only been read by Catholics of the time, but by persons of all sects in every age. In his *De l'Éducation des Filles* ('On the Education of Girls') Fénelon holds: —

Fénelon holds in his Education of Girls that they should be educated for real duties, and that their impulses should not be altogether repressed.

"Women, as a rule, have still weaker and more inquisitive minds than men; therefore it is not expedient to engage them in studies

---

[1] See p. 228.
[2] The *Letters* of Madame de Sévigné have been excellently translated and edited by Mrs. S. J. Hale (Boston, 1878).
[3] This was the name of the family estate; Fénelon's own name was *François de Salignac de la Motte*.

that may turn their heads. . . . Their bodies as well as their minds are less strong and robust than those of men. As a compensation, nature has given them for their portion neatness, industry, and thrift, in order to keep them quietly occupied in their homes. But what follows from this natural weakness of women? The weaker they are, the more important it is to strengthen them. Have they not duties to fulfill, and duties, too, that lie at the foundation of all life? . . . We must consider, besides the good that women do if properly brought up, the evil they may cause in the world when they lack a training that inspires virtue."

The objective method, the appeal to curiosity, and instruction through fables and dialogues.
Girls should, therefore, from earliest infancy, be trained for real duties in a real world. Their natural impulses should not be altogether repressed, as in the convent education of the times, but only directed. He emphasizes the objective method, and bases it upon the instinct of curiosity, and attempts to make study agreeable. All instruction, both intellectual and moral, he holds, should be given indirectly, and to that end, he believes in making use of fables and dialogues. Later, when he became tutor to the grandson of Louis XIV, he wrote collections of *Fables, Dialogues des Morts* ('Dialogues of the Dead'), and his famous *Aventures de Télémaque* ('Adventures of Telemachus'), and in other ways tried to carry his theories of informal education into effect.[1]

Fénelon's theory had little influence upon the dogmatic and ascetic education of women.
Results of Fénelon's Theories.— However, Fénelon's works were in singular contrast to the constraint of the Catholic teaching orders and schools of the period. They had little influence upon the education of women at the time, except perhaps temporarily upon the school at St. Cyr. Even the *Convent of New Catholics*, of which Fénelon himself was the Superior at the time of producing his chief educational work, was a school for the education of women and girls proselyted from Protestantism, and was dogmatic and ascetic in character. In fact, Fénelon's own educational practice is in keep-

---

[1] Fénelon's training of this young duke of Burgundy was most successful. The prince has been described as "terrible from his birth, passionate, vindictive, and even cruel by nature." Fénelon, however, discovered the right modes of appeal, and soon made "another man of him and changed such fearful faults into contrary virtues."

ing with that of his day, and he took an active part in the Catholic reaction that had been begun by the Jesuits a century and a half before. He was a man of character and thoroughly amiable, but he held it his duty to force a universal acceptance of Catholicism throughout France. He and Madame de Maintenon were among those who persuaded the king in 1685 to revoke the toleration that had been granted by the Edict of Nantes for nearly a century. Such, however, was the sentiment of the times that even the most liberal Catholics, like Madame de Sévigné, rejoiced at the establishment of religious unity, and Fénelon was rewarded for his loyalty and zeal by appointment to the archbishopric of Cambrai.

The Religious and Repressive Aim of Catholic Education.— It is now obvious that the aim of the Catholic education had reverted to its old position. Its object became, in general, the training of youth in religious observances and in submission to the authority of the Catholic Church. To this ideal was added the purpose of ridding the world of the dangerous heresies of Protestantism. Reason was held, except by the Jansenists and Oratorians, who did not exert much influence, to be out of place and to be utterly unreliable as a guide in education and life. But the religious conception of education was held by the Protestants in common with the Catholics, and as the Protestant creeds became more fixed, dogmatic, and suspicious of reason, there was little difference in principle between the educational positions of the two great religious parties. *Catholic education aimed at a training in religion and authority, and opposed reason as a guide.*

The Organization of the Catholic Schools and Universities.— The Protestants, however, had found it wise to place the support and control of education in the hands of the princes and the State. They could no longer leave it, as the Catholics did, absolutely to the Church, which was a sort of state within the State. Owing to this secular control and their position on universal intelligence, the Protestants had generally established state school systems and held to the duty of providing *Few instances in Catholic states of elementary education at public expense.*

and requiring elementary education at public expense. Of this the Catholics, from their different administration of the schools and their different conception of religion, did not in general see the necessity, although the Christian Brothers and others undertook a great work in this direction, and Duke Albrecht V of Bavaria actually ordered throughout his state the establishment of 'German' schools with instruction in reading, writing, and the Catholic creed.

In secondary and higher education the individual was also subordinated to authority.

In secondary and higher education the Jesuits furnished the most thorough and well-organized schools for all countries, but here, too, the subordination of the individual to authority and the Church was insisted upon. The same attitude was taken in Germany and elsewhere by the universities that remained loyal to Catholicism and in the few new Catholic universities that were founded at this time.

Little attention to the education of women.

As compared with the Protestants, little was done by the Catholics for any stage of the education of women. Notwithstanding the excellent theories of Fénelon and the practical efforts of Jacqueline Pascal and Madame de Maintenon, the training of girls remained of the austere type of the convent, and did not give attention to much beyond the forms of religion.

As a whole, the courses of study consisted mostly of religion and formal humanism.

The Curricula. — The course of study in the Catholic institutions was the logical product of their ideals and organization, and of the times. While the schools of the Christian Brothers trained their pupils in the rudiments, as well as in religion, and the Oratorians and the Port Royalists somewhat emphasized the vernacular studies, history, and philosophy, yet, upon the whole, the content of education was largely religion and humanism of the most formal type. In this respect, the Jesuits, like the Protestant Sturm, had a tremendous influence upon the schools of Europe and America for two centuries, and it has been an open question as to which of the two was the more important factor in this coloring of the curricula.

The Teachers and Methods. — While the Jesuits and

the Christian Brothers were the first educators in history to undertake the training of teachers, and their work was most thoroughly done, both orders tended to preserve the most formal and stereotyped methods. In spite of the example of the Port Royalists, they emphasized memory at the expense of reason, and held to complete imitation without any allowance for individuality or originality. They insisted upon the importance of tradition and authority, although, like the Protestants, they endeavored to cultivate controversial skill. In all instances, as a matter of course, the teachers were of the Catholic clergy and usually from the regular teaching orders. *[Memory, rather than reason, and controversial skill cultivated.]* *[The teachers were usually from the teaching orders.]*

Results of Education during the Reformation. — Hence, except for launching the idea of civil support and control, the Reformation accomplished but little directly making for individualism and progress either through the Protestant revolts or the Catholic awakening. Education fell back before long into the grooves of formalism, repression, and distrust of reason. There resulted a tendency to test life and the educational preparation for living by a formulation of belief almost as much as in the days of scholasticism. A new measure for realizing individualism and freedom from the bondage of tradition, and an opportunity to investigate and search for truth, were needed. Such a further fulfillment of the spirit of the awakening was to be found in the parallel and later educational movement now usually known as *realism*. *[The Reformation accomplished little for individualism and progress.]*

SUPPLEMENTARY READING

I. SOURCES

BARNARD, H. *American Journal of Education* (Volume XXVII, pp. 165-175, contains a translation of the Jesuit *Ratio Studiorum* as it appears in the *Constitution* of 1558).
CADET, F. *Port Royal Education* (contains extracts from the leading Port Royal educators, translated by A. D. Jones).
LA SALLE, J. B. *Conduct of Schools.*
LUPTON, K. *Fénelon's Education of Girls.*
M'CRIE, T. *Provincial Letters of Pascal.*

PACHTLER, G. M. *Ratio Studiorum* (*Monumenta Germaniæ Pedagogica*, II, V, IX, and XVI).
ROBINSON, J. H. *Readings in European History*. Chaps. XXVIII-XXIX.
ROBINSON, J. H., and WHITCOMB, M. *Early Reformation in Germany* (Translation and Reprints, II, No. 6).
ROLLIN, C. *Traité des Études* (Nouvelle édition par Letronne).
WATERWORTH, J. (Translator). *Decrees and Canons of the Council of Trent*.
WIGHT, O. W. (Editor). *Adventures of Telemachus* (translated by Hawkesworth).
WIGHT, O. W. (Translator). *Thoughts of Pascal*.

II. AUTHORITIES

ARNOLD, M. *Popular Education in France*.
AZARIAS, BROTHER. *Essays Educational*.
BARNARD, H. *American Journal of Education*. Vols. XIII, 477-486; XIV, 455-483; XX, 211-216; XXIII, 17-46; XXVII, 165-175; XXVIII, 1-16; XXX, 481-490, and 705-736.
BARNARD, H. *German Teachers and Educators*. Pp. 229-256.
BEARD, C. *Port Royal*. II, Chap. II.
BROWN, H. C. *The Jansenists and Their Schools* (*The Educational Review*, Vol. VI, pp. 485-492; VII, pp. 64-70).
BROWNING, O. *Educational Theories*. Chap. VIII.
CADET, F. *Port Royal Education* (translated by A. D. Jones).
CARTWRIGHT, W. C. *The Jesuits, Their Constitution and Teaching*. Chaps. II-III.
COMPAYRÉ, G. *The History of Pedagogy* (translated by Payne). Chaps. VII-VIII, and X-XII.
CREIGHTON, M. *A History of the Papacy during the Period of the Reformation*.
FISHER, G. P. *The Reformation*. Chap. XI.
GRIESINGER, T. *The Jesuits*.
GUILLAUME, L. *Les Jésuites et les Classiques Chrétiens*.
HUGHES, T. *Loyola and the Educational System of the Jesuits*.
LAURIE, S. S. *Educational Opinion from the Renaissance*. Chap. VIII.
LINDSAY, T. M. *A History of the Reformation*. Bk. VI.
MAGEVNEY, E. *The Jesuits as Educators*.
MERTZ, G. K. *Die Pädagogik der Jesuiten*.
MUNROE, J. P. *The Educational Ideal*. Chap. VI.
NOHLE, E. *History of the German School System*. (Report of the U. S. Commissioner of Education, 1897-1898, pp. 29-39.)
QUICK, R. H. *Educational Reformers*. Chaps. IV and XI.
RAVELET, A. *Blessed J. B. de la Salle*.
RUSSELL, J. E. *German Higher Schools*. Pp. 36-41, 50-58, and 137-141.

Sainte-Beuve, C. A. *Port Royal.*
Schwickerath, R. *Jesuit Education.*
Symonds, J. A. *Renaissance in Italy.* The Catholic Reaction, Vol. I.
Tollemache, M. *French Jansenists.*
Ward, A. W. *The Counter-Reformation.*
Wilson, Mrs. R. F. *The Christian Brothers.*

CHAPTER XVII

THE BEGINNINGS OF REALISTIC EDUCATION

The Relation of Realism to the Renaissance and the Reformation. — From what has preceded, it will readily appear that the movement of the seventeenth century called *realism* was an outgrowth of the same underlying forces as the humanistic awakening of the fifteenth and sixteenth centuries, and the social and religious reformation of the sixteenth and seventeenth. In the last four chapters we have noted how, through literary and æsthetic means, the intellectual quickening in Italy issued in individual development, and how later the same unfolding in the North came to stress "the infinite value of each human soul," and the importance of every individual's judging for himself in religious and theological matters. Now it was while the movement of the Renaissance was everywhere losing its vitality and declining into a narrow 'Ciceronianism,'[1] and the Reformation was hardening once more into fixed concepts and a dogmatic formalism, appealing to authority and systems of belief,[2] that the awakened intellect of Europe tended, through the channel of 'realism,' to find still another mode of expression. The process of emancipating the individual from tradition and repressive authority had not altogether ceased, but had simply varied its form of manifestation.

While the Renaissance and the Reformation were hardening into formalism, a new means of expression was found in 'realism.'

The Nature of Realism. — This new movement of realism also held to the reliability of the individual judgment. It implied a search for a method by which *real things* may be known, and held that real knowledge comes through the reason or through the senses rather than

This movement implied a method by which 'real' things may be known,

[1] See pp. 135-137 and 176.   [2] See pp. 204 f. and 237.

through memory and reliance upon tradition.¹ The most distinct form of realism interpreted 'real things' as individual objects, and was an application of the new spirit and methods of the awakening to investigation in the natural sciences.² In fact, 'realism' in its strictest connotation might well be denominated the 'early scientific' movement.³ This would, however, seem to limit the term to the later and more definite development that it reached in what has been called 'real' or 'sense' realism, and to obscure its origin and its close connection with the Renaissance and Reformation as part of the same freeing of the human intellect from the bonds of dogma. And while 'sense' realism cannot be said to appear as a distinct movement until the formulation of the scientific method by Bacon early in the seventeenth century, its roots run back into the other movements of the awakening for at least a century before that time. Even in the humanistic movement, although there is not much evidence of interest in objects as the true realities, there seems to be a tendency to break from a restriction to words and set forms and an effort to seek for the ideas, or 'real things,' back of the written words. It was such a broad type of humanism, of course, that marked the Renaissance in the first place, and it was not until the sixteenth century that it tended to harden into a formalism. But during the period of decline there is also a clearly marked effort to return

and in its strictest connotation might be called the 'early scientific' movement, did this not obscure the connection with the Renaissance and Reformation.

---

¹ Philosophically, this position has been known as 'rationalism' when, as with Descartes and his school, it was held that whatever appears clearly and distinctly is true, or as 'empiricism' when the reliability of the individual was transferred to sense experience, as in the case of Locke and Hume.

² The movement is, therefore, almost the opposite of scholastic 'realism' (see pp. 52 f.) in the Middle Ages, and should not be confused with it. In each case, the significance depends upon what is to be considered the 'real' thing,— ideas or individual objects.

³ With this interpretation in mind, Browning (*Educational Theories*, Chapters III–VII) divides educational thinkers into three classes, 'humanists,' who wish to educate by means of the classics; 'realists,' who would use the works of nature; and 'naturalists,' who aim rather at a training, outside of schools and knowledge, for the development of character.

to the better ideals of the earlier days and to oppose the artificial formulations into which humanism was crystallizing. By advocates of this broader humanism, form was considered of importance only as a doorway to content, and it was hoped to make the classical literatures a means of studying human life, motives, and institutions.

The broader humanism, or 'humanistic' realism, and the attempt to adapt education to actual living, known as 'social' realism, together form a bridge from humanism to sense realism.

The Earlier Realism, Verbal and Social. — This broader humanism may, therefore, as properly be called 'verbal' or 'humanistic' realism, and may be regarded as the forerunner of sense realism. With its emphasis upon content often went the study of social and physical phenomena, in order to throw light upon the meaning of the passages under consideration. There seems also to have been an attempt on the part of several writers to adapt education to actual living in a real world and to prepare young people for the concrete duties of life. This latter phase of the renewed humanism was most frequently stressed in the education of young aristocrats. It usually involved a study of the customs, institutions, and languages of other countries through travel under the care of a tutor or residence in a foreign school. Such a movement has been known as 'social' realism, but it cannot easily be distinguished from 'verbal' realism. While one element or the other may seem to be more prominent in a certain treatise, the two phases of education are largely bound up in each other, and both tendencies appear in most authors of the times. They seem to be but two sides of the same thing and to constitute together a natural bridge from humanism to sense realism.

The Earlier Realists. — Hence it happens that while most educators continued during the sixteenth and seventeenth centuries to make up the course of study from classical elements, the attitude, in the case of some, at least, was very different from what it had been. These reformed humanists or early realists wished to use the classical authors to understand life and nature through an appreciation of what had been the highest produc-

The early realists used the classical

THE BEGINNINGS OF REALISTIC EDUCATION 243

tions of the human mind, and to make education a preparation for real living. Erasmus, for example, is scathing in his ironical description of Ciceronianism, and justifies grammar simply as a gateway to ideas and real things. He declares:— *authors to understand life. Position of Erasmus,*

> "Knowledge seems to be of two kinds: that of things and that of words. That of words comes first, that of things is the more important. . . . So, then, grammar claims the first place and should be taught to youth in both Greek and Latin. . . . Having acquired the ability to speak, if not volubly, certainly with correctness, next the mind must be directed to a knowledge of things."

Elsewhere[1] we have seen that Erasmus was vehemently opposed to wasting time upon the details of accidence and syntax, and that he felt the main purpose of grammar was to unlock the content of the classics. Through this literature he believed that a knowledge of reality came, and that geography, natural history, and agriculture should be studied for the sake of the light they throw upon it. Similarly, Melanchthon states:— *Melanchthon,*

> "I always endeavor to introduce you to such authors as will increase your comprehension of things while they contribute toward enlarging your language. These two parts belong together, and have sworn friendship, as Horace says, so that one stands and is supported by the other, because no one can speak well if he does not understand what he wishes to say, and again knowledge is lame without the light of speech."

Neander, too, ventured to question the value of the classics where no real knowledge was obtained, and recommended the study of history, geography, science, and music for making clear the ideas of the ancients.[2] Elyot was also found to advocate Greek and Latin for their content and preparation for life,[3] and Ascham criticises the schools of the day for their grammatical grind and their neglect to bring the student into an understanding of the authors themselves.[4] *Neander, Elyot, and Ascham.*

Rabelais and His Works. — More radical innovations than any that appear in these other early realists, how- *The life of Rabelais.*

[1] See pp. 152 f.
[2] See p. 189.
[3] See p. 165.
[4] See p. 167.

ever, are implied in the skits of Luther's contemporary, the madcap Rabelais, upon the formal classicism, and in his suggestions for a more rounded and valuable course of study. *François Rabelais* (1495-1553) was the son of a French innkeeper, but was educated for a career in the Church. His appetite for letters and science, together with his interest in the beautiful scenery amid which he was reared, led to his abandonment of the monastery and to entrance upon a roving existence. He studied medicine, but, while engaged in its practice, spent most of his time in producing works of scholarship, and his world-famed *Gargantua* and *Pantagruel*. These were the stock names for giants in the romantic writings of the day, and by caricaturing these stories he found a most effective way of appealing to the people of his generation and drawing attention to the current abuses. For the same reason, these works are indecent almost beyond hope of intelligent expurgation,[1] but beneath all the obscene farce there runs a serious purpose.

His *Gargantua* and *Pantagruel*.

The Training of the Whole Man. — The *Gargantua* and *Pantagruel*, which are continuous in plot,[2] constitute a revolt from the narrower humanism and ecclesiastical abuses. They are filled with biting sarcasm against the monasteries and their courses of study, but are no more sparing in their ridicule of the Calvinistic and Lutheran dogmatism. But these works are not altogether negative, for Rabelais does endeavor also to construct a theory of education on broad principles. In his scheme the whole man is to benefit. Together with the intellect, the senses are to be trained; the body, as well as the mind, is to be nurtured; character and a religious spirit are to be developed; and the pupil made competent to take his place in a world of men, and to perform with ease and dignity all that manhood demands.

Rabelais constructed a theory of education in which the whole man was to benefit.

---

[1] Fleury (*Rabelais et Ses Œuvres*) has most nearly succeeded in a disinfected version. Cf. also Besant's *Readings in Rabelais*.

[2] The series contains five books in all, the last four of which belong to the *Pantagruel*. The third is the masterpiece, while the last two are much inferior and do not concern us here.

THE BEGINNINGS OF REALISTIC EDUCATION   245

The Informal Method of the *Gargantua*. — To achieve this for Gargantua, his father, after finding the ordinary grammatical drill a humiliating failure, finally has the boy begin a course of informal training quite in contrast to the former plan. The Scriptures are read and explained to him during his bath upon arising, and the sky is observed and its appearance compared with that of the evening before. While dressing he is exercised in a review of the previous day's work, and after breakfast he is read to for three hours. Then he and his tutor adjourn to the tennis-ground and play until they are in a profuse perspiration. While rubbing down and dressing for dinner, they repeat extracts from the lessons learned earlier in the day. At the dinner-table they discuss the origin, history, and use of various comestibles, and then give thanks to God for his bounty. Next, Gargantua spends an hour playing cards, thereby learning the science of numbers, while the three hours following are given to writing, drawing, and lettering. The remnant of the afternoon is spent in out-of-door sports, and after the evening meal come cards, music, a short practical lesson on astronomy, and a review of the day's proceedings.

_{Instead of a grammatical drill, the boy is to receive an informal training with a tutor.}

Thus Rabelais would, by a most natural method, afford a well-rounded education. Instruction is divorced from formal humanism, although six hours a day is devoted to books. Due attention is paid to the common affairs of life and to physical training, and, while no time is spent upon mass and daily services, expositions of the Bible, brief prayers at the proper times, and other religious lessons are given. No moment of the day is wasted, and no corporal punishment seems necessary.

The Broad Education to be Secured. — Gargantua's education is interrupted by war, but in the *Pantagruel*[1] a letter that the giant writes his son gives a specific statement of the subjects Rabelais thought should be mastered under this scheme of education. He declares : —

_{The pupil is to learn the ancient languages, history, cosmography, geometry,}

[1] See Bk. II, Chap. VIII.

246   A HISTORY OF EDUCATION

<small>arithmetic, music, the sciences, and religion.</small>

"First, Greek, as Quintilian advises; secondly, Latin; and then, Hebrew, because of the Holy Scriptures. Likewise, Chaldee, and Arabic; and form thy style, as to Greek, after Plato; as to Latin, after Cicero. Let there be no history which is not firm in thy memory, to which end cosmography will help thee. Of the liberal arts, I gave thee a taste of geometry, arithmetic, and music, when thou wast still little, no older than five or six; pursue the rest and search out all the laws of astronomy."

Besides this study of languages for the sake of the content, and of history, geography, and the mathematical subjects, Gargantua is represented as insisting upon a careful training in zoölogy, botany, geology, and religion, and issuing a final injunction: "In short, let me see thee an abyss of learning."

<small>Rabelais was in advance of his time, and had little effect upon the schools of the period.</small>

The Influence of Rabelais.— In the construction of such an educational scheme, however, Rabelais shows himself as extreme as in his wholesale condemnation of everything done in his time, and we may well take issue with him in regard to the amount and character of the studies he proposes for the curriculum, but his basal principle that one's entire nature should feel the benefit of education marks him as many generations in advance of his time. His curriculum, too, while humanistic, is far from being of the narrow and formal sort, and by its study of nature helps to open the way to realism. It is not easy, however, to point out any direct effect that this broader humanism, or early realism, of Rabelais may have had upon the schools of the period. But the writings of Montaigne, Locke, Rousseau, and other educational theorists show the stamp of his influence.

<small>The life and *Essais* of Montaigne.</small>

Montaigne and His Educational Essays.— Toward the end of the sixteenth century and during the seventeenth, this tendency to interpret humanism more realistically and to make education a means of coming in touch with society, takes more definite form in such exponents as Montaigne in France, and Mulcaster, Milton, and Locke in England. *Michel, Seigneur de Montaigne* (1533–1592), as his title implies, belonged to the aristocracy, and assumed a more refined attitude than his *bourgeois* compatriot, Rabelais. He traveled much, wrote upon a variety of literary topics, and became one of the most brilliant prose authors the world has known. His chief work consists of three volumes of *Essais*, of which *On Pedantry* and *On the Education of Children*[1] especially give his educational views.

Opposition to Formal Humanism. — While Montaigne is never as extreme as Rabelais, throughout these essays he launches ridicule and even invective against the prevailing narrow humanistic education, with its memorizing of words and forms. Of this 'pedantry' he says: — *(He ridicules the formal humanistic education of the times;)*

> "We only toil and labor to stuff the memory, and in the meantime leave the conscience and understanding unfurnished and void. And like birds who fly abroad to forage for grain, and bring it home in their beak without tasting it themselves to feed to their young; so our pedants go picking knowledge here and there out of several authors, and hold it at the tongue's end, only to distribute it among their pupils. . . . But the worst of it is, their scholars are no better nourished by it than themselves: it makes no deeper impression upon them than upon the other, but passes from hand to hand, only to make a show, to be tolerable company, and to tell pretty stories; like a counterfeit coin, of no other use or value but as counters to reckon with or set up at cards."

With such a training, Montaigne holds that it is not remarkable that "when the youth comes back from school after fifteen or sixteen years, there is nothing so awkward and maladroit, so unfit for company or employment; and all that you shall find he has obtained is that his Latin and Greek have made him a more conceited blockhead than before."

Ideas as the Aim of Education. — This is a typical illustration of the early realist's attitude, with its protest against mere memorizing without understanding and the failure to prepare for concrete living. From such a point of view, unless the thought of the author is grasped by the pupil and has become a part of him, the classical *(and holds that ideas are more important than words,)*

---

[1] The latter essay (Bk. I, Chap. XXV) is an expansion of a part of the former (Bk. I, Chap. XXIV), written for his patroness, and, as the title indicates, is more constructive. There are, likewise, many hints of his educational positions in the brief treatise *On the Affection of Fathers to Their Children* (Bk. II, Chap. VIII) and in other essays.

education has failed of its purpose. "Let the master not only examine him about the words of his lesson," says Montaigne, "but also as to the sense and meaning of them, and let him judge of the profit he has made, not by the testimony of his memory, but that of his understanding." And he further insists: "Let but our pupil be well furnished with things, words will follow but too fast. . . . I hold whoever has in his mind a clear and vivid idea, will express it in one way or another." From this it can be seen how Montaigne, like other early realists, uses 'things' as synonymous with 'ideas,' and how the broader humanism shades over into sense realism.

and character than books, and recommends travel under a tutor rather than schools.

Travel the Best Means of Education. — But Montaigne also holds that, even under the most favorable circumstances, books and the mere acquisition of knowledge are not the most important things in life, and should not be the final aim of education. The real purpose of all training is to shape our character and make us useful and efficient. "The advantages of study are to become better and wiser," and it is the part of the teacher to inspire a love for moral living in his pupil and make him see "that the height and value of true virtue consists in the facility, utility, and pleasure of its exercise." Since virtue comes from experience and breadth of vision rather than from reading, Montaigne advocates travel[1] rather than schools as a means of education. He declares: —

"That we may whet and sharpen our wits by rubbing them on those of others, I would that a boy should be sent abroad very young. . . . I would have this the book my young gentleman should study with most attention; for so many humors, so many sects, so many judgments, opinions, laws, and customs, teach us to judge aright of our own, and inform our understanding to discover its imperfection and natural infirmity."

Like Rabelais, Locke, and Rousseau, Montaigne intended that this travel and the rest of education should

[1] Rabelais had previously implied this, and Milton, Comenius, Locke, and Rousseau afterward gave similar advice.

be private and under the care of a tutor. This preceptor, he held, should be a man of the world, one "whose head is well tempered rather than well filled."

Subjects and Training to be Acquired. — Montaigne's belief in educating for character by means of experience explains his idea that the chief study should be "philosophy, or at least that part which treats of man and his offices and duties." He even asks: "Since philosophy is that which instructs us to live, why is it not communicated to children? . . . Philosophy has discourses equally proper for childhood and for old age." But "having taught the pupil what will make him more wise and good," Montaigne believes that some of the traditional subjects, — logic, rhetoric, geometry, and physics, may be imparted, but they are of less importance. He even admits the need of Latin and Greek in the education of a gentleman,[1] although he maintains that one should first study his own language and those of his neighbors. He also stresses physical exercise and adds:

The chief study should be 'philosophy,' but some traditional subjects should also be imparted.

"I would have his outward behavior and mien, and the disposition of his limbs formed at the same time. It is not a soul, it is not a body that we are training; it is a man, and we ought not to divide him into two parts."

Physical exercise and the 'hardening process.'

In this respect he was followed by Locke and Rousseau, who may likewise have taken from him the 'hardening process,' or the inuring of the boy to heat and cold, to make him hardy and vigorous.

Advanced Methods of Teaching. — Montaigne's suggestions as to method were also advanced. We have already seen his disapproval of the *memoriter* plan in vogue.[2] Elsewhere he asserts that "to know by rote is no knowledge," and he recommends the more flexible method of "instructing him sometimes by discourse and sometimes by reading; sometimes his tutor shall put the author himself into his hands, and sometimes only the marrow and substance of him." He further holds that "a man should not so much repeat his lesson as practice

Disapproval of memorizing.

Latin and Greek learned by speaking them.

---

[1] Locke makes a similar argument for Latin. See p. 258. [2] See p. 247.

it," and so recommends that Latin and Greek be learned by speaking them.¹ If such effective and pleasant methods were adopted, Montaigne believes that the existing discipline, " presenting nothing but rods and ferules," would be unnecessary, and that schools would no longer be 'mere prisons.'

While Montaigne's doctrines influenced the schools but little, they popularized many educational improvements.

The Effects of Montaigne's Theories.— It may not be possible to show the influence of Montaigne's educational doctrines upon the schools of the times, but they must have been widely read and have done much to popularize many improvements in the content and methods of education. While Montaigne was not himself a teacher, these confidential discourses have made a large contribution to educational theory and practice. They seem to have directly influenced Locke and Rousseau, and many others through them, and it is quite apparent that Montaigne's practical program of studies led naturally into the sense realism of Bacon and Comenius.

Mulcaster in his Positions and Elementarie shatters the restricted humanism and approaches sense realism.

Mulcaster's Advanced Position. — In England an excellent instance of these tendencies of the earlier realism is seen in the advanced theories of the English schoolmaster, *Richard Mulcaster* (1530–1611). This writer seems not only to have shattered the old idols of the restricted humanism, but to have been approaching some of the new constructions of sense realism. Mulcaster was given a classical education at Eton, Oxford, and Cambridge, and almost up to his death was in charge of one of the most famous 'grammar' schools in London. From 1561 to 1586 he was headmaster of Merchant Taylors', and during the years 1596–1608 he held the same office at St. Paul's. Nevertheless, in both his great educational works, *Positions* (1581) and *Elementarie* (1582),² he gives especial attention to primary

---

¹ This method was probably suggested to him by his own experience in studying with a German tutor who knew no French and had to communicate with him in Latin.
² The full titles are *Positions Wherein Those Circumstances are Examined for the Training up of Children either for Skill in their Booke or*

training, praises English as a means of education, and expressly flouts authority. "It is not so," he says, "because a writer said so, but because the truth is so."

His Advocacy of a Natural Education. — Mulcaster's attitude in these matters proceeds from his general advocacy of an education more in keeping with nature than was that in vogue. He states: —

> "The end of education and training is to help nature to her perfection, which is, when all her abilities be perfected in their habit.
> ... Consideration and judgment must wisely mark whereunto Nature is either evidently given or secretly affectionate, and must frame an education consonant thereto." [1]

He, therefore, holds that the 'ingenerate' abilities of each child should be examined, that a proper education may be given him, and he attempts a psychological analysis as the basis of his philosophy of education. He finds that there are to be considered three main powers of the mind, — "wit to take (or perception), memorie to keep, and discretion to discern (or judgment)." On the development of the last, which functions in morality, he lays considerable stress, in order that the children may "learn to discern that which is well from ill, good from bad, religious from profane, honest from dishonest, commendable from blameworthy, seemly from unseemly." Like Montaigne, too, he believes in physical education and the training of the whole man on the ground of "the soul and body being co-partners in good and ill." *He analyzes the mind into 'wit,' 'memorie,' and 'discretion,' and recommends a natural development. Physical education.*

His Emphasis upon Elementary Education. — Like the other humanistic realists, Mulcaster lacks faith in the classical fetish of the times. Moreover, he seems to imply that too many are receiving a classical education for the good of the country or themselves, by asking: — *He thinks that too many receive a classical education, but holds that all should have an elementary training.*

Health in their Bodie, and *The Elementarie, Which Entreateth Chiefly of the Right Writing of the English Tung.* Only the first part of the latter work was ever completed.

[1] When necessary for intelligibility, Mulcaster's orthography has been modernized.

"To have so many gaping for preferment, how can it be but that such shifters must needs shake the very strongest pillar in that state where they live? . . . If that wit fall to preach which were fitter for the plough, and he to climb a pulpit, who is meant to scale a wall, is not a good carter ill lost, and a good soldier ill placed?"

Mulcaster holds, however, that all should have elementary training in reading and writing English, and in drawing and music. Those who can go no further will need this training in the vernacular "for religion's sake and their necessary affairs," while those who are to take up Latin and the higher education should have it first, because "we are directed by nature and propertie to read that first which we speak first, and to care for that most which we ever use most." And his pride in the mother tongue blazes forth more clearly in his *Elementarie*, where he exclaims: —

Pride in the mother tongue.

"I do not think that any language is better able to utter all arguments either with more pith or greater plainness than our English tongue."

'Grammar' school after twelve, and university after sixteen.

Higher and Other Training. — This elementary education is to engage the pupil until he is twelve, when those fitted for it are to begin the 'grammar' school. They will, Mulcaster believes, then acquire more in a secondary education between twelve and sixteen than if they started Latin at seven. The university, which next follows for those of ability, is to include "colleges for tongues, for mathematics, for philosophy, for teachers, for physicians, for lawyers, for divines." Mulcaster does not, however, believe foreign travel as essential to education, as do Montaigne, Locke, or even Milton, although he admits its value. But Mulcaster devotes much more space than Montaigne or Milton, and fully as much as Locke, to a description of the proper physical training.[1] Although his account does not embody any peculiar doctrine, like the 'hardening process,'[2] it is very broad, and includes dancing, wrestling, fencing,

[1] Some two thirds of his forty-five *Positions*, although not much over one third of the actual number of pages, are included in this part of his work. [2] See pp. 249 and 308.

running, leaping, swimming, riding, hunting, and shooting, and an outline of the necessary knowledge of anatomy, physiology, and hygiene.

The Education of Girls. — While Mulcaster gives first attention to the boys, because of their greater political importance, he is progressive enough to "admit young maidens to learn," and this he defends on four grounds, — "the custom of our country, our duty towards them, their natural ability, and the worthy effects of such as have been well trained." As in the case of their brothers, too, the girls are to be trained somewhat with reference to their ability and aim in life. They are to be taught reading, writing, drawing, and music, just as the boys are, but the study of the professions is to be replaced by that of housewifery. In some cases they may even be taught the classic and other languages. *(Girls to be trained with reference to their ability and aim in life.)*

Improvements in Teaching. — Mulcaster wishes the method of education to be equally in conformity with nature, and he insists that the pupil shall be neither forced nor repressed. In the matter of discipline, while he feels that "the rod may no more be spared in schools than the sword may in the princes' hand," the offenses that he has in mind for its administration are altogether those against morality. It is also of interest to notice the importance that Mulcaster attached to securing good teachers, and his insistence that elementary work is the most difficult and that the teachers of this stage should have the smallest number of pupils and be paid more than any of the others. He wished also, as has been indicated, to have teachers trained in a separate college of the university upon the same professional basis as doctors, lawyers, and clergymen. *(The pupil should be neither forced nor repressed. Teachers and their training.)*

The Results of Mulcaster's Positions. — The advanced theories and suggestions of Mulcaster seem to have been but little reflected in the immediate education of the times. Even the schools of which he was the head were distinctly Latin schools, and were for the most part conducted upon the traditional basis. However, he must, through his proposed reforms in aim, organization, and *(Mulcaster's theories had little effect at the time, but greatly influenced the later realists.)*

method, have had a far-reaching effect upon the later realists and the realistic trend in modern education. In fact, while there is not as much direct reference to sense training and a scientific content in Mulcaster's course of study as in even that of Rabelais and Milton, by his advocacy of the vernacular and especially by his attempt at a science of education, he may be regarded as more nearly approaching sense realism than any other of the broader humanists. According to some authorities, Mulcaster, rather than Bacon, Ratich, or Comenius, should be considered the first writer to embody the genuine spirit of sense realism in his works. Some of his ideas, too, seem not to have been utilized until much later than the period of sense realism. His suggestions that girls should have a complete training, that the initial work in education is the most important and difficult, and that teachers should be trained for every stage of the work, it has remained for the nineteenth and twentieth centuries to realize.

Some of his ideas not utilized before the nineteenth century.

Milton's Opposition to the Formal Humanism. — Another important illustration of the broader humanism, while not containing propositions as advanced as those of Mulcaster, is found some three quarters of a century later in the *Tractate of Education* by the great poet and scholar,[1] *John Milton* (1608-1674). While a remarkable classicist himself, Milton objects to the usual humanistic education with its " grammatic flats and shallows where they stuck unreasonably to learn a few words with lamentable construction," and declares that the boys " do for the most part grow into hatred and contempt of learning." He claims that " we do amiss to spend seven or eight years in scraping together so much miserable Latin and Greek as might be learned otherwise easily and delightfully in one year." He especially stigmatizes, as Locke did later, the formal work in Latin composition, " forcing the empty wits of children to compose

Milton's Tractate opposes the formal humanism,

---

[1] Milton's fame as the author of *Paradise Lost* and other poems has obscured the fact that he conducted a private school for nine years, and was an industrious scholar and an active pamphleteer during middle life.

themes, verses, and orations, which are the acts of ripest judgment and the final work of a head filled by long reading and observing."

An Encyclopædic but Humanistic Program. — It is not, however, the study of classics in itself that Milton opposes, but the constant harping upon grammar without regard to the thought of the authors, for "though a linguist should pride himself to have all the tongues that Babel cleft the world into, yet if he have not studied the solid *things* [1] in them as well as the words and lexicons, he were nothing so much to be esteemed as any yeoman or tradesman competently wise in his mother dialect only." In this statement, as well as elsewhere, it is obvious that by 'things' Milton, like Montaigne,[2] meant ideas and not objects. Even in his recommendation of a most encyclopædic program of studies, which is usually one of the marks of the sense realist, he seems to imply the humanistic rather than the later realism, although he wrote half a century after Bacon and was a younger contemporary of Comenius.[3] While this curriculum includes large elements of science and manual training, and especially emphasizes a knowledge of nature, it affords the broadest training in Latin and Greek, and, after the fashion of broader humanism in general, undertakes to teach agriculture through Latin, and natural history, geography, and medicine through Greek. On the whole, it is an education of books, and the enormous load of languages, — Italian, Hebrew, Chaldee, and Syriac, as well as Latin and Greek, — together with mathematics, sciences, and other studies, would make such a course impossible, except, as some one has said, for a 'college of Miltons.' As with some of the other humanistic realists, notably Montaigne, Milton also would have considerable time given, toward the end of the course, to the social sciences, — history, ethics, politics, economics, theology, — and to such practical training as would bring one in touch

and advocates ideas rather than words.

He recommends an encyclopædic program, including sciences, but also a broad training in Latin and Greek, and much time on the social sciences.

---

[1] Italics mine. [2] See p. 248.
[3] The *Tractate* is dedicated to Samuel Hartlib, who was also the friend and patron of Comenius, and a well-known sense realist.

with life. He likewise advocates the experience and knowledge that would come from travel in England and abroad.

Milton's Definition of Education. — Thus, in the place of the usual restricted conception of humanistic education, Milton would substitute a genuine study and understanding of the classical authors and a real preparation for life. While he piously states the aim of learning as "to repair the ruins of our first parents by regaining to know God aright," he is more specific later when he frames his famous definition: —

> "I call therefore a complete and generous education that which fits a man to perform justly, skilfully, and magnanimously all the offices both private and public of peace and war."

The Academy of Milton. — The school in which Milton would carry out his ideal education he calls an *Academy*, and states that it should be held in "a spatious house and ground about it, big enough to lodge one hundred and fifty persons." This institution should keep the boys from the age of twelve to twenty-one, and should provide both secondary and higher education, "not heeding a remove to any other house of scholarship, except it be some peculiar college of Law or Physic." And he adds: "After this pattern as many edifices may be converted to this use, as shall be needful in every city throughout this land." Strangely enough, as will be seen later,[1] this curriculum and organization of Milton's, exaggerated as they were, found a partial embodiment and a function in a new educational institution. 'Academies' based upon this general plan were organized to meet the exigencies of the English nonconformists, and afterward afforded the name and pattern of a species of secondary school that was for a time predominant in America.

Early Realism in Locke's *Thoughts*. — The broader or realistic humanism also appears later than Milton's time in *John Locke* (1632–1704). As will be shown

---
[1] See pp. 291–293.

THE BEGINNINGS OF REALISTIC EDUCATION 257

later,[1] Locke based most of his educational positions upon sense realism or upon formal discipline, but in *Some Thoughts concerning Education*, he has many elements that remind us strongly of Montaigne, Milton, and Mulcaster. The resemblance to Montaigne is especially noticeable, although he lived a century later than the French writer. The *Thoughts* embodied Locke's experience as a private tutor in the family of the Earl of Shaftesbury, and consists of a set of practical suggestions for the education of a gentleman, rather than a scholar. The recommendations, therefore, appear to be somewhat at variance with the underlying principles of Locke's philosophy and the intellectual training suggested in his other educational work, *Conduct of the Understanding*.[2] {Locke holds in his *Thoughts* that}

The Chief Aim of Education. — Like Montaigne, Locke holds that book education and intellectual training are of less importance than the development of character and polish. After treating bodily education at considerable length, he states the aims of education in the order of their value as " *Virtue, Wisdom (i.e.* worldly wisdom), *Breeding*, and *Learning*," and later adds : — {character is of most importance in education.}

"Learning must be had, but in the second place, as subservient only to greater Qualities. Seek out somebody that may know how discreetly to frame his Manners : Place him in Hands where you may, as much as possible, secure his Innocence, cherish and nurse up the good, and gently correct and weed out any bad Inclinations, and settle in him good Habits. This is the main Point, and this provided for, Learning may be had into the Bargain."

Education through a Tutor and Travel. — Such a training, Locke agrees with Montaigne, can be secured only through personal attention, and the young gentleman should be given a tutor when his father cannot properly look after his training. Likewise, he feels that, "to form a young Gentleman as he should be, 'tis fit his *Governor* should himself be well-bred, understanding the Ways of {The proper training comes through a tutor rather than schools.}

---
[1] See pp. 287–289 and 306–310.
[2] The *Conduct* grows directly out of the philosophy of Locke, as given in his famous *Essay concerning the Human Understanding.*

s

Carriage and Measures of Civility in all the Variety of Persons, Times, and Places; and keep his Pupil, as much as his Age requires, constantly to the Observation of them." This private training is infinitely to be preferred, Locke holds, to that "from such a Troop of Play-fellows as schools usually assemble from Parents of all kinds." Locke also believes, with Montaigne and Milton, in foreign travel as a means of broad education and adaptation to living. He thinks, however, that it should not, as it usually did, come at the critical period between sixteen and twenty-one, but either earlier, when the boy is better able to learn foreign languages, or later, when he can intelligently observe the laws and customs of other countries.

Travel at the right time.

Broader Humanism and Improved Methods in Intellectual Education. — Locke approaches the earlier realists even more closely in showing scant respect for the narrow humanism and tedious methods of the grammar schools. He declares specifically : —

Locke is opposed to the narrow humanism, but thinks Latin necessary to a gentleman, and should be taught by speaking.

"When I consider what ado is made about a little *Latin* and *Greek*, how many Years are spent in it, and what a Noise and Business it makes to no Purpose, I can hardly forbear thinking that the Parents of Children still live in fear of the Schoolmaster's Rod, which they look on as the only Instrument of Education ; as a language or two to be its whole Business."

Yet Locke agrees with Montaigne again[1] in thinking Latin is, after all, "absolutely necessary to a Gentleman," but that "'tis a Wonder Parents, when they have had the Experience in French should not think (it) ought to be learned the same way, by talking and reading,"[2] instead of through grammar, theme-writing, versification, and memorizing long passages. Greek, however, Locke does not regard as essential to a gentleman's education, although he may in manhood take it up by himself.

Other Acquisitions. — As a further part of 'intellectual

---

[1] See pp. 249 f.
[2] When conversation is impossible, he recommends the use of interlinear translations.

THE BEGINNINGS OF REALISTIC EDUCATION 259

education,' Locke holds that, "besides what is to be had from Study and Books, there are other *Accomplishments* necessary for a Gentleman," — dancing, horseback riding, fencing, and wrestling. The pupil should also, he contends, "*learn a Trade, a manual Trade;* nay, two or three, but one more particularly." This the future gentleman should acquire, not with the idea of ever engaging in it, but for the sake of health and of "easing the wearied Part by Change of Business."[1] Dancing, horseback riding, fencing, wrestling, and a trade.

Influence of Locke's *Thoughts*. — Thus throughout the 'intellectual education' in his *Thoughts*, Locke appears mostly as a humanistic realist after the pattern of Montaigne and Milton. On the other hand, his methods in 'physical education' and 'moral education' in this work, and his attitude toward intellectual education in his *Conduct of the Understanding*, are largely disciplinary or sense realistic and can be better discussed elsewhere.[2] The influence of the elements of humanistic realism in him, as in Montaigne, Mulcaster, and Milton, was not immediate, but appears rather in his successors among educational theorists and in the later organization and curriculum of English education. Rousseau and other reformers clearly owe many incidental suggestions and details to Locke,[3] and to him is in some measure due the great development of the physical and ethical sides of education in the public and grammar schools of England, together with the tendency of these institutions to consider such aspects of rather more importance than the purely intellectual. His plea for a tutor as the means of shaping manners and morals has also probably had its effect upon the education of the English aristocracy. As a humanistic realist, Locke influenced his successors in theory, and the grammar schools in practice.

The Effect of the Earlier Realism. — Thus there seems to have been in the sixteenth and seventeenth centuries The early realism was a return to

---

[1] Rousseau, however, when he borrowed the suggestion, put it upon the economic ground that if the pupil lost his fortune, he would have the trade to fall back upon.   [2] See pp. 306–311.

[3] This Rousseau fully acknowledges in the *Émile*, although he does not hesitate to criticize the English realist and to base his system on a very different set of underlying principles.

the broader humanism, and held to 'real things,' or ideas, and to real living, rather than to words and memorizing.

a decided tendency toward a disruption of the traditionalism and formalism into which humanism had crystallized. In this movement appears also an effort to bring education into touch with society and to make it a preparation for real life. While this whole tendency seems to be a reaction to the formalized products of the Renaissance, it was caused by the same awakening of the human intelligence from which humanism had originally sprung, and to a large extent advocated the same material in education. It was its attitude in insisting upon content rather than form that was so different, although this, too, was similar to that with which humanism had begun. 'Real things,' or ideas, rather than words and phrases, and real living rather than mere memorizing, were now emphasized. The movement, therefore, seems to be a species of return to the animating spirit and method of the Renaissance, and to constitute a natural bridge between the emphasis upon verbal forms in narrower humanism and that upon individual objects in sense realism. It was at once a species of realistic humanism and of humanistic realism.

Since the change was in method rather than content, it is difficult to determine how far the education of the day was affected.

Since this change was more in the method of presenting the subject matter than in the content of the course itself, it is difficult to determine to what extent the education of the day was affected. But so many theorists espousing the cause of the broader humanism could not have existed without some support from the educational sentiment of the times, or without having in time some reflex influence upon the institutions. With all the proverbial conservatism and slowness of schools, they must have responded somewhat to the contemporary spirit, and the classics were probably taught everywhere with more regard to the underlying thought and the bearing of their content upon actual life. Without this attitude upon the part of the schools, it would be impossible to account for their adoption of sense realism as a matter of natural evolution.

THE BEGINNINGS OF REALISTIC EDUCATION

SUPPLEMENTARY READING

I. SOURCES

BESANT, W. *Rabelais* (in *Foreign Classics Series*).
FOWLER, T. *Locke's Conduct of the Understanding.*
MORRIS, E. E. *Milton's Tractate of Education.*
QUICK, R. H. (Editor). *Locke's Some Thoughts concerning Education.*
QUICK, R. H. (Editor). *Mulcaster's Positions and Elementarie.*
RECTOR, L. E. (Translator). *Montaigne's Education of Children.*
URQUHART, T. (Translator). *Works of Rabelais.*
WOODWARD, W. H. *Erasmus concerning Education* (contains the *De Ratione* and *De Pueris*).

II. AUTHORITIES

ADAMSON, J. W. *Pioneers of Modern Education.* Chaps. I, VII, X, and XIV.
BARNARD, H. *American Journal of Education.* Vol. II, pp. 76–85; IV, 461–478; XIV, 147–158; XXII, 181–190; XXIII, 151–160; XXIV, 179–184; XXVIII, 745–748.
BARNARD, H. *English Pedagogy.* Pp. 145–198. Second Series, pp. 177–324.
BROOKS, P. *Milton as an Educator* (in *Essays and Addresses*, pp. 300–319).
BROWNING, O. *History of Educational Theories.* Chaps. V–VII.
COMPAYRÉ, G. *History of Pedagogy.* Pp. 91–110.
FOWLER, T. *Locke* (in *English Men of Letters Series*).
FRAZER, A. C. *Locke.*
HAZLITT, W. C. *The Works of Montaigne.* Introduction.
LAURIE, S. S. *Educational Opinion since the Renaissance.* Chaps. V–VI, IX, and XII–XIV.
LAURIE, S. S. *Essays and Addresses.* Chap. IX.
LOWNDES, M. E. *Michel de Montaigne.*
MASSON, D. *The Life of Milton.* Vol. III, pp. 186–255.
MONROE, P. *Text-book in the History of Education.* Chap. VIII, pp. 442–461.
MORRIS, E. E. *Milton's Tractate of Education.* Introduction, I–III.
MUNROE, J. P. *The Educational Ideal.* Chaps. II and V.
OLIPHANT, J. *The Educational Writings of Richard Mulcaster.*
OWEN, J. *Skeptics of the French Renaissance.* Chap. I.
QUICK, R. H. *Educational Reformers.* Chaps. I–II, V–VI, VIII, and XII–XIII.
STREET, A. E. *The Education of Gargantua* (in *Critical Sketches*).
WATSON, F. *Mulcaster and Ascham.*
WOODWARD, W. H. *Education during the Renaissance.* Chaps. XII–XIII.
WOODWARD, W. H. *Erasmus concerning Education.* Chaps. II and V.

CHAPTER XVIII

SENSE REALISM IN EDUCATION

'Sense' realism was a reflection of the scientific development in the sixteenth and seventeenth centuries. It led to new principles, content, method, and texts in education.

The Development of Realism.— But the realistic awakening did not stop with reviving the idea back of the word or with the endeavor to bring the pupil into touch with the life he was to lead. The earlier or humanistic realism simply represents a stage in the process of transition from the narrow and formal humanism to the movement of sense realism. This later form of realism was a reflection of the great scientific development of the latter part of the sixteenth and the first half of the seventeenth centuries, with its variety of discoveries and inventions. The first great step in this movement was that taken by Copernicus. Not until 1543 was his hypothesis of a solar system published, but as early as 1496 there had been a dissatisfaction with the existing Ptolemaic interpretation, and a groping after a more satisfactory explanation of the universe. After Copernicus, other great discoverers rapidly arose in Italy, France, Holland, and England, and the spirit of the new movement was felt in philosophy and education. Many new discoveries in science and inventions were made, and philosophy began to base itself upon reason and the senses. Kepler made it possible to search the heavens, Galileo reorganized the science of physics, and an air-pump was invented by Guericke. This scientific progress was accompanied on the philosophic side by the rationalism of Descartes and the empiricism of Locke. The educational theorists, as a result, began to introduce science and a knowledge of real things into the curriculum. It was felt that humanism gave a knowledge only of words, books, and opinions, and did not even at its best lead to a study of real things. Hence new methods and new books were produced, to shorten and improve the study of the classical languages, and new content was imported into the courses of study. The movement also included an attempt at a formulation of scientific principles in education and an adaptation of education to the nature of the child.

Bacon and His New Method.—The new tendency, however, did not appear in education until after the time of *Francis Bacon* (1561-1626). The use of the scientific method by the various discoverers was largely unconscious, and it remained for Bacon to formulate what he called the method of 'induction', and, by advocating its use, to point the way to its development as a scientific theory of education. He is, therefore, ordinarily known as the first sense realist. According to Dr. Rawley, his biographer, Bacon, while still at the University of Cambridge, conceived a disgust for Aristotle's philosophy as it was then taught At any rate, it is known that even during the busiest part of his public career he undertook in sporadic works to combat the Aristotelian method, and to form a new procedure on the basis of the scientific discoveries of the day. Not until 1620, however, did he publish his great treatise on inductive reasoning called *Novum Organum* ('new instrument') in opposition to Aristotle's work on deduction. In behalf of his treatise Bacon argues that, as the hand is helpless without the right tool to aid it, so the human intellect is inefficient when it does not possess its proper instrument or method, and, in his opinion, all men are practically equal in attaining to complete knowledge and truth, if they will but use the mode of procedure that he describes. This new method of seeking knowledge he contrasts with that in vogue, as follows:

Bacon, in opposition to the Aristotelian method, published his Novum Organum, *by means of which he thought all men might attain to complete knowledge and truth.*

"There are and can be only two ways of searching into and discovering truth. The one flies from the senses and particulars to the most general axioms, and from these principles, the truth of which it takes for settled and immovable, proceeds to judgment and the discovery of middle axioms. And this way is now in fashion. The other derives axioms from the senses and particulars, rising by a gradual and unbroken ascent, so that it arrives at the most general axioms last of all. This is the true way, but as yet untried."

Hence Bacon would begin with particulars, rather than use the *a priori* reasoning of the syllogism, as advocated by the schoolmen under the impression that this was the method of Aristotle. Before, however, one's observations can be accurately made, Bacon felt it would be necessary to divest oneself of certain false and ill-defined notions to which humanity is liable. These preconceptions of which it is necessary to be rid are his famous 'idols,' which he declares to be of four classes:—

<small>First, however, one must divest himself of certain preconceptions, or 'idols.'</small>

"Idols of the Tribe, which have their foundation in human nature itself; Idols of the Cave, for every one, besides the faults he shares with his race, has a cave or den of his own; Idols of the Market-place, formed by the intercourse and association of men with each other; and Idols of the Theatre, which have immigrated into men's minds from the various dogmas of philosophies and also from wrong laws of demonstration."

<small>And one must not stop with particulars.</small>

Nor should the new method end with a mere collection of particulars. This proceeding Bacon believes to be useless and fully as dangerous for science as to generalize *a priori*, and holds that these two polar errors together account very largely for the ill success of science in the past. He declares:—

"Those who have handled sciences have been either men of experiment or men of dogmas. The men of experiment are like the ant; they only collect and use: the reasoners resemble spiders; who make cobwebs out of their substance. But the bee takes a middle course; it gathers its material from the flowers of the garden and the field, but transforms and digests it by a power of its own. Not unlike that is the true business of philosophy; for it neither relies solely or chiefly on the powers of the mind, nor does it take the matter which it gathers from natural history and mechanical experiments and lay it up in the memory whole, as it finds it; but lays it up in the understanding altered and digested. Therefore, from a closer and purer league between these two faculties, the experimental and the rational (such as has never yet been made), much may be hoped."

<small>The facts must be tabulated and the 'forms' discovered.</small>

In the second book of the *Novum Organum* Bacon begins, though he does not complete, a more definite statement of his method. Briefly stated, his plan was, after ridding the mind of its prepossessions, to tabulate carefully lists of all the facts of nature. It seemed to him a comparatively easy task to make, through the coöperation of scientific men, a complete accumulation of all the facts of science. After this data was secured, the next step would be to discover the 'forms' of things, by which he means the underlying essence or law of each particular quality or simple nature. Such an abstraction could be achieved by a process of comparing the cases where the quality appears and where it does not appear and of excluding the instances that fall under both heads until some 'form' is clearly present only when the quality is. Then, as a proof, another list may be drawn up where the quality appears in different degrees and where the 'form' should vary correspondingly.

Solomon's House and the Pansophic Course. — A description of what Bacon thinks may be expected when this scientific method is systematically carried out can be found in his fable of *The New Atlantis*. The inhabitants of this mythical island are described as having in the course of ages created a state in which ideal sanitary, economic, political, and social conditions obtained. The most important institution of this society is its 'Solomon's House,' an organization in which the members devoted themselves to scientific research and invention, and in their supposed investigations Bacon anticipates much that scientists and inventors have to-day only just begun to realize. He represents these Utopian scientists as making all sorts of physical, chemical, astronomical, medical, and engineering experiments and discoveries, including the artificial production of metals, the forcing of plants, grafting and variation of species, the infusion of serums, vivisection, telescopes, microphones, telephones, flying-machines, submarine boats, steam-engines, and perpetual-motion machines.

_{The members of 'Solomon's House' on the *New Atlantis* devote themselves to scientific research.}

While Bacon was not a teacher and nowhere explicitly states his views on education, it would seem from the description of 'Solomon's House' as if this English philosopher must have believed that education ought to be organized upon the basis of society's gradually accumulating a knowledge of nature and imparting it to all

_{Probably Bacon believed that education should have a similar organization.}

pupils at every stage, as far as they could comprehend it. Such certainly was the plan of Ratich and Comenius, who later on worked out the Baconian plans in education, and this dream of *pansophia* ('all wisdom') for all schools was ardently desired by the later realists in general as the foundation of their educational organization and of their course of study.

The Value of Bacon's Method. — In estimating the method of Bacon, it is difficult to be fair. The importance of his work has been as much exaggerated by some as it has been undervalued by others. He reacted from the current view of Aristotle's reasoning, and, taking his cue from the many scientific workers of his time, formulated a new method in opposition to what he mistook as the position of the great logician. He very properly rejected the contemporary method of attempting to establish *a priori* the first principles of a science and then deduce from them by means of the syllogism all the propositions which that science could contain. But in endeavoring to create a method whereby any one could attain all the knowledge of which the human mind was capable, he undertook far too much. His effort to put all men on a level in reaching truth resulted in a most mechanical mode of procedure and neglected the part played by scientific imagination in the framing of hypotheses. Scientific method is not at present satisfied to hold, as Bacon did, that because all observed cases under certain conditions produce a particular effect, every other instance not yet observed will necessarily have the same property or effect. The modern procedure is rather that, when certain effects are observed, of which the cause or law is unknown, the scientist frames an hypothesis to account for them; then, by the process of deduction, tries this on the facts that he has collected; and if the hypothesis is verified, maintains that he has discovered the cause or law. Yet this is only a more explicit statement of what has always been implied in every process of reasoning. The method had certainly been used by the later Greek philosophers, and it, as well as the

<small>Bacon properly rejected the contemporary *a priori* method, but, in attempting to put all men on a level in attaining truth, he undertook too much, and made a most mechanical procedure.</small>

syllogism, had even been formulated by Aristotle, although this part of his work was not known in Bacon's day.

Bacon cannot, therefore, really be said to have invented a new method. It is also evident that he failed to appreciate the work of Aristotle and the function of genius in scientific discovery. But he did largely put an end to the vestigial process of *a priori* reasoning, and he did call attention to the necessity of careful experimentation and induction. Probably no book ever made a greater revolution in modes of thinking or overthrew more prejudices than Bacon's *Novum Organum*. It represents the culmination of the reaction that had been growing up through the Renaissance, the Reformation, and the earlier realism.

As far as education is concerned, while not skilled or interested in the work himself, Bacon affected profoundly the writing and practice of many who were, and has done much to shape the spirit of modern education. His method was first applied directly to education by a German known as Ratich, and, in a more effective way, by Comenius, a Moravian.

Ratich's Attempts at School Reform. — *Wolfgang von Ratke* (1571–1635), generally called *Ratich* from an abbreviation of his Latinized name,[1] was born in Wilster, Holstein, and first studied for the ministry at the University of Rostock. Later, he continued his studies in England, where he probably became acquainted with the work of Bacon. Before long, realizing that he had an incurable defect in speech which would keep him from success in the pulpit, he decided to devote himself to educational reform. He planned to apply the principles of Bacon to the problems of education in general, but he intended especially to reform the methods of language teaching.

In 1612 Ratich memorialized the imperial diet, while it was sitting at Frankfurt, and asked for an investigation of his methods. Two professors from the University

Ratich applied the Baconian method to the problems of education, especially language teaching.

---
[1] I.e. *Ratichius*.

of Giessen were commissioned to examine his propositions, and afterward the University of Jena similarly had four of its staff look into the matter, and in each case a favorable, not to say enthusiastic, verdict was reached.

<small>His attempts to apply his principles were uniformly unsuccessful.</small> When, however, on the strength of such reports, the town council of Augsburg gave him control of the schools of that city, he was not able to justify his claims, and the arrangement was abandoned at the end of a year. Having appealed to the diet again without encouragement, Ratich began traveling from place to place, trying to interest various princes or cities in his system. He was befriended by Dorothea, Duchess of Weimar, who induced her brother, Prince Ludwig of Anhalt-Köthen, to provide a school for Ratich. This institution was furnished with an expensive equipment, including a large printing plant; a set of teachers that had been trained in the Ratichian methods and sworn to secrecy were engaged; and some five hundred school children of Köthen were started on this royal road to learning. The experiment lasted only eighteen months, and, largely owing to Ratich's inexperience as a schoolmaster, was a dismal failure. The prince was so enraged at his pecuniary loss and the ridiculous light in which he was placed that he threw the unhappy reformer into prison, and released him only at the end of three months upon his signing a statement that he had undertaken more than he could perform. After this, Ratich tried his hand at Magdeburg, where he failed again, mostly as the result of theological differences, and then was enabled to present his principles to Oxenstiern, the chancellor of Sweden, but he never really recovered from his disappointment in Köthen, and died of paralysis in Erfurt before he could hear from Stockholm.

<small>His claims concerning the teaching of languages, the arts and sciences, and uniformity, seem</small> **His Claims.**—Although there was considerable merit in the principles of Ratich, he had many of the earmarks of a mountebank. Such may be considered his constant attempts to keep his methods a profound secret, and the spectacular ways he had of presenting the ends they were bound to accomplish. In writing the

diet, he promised by means of his system: — first, to teach young or old Hebrew, Greek, and Latin without difficulty and in a shorter time than was ordinarily devoted to any one language; secondly, to introduce schools in which all arts and sciences should be thoroughly taught and extended; and, lastly, to establish uniformity in speech, religion, and government. As Ratich stated them, these claims seem decidedly extravagant, but as far as he expected to carry them out, they were but the natural aims of an education based upon realism and the Baconian method. *extravagant, but were in keeping with realism.*

His Realistic Methods of Teaching Languages and Other Subjects. — The rules of procedure used by Ratich and his disciples have been extracted by Von Raumer from a work on the Ratichian methods published after the system had become somewhat known.[1] In linguistic training he insisted, like all realists, that one "should first study the vernacular" as an introduction to other languages. He also held to the principle of "one thing at a time and often repeated." By this he meant that, in studying a language, one should master a single book. At Köthen, as soon as the children knew their letters, they were required to learn *Genesis* thoroughly for the sake of their German. Each chapter was read twice by the teacher, while the pupils followed the text with their finger. When they could read the book perfectly, they were taught grammar from it as a text. The teacher pointed out the various parts of speech and made the children find other examples, and then had them decline, conjugate, and parse. In taking up Latin, a play of Terence was used in a similar fashion. A translation was read to the pupils several times before they were shown the original; then the Latin was translated to them from the text; next, the class was drilled in grammar; and finally, the boys were required to turn German sentences into Latin after the style of Terence. This method may have produced a high degree of concen- *"First study the vernacular" and "one thing at a time" were the principles back of his practice at Köthen.*

---

[1] *Methodus Institutionis Nova Ratichii et Ratichianorum*, published by Johannes Rhenius at Leipzig in 1626.

tration, but it was liable to result in monotony and want of interest, unless skillfully administered.

His other principles.

Another methodological formulation of Ratich's, whereby he insisted upon "uniformity and harmony in all things," must have been of especial value in teaching the grammar of different languages, where the methods and even the terminology are often so diverse. Similarly, his idea that one should "learn first the thing and then its explanation," which was his way of advising that the details and exceptions be deferred until the entire outline of a subject is well in hand, would undoubtedly save a pupil from much confusion in acquiring a new language. And some of his other principles, which applied to education in general, are even more distinctly realistic. For example, he laid down the precept, "follow the order of nature." Although his idea of 'nature' was rather hazy, and his methods often consisted in making fanciful analogies with natural phenomena, yet his injunction to make nature the guide seems to point the way to realism. Moreover, his attitude on "everything by experiment and induction," which completely repudiates all authority, went even farther and quite out-Baconed Bacon. And his additional recommendation that "nothing is to be learned by rote" looked in the same direction. Finally, these realistic methods were naturally accompanied by the humane injunction of "nothing by compulsion."

Ratich anticipated much of modern pedagogy, but because of charlatanism, inexperience, and the opposition of others, he failed to carry out his principles.

The Educational Influence of Ratich.—Thus Ratich not only helped shape some of the best methods for teaching languages, but he also anticipated many of the main principles of modern pedagogy. In carrying out his ideas, however, he was uniformly unsuccessful. This was somewhat due to his charlatan method of presentation, but more because of errors in his principles, his want of training and experience as a teacher, and the impatience, jealousy, and conservatism of others. He must have been regarded by his contemporaries in general as a complete failure, whenever they contrasted his promises with his performances. Nevertheless, it is clear that he stirred up considerable thought and had a wide influence. He won a great many converts to his principles, and, through the texts and treatises written as a result of the movement he stimulated, his ideas were largely perpetuated and expanded. In the next generation came Comenius, who carried out practically all the principles of Ratich more fully, and thus, in a way, the German innovator, unpractical as he was, became a sort of spiritual ancestor to Pestalozzi, Froebel, and Herbart.

The Education and Earliest Work of Comenius.—*Jan Amos Komensky* (1592–1671), better known by his Latinized name of *Comenius*, was born at Nivnitz, a village of Moravia. He was, by religious inheritance, a devoted adherent of the Protestant sect called *Moravian Brethren*.[1] While he became bishop of the Moravians, and devoted many of his writings to religion or theological polemics, this does not concern us here, except as it affected his attitude as an educational reformer and a sense realist. In his schooling, as the result of careless guardianship of his inheritance, Comenius did not come to the study of Latin, the all-important subject in his day, until he was sixteen. This delay must, however, be regarded as most fortunate for education, as his maturity enabled him to perceive the amount of time then wasted upon grammatical complications and other absurdities in teaching languages, and was instrumental in causing him to undertake an improvement of method. After his course in the Latin school, Comenius spent a couple of years in higher education in the Lutheran College of Herborn in the duchy of Nassau,[2] where he went to

Comenius was trained in a Latin school and at Herborn.

---

[1] The Moravian or Bohemian Church, officially known as *Unitas Fratrum*, is generally considered Lutheran in doctrine, but its religious descent goes back of Luther's time to the Bohemian martyr, Huss, and it has always preserved a separate organization. There are now three 'provinces' of Moravians, the German, British, and American. They number in all about thirty-five thousand members, of whom some twenty thousand are in the United States.

[2] The University of Prague, to which Comenius would naturally have gone, was at this time in the control of the Utraquists, a Hussite sect opposed to the Moravians.

272   A HISTORY OF EDUCATION

He taught at Prerau and wrote his *Easier Grammar*

prepare for the ministry of his denomination, and at the University of Heidelberg. Then, as he was still rather young for the cares of the pastorate, he taught for four years (1614-1618) in the school at Prerau, Moravia. Here he soon made his first attempt at a simplification of Latin teaching by the production of a work called *Grammaticæ Facilioris Præcepta* ('Precepts of Easier Grammar'). Next (1618-1621) he became pastor at Fulneck, and, after a series of persecutions, resulting from the Thirty Years' War, during which he and his fellow pastors were driven from pillar to post, he settled in 1627 at the Polish town of Leszno.[1]

In the *Janua*, the first of his remarkable series of texts on the study of Latin, he was influenced by Ratich and Bateus.

The *Janua Linguarum*. — This place became the center from which most of his great contributions to education emanated. During his residence of fourteen years as rector of the Moravian Gymnasium here, he accomplished many reforms in the schools, and began to embody his ideas in a series of remarkable textbooks. The first of these works was produced in 1631, and has generally been known by the name of *Janua Linguarum Reserata* ('Gate of Languages Unlocked'). It was intended as an introductory book to the study of Latin,[2] and consisted of an arrangement into sentences of several thousand Latin words for the most familiar objects and ideas. The Latin was printed on the right-hand side of the page, and on the left was given a translation in the vernacular. By this means the pupil obtained a grasp of all ordinary knowledge and at the same time a start in his Latin vocabulary. In writing this text, Comenius may have been somewhat influenced by Ratich, the criticism of whose methods by the professors at Giessen[3] he had read while at Herborn,[4] but he seems to have been more specifically indebted both for his

[1] This town, now called *Lissa*, is a part of Prussia.
[2] In the first edition it was called *Janua Linguæ Latinæ Reserata*.
[3] See pp. 267 f.
[4] As, however, Ratich had failed to answer the letter of inquiry he wrote him from Leszno, Comenius must have largely worked out the plan independently.

method and the felicitous name of his book to a Jesuit known as Bateus,[1] who had written a similar work.

The *Vestibulum*, *Atrium*, *Orbis Pictus*, and Other Janual Texts. — It was soon apparent that the *Janua* would be too difficult for beginners, and two years later Comenius issued his *Vestibulum* ('Vestibule') as an introduction to it. While the *Janua* contained all the ordinary words of the language, — some eight thousand, — there were but a few hundred of the most common in the *Vestibulum*. Both of the works, however, were several times revised, modified, and enlarged. Also grammars, lexicons, and treatises to accompany them were written during later periods of Comenius' literary career. Much work of this sort was done between 1642 and 1650. During this period Comenius had accepted the invitation of Sweden to settle, under the patronage of his friend, Ludovic De Geer, at Elbing, a quiet town on the Baltic, and develop his ideas on method and school improvement. Here the *Vestibulum* and *Janua* were revised,[2] and the third of his Latin readers, the *Atrium* ('Entrance Hall'),[3] which took the pupil one stage beyond the *Janua*, was probably started. But the *Atrium* was not finished and published until Comenius began his residence of four years at Saros-Patak, where he was in 1650 urged by the prince of Transylvania to come and reform the schools of the country.

From his description of an ideal school for Patak,[4] and from other works, it is known that he intended also

The Vestibulum was an introduction to the Janua; the Atrium, a third book; the Palatium, a fourth; the Orbis Pictus, an edition of the Janua with pictures; and the Schola Ludus, a dramatized Janua.

---

[1] Batty or Bateus was an Irishman, although at the College of Salamanca in Spain. Comenius makes acknowledgments to him in the *Janua*, but says his ideas had been outlined some time before his attention was called to the book of the Jesuit father.

[2] In Elbing the *Methodus Linguarum Novissima* ('Latest Method in Languages'), which outlines his idea of the purpose and principles of language teaching, together with several other didactic works, was also produced.

[3] When planning this work in the *Didactica Magna* (Chapter XXII, 19 and 22-24), he refers to it as *Palatium*, and the fourth book, afterward called *Palatium*, he there speaks of as *Thesaurus*.

[4] *Scholæ Pansophicæ Delineatio*.

T

to write a fourth [1] work in the Janual series, but he never completed it. This was to be known as *Sapientiæ Palatium* ('Palace of Wisdom'), and was to consist of selections from Cæsar, Sallust, Cicero, and others of the best prose writers. While in Patak, however, Comenius did write two supplementary textbooks, the *Orbis Sensualium Pictus* ('The World of Sense Objects Pictured') and the *Schola Ludus* ('School Plays'). The latter, which is an attempt to dramatize the *Janua*, soon fell into disuse, but the former, in which Comenius applied his principles of sense realism more fully than in any other of his readers, remained a very popular text for two centuries, and is most typical of the Comenian principles. It is practically an edition of the *Janua* accompanied with pictures, but is simpler and more extensive than the first issue of that book. Each object in a picture is marked with a number corresponding to one in the text.[2] It is the first illustrated reading-book on record.

The *Didactica* gives his principles, organization, content, and methods of education.

The *Didactica Magna*. — Thus throughout his life Comenius was more or less engaged at every period in writing texts for the study of Latin. But these books connected with method were only a part of the work he contemplated. During his whole career he had in mind a complete system of the principles of education, and of what, in consequence, he wished the organization, subject matter, and methods to be. His ideas on the whole question of education were early formulated at Leszno in his *Didactica Magna*[3] ('Great Didactic'). While

---

[1] It would be the fifth, if we should count the unimportant *Auctarium* ('Supplement'), which he afterward (1656) produced in Amsterdam and inserted between the *Vestibulum* and the *Janua*.

[2] The reprint of the English edition, published by Bardeen (Syracuse, 1887), should be consulted. This method of presentation is referred to by Comenius as early as the *Vestibulum* as a desirable one, which at that time could not be carried out for lack of a skillful engraver. It may have been suggested to Comenius in the first instance by a Greek Testament edited early in the seventeenth century by a Professor Lubinus of the University of Rostock.

[3] This is a singular, the noun *ars* being understood. The original title has in it over one hundred words, beginning *Didactica Magna; Omnes Omnia Docendi Exhibens*. For a translation of the entire title, see Keatinge, *The Great Didactic of Comenius*, p. 155.

this work has many original features and is more carefully worked out than anything similar, Comenius frankly recognizes his obligations to many who have written previously. In fact, he rather strove to assimilate all that was good in the realistic movement and use it as a foundation. In this way the *Didactica* may be said to develop many of the scientific principles and methods found in Vives,[1] Bateus, Ratich, Andreæ,[2] Frey,[3] and Bodinus,[4] but it owes a greater debt for its pansophic basis of education to the works of Bacon and even more to the *Encyclopædia* of Johann Heinrich Alsted, under whom Comenius had studied at Herborn. The *Didactica* seems to have been completed in the Moravian dialect[5] about the time the *Janua* first appeared, and must have been contemplated somewhat earlier. Hence, while this work was not translated into Latin and published until 1657, and was never printed in the language in which it was originally written until a century and three quarters after the death of its author, the point of view must have been established even before Comenius came to Leszno, and influenced him throughout his career.

It owes much to the works of Bacon, the Encyclopædia of Alsted, and the writings of many others.

The *Didactica* as the Basis of All the Work of Comenius.—The rest of the books of Comenius may be regarded as amplifications of certain parts of the *Didactica*. To make his instructions on infant training more explicit, while still at Leszno, he wrote the *Informatorium Skoly Materske* ('Handbook of the Mother School').[6] He also

The Didactica was made explicit in the Mother School, the vernacular series, and the Janual series.

---

[1] See p. 166.
[2] Johann Valentin Andreæ (1586–1654), court preacher at Stuttgart, attacked the formal religion and education of the time in numerous pamphlets.
[3] Janus Cæcilius Frey (?–1631) was a German educationalist, living in Paris, who produced a number of practical works.
[4] Jean Bodin (1530–1596) was a French writer on political theory, who published also an unusual educational treatise called *Methodus ad facilem historiarum cognitionem*.
[5] *Czech* was spoken in Moravia.
[6] This work was written first in Czech, although not published in that dialect for two centuries and a quarter. It was issued in German in 1633, and in Latin in 1657. Will S. Monroe has translated the Latin edition into English under the title of *The School of Infancy* (Boston, 1896).

supplemented the *Didactica* with a set of texts for the 'vernacular school' similar to the Janual series, which were intended for the 'Latin School'; but, being written in an obscure dialect, these vernacular works were never revised and soon disappeared.[1] But the phase of the *Didactica* most often elaborated both in his other works and in his school organization was the realistic one of *pansophia* ('universal knowledge'). This was most manifest in his desire to teach at least the rudiments of all things to every one. It has already been seen how this principle was emphasized in his textbooks, such as the *Janua* and the *Orbis Pictus*. Also, after producing treatises upon *Astronomy* and *Physics*, he wrote, while at Leszno and Elbing, several works specifically on *pansophia*, of which the *Janua Rerum Reserata* ('Gate of Things Unlocked') is the most systematic and complete. These works, while diluted by traditional conceptions but little beyond those of scholasticism,[2] show how far Comenius had advanced beyond previous attempts by organizing his data about large principles, instead of merely accumulating facts. Further, in his *Didactica* he recommends that a great College of Pansophy, or scientific research,[3] be established, and in 1641, just before his call to Sweden, he went to England, at the invitation of Parliament, to start an institution of this character there. At Patak he even undertook to establish a pansophic school of secondary grade, as outlined in his *Pansophicæ Scholæ Delineatio* ('Plan of a Pansophic School').

Pansophia a Ruling Passion with Comenius. — This idea of *pansophia* seems to have been most keen and vivid with Comenius all his life, but he was always pre-

[1] The names of these texts, as he gives them in his *Scholæ Vernaculæ Delineatio*, were *Violarium* ('Violet-bed'), *Rosarium* ('Rose-bed'), *Viridarium* ('Grass-plot'), *Labyrinthus* ('Labyrinth'), *Balsamentum* ('Balsam-bed'), and *Paradisus Animæ* ('Paradise of the Soul'). Cf. also the *Didactica*, Chapter XXIX, 11.
[2] For example, with Comenius the constituents of the universe are reduced to matter, spirit, and light.
[3] He calls it a *collegium didacticum*. See p. 280.

vented from undertaking it to any extent by one accident or another, and was doomed to constant disappointment. Finally, shortly after his return from Patak, when Leszno was burned by the Poles,[1] Comenius barely escaped with his life, and his *silva*, or collection of pansophic materials, upon which he had worked for forty years, was completely destroyed. He was now in his sixty-fifth year and had not the strength or courage to pursue his favorite conception further.

The Threefold Aim of Education. — While mystic and narrow at times, Comenius was a sincere Christian, and his view of life is most consistently carried out in his conception of education. He hoped for a complete regeneration of mankind through an embodiment of religion in the purpose of education. This educational aim is shown in the following propositions, which he develops in successive chapters of the *Didactica:* —

Education should aim at knowledge, morality, and piety.

> " (I) Man is the highest, the most absolute, and the most excellent of things created; (II) the ultimate end of man is beyond this life; (III) this life is but a preparation for eternity; (IV) there are three stages in the preparation for eternity: to know oneself (and with oneself all things), to rule oneself, and to direct oneself to God;[2] (V) the seeds of these three (learning, virtue, religion[3]) are naturally implanted in us; (VI) if a man is to be produced, it is necessary that he be formed by education."

Thus, from his religious conception of society, Comenius works out as his aim of education *knowledge, morality, and piety,* and makes these ideals go hand in hand. It is to be noted, however, that his ideas about what constitutes religion have advanced a long way

The lower nature should be controlled by the higher.

---

[1] The Moravians, who had suffered so severely from the Catholics during the Thirty Years' War, were in secret sympathy with the Protestant Swedes during their invasion of Poland. After the peace was declared, and several towns, including Leszno, were ceded to Sweden, Comenius foolishly published a letter of congratulation to the Swedish king, Charles Gustavus, and in retaliation, the Poles attacked Leszno and plundered it.

[2] In the original, *Se et secum omnia, Nosse; Regere; et ad Deum Dirigere.* Cf.

> " Self-reverence, self-knowledge, self-control, —
> These three alone lead life to sovereign power."
> — Tennyson's *Œnone.*

[3] I.e. *eruditio, virtus seu mores honestas, religio seu pietas.*

beyond those of mediæval times. He regards education not as a means of ridding oneself of all natural instincts, and of exalting the soul by degrading the body, but as a system for controlling the lower nature by the higher through a mental, moral, and religious training. Education should enable one to become pious through the establishment of moral habits, which are in turn to be formed and guided through adequate knowledge.

There should be one system of schools for all.

Universal Education. — But as with Comenius education is to prepare us to live as human beings, rather than to fit us for station, rank, or occupation, he further holds: —

"(VIII) The young must be educated in common, and for this schools are necessary; (IX) all the young of both sexes should be sent to school."

Under these headings he shows that, while the parents are responsible for the education of their children, it has been necessary to set aside a special class of people for teachers and to create a special institution known as the school, and that there should be one system of schools for all alike, — "boys and girls, both noble and ignoble, rich and poor, in all cities and towns, villages and hamlets."

The 'school of the mother's lap,' the 'vernacular school,' the 'Latin school,' and the 'academy.'

The Four Periods in the School System. — Later on,[1] the *Didactica* more fully describes the organization that Comenius believes would be most effective. The system should consist of four periods of six years each, ranging from birth to manhood. The first period of instruction is that through infancy, which lasts up to the age of six, and the school is that of the 'mother's lap.'[2] Next comes childhood, which continues until the pupil is twelve, and for this is to be organized the 'vernacular,' or elementary, school. From that time up to eighteen, comes the period of adolescence, with its 'Latin,' or secondary, school. Finally, during youth, from eighteen to twenty-four, the 'academy,' or university, together

[1] Chapters XXVII–XXXI.
[2] This was known as *Schola Materni Gremii* in the Latin translation.

with travel, should be the means of education. As to the distribution and scope of these institutions, Comenius declares : —

"A mother school should exist in every house, a vernacular school in every hamlet and village, a Latin school in every city, and a university in every kingdom or in every province. The mother school and the vernacular school embrace all the young of both sexes. The Latin school gives a more thorough education to those who aspire higher than the workshop; while the university trains up the teachers and learned men of the future, that our churches, schools, and states may never lack suitable leaders."

Hence only those of the greatest ability, 'the flower of mankind,' were to go to the university. "A public examination should be held for the students who leave the Latin school, and from its results the masters may decide which of them should be sent to the university and which should enter the other occupations of life. Those who are selected will pursue their studies, some choosing theology, some politics, and some medicine, in accordance with their natural inclination, and with the needs of the Church and of the State."

Such an organization of schools as that suggested by Comenius would tend to bring about the custom of educating according to ability, rather than social status, and would thus enable any people to secure the benefit of all their genius. It was a genuine 'ladder' system of education, open to all and leading from the kindergarten through the university, such as has been commended by Huxley in speaking of the American schools. At the day that Comenius proposed it, this organization was some three centuries in advance of the times. Such an idea of equal opportunities for all could have been possible in the seventeenth century only as the educational outgrowth of a religious attitude like that of Comenius, and may well have been promoted in his case by the simple democratic spirit of the little band of Christians whose leader he was.[1]

A 'ladder' system of education.

[1] In the old cemeteries of the Moravian communities in the United States, the departed lie side by side without distinction in regard to

A coöperative college of investigation known as a 'Schola Scholarum.'

The College of Pansophia. — But beyond the university, which, like the lower schools, was to make teaching its chief function, Comenius held it to be important that somewhere in the world there should be a *Schola Scholarum* or *Collegium Didacticum*, which should be devoted to scientific investigation. Through this pansophic college, learned men from all nations might coöperate, and, he holds, —

> "These men should . . . spread the light of wisdom throughout the human race with greater success than has hitherto been attained, and benefit humanity by new and useful inventions. For this no single man and no single generation is sufficient, and it is therefore essential that the work be carried on by many, working together and employing the researches of their predecessors as a starting-point."

This pansophic college was to form a logical climax to the system of schools.

Encyclopædic Course at Every Stage. — This plan of a 'Universal College' for research would seem to be a natural product of the pansophic ideal, which has been seen [1] to dominate all of the educational theory of Comenius. Such an institution would form a logical climax to his system of schools, bearing, as he says, the same relation to them that the stomach does to the other members of the body by "supplying blood, life, and strength to all," for he holds that a training in all subjects should be given at every stage of education. Such universal knowledge, however, Comenius believes, should be given only in outline at first, and then more and more elaborately and thoroughly as education proceeds. The *Didactica*, accordingly, states : —

> "These different schools are not to deal with different subjects, but should treat the same subjects in different ways, giving instruction in all that can produce true men, true Christians, and true scholars; throughout graduating the instruction to the age of the pupil and the knowledge that he already possesses. . . . In the earlier schools everything is taught in a general and undefined manner, while in those that follow the information is particularized and

position, wealth, or color. The tombstones are laid flat upon the graves, and are exactly alike, except for size, so that none in this Christian family may appear more prominent than the other. A similar interpretation of the Master's 'brotherhood of man' is evidenced in all the Moravian social life.   [1] See pp. 276 f.

exact; just as a tree puts forth more branches and shoots each successive year, and grows stronger and more fruitful."[1]

The Training of the Mother School. — In later chapters of the *Didactica* and in his works for the special stages, Comenius gives the details of the pansophic training in each period of education. Even in the mother school, it is expected that the infant shall be taught geography, history, and various sciences; grammar, rhetoric, and dialectic; music, arithmetic, geometry, and astronomy; and the rudiments of economics, politics, ethics, metaphysics, and religion, as well as encouraged in sports and the construction of buildings. The attainment at this stage is, of course, not expected to be as formidable as the names of the subjects sound. It is to consist merely in understanding simple causal, temporal, spatial, and numerical relations; in distinguishing sun, moon, and stars, hills, valleys, lakes, and rivers, and animals and plants; in learning to express oneself, and in acquiring proper habits. It is, in fact, very much like the training of the modern kindergarten. *(Even the course in the mother school is to be pansophic.)*

The Course of the Vernacular School. — Similarly, the vernacular school is to afford more advanced instruction in all literature, morals, and religion that will be of value throughout life, in case the pupil can go no further. The course is to include, beside the elements, morals, religion, and music, everyday civil government and economics, history and geography, with especial reference to the pupil's own country, and a general knowledge of the mechanic arts. All these studies are to be given in the native tongue, since it would take too long to acquire the Latin, and those who are to go on will learn Latin more readily for having a wide knowledge of things to which they have simply to apply new names instead of those of the vernacular. *(So the vernacular school is to afford instruction in all subjects, in case the pupil can go no farther.)*

The Course of the Latin School. — The Latin School, while including four languages, — the vernacular, Latin,

---

[1] Chapter XXVII, 4–5. This is practically the modern German method of teaching, known as that of 'concentric circles.'

282   A HISTORY OF EDUCATION

The Latin school offers four languages, but continues this encyclopædic training.

Greek, and Hebrew, is also to continue this encyclopædic training. The seven liberal arts are to be taught in more formal fashion, and considerable work is to be given in physics, geography, chronology, history, ethics, and theology. In his description of the pansophic school that he undertook to establish at Patak, Comenius gives an even more specific account of the range of knowledge that should be gained in secondary education. He maps out seven classes, of which the first three are to be called 'philological,' and the other four to be known as 'philosophical,' 'logical,' 'political,' and 'theological' respectively. In the philological grades, he indicates that Latin is to be taught; arithmetic, plane and solid geometry, and music are to be gradually acquired; and instruction is to be afforded in morality, the catechism, the Scriptures, and psalms, hymns, and prayers. So he gives exactly the amount of training in mathematics, the arts and sciences, and religion that is to appear in the next three classes, and arranges that Greek shall be studied and Hebrew begun. In the last class, the wide range of secular knowledge is to be continued, and such theological matters as the relation of souls to God are to be discussed.

In the university each student should devote himself to a specialty, but a few should pursue all branches.

The University Curriculum. — Finally, in the case of the university, Comenius maintains that "the curriculum should be really universal, and provision should be made for the study of every branch of human knowledge," but "each student should devote his undivided energies to that subject for which he is evidently suited by nature,"— theology, medicine, law, music, poetry, or oratory. However, "those of quite exceptional talent should be urged to pursue all the branches of study, that there may always be some men whose knowledge is encyclopædic."

The Method of Nature.—Thus at every stage of education Comenius believes that there should be pansophic instruction. The way in which this knowledge is to be acquired, he also intends to have in full accord with sense realism. He insists that, in order to reform the schools of the day, which were uninteresting, wasteful of time, and cruel, the 'method of nature' must be observed and followed, for "if we wish to find a remedy for the defects of Nature, it is in Nature herself that we must look for it, since it is certain that art can do nothing unless it imitate Nature." He then shows how Nature accomplishes all things "with certainty, ease, and thoroughness,"[1] in what respects the schools have deviated from the principles of nature, and how they can be rectified only by following her plans.

One should follow the 'method of nature,' which accomplishes all things "with certainty, ease, and thoroughness."

These principles concerning the working of nature were, however, not established inductively by Comenius, but laid down *a priori*, and were mostly superficial and fanciful analogies. The following quotation from the *First Principle* that he gives under the 'certainty' of nature, may serve as a specimen of his method:—

"*Nature observes a suitable time.* For example, a bird that wishes to multiply its species, does not set about it in winter, when everything is stiff with cold, nor in summer, when everything is parched and withered with heat; nor yet in autumn, when the vital force of all creatures declines with the sun's declining rays, and a new winter with hostile mien is approaching; but in spring, when the sun brings back life and strength to all."

The analogy of the bird.

The schools deviate from this method of nature, he claims in the first place, because "the right time for mental exercise is not chosen," and to rectify the error,—

"(I) The education of men should be commenced in the springtime of life, that is to say, in boyhood (for boyhood is the equivalent of spring, youth of summer, manhood of autumn, and old age of winter). (II) The morning hours are the most suitable for study, for here again the morning is the equivalent of spring, midday of summer, the evening of autumn, and the night of winter."

It is not remarkable that, with all his realistic tendencies, Comenius did not employ the inductive method to any extent. He had inherited the notion that not all truth can be secured through the senses or by reason. He claimed that even Bacon's method could not be applied to the entire universe, all of which is included

The inductive method was not employed to any extent.

---

[1] I.e. *certo, facile, solide.* See *Didactica*, Chapters XIV–XVIII.

in his *pansophia*. There are, he held, three media for knowledge, — the senses, the intellect, and revelation, and "error will cease if the balance between them is preserved." The natural sciences were young in the day of Comenius, and he was very limited in his grasp of their content and method. It is a sufficient merit that, imbibing the spirit of sense realism, he had for the first time in history applied anything like induction to teaching, and produced the most systematic and thorough work upon educational method that had been known.

The Method Applied to Special Subjects. — After working out in the *Didactica* these general principles for following nature, Comenius renders his work much more practical by showing how such principles may be made effective in the ordinary schools. He then applies his general method to the specific teaching of various branches of knowledge, — sciences, arts (including reading, writing, singing, composition, and logic), and languages, and to instruction in morality and piety. On this practical side of his method, he applies more fully the induction of Bacon. After showing the necessity for careful observation in obtaining a knowledge of the sciences, he gives nine useful precepts for their study, and while they are stated as general principles, they are clearly the inductive result of his own experience as a teacher. Similarly, he formulates rules for instruction in the arts, languages, morality, and piety. The description of special method in sciences, too, is thoroughly in harmony with realism in its insistence that, in order to make a genuine impression upon the mind, one must deal with realities rather than books. The objects themselves, or, where this is not possible, such representations of them as can be conveyed by copies, models, and pictures, must be studied. In the case of the languages, arts, morality, and piety, impression must be insured by expression. "What has to be done, must be learned by doing." Reading, writing, and singing are to be acquired by practice. The use of foreign languages affords a better means of learning them than do the rules of grammar. Practice, good example, and sympathetic guidance teach us virtue better than do precepts. Piety is instilled by meditation, prayer, and self-examination.

Correlation. — As would be expected from the threefold interrelated aim and the encyclopædic content of education, Comenius everywhere in his method intends that all subjects shall be correlated. In particular, he holds: — *[The study of languages to be correlated with that of objects.]*

"The study of languages, especially in youth, should be joined to that of objects, that our acquaintance with the objective world and with language, that is to say, our knowledge of facts and our power to express them, may progress side by side."[1]

Discipline. — In the matter of discipline, as a natural accompaniment of his improvements in method, Comenius was in advance of his time. He holds that the end of discipline is to prevent a recurrence of the fault, and it must be inflicted in such a way that the pupil will recognize that it is for his own good. Severe punishment must not be administered for a failure in studies, but only for a moral breach, and exhortation and reproof are to be used before resorting to more stringent measures. *[Discipline is to prevent a recurrence, and should be administered only for a moral breach.]*

The Comenian Principles and Their Effect upon Education. — Such was the work of Comenius, who may in the fullest sense be considered the first great educational reformer and the real progenitor of modern education. His position grew out of sense realism, but to the encyclopædic content and the natural method of Bacon, Ratich, and others, which he rendered more elaborate, consistent, and rational, he added his natural endowment of innate piety and a sense of the 'brotherhood of man.' Comenius made it evident that education should be a natural, not an artificial and traditional, process in harmony with man's very constitution and destiny, and that a well-rounded training for complete living should be everywhere afforded to all, without regard to sex, social position, or wealth, because of their very humanity. *[To sense realism Comenius added the endowment of piety. Education should be in harmony with one's nature, and should be universal.]*

[1] This principle, it has been seen (pp. 272–274), Comenius carried out in his series of Latin textbooks.

He outlined a regular system of schools and described their grading, and was the first to suggest a training for very young children. He held that bodily vigor and physical education were essential, and made sense training an important part of the course. He further broadened and enriched the entire curriculum by subordinating Latin to the vernacular and insisting upon geography, history, the elements of all arts and sciences, and such other studies as would fit one for the activities of life. He correlated and coördinated all subjects, and combined even the training in Latin with a knowledge of real things. This he accomplished through a series of textbooks that were a great advance over anything previously produced. Thus he greatly contributed to make education more effective, interesting, pleasant, and natural.

However, for nearly two centuries Comenius had but little direct effect upon the schools, except for his language methods and his texts. The *Janua* was translated into a dozen European, and at least three Asiatic, languages; the *Orbis Pictus* proved even more popular, and went through an almost unlimited number of editions in various tongues; and the whole series became for many generations the favorite means of introducing young people to the study of Latin. But until about half a century ago, the work of Comenius as a whole had purely an historical interest, and was known almost solely through the *Orbis Pictus*. The great reformer was viewed as a fanatic, especially as the pansophic ideal turned out to be of only ephemeral interest. Humanism was too thoroughly intrenched to give way at once to realism.

Nevertheless, the principles of Comenius were unconsciously taken up by others and have become the basis of modern education. Francke was anticipated by Comenius in suggesting a curriculum that would fit one for life; before Rousseau, Comenius intimated that the school system should be adapted to the child rather than the child to the system; Basedow largely modeled his encyclopædic content and natural method after the *Orbis Pictus;* Pestalozzi revived the universal education, love of the child, and study of nature that appear in the works of the old bishop; Herbart's emphasis upon character and upon observation seem like an echo of Comenius; while the kindergarten, self-activity, and play, suggested by Froebel, had been previously outlined by the Moravian. Hence it happened that in the middle of the nineteenth century, when the works of Comenius were once more brought to light by German investigators, it was discovered that the old realist of the seventeenth century had been the first to deal with education in a scientific spirit, and work out its problems practically in the schools. His evidently was the clearest of visions and broadest of intellects. While it is easy to criticize him now, in the light of history Comenius is perhaps the most important individual in the development of modern education.

Pestalozzi, Herbart, and Froebel.

Locke as a Sense Realist. — Among those who most directly felt the influence of Comenius was Locke. There are elements throughout the *Thoughts,* and to some extent in the *Conduct,* where he seems to have been affected by the concrete material and interesting methods of the great sense realist as clearly as he was elsewhere by the humanistic realism of Montaigne.¹ Even in the subjects he recommends for the education of a gentleman, where he was especially following Montaigne, Locke makes a selection, utilitarian in nature and wide in range, that reminds one of the encyclopædic advice of Bacon, Ratich, and Comenius. He also resembles the sense realists in desiring to begin with the vernacular studies, which with him are reading, writing, drawing, and possibly shorthand. And when the pupil is able to take up a foreign language, Locke believes, with Comenius, that this should not be Latin, but the language of his nearest neighbor, — in the case of the English boy, French. After the neighboring language has been learned, Latin may be studied. Like the Moravian, too, Locke believes

Locke was influenced by sense realism, to the extent of introducing a utilitarian and encyclopædic curriculum, and in beginning with the vernacular studies and the languages of one's nearest neighbors,

¹ See pp. 256–259.

288 A HISTORY OF EDUCATION

in correlating content studies with the study of languages. He suggests: —

"At the same time that he is learning *French* and *Latin*, a Child, as has been said, may also be enter'd in *Arithmetick, Geography, Chronology, History,* and *Geometry,* too. For if these be taught him in French or Latin, when he begins once to understand either of these Tongues, he will get a Knowledge in these sciences, and the Languages to boot."

and in his pleasant methods of teaching.

In the matter of method also, Locke reminds one of Comenius and the other sense realists. He believes that "contrivances might be made *to teach Children to read,* whilst they thought they were only playing," and makes the suggestion of pasting the letters of the alphabet upon the sides of the dice. And further, — "when by these gentle Ways he begins to *read,* some easy pleasant Book, suited to his Capacity, should be put into his Hands, wherein the entertainment he finds might draw him on."

He also holds that impressions are made through the senses by observation.

Moreover, Locke is most thoroughly a sense realist in his theory of knowledge and the pedagogical recommendations that grow out of it. He holds that impressions are made through the senses by observation, and are only combined afterward by reflection.[1] The development, therefore, of such knowledge to the most complex ideas comes through induction, and in this way the sciences should be studied. In the *Conduct,*[2] he states: —

"The surest way for a learner, in this as in all other cases, is not to advance by jumps, and large strides; let that which he sets himself to learn next be indeed the next; *i.e.,* as nearly conjoined with what he knows already as it is possible; let it be distinct, but not remote from it; let it be new and what he did not know before, that understanding may advance; but let it be as little at once as may be, that its advances may be clear and sure."

Discipline should be mild, and not for intellectual remissness.

It is not surprising that, with such pleasant methods, Locke, like the realists generally, declares in his *Thoughts* that "great *Severity of Punishment* does but very little Good, nay, great Harm in Education."[3] He

[1] This, of course, is brought out more clearly in his philosophical work, *Essay concerning the Human Understanding.*   [2] § XXXIX.

[3] His ideas in the *Conduct* would point to quite a different type of method and discipline.

prefers "*Esteem* or *Disgrace*" as the proper means of discipline, and maintains, as Comenius did, that corporal punishment should be for moral rather than intellectual remissness.

Realistic Tendencies in the Elementary Schools. — Obvious as the movement is in the seventeenth century, the effect of sense realism upon the schools seems to have been slow and indirect. The schools of those days, as of other periods, had become highly institutionalized, and the teachers were loath to break through any of their established habits in respect to either content or method. But in Germany during the seventeenth century there came a decided tendency throughout the elementary schools to increase instruction in the vernacular, as recommended by Ratich and Comenius, and to learn first the German grammar rather than the Latin. With this movement was joined the increase in universal and compulsory education urged by the reformers, and an introduction of elementary science, in addition to the reading, writing, arithmetic, religion, and singing. At Weimar in 1619, through a pupil of Ratich, a new system with universal education was organized, and in 1640 Duke Ernst, the Pious, of Gotha ordered Andreas Reyher to prepare a *Schulmethodus* based upon new lines.[1] Under this plan, which was completed two years later, elementary instruction was afforded to both sexes throughout the duchy in the natural sciences, as well as in the usual rudiments and religion. This work in 'science' consisted in teaching the children to measure with the hour-glass and sun-dial, to observe the ordinary plants and animals, and to carry on other objective studies of a simple character. Many other attempts were made elsewhere in the German states, both in private and public education, and the same tendency appeared in the states of Italy, and in France, Holland, and England.

The effect of sense realism was slow and indirect, but in the German elementary schools there was increased instruction in the vernacular and an introduction of elementary science.

Secondary Schools. — But the new realistic tendencies

[1] See p. 199.

Realistic tendencies in the 'Gymnasien,' in the 'Ritterakademien' that were developed, in the schools of the Pietists, and in the 'Realschulen';

appear also in German secondary education. While it was not until the close of the seventeenth century that there are any evidences of it in the *Gymnasien* and other preparatory schools, it becomes apparent by the middle of the century in the renewed activity of academies for the nobles.[1] After the Thirty Years' War, owing to the havoc wrought in the cities, the importance of the burghers gives way decidedly to that of the nobles, who find a compensation for the devastation of the country in a new splendor of living and a brilliant literature borrowed from the court of Louis XIV (1643–1715), then at its height. For a century French influence dominated the courts of the German states, and, in place of humanistic education, there was developed a special training for the young nobles in French, Italian, Spanish, and English, in such accomplishments as courtly conduct, dancing, fencing, and riding, and in philosophy, mathematics, physics, geography, statistics, law, genealogy, and heraldry. This realistic training, while it includes the sciences, is seen to lean rather toward the social features in the earlier realism of Montaigne[2] than the objective character of sense realism. The educational institutions in which it was embodied were not known as *Fürstenschulen*, but *Ritterakademien* ('academies for the nobles'). Such academies were founded at Colberg, Lüneburg, Vienna, Wolffenbüttel, and many other centers, before the close of the century. They originally covered the work of the *Gymnasien*, although they substituted modern languages, sciences, and knightly arts for the Greek and Hebrew, and added a little from the course of the university, but gradually they became part of the regular secondary system. Both in these schools and the *Gymnasien* the Comenian texts were used, but this was rather for the sake of their method of presenting Latin than because of the scientific content of these works.

Later on, the *Pietists' schools*[3] also embodied all the

---

[1] See p. 154.   [2] See pp. 246–250.   [3] See pp. 300–305.

realistic elements which were borrowed by Francke from the suggestions in the writings of Comenius. The Pietists, however, adopted these ideas of the Moravian bishop largely for their religious side as a protest and reaction to the *Ritterakademien* and the 'rationalistic' movement, although they did not hesitate also to stress the science content and the study of the vernacular. These realistic ideas, started by Francke at Halle, were modified and expanded by his colleagues, Semler and Hecker, and found their way to Berlin toward the middle of the eighteenth century. They then spread throughout Germany until, before the close of that century, they were embodied by means of the *Realschulen* ('realistic schools') in the regular school system of the different states.¹ These institutions, while retaining French and some Latin, have added also the vernacular, history, geography, geometry, mechanics, architecture, and various natural sciences, to their curriculum.

In England such recommendations as those in Locke's *Thoughts* concerning moral and physical education, as we have already noted, did much toward reshaping the practice of the grammar and public schools, but probably very few introduced even the elements of science into their course. On the other hand, the *academy* recommended in Milton's *Tractate of Education* was actually organized in many places by the Puritans. The two thousand non-conforming clergymen who were driven from their parishes by the harsh Act of Uniformity in 1662, in many instances found school-teaching a congenial means of earning a livelihood, and at the same time of furnishing higher education to the young dissenters who were excluded from the universities and grammar schools. The first of these academies was that established by Richard Frankland at Rathmill in 1665, and this was followed by the institutions of John Woodhouse at Sheriffhales, of Charles Morton at New- *(in the grammar and public schools, and in the nonconformist 'academies';)*

---

¹ See p. 304.

ington Green, and of some thirty other educators of whom we have record. While these academies usually followed the humanistic realism of Milton, and, since their chief function was to fit for the ministry, included Latin, Greek, and Hebrew in their course, they were also rich in sciences and mathematics and the study of the social sciences, and the vernacular was especially emphasized.[1] The new tendency was also broadened and amplified by the writings of Locke, whose *Thoughts* became the great guide for the managers of the Puritan academies. In 1689, when the Act of Toleration put non-conformity upon a legal footing, the academies were allowed to be regularly incorporated.

and in the academies of America. So in America, when the number of religious denominations had greatly increased and the demands upon secondary education had expanded, the 'grammar' schools, with their narrow denominational ideals and their limitation to a classical training and college preparation, proved inadequate, and an imitation of the English *academy* arose as a supplement. The first suggestion of an 'academy' was made in 1743 by Benjamin Franklin. He wished to inaugurate an education that would prepare for life, and not merely for college. He accordingly proposed for the youth of Pennsylvania a course in which English grammar and composition, penmanship, arithmetic, drawing, geography, history, the natural sciences, oratory, civics, and logic were to be emphasized. He would gladly have excluded the languages altogether and made the course completely realistic, but for politic reasons he made these subjects elective. His academy was opened at Philadelphia in 1751, and similar institutions sprang up rapidly through the other colonies during the latter half of the eighteenth century. Shortly after the Revolution, partly owing to the inability or the unwillingness of the towns or the counties to maintain grammar schools, the academy quite eclipsed these

---

[1] A detailed account of the history and curriculum of these academies is given in Brown, *Making of Our Middle Schools*, Chapter VIII.

institutions, and became for a time the representative type of secondary school in the United States.[1]

The Universities. — The conservatism of the universities toward realism has been even more striking than that of secondary education. These higher institutions, it has previously been observed, were exceedingly reluctant to take up the classics, but after having adopted them as the substance of the course for a couple of centuries, they were long unwilling to exchange these subjects for others, or to make room for the sciences in any way.

In Germany, as the result of its Pietistic origin, the University of Halle was realistic almost from its beginning in 1692. Göttingen, the next institution to become hospitable to the new movement, did not start it until 1737. But soon afterward the tendency became general, and by the end of the eighteenth century all the German universities,—at least, all under Protestant auspices, had created professorships in the sciences. The English universities, Oxford and Cambridge, were much slower than those of Germany in adopting the new subjects, and even at the present day the sciences have not altogether obtained the standing of the classics. During the professorship of Isaac Newton in the last half of the seventeenth century, however, much was done toward making Cambridge mathematical and scientific, and during the eighteenth century many chairs were established in the sciences, but it was not until toward the end of the nineteenth that this institution became famous for its science. The foundation of efficient municipal universities in such cities as London, Liverpool, Manchester, and Birmingham, has greatly hastened the realistic movement in England during the past half century. Likewise, the bitter contest over the admission of science in the universities of the United States, in spite of their greater freedom from tradition and precedent, is still within the memory of many.

The universities were very conservative in the adoption of the sciences.

In Germany by the end of the eighteenth century the tendency became general.

Oxford and Cambridge were slower, but the new municipal universities have hastened the realistic movement.

The admission of sciences in the United States is recent.

---

[1] See Brown, *op. cit.*, Chapter IX.

SUPPLEMENTARY READING

I. SOURCES

BACON, F. *Philosophical Works* (edited by Spedding, Ellis, and Heath).
COMENIUS, J. A. *Great Didactic* (translated by M. W. Keatinge), *Orbis Pictus* (English edition reprinted by C. W. Bardeen), and *School of Infancy* (translated by W. S. Monroe).
LOCKE, J. *Conduct of the Understanding* (edited by Fowler), and *Some Thoughts concerning Education* (edited by Quick).
RICHTER, A. *Ratichianische Studien* (Pts. 9 and 12 of *Neudrücke Pädagogischer Schriften*).

II. AUTHORITIES

ADAMSON, J. W. *Pioneers of Modern Education.* Chaps. I–X.
BALL, W. W. R. *Short History of Mathematics.*
BARNARD, H. *American Journal of Education.* Vols. V, 229–298 and 663–681, and VI, 459–466.
BARNARD, H. *German Teachers and Educators.* Pp. 311–388.
BEARD, C. *The Reformation of the Sixteenth Century.* Chap. XI.
BROWN, E. E. *The Making of Our Middle Schools.* Chaps. VIII and IX.
BROWNING, O. *Educational Theories.* Chap. IV.
BUTLER, N. M. *The Place of Comenius in the History of Education.*
CAIRD, E. *University Addresses.* Pp. 124–156.
CAJORI, F. *A History of Physics.*
CHURCH, R. W. *Bacon.*
COMPAYRÉ, G. *History of Pedagogy.* Pp. 121–137.
DAVIDSON, T. *History of Education.* Division III, Chap. I.
FISCHER, K. *Descartes and His School.*
FOWLER, T. *Bacon's Novum Organum.*
HANUS, P. H. *The Permanent Influence of Comenius* (*Educational Aims and Values*, VIII, 193–211).
KAYSER, W. *Johann Amos Comenius.* Pp. 1–148.
LAURIE, S. S. *Educational Opinion since the Renaissance.* Chaps. X–XI and XIII–XIV.
LAURIE, S. S. *John Amos Comenius.*
LAURIE, S. S. *Teachers' Guild Addresses.* Chap. VI.
LIPPERT, F. A. M. *Johann Heinrich Alsteds pädagogischdidaktische Reform-Bestrebungen und ihr Einfluss auf J.A. Comenius.*
MONROE, P. *Text-book in the History of Education.* Chap. VIII.
MONROE, W. S. *Comenius and the Beginnings of Educational Reform.*
MUNROE, J. P. *The Educational Ideal.* Chaps. III–V.
NICHOL, J. *Francis Bacon.*

NOHLE, E. *History of the German School System* (Report of the U. S. Commissioner of Education, 1897–98, pp. 39–44).
PAULSEN, F. *German Education* (translated by Lorenz). Bk. III.
QUICK, R. H. *Educational Reformers*. Chaps. IX, X, and XIII.
RUSSELL, J. E. *German Higher Schools*. Chap. III.
SPEDDING, J. (Editor). *Life and Times of Francis Bacon*.

CHAPTER XIX

EDUCATIONAL INFLUENCES OF PURITANISM, PIETISM, AND RATIONALISM

The awakening in religion and government in the seventeenth and eighteenth centuries.

DURING the seventeenth and eighteenth centuries there also occurred a decided awakening in the religion and government of Europe. This, however, would seem to have been the product of the same causes as the revival in intellectual, moral, and social conditions marked by the Renaissance, the Reformation, and the rise of realism. It somewhat overlapped these other movements, and was in part connected with them, and in part was a reaction from them when they had become stereotyped and fixed.

Catholic and Protestant states alike had become set and literal in their religion, and many states had developed into despotisms.

Reaction to the Conditions in Church and State. — We have already had occasion to notice how the stimulus in matters religious that took place during the Protestant revolts and the Catholic reformation had largely lost its vitality and lapsed once more into formalism. In France, Italy, Spain, and other Catholic countries, the Mother Church had again sunk into a traditionalism and authoritativeness almost as repressive as before the Reformation; in England, the National Church, while at first growing less and less ceremonial, had under the Stuarts become dogmatic and formal again; while in Germany, the Protestant and Catholic states alike were set and literal in their interpretation of religion. A similar formalism and despotism had for a longer period been growing up politically. Many states of Europe had at length become more unified through the development of strong national governments under absolute monarchs, and although these more stable conditions may be considered to point in the direction of higher civilization, they proved anything but an unalloyed blessing.

EDUCATIONAL INFLUENCES OF PURITANISM 297

While this religious and political situation obtained even in the small and disunited states of Germany and Italy, and in the Hapsburg dominions of Spain and Austria, it was more noticeable in such highly centralized governments as those of France and England. In France, the king had become more and more thoroughly a despot, who, by the end of the seventeenth century, no longer even went through the form of summoning the Estates-General, but made laws and levied taxes practically to suit himself. The nobility and the clergy, however, were exempt from taxation, and while still collecting their feudal dues or ecclesiastical tithes from the people, furnished them little protection or spiritual comfort in return. The Catholic Church was all-powerful, and Protestants could not be legally married, have births recorded, or make wills. In England the power of Parliament over taxes and legislation, which had been built up during the Middle Ages, became nominal during the Tudor period, and the sovereigns, by the exercise of tact, had been able to rule as practically absolute monarchs. The situation was further complicated and rendered more intolerable through religious oppression. The Tudors had established a national church, in which the authority of the pope was denied, but many of the old forms and ceremonies were continued. The 'Puritans,'[1] who were dissatisfied with this half-way reform,[2] were required by Charles I (1625–1649) and his Archbishop Laud to conform to the national church. This led to a political and religious revolt, in which the Puritans were for a time successful, and controlled England under Oliver Cromwell and his son (1649–1660). But a reaction against the Puritan régime led to the restoration of the Stuarts and the expulsion of the Puritans from their parishes or even from the country, and conditions became more oppressive than ever. Even in Germany,

In France,

England,

Germany,

---

[1] The term was originally applied to Low Churchmen, who objected to some of the doctrine and ritual, but it was soon loosely used and extended so as to include the Presbyterians and Independents as well.

[2] See pp. 196 f.

where the various states were not yet centralized under a single head,¹ religion had become largely crystallized and formal. Most of the fervor of the Reformation had spent itself, and the prevailing Lutheranism had become bound down by creed and sacrament. Exactness of definition and correctness of belief had come to weigh more than religious emotion and purity of life. Similar conditions existed in all other countries and were bound to lead to a reaction. With the growth of intelligence and civilization, discontent with these despotic civil and ecclesiastical conditions in Europe was inevitable. In opposition to the prevailing formalism, great movements of protest, such as Puritanism in England, Pietism in Germany, and Rationalism in England and France grew up.

and elsewhere had grown up movements of protest.

Puritanism and Its Effects.—*Puritanism* was originally an attempt to bring about a more active piety and a 'purer' conduct, but through a gradual increase in strength and the persecutions of the government, it became involved in politics and was most potent in the overthrow of the Stuarts. From its ranks, too, came several who contributed greatly to educational theory and to the improvement of the schools themselves. For example, the poet Milton was a stanch Puritan, and his *Tractate of Education*,² which showed his opposition to the formal schools of the day, was but one of the several pamphlets of protest from his pen. He also wrote upon the freedom of the press, the tenure of kings, and religious toleration, and against the episcopacy.³ Moreover, as has already appeared,⁴ the 'acad-

Puritanism had become potent in the overthrow of the Stuarts, and had developed education and the schools.

Milton, his Tractate, and the 'Academy.'

---

¹ Of course the Hapsburg control of Germany was mostly nominal.
² See pp. 254–256.
³ On the other hand, the great social philosopher *Hobbes* was stimulated to write through his royalist associations. He defended the absolutism of the monarch on the theory that the people had in the dim past agreed to hand over all their rights to a single person, in order to escape from continual warfare with one another, and could never be released from their obedience. Therefore, with him, right and morality are the creation of the State, and religion and education should be controlled by the State. ⁴ See pp. 291–293.

EDUCATIONAL INFLUENCES OF PURITANISM 299

emy' that he recommended in his *Tractate* formed a sort of model for the later non-conformist schools, and for the second stage of American secondary education.

The Puritans thus greatly aided in bringing both civil and religious liberty to England and in improving the tone of morals and education. Nevertheless, the movement, like the revivals that had preceded it, seems to have degenerated, whenever it became dominant, into a formalism quite as marked as that against which it was a protest. It affected impossible and absurd ideals, and condemned all harmless amusements and pleasures. Ball-playing, bell-ringing, hunting, theater attendance, and dancing were placed in the same category with drunkenness, licentiousness, theft, lying, and profanity. Use of the Book of Common Prayer or scoffing at Puritans came to be considered equally heinous with looseness of living. The effort to stimulate 'pure religion and undefiled' deteriorated into pride, narrowness, intolerance, exaggeration, and occasional hypocrisy. The everyday conversation of the Puritans must have been filled with the fanaticism and cant that appears in the literature of the day, and wide was the divergence between preaching and practice. Puritanism had largely become externality and form.

The degeneracy of Puritanism into formalism.

Rise of the Pietists. — Meanwhile, a great religious revival was taking place also in Germany. In the midst of the formalism into which Lutheranism had fallen, there arose a set of theologians who were convinced of the need of moral and religious reform, and desired to make religion a matter of life rather than of creed. Among their number early appeared *Philipp Jakob Spener* (1635-1705), a pastor in Frankfurt, who instituted at his home a series of so-called *collegia pietatis* ('religious assemblies'), in which were formulated propositions of reform. The views here represented seem to have been largely borrowed from Puritan writers. They did not advocate any new doctrine, but simply subordinated orthodoxy to spiritual religion and practical

Spener and his 'collegia pietatis.'

morality. The movement spread rapidly, and made a great impression throughout Germany. The old orthodox theologians and pastors were grievously offended, and, from the name of the gatherings, the reformers became known in reproach as *Pietists*.[1]

Francke's education and early career.

Francke. — From the standpoint of education, however, the most important Pietist was *August Hermann Francke* (1663-1727). Francke received an excellent education at Gotha Gymnasium, where he became acquainted with the reforms of Ratich and Comenius, and at the universities of Erfurt, Kiel, and Leipzig, in which he studied theology and the languages, especially Greek and Hebrew. He first came into notice at Leipzig, where he had become a *Privatdocent*, by starting a Pietist society for careful discussion and pious application of the Scriptures. His attitude aroused the ill-will of the older professors and caused his dismissal. After a brief but stormy career as a preacher at Erfurt and as a teacher at Hamburg, he assisted in founding the University of Halle, which became the center from which Pietism was diffused throughout Germany.

Through his pastorate in Glaucha, he was led to found an 'Armenschule,' a 'Bürgerschule,' and a 'Waisenanstalt.'

Organization of His Institutions. — Here in 1692 Francke became a professor of the Greek and Hebrew languages, but was afterward transferred to his favorite subject of theology. To make ends meet, he was also appointed pastor in the suburb of Glaucha, and through this latter position his real work as an educator began. While catechizing the children who came to the parsonage to beg, he was shocked at their ignorance, poverty, and immorality, and resolved to raise them from their degradation by education. One day early in 1695, upon finding a contribution of seven guldens ($2.80) in his alms box, he started an *Armenschule* ('school for the poor') in his own house and engaged a student of the university to teach it. As he was soon requested to open another school for those whose parents could afford to pay, he rented two rooms in a neighboring building, —

---

[1] Like the names *Puritan* and *Methodist*, however, it was afterward adopted as a term of honor.

one for the *Armenschule* and one for the *Bürgerschule* ('school for citizens'). Further, believing it of advantage to remove orphans from their old associations, he established a third institution for them, called the *Waisenanstalt* ('orphanage'), and later he subdivided all three organizations upon the basis of sex.

Still in this same year, he undertook for a wealthy widow of noble family to educate her son together with some other boys, and his work in this direction grew rapidly into a secondary school, which came to be known as the *Pädagogium*. Two years later he started another secondary course for the purpose of preparing the brighter boys from the orphan and poor schools for the university, and this was called the *Lateinische Hauptschule*, or *Schola Latina*, to distinguish it from the elementary schools, in which no foreign language was taught. As early as 1698, Francke likewise wished to organize a boarding-school where girls whose parents could afford it might obtain a training in Latin, Greek, Hebrew, and other secondary subjects, and while at first this enterprise was on a small scale, within a dozen years the *Höhere Töchterschule* ('higher school for girls') became a regular part of his system. Moreover, through his colleague, Semler, a secondary school of a more practical type, called the *Realschule*, in which the pure and applied sciences were taught, became associated in 1708 with the institutions of Francke.

He also founded secondary schools,— 'Pädagogium,' 'Schola Latina,' 'Töchterschule,' and 'Realschule,'

In addition to these elementary and secondary schools, Francke was also enabled, through a gift of four thousand marks ($1000), to institute in 1695 a *Seminarium Præceptorum* ('seminary for teachers'), in which the theological students that taught in his schools might be trained. These students practiced teaching for two hours each day under the supervision and criticism of inspectors, and were boarded at a *Frei-tisch* ('free table'), established by means of the endowment.

and a 'Seminarium Præceptorum.'

His Religious Aim in Education.— Even if we were not acquainted with the origin of Pietism, or with the practice in Francke's schools, the explicit statements in

His *Christian Education* holds

302   A HISTORY OF EDUCATION

religion to be the chief aim, but declares that the pupil's station must be considered.

his *Brief and Simple Treatise on Christian Education*[1] would make it evident that the educational aim underlying all his work was primarily religious training. "The chief object in view," says Francke, "is that children may be instructed above all things in the vital knowledge of God and Christ, and be initiated into the principles of true religion." He goes so far as to insist:

"Only the pious man is a good member of society. Without sincere piety, all knowledge, all prudence, all worldly culture, is more hurtful than useful, and we are never secure against its misuse."

His position is, therefore, a real return to the Reformation emphasis upon faith and non-ceremonial worship. Nevertheless, it has been clear that he was sufficiently affected by the times to found his schools somewhat with reference to existing social strata, and he distinctly declares: "In all instruction we must keep the pupil's station and future calling in mind."

The Bible and catechism as material, and reading and writing based on the Scriptures.

Course in His Different Schools.—Naturally, then, the subject most emphasized in all of Francke's schools was religion. In the elementary schools, four out of seven hours each day were given to Bible study, catechism, prayer, and pious observances, and the reading and writing were based upon the Scriptures as material. After learning to read, a pupil studied arithmetic for four hours, and vocal music for two hours each week. Incidentally, the course was enriched with a knowledge of 'real' or useful things, such as the simplest facts of astronomy and physics, bits of geographical and historical information, and various household arts.

Realistic studies.

In the Pädagogium, Greek and Hebrew for exegesis, and Latin and French through the Bible.

In the *Pädagogium*, not only was religion the chief study, but Greek and Hebrew were taught largely for the sake of exegesis, compositions were written in Latin upon Bible subjects, and French was learned through a New Testament in that language. The realistic turn to Francke's work also appeared in the training in the vernacular, in such studies as mathematics, German oratory,

[1] The full title is *Kurzer und einfältiger Unterricht wie die Kinder zur wahren Gottseligkeit und Christlichen Klugheit anzuführen sind.*

history, and geography, and in the elements of natural science, arts, and crafts, and of astronomy, anatomy, and materia medica. He also added the management of estates, gardens, and vineyards, and such other knowledge as the upper classes of society would find useful. As the pupils in the *Schola Latina* were not of sufficient social standing to demand it, the French and some of the practical studies of the *Pädagogium* were omitted, but the curriculum was otherwise the same. The *Realschule* went more fully into the mathematics, sciences, and useful subjects than did the *Pädagogium*. The work in the *Töchterschule* was not unlike that in the Latin school, but included the household arts and other occupational studies and 'accomplishments.' *Realistic and practical studies. Course of the Schola Latina, the Realschule, and the Töchterschule.*

Character of His Methods. — While the course in all of Francke's schools was distinctly disciplinary in theory, good pedagogy was not altogether neglected. The teachers were directed by his treatise to study each individual pupil, and were advised how to train children to concentrate, observe, and reason. Although much memorizing was practiced, "children were not to be permitted to learn to prattle words without understanding them." This comprehension of the work was, of course, increased by applying all studies to everyday life. The pupils wrote formal letters, receipts, and bonds, and their mathematical problems were based upon practical transactions. The discipline in all the schools of Francke, in consequence, though strict, was mild and humane. *The individual pupil was studied. Memorizing without understanding was not allowed. Application of studies to daily life. Mild discipline.*

The Influence of Francke's Institutions. — From these schools, together with the orphanage, seminary, and 'free table' as a nucleus, have developed the now celebrated organization known as *Franckesche Stiftungen* ('Francke's Institutions'). "It is difficult to decide," says Adamson, "whether the most surprising feature is their humble beginning, or their rapid growth and steady adaptation of means to ends." In spite of many controversies resulting from the Pietistic auspices of the institutions, at the death of Francke in 1727, there were *'Francke's Institutions' grew rapidly, increased in number, and have done a most effective work.*

already in the elementary schools some seventeen hundred and twenty-five pupils of both sexes, in the orphanage were maintained one hundred boys and thirty-four girls, while the *Pädagogium* had eighty-two, and the *Schola Latina* four hundred, boys, and two hundred and fifty students boarded at the 'free table.'

These institutions have since been increased in number, and there are now some twenty-five enterprises conducted in a large group of structures built about a double court. Among the additions are a printing-plant and bindery, a book-store, a Bible house, a drug-store and dispensary, and a home for women, as well as a *Realgymnasium*[1] and a *Vorschule*.[2] Through these institutions more than four thousand persons are being provided with the means of an education or livelihood, and many good causes are advanced. Over one million marks ($250,000), coming from the endowment, state appropriations, tuition fees, and profits upon the enterprises, are expended each year in maintaining the institutions.

The 'modern' studies have influenced the 'Gymnasien,' the 'Realschule' has spread throughout Prussia, and the 'Seminarium' has been adopted by practically all the German states.

This work of Francke has had a great influence upon German education in several directions. The 'modern' studies of the *Pädagogium* and *Schola Latina* have been a model for Prussia and all Protestant Germany, and have somewhat affected the curricula of the *Gymnasien*. The *Realschule* of Semler was brought in a slightly modified form to Berlin by Hecker, one of the teachers in the *Pädagogium*. From the capital it spread gradually throughout Prussia, until it was taken into the public system, and is to-day one of the most important features. The seminary, or training-school for teachers, has been adopted by practically every one of the German states. Further, since in the various schools of Francke were realized the chief ideals of most educational reformers up to that time, Germany was thereby given

---

[1] A compromise between the *Gymnasium* and the *Realschule*, which has been quite common in Germany, but is now disappearing.

[2] A preparatory school for the secondary schools, attended by children between six and nine.

a concrete example of what it might best strive to imitate. Again, by means of teachers trained in his system by the seminary, all Germany has been leavened by the spirit of the great Pietist.

Decline of Pietism. — As to Pietism itself, however, while originally a protest against creed and ceremonial, in later years it lost much of its living power and deteriorated into a formalism in religious life and thought. It magnified even the smallest of daily doings into expressions of piety, and became, like Puritanism, pervaded with affectation and cant. To a great extent, its schools, with their spiritual purpose and content, then lapsed into merely inefficient classes in formal catechism, and all hold upon real living was lost. The religious revival of Spener and the educational impulse of Francke had become crystallized and fixed.

Rationalism in England and France and Its Effects; John Locke. — It was also during this period of Puritanism and Pietism that the world heard from the great rationalistic philosopher and educationalist, *John Locke*. While Locke's ancestry was Puritan, this seems to have had little influence upon his life and philosophy, except as he was ever the advocate of civil, religious, and philosophic freedom. This tendency was increased by his close personal relations with the noted liberal, Lord Shaftesbury.[1] In accordance with his convictions, Locke wrote two *Treatises on Government*, three *Letters on Toleration*, and an essay upon *The Reasonableness of Christianity*. Each of these works vigorously opposed absolutism and dogmatism, but they are all simply applications of the thought underlying his great *Essay concerning the Human Understanding*. In this treatise, which was the product of his reflection during a score of years, he holds, as in the more special works, to the fruitlessness of traditional opinions and empty phraseology. He rejects all 'innate ideas,' or axiomatic principles, and charges that this tenet was imposed by

All Germany has been leavened.

But Pietism, too, became crystallized and fixed.

Locke, as an advocate of civil and religious freedom, wrote several treatises, but they are all applications of the rationalistic philosophy in his Essay.

---

[1] See p. 257.

masters and teachers upon their followers, "to take them off their own reason and judgment, and put them on believing and taking them upon trust without further examination." All knowledge, claims the *Essay*, comes rather from experience, and the mind is like white paper upon which ideas can be painted by 'sensation' and 'reflection.'[1] Locke further finds it necessary to determine, when the ideas are once in mind, what they tell us in the way of truth. He holds that "knowledge is real only so far as there is a conformity between our ideas and the reality of things," and that, as we cannot always be sure of this correspondence, much of our knowledge is probable and not certain. We must, therefore, in each case carefully consider the grounds of probability, — "the conformity of anything with our own knowledge, observation, and the testimony of others."

He holds in his Conduct that the mind, like the body, grows through exercise,

Locke's Disciplinary Theory in Intellectual Education.— To train the mind to make the proper discriminations in these matters, Locke claims that a formal discipline must be furnished by education. This attitude is made clear in his posthumous educational work, *Conduct of the Understanding*. As regards the aim of intellectual education, he holds in this work: —

"As it is in the body, so it is in the mind; practice makes it what it is, and most even of those excellences which are looked on as natural endowments will be found, when examined into more narrowly, to be the product of exercise, and to be raised to that pitch only by repeated actions. Few men are from their youth accustomed to strict reasoning, and to trace the dependence of any truth in a long train of consequences to its remote principles and to observe its connection; and he that by frequent practice has not been used to this employment of his understanding, it is no more wonder that he should not, when he is grown into years, be able to bring his mind to it, than that he should not be able on a sudden to grave and design, dance on the ropes, or write a good hand, who has never practiced either of them."

Concerning the best studies for producing this mental gymnastic, Locke says: —

[1] This is his famous doctrine of the *tabula rasa*.

"Would you have a man reason well, you must use him to it betimes, exercise his mind in observing the connection of ideas and following them in train. Nothing does this better than mathematics, which therefore I think should be taught all those who have the time and opportunity, not so much to make them mathematicians as to make them reasonable creatures . . ., that having got the way of reasoning, which that study necessarily brings the mind to, they might be able to transfer it to other parts of knowledge as they shall have occasion."

and that the best gymnastic for reasoning is found in mathematics.

So Locke advises a wide range of sciences, not for the sake of the realistic knowledge obtained, but for intellectual discipline, "to accustom our minds to all sorts of ideas and the proper ways of examining their habitudes and relations; . . . not to make them perfect in any one of the sciences, but so to open and dispose their minds as may best make them capable of any, when they shall apply themselves to it." Similarly, he implies that reading may become a means of discrimination. "Those who have got this faculty, one may say, have got the true key of books, and the clue to lead them through the mizemaze of variety of opinions and authors to truth and certainty."

He also advises a range of sciences to dispose the mind so as to be capable of any science.

Formal Discipline in Moral and Physical Training. — The same disciplinary conception of the aim of education underlies most of Locke's recommendations on moral and physical training in *Some Thoughts concerning Education*. When in this work he comes to treat moral education, he declares at the start: —

Moral training he declares to be obtained by denying one's desires.

"As the strength of the body lies chiefly in being able to endure Hardships, so also does that of the Mind. And the great Principle and Foundation of all Virtue and Worth is plac'd in this: That a Man is able to *deny* himself his own *Desires*, cross his own Inclinations, and purely follow what Reason directs as Best, tho' the Appetite lean the other Way. . . . This Power is to be got and improv'd by Custom, made easy and familiar by an *early* Practice. If, therefore, I might be heard, I would advise that, contrary to the ordinary Way, Children should be us'd to submit their Desires, and go without their Longings, *even from their very Cradles*. The first Thing they should learn to know, should be that they were not to have any Thing because it pleas'd them, but because it was thought fit for them."

Hence, in Locke's opinion, morality comes about

through submitting the natural desires to the control of reason, and thereby forming virtuous habits. In this light he discusses various virtues and vices as they occur to him, and insists that, in order that the proper habits may be ingrained in them, children should recognize the absolute authority of their fathers and tutors.

and physical training by the 'hardening process.' The ideal upon which Locke bases his physical training is also that of formal discipline, and has since been generally known as the 'hardening process.' His advice concerning this part of a pupil's training might be abridged as follows : —

"Most Children's Constitutions are either spoil'd or at least harm'd by *Cockering* and *Tenderness*. The first Thing to be taken Care of is that Children be not *too warmly clad or cover'd*, Winter or Summer. The Face when we are born, is no less tender than any other Part of the Body. 'Tis Use alone hardens it, and makes it more able to endure the Cold. I will also advise his *Feet to be wash'd* every Day in cold Water, and to have his Shoes so thin that they might leak and let in Water, whenever he comes near it. I should advise him to play in the *Wind and Sun without a Hat*. His Diet ought to be very plain and simple, — if he must needs have Flesh, let it be but once a Day, and of one Sort at a Meal without other Sauce than Hunger. His Meals should not be kept constantly to an Hour. Let his *Bed* be *hard*, and rather Quilts than feathers, — hard Lodging strengthens the Parts."

Judged by the Thoughts rather than the Conduct, Locke has been classed as a realist or a naturalist, instead of an advocate of 'formal discipline,' as is clearly the case with the Conduct and the moral and physical training in the Thoughts. **Effects of Locke's Educational Theories.** — The intellectual education advocated by Locke in his *Conduct of the Understanding* is evidently very different in content and method from that in the *Thoughts*. And although the *Thoughts*, as has been pointed out, arose from special circumstances, it is from this work, rather than the *Conduct*, that the educational position of Locke has ordinarily been estimated. In consequence, he has been classed by most educational writers as a realist of the humanistic or the sense type, with leanings toward Montaigne or Comenius, according to which set of ideas seemed to have been most emphasized in this work.[1] In truth, if we regard only the intellectual education of Locke's *Thoughts* and the resemblance it bears in inci-

[1] See pp. 256–259 and 287–289.

EDUCATIONAL INFLUENCES OF RATIONALISM 309

dentals or details to the recommendations of the realists, there is sufficient reason for these classifications. On similar grounds, Locke might be placed in the 'naturalistic' class with Rousseau, who, while criticizing him severely at times, admits a great indebtedness to him and has clearly taken many ideas from him with little modification.

Locke as the Advocate of Formal Discipline. — But, although Locke stands in the apostolic succession of great educational theorists, selecting from the realists and influencing the naturalists, these interpretations cannot be considered at all adequate or in harmony with the whole spirit of Locke's rationalistic philosophy or his works upon other subjects. His peculiar point of view is exhibited in the *Conduct*, which was originally intended as an additional chapter and an application of the *Essay*, and in the positions taken on physical and moral training in the *Thoughts*. And the idea he gives here of training the mind by means of mathematics and other subjects so as to cultivate 'general power,' together with his 'denial of desires' in moral education and the 'hardening process' in physical training, would seem to make Locke the first writer to advocate the doctrine of 'formal discipline.'

Adherents of this theory hold that the study of certain subjects yields results out of all proportion to the effort expended, and gives a power that may be applied in any direction. It has been argued by formal disciplinarians, accordingly, that every one should take these all-important studies, regardless of his interest, ability, or purpose in life, and that all who are unfitted for these particular subjects are not qualified for the higher duties and responsibilities, and are unworthy of educational consideration. These subjects are usually held to be the classic languages, to improve the 'faculty of memory,' and mathematics to sharpen the 'faculty of reason,' although strenuous efforts have been made by the scientists and others [1] to meet this argument by point-

[1] See *Proceedings of the International Congress of Charities*, 1893.

ing out the 'formal discipline' in their own favorite studies.

The effect of formal discipline upon the English grammar and public schools and the universities, the German Gymnasien, and the high schools, colleges, and universities in the United States.

This doctrine of the formal discipline has had a tremendous effect upon each stage of education in practically every country and during every period almost up to the last decade, when a decided reaction began.[1] The formal classicism of the English grammar and public schools and universities, and of the German *Gymnasien,* afford excellent examples of the influence of formal discipline. While in the United States a newer and more flexible society has enabled changes to be more readily made, but a quarter of a century ago Greek, Latin, and mathematics made up most of the course in high schools, colleges, and universities, and until very recently the effete portion of arithmetic and the husks of formal grammar were defended in our elementary education upon the score of 'formal discipline.' But, with the growth of science, the abandonment of the 'faculty' psychology,[2] and the development of educational theory, the curriculum has everywhere been broadened, and the content of studies rather than the process of acquisition has come to be emphasized.

But Locke's formal discipline was not a defense of the public schools, but arose from his desire to root out the traditional and false, and is connected with

It should, however, be recognized that Locke did not defend, but vigorously assailed, the grammatical and linguistic grind in the English public schools.[3] His attitude toward formal discipline sprang from his desire to root out the traditional and false, rather than to support the narrow humanistic curricula of the times.

Section VII. E. B. Andrews makes this argument even for the study of Sociology.

[1] See Adams, *Herbartian Psychology,* Chap. V; Bagley, *Educative Process,* Chaps. XIII-XIV; Horne, *Training of the Will* (*School Review,* XIII, pp. 616-628); O'Shea, *Education as Adjustment,* Chaps. XIII and XIV; Thorndike, *Educational Psychology,* Chap. VIII; Wardlow, *Is Mental Discipline a Myth?* (*Educational Review,* XXXV, pp. 22-32). Read also the more recent investigations, which tend to show that we have reacted too far. See the contributions of Angell, Pillsbury, Judd, and Ruediger in *Educational Review,* XXXVI, pp. 1-43, and 364-372, and Winch in *The British Journal of Psychology,* Vol. II, pp. 284-293.

[2] See Graves, *History of Education before the Middle Ages,* pp. 196 and 213, for the origin and meaning of the 'faculty' psychology.

[3] See pp. 170-172.

His philosophy and educational doctrines grew out of his purpose to aid the cause of liberty and reason, and his esteem for mathematics as an intellectual training shows his connection with Descartes.[1] It was, moreover, his doctrine that, developed to an extreme, eventuated in the destructive philosophy of the French rationalists and the skepticism of Hume. While, therefore, Locke's imagery of the *tabula rasa* and his disciplinary theory have had an influence far beyond his times, it can hardly be supposed that he took that position in conscious support of the conservative formal education of the English schools. He was in this, as in all his positions, a radical and a rationalist.

the rationalism of Descartes and the skepticism of Hume.

Voltaire and the Encyclopedists. — But *Rationalism* did not in England take the same direction or go to the extreme it did in France. While the French were slower than the English to revolt against absolutism and ecclesiasticism, their conditions were more intolerable, and when the outbreak came, it was much more acute. As the eighteenth century wore on, the reaction to the traditional, irrational, and formal in Church and State, on the one hand, and to the fanaticism, hypocrisy, and formalism of Puritanism and Pietism on the other, grew and became popular. Efforts came to be made to interpret life in the light of reason and to overthrow all customs and institutions that did not square with this test.

The French outbreak against absolutism was more acute; it was a reaction to the traditionalism of Church and State, and to the fanaticism of the Puritans.

The rationalistic movement, which had started in English philosophic thought, was here popularized and put into actual practice. The sensationalism and rationalism of Locke were greatly developed by Montesquieu, Voltaire, Diderot, Condillac, D'Alembert, and others of the French 'encyclopedists.' The most keen and brilliant of all these writers was *Voltaire* (1694-1778), who well

The rationalism of Locke was developed by Voltaire and the 'encyclopedists.'

---

[1] Locke had first been stimulated by Descartes, who was reacting from his Jesuit traditions. The effort to strip off preconceived opinions is similar in both, and while Locke rejects the 'innate ideas,' to whose certainty Descartes holds, he also believes in mathematics as the best means of disciplining the mind and of getting rid of the false.

serves as a type of the whole movement. With matchless wit and literary skill, in a remarkable range of writings, he championed reason against the traditional institutions of State and Church. Voltaire's chief object of attack was the powerful Roman Catholic Church, which at this time seemed to stand seriously in the way of all liberty, individualism and progress, and the slogan with which he often closed his letters was, "crush the infamous thing." The Protestant beliefs he likewise repudiated as irrational. The other rationalistic writers had similar doctrines, and although the details of their ideas are hardly worthy of consideration here, they all produced writings upon education. In these they freely criticized the traditional school systems, and proposed new theories of organization, content, and method that must later have assisted to demolish the existing theory and practice in France.

The rationalistic attitude toward the Church and the traditional school systems.

Thus Rationalism sought to destroy despotism, superstition, and hypocrisy, and to establish in their place freedom in action, justice in society, and toleration in religion. But in casting away the old, it swung to the opposite extreme and degenerated into anarchy and skepticism, and at times even into materialism and license. In their fight against the despotic ecclesiasticism, the rationalists failed to distinguish it from Christianity, and wished in its place to create a religion of reason or nature. Their real opposition to the Church, however, was because it was irrational rather than because it was insincere, and they felt that it might have a mission with the masses, who were too dull and uneducated to be able to reason. So while Rationalism wielded a mighty weapon against the fettering of the human intellect, it cared little about improving the condition of the lower classes, who were sunk in poverty and ignorance, and universally oppressed. It endeavored to replace the traditionalism and despotism of the clergy and monarch with the tyranny and dogmatism of an intellectual few. While brilliant, the movement was also artificial and stilted. Morality came to be merely a veneer, — an observance of proper forms. The most vicious living was tolerated,

Rationalism reacted too far, and degenerated into anarchy and skepticism.

The despotism of the Church was replaced by the dogmatism of the intellectual few.

providing appearances were maintained. There came about merely the exchange of one kind of formalism for another.

The Hardening of the Puritan, Pietistic, and Rationalistic Movements. — Hence the reactions to formalism in the seventeenth and eighteenth centuries eventually hardened in each case into formalism of a new type. Puritanism and Pietism to a great extent deteriorated into fanaticism and hypocrisy, while Rationalism spread into skepticism and looseness of living. But during this period, as at other times in history, there was not a complete return to the point of departure. The stimulus in religion and political conditions disappeared again, but it not only left behind important by-products for society and education, but it also prepared the way for a higher development in the future.

Puritanism and Pietism deteriorated into fanaticism, and Rationalism into skepticism.

SUPPLEMENTARY READING

I. Sources

DESCARTES, R. *Meditations.*
LOCKE, J. *Conduct of the Understanding* (edited by Fowler), and *Some Thoughts concerning Education* (edited by Quick).
RICHTER, A. *August Hermann Francke, Kurzer und Einfältiger Unterricht* (Pt. X of *Neudrücke Pädagogischer Schriften*).

II. Authorities

BAGLEY, W. C. *The Educative Process.* Chaps. XIII–XIV.
BOURNE, H. R. F. *The Life of John Locke.* Vol. II, pp. 253–269.
BROWNING, O. *Educational Theories.* Chap. VII.
COMPAYRÉ, G. *History of Pedagogy.* Pp. 194–211.
ERDMANN, J. E. *History of Philosophy* (translated by Hough). Vol. II, pp. 104–116 and 153–170.
FOWLER, T. *John Locke.* Chaps. I–X.
FRANCKE, K. *German Literature as Determined by Social Forces.* Chaps. VI–VIII.
FRASER, A. C. *Locke.* Pts. I and II.
KRAMER, G. *August Hermann Francke; ein Lebensbild.*
LAURIE, S. S. *Educational Opinion from the Renaissance.* Chap. XV.
LEITCH, J. *Practical Educationalists and their Systems.* Pp. 1–51.
LOWELL, E. J. *Eve of the French Revolution.*

MACDONALD, F. *Studies in the France of Voltaire and Rousseau.*
MAY, T. E. *Democracy in Europe.* Vol. II, Chap. XII.
MONROE, P. *Text-book in the History of Education.* Chaps. VIII and IX.
MUNROE, J. P. *The Educational Ideal.* Pp. 106–118.
NOHLE, E. *History of the German School System* (Report of the U. S. Commissioner of Education, 1897–98, pp. 45–62).
O'SHEA, M. V. *Education as Adjustment.* Chaps. XIII–XIV.
PAULSEN, F. *German Education.* Bk. III.
QUICK, R. H. *Educational Reformers.* Chap. XIII.
RUSSELL, J. E. *German Higher Schools.* Pp. 60–66.
SCHLOSSER, F. C. *History of the Eighteenth Century.* Bk. I, Chaps. II and III.
THORNDIKE, E. L. *Educational Psychology.* Chaps. III and VIII.
WILLIAMS, S. G. *History of Modern Education.* Chap. X.

CHAPTER XX

THE PROGRESS BEFORE MODERN TIMES

The Middle Ages. — It may be well now to pause at the gateway of modern civilization and education and make a brief survey of the progress that has taken place since pre-mediæval days. During the Middle Ages, it has been seen that the key-note was adherence to authority and preparation for the life to come. Individualism was mostly repressed, and intellectual training was held within the confines of a few activities of a stereotyped sort. The cultural products of Greece and Rome largely disappeared or were deprived of their vitality, and all civilization was restricted, fixed, and formal. *The key-note of the Middle Ages was authority and repression.*

The Awakening. — But the human spirit could not be forever held in bondage, and, after almost a millennium of repression and uniformity, various factors that had accumulated within the Middle Ages produced an intellectual awakening. Some expression of individualism was once more attained, and the classics of Greece and Rome were again sought to nourish the renewed vigor. This period of intellectual restoration has been described by the word 'Renaissance,' and its vitality lasted during the fifteenth century in Italy and to the close of the sixteenth in the Northern countries. By the dawn of the seventeenth century, however, it had everywhere degenerated into 'Ciceronianism.' This constituted a formalism almost as dense as that it had superseded, except that linguistic and literary studies had replaced dialectic and theology. *The period of intellectual awakening, or the 'Renaissance,' degenerated into Ciceronianism;*

A little later than the spread of the Renaissance through the North, yet overlapping it somewhat, came the allied movement of the 'Reformation.' This grew in part out of the disposition of the Northern Renaissance *the 'Reformation,' or the religious and theological awakening,*

316   A HISTORY OF EDUCATION

<small>hardened into formalism;</small> to turn to social and moral account the revived intelligence and learning. A movement to reform church practice and doctrine appeared in the Protestant revolts and the Catholic reaction. Yet here also the revival abandoned its mission, and the tendency to rely upon reason rather than dogma hardened into formalism and a distrust of individualism.

<small>and in the seventeenth century the search for 'real things,' or 'realism,' arose.</small> Again, in the seventeenth century, apparently as an outgrowth of the same forces as produced the humanistic and religious revivals of the two preceding centuries, came the movement known as 'realism.' When the Renaissance and Reformation had deteriorated into narrow Ciceronianism on the one hand and dogmatic formalism on the other, the activity of the times took the form of a search for 'real things.' By this at first was merely intended a broader humanism and an effort to realize the idea back of the word, but it came before long to be expanded into a desire to deal with concrete objects. In a small and crude way the modern scientific movement had begun.

<small>Associated with realism came the religious and political awakening that took the forms of Puritanism, Pietism, and Rationalism, which also became formal and degenerate.</small> **Preparation for Rousseau and the French Revolution.** — Associated with this realistic tendency, on the religious and political sides came a quickening known in various forms and countries as Puritanism, Pietism, and Rationalism. These movements went on through the seventeenth and eighteenth centuries, but eventually degenerated into fanaticism and hypocrisy or skepticism and anarchy.

While it can be seen that the revival in each of these periods lapsed and hardened once more into a new sort of formalism, something in every era was accomplished for progress, and the social pendulum never swung back as far as the point from which it had started. <small>Thus was the way prepared for the complete reaction of Rousseau and the French Revolution.</small> Thus was the way opened for the absolute break from tradition and authority that occurred during the latter part of the eighteenth century. At that time came *Jean Jacques Rousseau* (1712–1776) and the extreme reaction from all that had been built up during the centuries preceding. Of this complete repudiation of the past and of the existing order of society, voiced by the Swiss-French philosopher, the most violent and marked symptom is found in the French revolution.

The Modern Spirit. — This destruction of the entire social fabric, while most disastrous and costly at the time, was an inevitable result of the unwillingness to reshape society in accordance with changing ideals and conditions, and out of the ruins grew a nobler structure. The social world must have come to an end, had it paused with Rousseau and the French upheaval, but through this very demolition was ushered in the spirit of the nineteenth century together with modern civilization and progress. Individualism had at length triumphed and for a time ground authority under its heel, but when this extremity had been passed, the problem became how to harmonize the individual with society, and how to develop personality progressively in keeping with its environment. That constituted the task for the modern reformers, and is the underlying *desideratum* for which modern society and education have ardently been striving.

Out of the ruins grew modern civilization and the effort to harmonize the individual with society.

INDEX

Abbot, 6 (footnote).
ABC shooters, 86 (footnote).
Abelard, 53, 57, 79, 80.
Academiæ, 218.
Academies, in England, 291, 298; in America, 174, 292 f., 298.
Academy, with Milton, 256, 291, 298; with Comenius, 278, 282.
Acquaviva, Claudio, 210, 220.
Adagia, 151.
Adams, George Burton, quoted, 1, 107.
Adnotationes, of Valla, 129, 151.
Adolescentia, of Wimpfeling, 149.
Æmuli, 218.
Æneas Sylvius, 130, 131, 132 f., 143 (footnote), 162.
Africa, of Petrarch, 116.
Agricola, 147 f., 149.
Albertus Magnus, 54, 73.
Albigenses, 72; 179 (footnote).
Albrecht V, of Bavaria, 236.
Alcuin, 28, 29, 30, 32, 33.
Alexander of Hales, 54, 73.
Alexandria, 43, 76.
Alfonso of Naples, 123.
Alfred, education under, 36 ff.
Algazzali, 42.
Alsted, Johann Heinrich, 275.
Altdorf, university of, 202.
Alva, duke of, 199, 208.
A. M. D. G., 221.
America, education in, 199 f.
Anabaptists, 184 (footnote).
Andreæ, 275.
Angelique, Mère, 224 (footnote).
Anglo-Saxon Chronicle, The, 38.
Anhalt-Köthen. *See* Köthen.
Anselm, 51.
Anthony, 6.
Antidotarium, 90.
'Apprentice' 92, 97.
Aquinas, Thomas, 54 f., 73.

Aretino, 120 (footnote).
Arezzo, university of, 81.
Aristotle, 18, 20, 41, 42, 115, 263, 264.
Arithmetic, in pagan course, 15, 18.
Armenschule, 300 ff.
Arnauld, 224 (footnote), 226, 227.
Art, mediæval, 103.
Asceticism, in Christianity, 5.
Ascham, Roger, 164, 166 f., 243.
Asser, 37.
Assimilation, key to Middle Ages, 3.
Astronomy, in pagan course, 15; in later course, 17.
Athanasius, 7.
Atrium, 273.
Auctarium, 274 (footnote).
Augsburg, 161 (footnote), 268; peace of, 183 (footnote).
Augustine, 8 (footnote).
Augustine. *See* St. Augustine.
Augustinians, 8, 181.
Austin friars, 74.
Authority, insistence upon, 219.
Averroës, 43, 45.
Avicenna, 42, 90.
Avignon, papal court at, 180.
Aymeri de Narbonne, 101.

Bacon, Francis, 94, 254, 255, 263 ff., 267, 269, 270, 275, 285.
Bacon, Friar, 90, 94.
Baeda, 32, 38.
Balsamentum, 276 (footnote).
Barbarisms, of Donatus, 89.
Barbaro, 131.
'Barbarossa,' 82.
Barlaam, 118.
Barzizza, 117, 121, 123.
Basedow, 286.
Basel, 150.
Basil, 6, 7.
Bateus, 273, 275.

319

INDEX

Bec, 13, 31.
Bembo, 130, 135, 161.
Benedict, 7, 8, 9, 12.
Benedict of Aniane, 8.
Benedict XII, 94.
Beowulf, Story of, 101.
Bernard of Clairvaux, 50.
Bérulle, 222.
Best Method of Opening an Institution of Learning, 159.
Birmingham, university of, 293.
Bobbio, 12.
Boccaccio, 93, 116 ff., 118, 119, 137.
Bodinus, 275.
Boethius, 16, 38, 89; *De Musica*, 21.
Bologna, university of, 78 f., 81, 82, 150.
Bonaventura, 50, 54, 73.
Boniface, 7.
Bossuet, 221.
Boston Latin School, 173.
Bremen, education at, 198.
Brethren of the Common Lot, 145 ff.
Brinsley, John, 172.
Brothers of Sincerity, 42 f.
Bruni, 120, 131, 132, 133, 143 (footnote).
Brunswick, schools at, 188, 198.
Budæus, 143, 166.
Bürgerschule, Francke's, 300 ff.
Bugenhagen, educational work of, 188, 198, 201.
Burckhardt, quoted, 113 f.
Burgher, class, 97; schools, 97 ff.

Cairo, 43.
Calasanzio, José, 229.
Calderon, 221.
Calvin, 143, 191 f., 204, 224; educational work of, 192 ff.
Calvinist education, spread of, 193 f.
Cambrai, 146.
Cambridge, university of, 81, 84, 163 f., 202, 250, 263, 293.
Canisius, 228.
Canterbury, 13.
Canterbury Tales, 102 (footnote).
Canzoniere, 115.
Carlstadt, 184 (footnote).
Carmelites, 74.
Carthusians, 8.
Cassian, 7.

Cassiodorus, 16, 32.
Cathedral schools, under Charlemagne, 30 f.
Catholic education, aim, 235; organization, 235 f.; content, 236; methods, 236 f.; results, 237.
Celestine III, 80.
Cessatio, 84 f.
Chanson de Roland, 64 f., 101.
Chansons de geste, 101.
Chantry schools, 98, 195.
Charlemagne, 25 ff., 63, 101, 104; education under, 27 ff.
Charles Gustavus, 277 (footnote).
Charles V, 183.
Charles VIII, 142.
Charterhouse, 173.
Cheke, Sir John, 164.
Cheltenham, 173.
Chivalric education, preparatory stages, 65 ff.; knighthood, 67 f.; training of women, 68; effects of, 68 ff.
Chivalry, 64 ff.
Christian Brothers, 228 ff., 236; educational aim, 229 f.; organization, 230; content and methods, 231 f.; results, 232.
Christian Education, Brief Treatise on, 302.
Christian Education of Youth, Zwingli's treatise, 190 f.
Christianity, religion of Roman world, 4.
Christ's Hospital, 173.
Chrysoloras, Emanuel, 119 ff., 126.
Cicero, 20, 176.
Ciceronianism, 130, 136 f., 160 f., 213 f., 243, 246, 315.
Ciceronianus, Dialogus, 130 (footnote), 136, 151.
Cistercians, 8.
Cities, growth of, 96 f.
Classe, 13.
Classic Letters, 159.
Clement XIV, 221 f.
Clifton, 173.
Cluny, 8, 13.
Coadjutores spirituales, 212.
Code, of Justinian, 90.
Cœnobitic, 6.
Colberg, 290.

INDEX

Lolet, 150, 163, 167 ff., 175.
Collège de Guyenne, 144 f.
Collège de la Rive, 192, 193.
Collège de Montaigu, 146, 149.
Collèges, 175, 193, 201.
Colleges, Moorish, 41; of the Jesuits, 211 ff.
Collegia pietatis, 299.
Colloquia, of Corderius, 144, 172, 174, 192; of Erasmus, 150, 151, 158.
Cologne, university of, 82, 163.
Columba, 7.
Comenius, 254, 255, 266, 271 ff., 287, 300.
Commerce in the Middle Ages, 96.
Conceptualism, 53.
Concertatio, 218.
Condillac, 311.
Conduct of Schools, 231, 232.
Conduct of the Understanding, Locke's, 257, 259, 287, 307 f., 308, 309.
Consiliarius, 88.
Constance, Council of, 180.
Constantinople, taken by Venetians, 45; taken by Turks, 118.
Constantinus Africanus, 77.
Constitutiones, the Jesuit, 210, 212, 213.
Convent of New Catholics, 234.
Convictus, 214.
Copernicus, 94, 262.
Corbie, 13, 31.
Corderius, 143 f., 192.
Cordova, 43, 76.
Corneille, 221.
Corporal punishment, 166, 218, 285, 288 f.
Corpus Juris Canonici, 79 (footnote).
Corpus Juris Civilis, 78, 79, 90.
Corrector, 219.
Correlation, with Comenius, 285.
Counter-reformation, 208 (footnote).
Court, humanistic influences at the, 164.
Court schools, 123; relation to the universities, 127 f.
Croke, Richard, 163.
Croyland, 10, 13.
Crusades, 65, 100 f., 104.
Crusius, 161 (footnote).
Cur Deus Homo, 52 (footnote).
Czech, 275 (footnote).

D'Alembert, 311.
Dante, 93, 114 (footnote).
D'Arezzo, 120 (footnote).
'Dark Ages,' 12, 103.
Decamerone, 102 (footnote), 117.
Decanus, 88.
De Civilitate, 151.
De Copia Verborum, 150.
Decretum Gratiani, 79, 90.
Decuriones, 218.
De Emendatione, 144, 192.
De Formando Studio, 147 f.
De Geer, Ludovic, 273.
Degrees, mediæval universities, 92 f.
De Ingenuis Moribus, 121.
De Liberorum Educatione, 130.
De l'Institution du Prince, 143.
Démia, Charles, 229.
De Ordine Docendi, 121.
De Pueris, 151.
De Ratione, 151.
Descartes, Réné, 222, 224, 262, 311.
De Studiis et Literis, 120.
De Tradendis Disciplinis, 166.
De Utilitate Græcæ, 148.
Deventer, 146, 147, 148, 149.
De Viris Illustribus, 116.
Dialectic, in pagan course, 15; meaning of, 18.
Dialogues of the Dead, 234.
Didactica Magna, 273 (footnote), 274 ff.
Didacticum, collegium, 276 (footnote), 280.
Diderot, 221, 311.
Dietarum Liber, 90.
Digest, of Justinian, 90.
Disciplinary theory. See Formal discipline.
Disputationes, 218.
Disputation of Pippin, 29.
'Doctor,' 92, 215.
Doctor scholasticus, 50.
Dominicans, 8, 73 ff., 221.
Donation of Constantine, 129.
Donatus, 20, 89.
Don Juan of Austria, 221.
Dorpat, university of, 202.
Dort, synod of, 199.
'Double translation,' 166 f.
Dulwich, 173.

Y

322 INDEX

Duns Scotus, 55.
Dunstan, 8.

Eck, 182.
Education of Children, 247 f.
Education of Girls, 233 f.
Edward VI, 195 ff., 202.
Einhard, 29.
Eisleben, 155, 157, 187, 198.
Elbing, 273.
Elegantiæ Latinæ, 135.
Elementarie, Mulcaster's, 250 ff.
Elementary education, under Charlemagne, 31 f.; under Alfred, 37 f.; under Moslems, 44.
Elizabeth, queen, 167, 196.
'Eloquence,' as educational aim, 159.
Elyot, Sir Thomas, 165, 166.
Émile, Rousseau's, 259 (footnote).
Empiricism, 241 (footnote), 262.
Emulation, in Jesuit education, 217 f.
Encomium Moriæ, 151.
Encyclopedists, 311.
Epistolæ, Petrarch's, 116.
Erasmus, 93, 148, 149 ff., 156, 159, 161, 163, 166, 168, 170, 171, 243.
Erfurt, university of, 82, 145, 148, 181, 300.
Erigena, Joannes Scotus, 34, 49, 51.
Ernst the Pious, 199, 289.
Erotemata, 119.
Essais, Montaigne's, 247.
Essay concerning the Human Understanding, 305, 309.
Estiennes, 143.
Ethics, Aristotle's, 89.
Eton, 173, 250.
Eucharist, Zwingli's position on the, 190, 204.
Externi, 13, 212.

Fabliaux, 102.
Factors in modern civilization, 1.
Faculties, 88.
'Faculty,' 309, 310.
Febrium, Liber, 90.
Federigo da Montefeltro, 123.
Fénelon, François, 233 ff., 236.
Ferrara, 121, 123, 127, 147.
Ferrières, 13.
Feudalism, 63 f., 100.

Filelfo, 121, 124 (footnote), 129.
Fisher, Bishop, 163.
Fleury, 13.
Florence, 119, 120, 122, 123, 128, 142, 150, 162.
Fontenelle, 13.
'Formal discipline,' 306 ff.
Formalism, 135 f., 176, 203 f., 237.
'Forms,' 265.
Francis I, 142, 191.
Franciscans, 8, 72 ff., 222.
Francke, August Hermann, 286, 300 ff.; aim in education, 301 f.; course, 302 f.; methods, 303; influence of, 303 f.
Franckesche Stiftungen, 303 f.
Frankfurt, diet of, 267.
Franks, 25 ff.
Frederick I, 79, 82.
Frederick II, 44, 77.
Friars, mendicant, 72.
Froebel, 271, 287.
Fürstenschulen, 153 ff., 175, 201, 290.
Fulda, 10, 13, 31, 33, 34.
Fust, Johann, 140.

Galileo, 94, 262.
Gandersheim, 13.
Gargantua, 244 ff.
Gaunilo, 52 (footnote).
Geert Geerts, 149 (footnote).
'General,' the Jesuit, 211.
Geneva, Calvin at, 192 ff.
Geometry, in pagan course, 15; later, 18.
'Germaniæ præceptor,' 149, 157.
German universities, classics in, 145.
Gerson, 55 (footnote).
Gesta Romanorum, 12.
Giessen, university of, 267 f., 272.
Gilds, 92, 97.
Gild schools, 97 f., 195.
Giocosa, la casa, 124.
Glastonbury, 13.
Gnostics, 5.
Göttingen, education at, 188; university of, 293.
Goldberg, 188.
Goliardi, 86.
Golias, 86 (footnote).
Gonzaga, 124.

INDEX 323

Gotha, education at, 198 f.
Gouvéa, 144.
Governour, The, 165.
Grammar, in pagan course, 15; meaning of, 17.
Grammar schools, in England, 170 ff., 175, 197 f., 201, 291; in America, 173 f.
Grammaticæ Facilioris Præcepta, 272.
Granada, 43, 76.
Gratian, 79.
Gratis accepistis, 213.
Great Didactic, The. See *Didactica Magna*.
Greek, in Italy, 117 ff.; at Oxford, 162 f.; at Cambridge, 163 f.
Gregorio of Tiferno, 142.
Gregory I, the Great, 8 (footnote), 38.
Gregory IX, 81 f.
Grimbald, 37.
Grimma, 155.
Grocyn, William, 150, 162, 165, 168.
Groot, Geert, 146.
Guarino, Battista, 109 (footnote), 121, 131, 132, 143 (footnote).
Guarino da Verona, 120 f., 123, 124, 126, 128, 131.
Guericke, 262.
Gymnasien, 153 ff., 157, 175, 201, 290.

Habita, Authentic, 82, 83.
Haileybury, 173.
Halle, university of, 293, 300.
Hamburg, schools at, 188.
'Hardening process,' 252.
Harold, king of England, 70.
Harrow, 173.
Hartlib, Samuel, 255 (footnote).
Hecker, 291, 304.
Hegius, Alexander, 148.
Heidelberg, university of, 82, 83, 145, 147, 148, 156, 272.
Helmstadt, university of, 202.
Henry III, of England, 85.
Henry VIII, 174, 195 ff., 202, 204.
Heptameron, 102 (footnote).
Herbart, 271, 287.
Herborn, college of, 271 f., 272, 275.
Hermits, first Christian, 5 f.
Hermonymus, 142.
Hersfeld, 13.

Hessen-Cassel, education at, 198.
Hessen-Darmstadt, education at, 198.
Hieronymian schools, 145 ff., 154, 175, 213.
Hirschau, 13, 31.
Hobbes, 298 (footnote).
Holland, school system of, 193, 199 f.
Holstein, education at, 188, 198, 267.
Holy Roman Empire, 26.
Hornbach, 161 (footnote).
Hughes, quoted, 214 (footnote).
Humanism, 108 f.; in Italy, 110 ff.; in North, 140 ff.; in France, 141 ff.; in Teutonic countries, 145 ff.; in England, 161 ff.
Humanistic education, ideals of, 130 ff., 174 f.; content, 132 ff., 175 f.; method, 134; organization, 134 f., 175; results, 135 ff., 176.
Hume, 311.
Humphrey, duke of Gloucester, 161.
Huss, Johann, 93, 180.

'Idols,' Bacon's, 264.
Il Convito, Dante's, 114 (footnote).
Ilfeld, 189.
'Induction,' 263 ff., 270, 283 ff., 288.
'Indulgence,' 182.
Industrial education, 97.
Inferiora studia, 212 ff.
Informatorium Skoly Materske, 275.
Ingoldstadt, university of, 145, 148.
'Innate ideas,' 305, 311 (footnote).
Innocent IV, 100.
Institutes, of Justinian, 90.
Isaac Judæus, 90.
Isidoneus Germanicus, 149.
Isidore of Seville, 16.

Jacqueline Pascal, 226, 228, 233.
Jansenists, 222, 223 ff., 228, 237.
Janua Linguæ Latinæ Reserata, 272 (footnote).
Janua Linguarum Reserata, 272, 273, 286.
Janua Rerum Reserata, 276.
Jena, university of, 145, 202, 268.
Jerome, 7.
Jesuit education, aim of, 210; organization, 210 ff.; content, 213 ff.; method, 215 ff.; results, 219 ff.

INDEX

Jesuits, 155, 175, 209 ff., 228, 229, 231, 235, 236.
John the Saxon, 38.
John XXII, 94.
John XXIII, 94.
'Journeyman,' 92, 97.
Juilly, college at, 223.
Jurisdictio, 63 (footnote).
'Justification by faith,' 181, 191.
Justinian's *Decree*, 4.
Jus ubique docendi, 84.

Kepler, 262.
Klosterschulen, 154.
'Knowledge,' as educational aim, 151, 160, 277 f.
Knox, John, 194, 204.
Königsberg, university of, 145, 202.
Köthen, Ratich at, 268, 269.
Koran, 40, 44.

Labyrinthus, 276 (footnote).
Lamy, 223.
Lancelot, 226, 227 f.
Landesschulen, 154 (footnote).
La Salle, 228 ff.
Lateinische Hauptschule. *See* Schola Latina.
Latimer, William, 163.
'Latin school' of Comenius, 276, 278, 281 f.
Lauingen, 161 (footnote).
Lausanne, collège at, 192.
Laynez, Diego, 209 (footnote), 210, 214.
Leach, quoted, 195 (footnote).
Lecointe, 223.
Lefèvre, 175.
Leipzig, university of, 145, 163, 300.
Lelong, 223.
Leo X, 130, 135.
Leszno, 272, 274, 275, 276, 277 (footnote).
Letter to Mayors and Aldermen, 184, 187, 201.
Liberatura, 69 (footnote).
Libraries, in monasteries, 10 f.
Liège, 146, 158.
Lily, William, 150, 169, 174.
Linacre, Thomas, 150, 162 f., 165.
Lisbon, university of, 81.
Lissa. *See* Leszno.

'Little Schools,' 224 ff.
Liverpool, university of, 293.
Locke, 246, 249, 252, 254, 256 ff., 262, 287 ff., 292, 305 ff., 312.
Lollards, 180, 194 (footnote).
London, university of, 293.
Louis VII, 80.
Louis XII, 142.
Louis XIV, 227, 290.
Louvain, 146, 150, 158.
Loyola, Ignatius, 209 ff.
Ludus literarius, 172.
Lübeck, education at, 188.
Lüneburg, 290.
L'uomo universale, 114.
Luther, Martin, 93, 156, 175, 181 ff., 201, 208; religious works of, 183; educational works, 183 f.; theory of education, 184 ff.
Luxembourg, duc de, 221.

McCabe, quoted, 80.
Magdeburg, 198, 268.
Maintenon, Madame de, 233, 235, 236.
Malebranche, 223.
Malmesbury, 13.
Manchester, university of, 293.
Mansfeld, count of, 157, 187.
Mantua, court school at, 123 ff.
Manuscripts, in monasteries, 10 ff.
Marburg, university of, 145, 202.
Marlborough, 173.
Mary, queen of England, 193, 196 (footnote).
Mary, queen of Scots, 193, 208.
Mascaron, 223.
Massachusetts, educational act of 1647, 174, 200.
Massillon, 223.
'Master,' 92, 97.
'Master-universities,' 81.
Mechlin, 146.
Mecklenburg, education at, 198.
Medicean library, 122 (footnote).
Medici, Cosimo de', 119, 122; Lorenzo de', 122 f.
Meissen, 155.
Melanchthon, 155, 157, 175, 187, 189, 192, 198, 204, 243.
Meminger, 161 (footnote).
Memorizing, 216, 237.

INDEX 325

Merchant Taylors', 98, 173, 250.
Methodus Linguarum Novissima, 273 (footnote).
Middle Ages, as period of assimilation, 1 f.; as period of repression, 2 f., 315.
Milan, 142.
Milton, John, 246, 252, 254 ff., 257, 259, 298 f.
Minden, education at, 188.
Minnesingers, 65, 102.
Monasteries, 6; effect of, 9; manuscripts in, 10 ff.; original writings in, 12.
Monastic education, organization of, 12; ideals, 13; content, 14 ff.; methods, 19 ff.; results of, 21 ff.; under Charlemagne, 30 f., 32.
Monasticism, rise of, 4; cœnobitic, 6 f.; in West, 6 f.; effects of, 21 ff.
'Monitor,' the Jesuit, 211.
Monologion, Anselm's, 51.
Montaigne, 246 ff., 250, 251, 252, 255, 257, 258, 259, 287.
Montanists, 5.
Monte Cassino, 12.
Montesquieu, 311.
Montpelier, university of, 82.
'Morality,' as educational aim, 151, 277 f.
Moravian Brethren, 271, 277 (footnote), 279.
More, Sir Thomas, 150, 162, 164.
Moritz, duke of Saxony, 154.
Moslem schools, 40 ff.
'Mother School.' *See* School of Infancy.
Mulcaster, Richard, 246, 250 ff., 254, 259.
Music, in pagan course, 15; later, 19.
Mysticism, nature and rise of, 47 f.; education in, 49; development of, 49.

Nantes, edict of, 235.
Naples, 142; university of, 78, 81.
Nassau, 271.
National spirit, growth of, 100 f.
'Nationes,' 87.
Nature, method of, 263 ff., 270, 282.
Neander, educational work of, 189, 201, 243.

Nestorius, 41,
New Atlantis, The, 265.
Newton, Isaac, 293.
Niccolo de' Niccoli, 119 f.
Niccolo d' Este, 123.
Nicholas V, 120, 129 f., 135.
Nicolaus of Salerno, 90.
Nicolaus Syocerus, 118 (footnote).
Nicole, 226, 228.
Niebelungenlied, 102.
Nivnitz, 271.
Nominalism, scholastic, 52 f.
Northumbria, 8.
Notre Dame, cathedral school at, 80.
Novalese, 10.
Novum Organum, 263 ff., 267.
Nuremberg, 157.

Oblati, 13.
Odofredus, 91.
Oratorians, 222 ff., 235, 236.
Orbis Pictus, 274, 286, 287.
Organon, Aristotle's, 89, 263.
Orleans, 31.
Osnabrück, education at, 188.
Oxenstiern, 268.
Oxford, university of, 81, 84 f., 162 f., 202, 250, 293.

Pachomius, 6, 7.
Padua, 131, 150; university of, 81.
Pädagogium, 301, 302, 303, 304.
'Page,' stage of feudal education, 66.
Painting, during the Renaissance, 108 (footnote).
Palace school, 28 ff.
Palatium, 273 (footnote), 274.
Palencia, university of, 81.
Pandects, of Justinian, 78 (footnote).
Pansophia, 265 f., 276 f., 280, 284.
Pansophicæ Scholæ Delineatio, 276.
Pantagruel, 244 ff.
Paradisus Animi, 276 (footnote).
Paris, university of, 80 f., 84, 85, 87, 89, 94, 142, 146, 158.
Parish schools under Charlemagne, 30, 31.
Parsifal, 102.
Pascal, 226, 227.
Patak, 273, 274, 276, 282.
Patrocinium, 63 (footnote).

Paul, founder of hermit life, 6.
Paul the Deacon, 28.
Paul III, pope, 209.
Pavia, 128, 147.
Pedantry, Montaigne's, 247.
Pensées, Pascal's, 227.
Pestalozzi, 271, 287.
Peter of Pisa, 28, 30.
Peter the Lombard, 57, 80, 90.
Petrarch, 93, 114 ff., 137.
Pforta, 155.
Philip Augustus, 80, 83.
Philip II, 208.
Philip VI, 94.
Philo, 48 (footnote).
'Phonetic' method, 226.
Piarists, 222, 228 f.
Pietas literata, 192.
Pietists, 222, 290, 293, 298, 299 f., 313.
'Piety,' as educational aim, 151, 159, 277 f.
Pilato, 118.
Pisa, Council of, 180.
Pius II, 121, 129 f.
Pius VII, 222.
Platina, quoted, 127.
'Pleasant House,' 124 f., 127.
Plotinus, 48.
Poetics, Aristotle's, 89.
Poggio, 121, 124 (footnote), 129.
Politics, Aristotle's, 89.
Pomerania, education in, 188 f.
Pomposa, 12.
Porcia, 131.
Port Royal Grammar, 226.
Port Royalist education, aim, 223 f.; organization, 224; content, 225 f.; method, 226; results, 227 f.
Port Royal Logic, 226.
Positions, Mulcaster's, 250 ff.
Præcarium, 63 (footnote).
Prælectio, 216.
Prague, university of, 82.
'Preceptor,' the Jesuit, 211.
Predestination, 192.
'Prefect,' the Jesuit, 211.
Priscian, 20, 89.
Professi, 212 f.
'Professor,' the Jesuit, 92, 211.
Proslogion, 52 (footnote).

Protestant education, aim, 197; organization, content, and method, 197 ff.; effect of, 203 ff.
Provincial Letters, 227.
'Provincial,' the Jesuit, 211.
Pseudo-Dionysius, 48 f., 162, 168.
Ptolemy, 18, 21.
'Public,' schools in England, 172 f., 291, 310.
Puritan education, 196 f., 298.
Puritans, 297, 298 ff., 305, 316.

Quadrivialia, 89.
Quintilian, 20, 176.

Rabanus Maurus, 33 f.
Rabelais, 243 ff., 248, 254.
Raoul de Cambrai, 64 f., 101.
Rashdall, quoted, 3, 79.
Ratich, 254, 266, 268 ff., 272, 275, 287, 300.
Rationalism, 262, 298, 305 ff., 316.
Ratio Studiorum, 210, 219, 231.
Raymund of Toledo, 44.
Realgymnasium, 304.
Realism, 240, 316; relation to the Renaissance, 240; nature of, 240 f.; verbal and social, 242 ff.; effect of earlier, 259 ff. *See also* Sense realism.
Realism, scholastic, 52, 257 (footnote).
Realists, the earlier, 242 ff.
Realschulen, 303, 304.
'Rector,' 88, 211.
Reformation, 107, 315 f.; causes of, 179 ff.; Luther's revolt, 181 ff.; Zwingli's revolt, 189 ff.; Calvin's revolt, 191 ff.; Henry VIII's revolt, 194 ff.
Regulation of Studies, 227.
Reichenau, 13.
Renaissance, 105, 107, 260, 315.
Renan, quoted, 44.
Repetitio mater studiorum, 217.
Repression, key to Middle Ages, 3.
Reuchlin, 147 f., 155.
Reviews, in Jesuit education, 217.
Revival of Learning, 107 f.
Reyher, Andreas, 289.
Rheims, 230.
Rhetoric, Aristotle's, 89.

INDEX

Rhetoric, in pagan course, 15; meaning of, 18.
Richard the Lionhearted, 70.
Richelieu, 221.
Ritterakademien, 290, 291.
Ritwyse, John, 169.
Robert of Normandy, 77.
Rollin, Charles, 228.
Rome, university of, 128, 150.
Rosarium, 276 (footnote).
Roscellinus, 52, 80.
Rossall, 173.
Rossleben, 175.
Rostock, university of, 267.
Rousseau, 248, 249, 259 (footnote), 286, 316 f.
Rugby, 173.
Rule, of Benedict, 9; of St. Francis, 72.
Rupert I, 83.

St. Albans, 13.
St. Augustine, 7, 16, 32.
St. Bartholomew's Day, 208.
St. Bruno, 8.
St. Charles, Brethren of, 229.
St. Cyran, 224, 225.
St. Gall, 10, 13.
St. Maur, 7.
St. Paul's School, 150, 168 ff.; 173, 196, 250.
St. Victor, Hugo and Richard of, 50.
St. Yon, 230.
Salamanca, university of, 81, 209.
Salerno, university of, 77, 81.
Sapientiæ Palatium. See *Palatium*.
Saros-Patak. See Patak.
Saxony, the elector of, 157.
Schenck, 161 (footnote).
Schlettstadt, 148.
Scholæ Pansophicæ Delineatio, 273 (footnote), 276.
Schola Latina, 301, 303, 304.
Schola Ludus, 274.
Schola Materni Gremii, 278 (footnote).
Scholares vagantes, 86 (footnote).
Schola Scholarum, 280.
Scholastici, 212.
Scholasticism, character of, 50 f. ; history of, 50 ff.; tendency of, 56 f.; organization and content, 56 f.; method, 57 f.; influences, 58 ff.

Scholemaster, The, 164, 166 f.
Schoolmen, 50.
School of Infancy, The, 275 (footnote).
Schulmethodus, Reyher's, 289.
Schulplan, Melanchthon's, 157.
Schulvisitant, Melanchthon as, 157.
Schwartzerd, 155 (footnote).
Scotland, parish schools of, 194, 200.
Scriptorium, 11.
Seminarium Præceptorum, 301, 304.
Semler, 291, 301, 304.
Sense realism, development of, 262 ff.; representatives of, 263 ff.; in elementary education, 289 ; in secondary schools, 289 ff.; in universities, 293 f.
Sententiæ, Peter the Lombard's, 57, 90.
Sermon on Sending Children to School, 184, 187.
Servetus, 204.
Seven Liberal Arts, 15, 16.
Sévigné, Madame de, 233, 235.
Seville, 43, 76.
Shrewsbury, 173.
Sic et Non, Abelard's, 57, 79.
Silius Italicus, 117.
Silva, pansophic collection, 277.
'Simultaneous' method, 231.
Smith, Sir Thomas, 164.
Society of Jesus, 209 ff.
Soest, education at, 188.
'Solomon's House,' 265 f.
Song of the Open Road, 86.
Spener, Philipp Jakob, 299.
'Squire,' stage of feudal education, 66 f.
Stockholm, 268.
Strasburg, 155, 158, 187, 202.
Stuart kings, 196.
Sturm, Johann, 155, 158 ff., 166, 187, 192, 201, 213.
Summa Theologiæ, of Aquinas, 55, 57.
Sunday Sermons, 160.
Superiora studia, 212 ff.
Suppression of monasteries, 195 f.
Suzerains, 63.
Sweden, Ratich called to, 268; Comenius at, 273.
Switzerland, education in, 192 f.
Symbolum Apostolicum, 129.

Tabennæ, island in Nile, 6.
Tabula rasa, 306 (footnote), 311.
Tasso, 221.
Télémaque, 234.
Tetzel, 182.
Theodulf, 32, 33.
Therapeutæ, 5.
Thesaurus, 273 (footnote).
Thirty Years' War, 199, 209, 290.
Thoughts concerning Education, Locke's, 257, 259, 287, 292, 306 f., 308, 309.
Tilly, 221.
Töchterschule höhere, 301, 303.
Toledo, 43; archbishop of, 32 (footnote), 44.
Topics, of Boethius, 89.
Toul, 13.
Toulouse, university of, 81.
Tours, 13, 31.
Tractate of Education, Milton's, 254 ff., 291, 298 f.
Trasbach, 161 (footnote).
Trent, Council of, 208.
'Trojans,' party of, 164 (footnote).
Trotzendorf, educational work of, 188.
Troubadours, 65, 102.
Trouvères, 101.
Tübingen, university of, 145, 148, 156.
Tyrants, as humanists, 121 ff.

'Universitas,' 87.
Universities, mediæval, rise of, 76; history, 77 ff.; privileges, 82 ff.; organization, 86 ff.; courses of study, 88 ff.; methods, 90 ff.; degrees, 92 f.; effect, 93 f.
Urbino, duke of, 123.
Utopia, 165.

Vagantes, 86.
Valenciennes, 146.
Valla, 129, 135.
Valladolid, university of, 81.
Vegio, 131.
Venetians, take Constantinople, 45.
Venice, 123, 150.
Vergerius, 121, 123, 131, 132, 134.
Vergil, 18.
Vernaculæ Scholæ Delineatio, 276 (footnote).
'Vernacular school,' of Comenius, 276, 278 f., 281.

Verona, 123.
Vestibulum, 273.
Vienna, university of, 82, 145, 290.
Violarium, 276 (footnote).
Viridarium, 276 (footnote).
Visconti, 122, 123, 142.
Vittorino da Feltre, 120, 123 ff., 131, 132, 134.
Vives, 166, 275.
Volksschulen, rise of, 199.
Voltaire, 311 f.
Von Hutten, 184 (footnote).
Von Sickingen, 184 (footnote).
Vorschule, 304.
Vulgate, 129.

Waisenanstalt, 301.
Waldenses, 72, 179.
'Wandering students,' 85 f.
Warham, Archbishop, 165.
Wartburg, 183.
Wearmouth, 8, 13.
Weimar, education at, 198; duchess of, 268, 289.
Wellington, 173.
Wessel, 147.
Westminster, 173.
William of Champeaux, 80.
William of Normandy, 70.
William of Occam, 55, 73.
Wilster, 267.
Wimpfeling, 148 f., 150.
Winchester, 173.
Wissenbourg, 13.
Wittenberg, university of, 145, 156, 182.
Wolfenbüttel, education at, 290.
Wolfram von Eschenbach, 102.
Wolsey, Cardinal, 164.
Worms, 147; diet of, 183.
Würtemberg, school system of, 161, 198.
Wyclif, John, 93, 182.

Xavier, Francis, 209 (footnote).

Yarrow, 8, 13.
York, 13, 28.

Zurich, 190.
Zwingli, 189 ff., 204; theory of education, 190 ff.
Zwolle, 146, 147.

/370.9G776H>C1/